Taste of Home

Celebrations
COOKBOOK

Taste of Home
Celebrations
COOKBOOK

A READER'S DIGEST BOOK

Taste of Home Books
© 2005 Reiman Media Group, Inc.
5400 S. 60th Street, Greendale, WI 53129

Editor: Jean Steiner
Associate Editor: Beth Wittlinger
Art Director: Kathy Crawford
Graphic Art Associates: Ellen Lloyd, Catherine Fletcher
Senior Editor: Julie Schnittka
Senior Art Director: Linda Dzik
Craft Editor: Jane Craig
Food Editor: Janaan Cunningham
Associate Food Editors: Coleen Martin, Diane Werner
Assistant Food Editor: Karen Scales
Senior Recipe Editor: Sue A. Jurack
Recipe Editor: Janet Briggs
Test Kitchen Director: Mark Morgan
Test Kitchen Home Economists: Tamra Duncan, Peggy Fleming,
    Pat Schmeling, Wendy Stenman
Test Kitchen Assistants: Rita Krajcir, Megan Taylor
Food Stylists: Kristin Arnett, Joylyn Trickel
Set Stylists: Julie Ferron, Stephanie Marchese
Food Photography: Rob Hagen, Dan Roberts
Cover Design: George McKeon
Executive Editor, Books: Heidi Reuter Lloyd
Senior Vice President/Editor in Chief: Catherine Cassidy
President: Barbara Newton
Founder: Roy Reiman

Pictured on Front Cover:
Turkey Breast Roulade, Vegetable Bundles, Dilly Bread Ring,
Decadent Brownie Pie

Pictured on Back Cover:
Turkey with Apple Stuffing, Rabbit Rolls, Bread Pudding Pumpkin,
Tropical Fruit Salad, Spiderweb Pumpkin Cheesecake

International Standard Book Number: 0-89821-447-5

Library of Congress Control Number: 2005901782

For more Reader's Digest products and information,
visit our website at *www.rd.com*

Printed in China

1 3 5 7 9 10 8 6 4 2

SPRING

SUMMER

FALL

WINTER

YEAR-ROUND

Celebrate the Seasons with Special-Occasion Recipes

HOLIDAYS are special times to gather with family, catch up with dear friends and appreciate the blessings in our lives. An attractive spread of home-cooked foods helps make the occasions more joyful and the memories more vivid.

With that in mind, we compiled this *Taste of Home's Celebrations Cookbook*. This big, colorful, photo-filled treasury features 474 mouth-watering recipes to make your special events throughout the year easy and enjoyable. You see, we've done the planning for you, offered menu options and provided timetables to minimize any last-minute fuss.

- SPRING (pages 4-79). Some of the springtime celebrations that sprout up in this cookbook include St. Patrick's Day, Easter, Cinco de Mayo and Memorial Day.
- SUMMER (pages 80-133). Father's Day and the Fourth of July start off summer with a bang, while family reunions abound during the warm-weather months.
- FALL (pages 134-205). We guarantee you'll "fall" for the Halloween and Thanksgiving fare and festivities featured in the pages of this book.
- WINTER (pages 206-369). From Hanukkah and Christmas to New Year's and Valentine's Day—plus everything else in between—wintertime is a flurry of activity.
- YEAR-ROUND (pages 370-417). Birthdays, bridal showers, baby showers and wedding anniversaries fill up the calendar throughout the year.

To make these occasions even more special, we've included a host of ideas for creating simple centerpieces and other pretty table-toppers and table-setting suggestions, easy yet impressive napkin folds and more.

With a splendid assortment of appetizers, side dishes, entrees, desserts, party menus, decorating ideas and more, *Taste of Home's Celebrations Cookbook* will make entertaining more fun for you…and unforgettable for your family and friends!

SPRING
Celebrations

St. Patrick's Day Celebration 6-15

Brunch Celebrates the Season 16-31

Easter Feast Features Ham 32-39

Old-Fashioned Easter Egg Hunt 40-51

Exciting Ideas for Hard-Cooked Eggs . . .52-59

Cinco de Mayo Fiesta 60-69

Backyard Memorial Day Party 70-79

Tulip image: Index Stock Imagery, Inc./ChromaZone Images

St. Patrick's Day Celebration

YOU DON'T have to be Irish to join in the fun of St. Patrick's Day. (Plus, what better way to welcome the arrival of spring than by "The Wearing of the Green"?)

Bring a little luck of the Irish to your home...ask relatives and friends over to share in this flavorful feast.

Mint Tea Punch and Floating Four-Leaf Clovers will have leprechauns of every age leaping for joy.

Then dig in to the traditional tastes of Irish Soda Bread, Colcannon Potatoes and Spicy Corned Beef.

All eyes—whether they're Irish or not—will surely be smiling around your dinner table!

LUCK OF THE IRISH

(Clockwise from top right)

Irish Soda Bread (p. 8)

Colcannon Potatoes (p. 10)

Spicy Corned Beef (p. 12)

Mint Tea Punch and
Floating Four-Leaf Clovers (p. 9)

Irish Soda Bread

(Pictured on page 7)

Each St. Patrick's Day, I bake this bread for my neighbor, who is Irish. Then I make another loaf for my family to enjoy. Sweet raisins contrast nicely with the caraway.
— *Emma Dewees, Eagleville, Pennsylvania*

4 cups all-purpose flour
3 tablespoons sugar
3 teaspoons baking powder
1 teaspoon salt
3/4 teaspoon baking soda
6 tablespoons cold butter
1-1/2 cups raisins
1 tablespoon caraway seeds
2 eggs, beaten
1-1/2 cups buttermilk

In a large bowl, combine the first five ingredients. Cut in butter until mixture resembles coarse crumbs. Stir in the raisins and caraway seeds. Set aside 1 tablespoon beaten egg. In a bowl, combine buttermilk and remaining egg; stir into crumb mixture just until flour is moistened (dough will be sticky). Turn onto a well-floured surface; knead about 10 times. Shape into a ball.

Place the dough in a greased 9-in. round baking pan. Cut a 4-in. X, 1/4 in. deep, in the center of the ball. Brush the top with reserved egg. Bake at 350° for 1 hour and 20 minutes or until a toothpick inserted near the center comes out clean.

Cover loosely with foil during the last 20 minutes if top browns too quickly. Cool for 10 minutes before removing from pan to a wire rack to cool completely. **Yield:** 1 loaf.

THE IRISH SODA BREAD STORY

THIS CLASSIC quick bread from Ireland is so named because it uses baking soda for leavening. Legend has it that the X is cut into the top of the bread before baking to ward off evil spirits.

Horseradish-Mustard Sauce For Corned Beef

When you have a strong Irish heritage and a son named Patrick, you can't help but make a big fuss on March 17! This zesty sauce is the perfect accompaniment to corned beef.
— *Denise Bender, Bayville, New York*

1 cup (8 ounces) sour cream
2 tablespoons prepared horseradish
2 tablespoons prepared mustard

In a small bowl, combine the sour cream, horseradish and mustard. Serve with corned beef. **Yield:** 10 servings.

Mint Tea Punch

(Pictured at right and on page 6)

This pretty punch prepared with green tea has a hint of mint, making it the highlight of any spring meal.
—Sandra McKenzie
Braham, Minnesota

10 cups water, *divided*
 5 bags green tea with mint
 1 cup sugar
 1 cup pineapple juice
1/2 cup lemon juice
2-1/2 cups chilled ginger ale
 4 to 5 drops green food
   coloring, optional
Floating Four-Leaf Clovers
   (recipe below)

In a large saucepan, bring 5 cups water to a boil; add tea bags and steep for 5 minutes. Remove and discard tea bags. Stir in sugar, pineapple juice, lemon juice and remaining water. Cover and refrigerate for 4 hours.

Just before serving, add ginger ale and food coloring if desired. Add Floating Four-Leaf Clovers. **Yield:** about 3-1/2 quarts.

Floating Four-Leaf Clovers

(Pictured above and on page 6)

Instead of using regular ice cubes in Mint Tea Punch, our home economists stayed in the spirit of St. Patrick's Day and prepared these cute clover cubes. They're made with soda so they won't dilute your beverage. They can be made weeks in advance and stored in the freezer.

4 cups plus 2 tablespoons
   chilled lemon-lime soda, *divided*
12 lime slices
 1 strip lime peel (6 inches)

Pour 1/4 cup lemon-lime soda into 12 muffin cups; freeze until solid. On a work surface, cut lime slices into quarters. Rotate each quarter slice clockwise until one end of outer edge touches the center; place over frozen soda. To make a stem, cut the lime strip into 1/2-in. pieces. Place at one corner of clover. Freeze for 20 minutes. Slowly pour remaining soda into cups until lime is almost covered. Immediately freeze until solid. **Yield:** 12 clover cubes.

Colcannon Potatoes

(Pictured on page 7)

*Every Irish family has its own version of this classic side dish...my recipe comes from
my father's family in Ireland. It's part of my St. Pat's menu,
along with lamb chops, carrots and soda bread.*
—Marilou Robinson, Portland, Oregon

2 pounds cabbage, shredded
2 cups water
4 pounds potatoes, peeled and
   quartered
2 cups milk
1 cup chopped green onions
Salt and coarsely ground pepper
   to taste
1/4 cup butter, melted
Crumbled cooked bacon and
   minced fresh parsley

In a large saucepan, bring cabbage and water to a boil. Reduce heat; cover and simmer for 10-12 minutes or until tender. Drain, reserving cooking liquid. Keep cabbage warm. Place cooking liquid and potatoes in a large saucepan; add enough additional water to cover the potatoes. Bring to a boil. Reduce heat; cover and cook for 15-17 minutes or until tender. Drain and keep warm.

In a small saucepan, bring milk and onions to a boil; remove from the heat. In a large mixing bowl, mash potatoes. Add milk mixture; beat until blended. Add cabbage, salt and pepper; beat until blended. Top with melted butter, bacon and parsley. **Yield:** 12-16 servings.

DO YOU KNOW ABOUT COLCANNON?

COLCANNON—a combination of mashed potatoes and either cabbage or kale—is mostly associated with the harvest and is traditionally eaten in Ireland on Halloween.

Symbols of good fortune (a golden ring predicting marriage within a year, a sixpence for forthcoming wealth, a thimble for spinsterhood and a button for bachelorhood) are often hidden in the dish for folks to find.

Hot Pastrami Spread

(Pictured at right)

I first tasted this at a church party a few years ago. Everyone raves about it, and the dish is always scraped clean. You can also serve the savory spread with bite-size bagel pieces.
—Arlene Wilson
Center Barnstead, New Hampshire

  2 **packages (8 ounces *each*) cream cheese, softened**
1/2 **cup sour cream**
  2 **packages (2-1/2 ounces *each*) thinly sliced pastrami, chopped**
1/2 **cup finely chopped green pepper**
1/3 **cup chopped pecans *or* walnuts, optional**
Thinly sliced pumpernickel and light rye bread

In a small mixing bowl, beat cream cheese and sour cream until smooth. Add pastrami and green pepper; mix well. Transfer to a greased 1-qt. baking dish. Sprinkle with pecans if desired. Bake, uncovered, at 350° for 25-30 minutes or until heated through and edges are bubbly. Cut out bread with a shamrock-shaped cookie cutter if desired. Serve with spread. **Yield:** about 3-1/2 cups.

Reuben Chicken

With just four ingredients and little preparation time, this rich and cheesy main dish couldn't be easier. My family prefers it to traditional Reuben sandwiches made with corned beef.
—Dana Chandler, Wilmington, Delaware

  6 **boneless skinless chicken breast halves**
  1 **cup Thousand Island salad dressing**
  1 **can (14 ounces) sauerkraut, rinsed and drained**
  6 **slices Swiss cheese**

Pound chicken between two pieces of waxed paper to flatten. Place in a greased 13-in. x 9-in. x 2-in. baking dish. Spoon salad dressing over chicken; cover with sauerkraut. Cover and bake 350° for 30 minutes. Uncover; top with cheese. Bake 20-30 minutes longer or until chicken juices run clear. **Yield:** 6 servings.

Spicy Corned Beef

(Pictured on page 6)

This corned beef recipe is so easy to fix because it can be simmered one day and baked the next.
—Jacqueline Clark, Eugene, Oregon

2 corned beef briskets (about 3 pounds *each*)
1 medium onion, halved
1 medium carrot, cut into chunks
1 celery rib with leaves
1 tablespoon mixed pickling spices
1/3 cup packed brown sugar
1 tablespoon prepared mustard
1/2 cup sweet pickle juice

Place corned beef in a large Dutch oven; cover with water. Add the onion, carrot, celery and pickling spices. Bring to a boil. Reduce heat; cover and simmer for 2-1/2 to 3 hours or until meat is tender.

Transfer corned beef to a 13-in. x 9-in. x 2-in. baking dish; discard broth and vegetables. Score the surface of meat with shallow diagonal cuts. Combine brown sugar and mustard; spread over meat. Pour pickle juice into dish. Bake, uncovered, at 325° for 1 hour, basting occasionally. **Yield:** 18-20 servings.

Potato Asparagus Bake

Many of my springtime menus include this dish,
which can be made ahead, refrigerated and baked when ready.
—Deborah Sears, Heathsville, Virginia

1 pound potatoes, peeled and quartered
1 pound fresh asparagus, trimmed
2 tablespoons butter, *divided*
1 tablespoon all-purpose flour
3/4 cup heavy whipping cream
1/2 teaspoon salt
1/4 teaspoon pepper
3 tablespoons dry bread crumbs
3 tablespoons grated Parmesan cheese

Place potatoes in a saucepan and cover with water. Bring to a boil. Reduce heat; cover and cook for 15-20 minutes or until tender. Meanwhile, cut the tips off asparagus spears; set aside for garnish. Cut stalks into 1-in. pieces; place in a saucepan and cover with water. Bring to a boil. Reduce heat; cover and cook for 8-10 minutes or until tender. Drain asparagus and place in a food processor or blender. Cover and process until pureed; set aside. Drain potatoes; mash and set aside.

In a large saucepan, melt 1 tablespoon butter; whisk in flour until smooth. Gradually stir in cream. Bring to a boil; cook and stir for 2 minutes or until thickened. Stir in asparagus pieces, mashed potatoes, salt and pepper. Transfer to a greased shallow 1-1/2-qt. baking dish. Top with reserved asparagus tips.

Melt remaining butter; lightly brush some over top. Toss bread crumbs, Parmesan cheese and remaining butter; sprinkle over casserole. Bake, uncovered, at 350° for 25-30 minutes or until lightly browned. **Yield:** 8-10 servings.

Three's-a-Charm Shamrock Soup

(Pictured at right)

There's no better way to use up leftover St. Patrick's Day corned beef, cabbage and potatoes than to make a hearty soup. This second-time-around soup is one of my best.
— Deborah McMurtrey
Estes Park, Colorado

6 celery ribs, chopped
4 medium carrots, sliced
2 cups cubed peeled potatoes
5 cups water
3 cups cubed cooked
  corned beef
2 cups chopped cooked cabbage
1 teaspoon dill weed
1 teaspoon salt
1 teaspoon seasoned salt
1/2 teaspoon white pepper

In a large soup kettle, bring the celery, carrots, potatoes and water to a boil. Reduce heat; cover and simmer until the vegetables are tender, about 20 minutes. Stir in all of the remaining ingredients. Cover and simmer for 15-20 minutes or until heated through. **Yield:** 10 servings (2-1/2 quarts).

Irish Beef 'n' Carrot Stew

My husband was born on St. Patrick's Day, and this is the special meal I make to celebrate that occasion. My family looks forward to it all year.
—Marie Biggs, Anacortes, Washington

1 pound carrots, peeled and cut into 2-1/2-inch pieces
2 medium onions, chopped
3 tablespoons vegetable oil
3 tablespoons all-purpose flour
Salt and pepper to taste
1-1/2 pounds boneless beef chuck steak, cut into 1-inch strips
1/2 teaspoon chopped fresh basil
2/3 cup Guinness, other dark beer *or* beef broth
1 teaspoon honey
2/3 cup additional beef broth
Mashed *or* boiled potatoes

Place carrots in a greased shallow 2-qt. baking dish. In a skillet, saute onions in oil for 5 minutes or until tender. Using a slotted spoon, transfer onions to dish.

In a resealable plastic bag, combine the flour, salt and pepper. Add beef, a few pieces at a time, and shake to coat; reserve flour mixture. In the same skillet, brown meat in oil on all sides. Transfer to baking dish.

Stir reserved flour mixture into oil; cook and stir over medium heat for 1 minute. Add basil and beer or broth. Bring to a boil; cook and stir for 1 minute or until thickened. Stir in honey and additional broth; return to a boil, stirring constantly. Pour over beef. Cover and bake at 325° for 1-1/2 hours or until beef is tender. Serve with potatoes. **Yield:** 4-6 servings.

Chocolate Lime Dessert

(Pictured on opposite page)

The pretty pale green color of this refreshing lime gelatin dessert is perfect for a St. Patrick's Day party, but don't be surprised when your family requests it year-round!
—Jane Lochowicz, Brookfield, Wisconsin

1 package (3 ounces) lime gelatin
1-3/4 cups boiling water
2 cups crushed chocolate wafers
6 tablespoons butter, melted
1/4 cup lime juice
2 teaspoons lemon juice
1 cup sugar
1 can (12 ounces) evaporated milk
Pots o' Gold (recipe on opposite page)

In a small mixing bowl, dissolve gelatin in boiling water. Refrigerate until partially set, about 1-1/2 hours. In a bowl, combine wafer crumbs and butter; press into a 13-in. x 9-in. x 2-in. dish. Set aside.

Beat gelatin with an electric mixer until foamy. Add the lime and lemon juices. Gradually add sugar, beating until dissolved. While beating, slowly add the milk; mix well. Pour over prepared crust. Refrigerate until set. Garnish with Pots o' Gold. **Yield:** 12-15 servings.

Pots o' Gold

(Pictured at right)

*You won't find a real pot of gold at
the end of a rainbow; but this
chocolate garnish from our Test Kitchen
will make any dessert
look like a million bucks!*

1/2 cup semisweet chocolate chips
1/4 teaspoon shortening
**1/2 cup light green candy coating
disks**

Place a sheet of waxed paper on a baking sheet; draw a 1-in. pot with a 2-in. x 1-in. rainbow coming out of the pot. Place another sheet of waxed paper over the top. Secure both to a baking sheet with tape; set aside.

In a microwave, melt the chocolate chips and shortening; stir until smooth. Cut a hole in the corner of a pastry or plastic bag. Insert round tip #3 and add the melted chocolate. Pipe chocolate over outlines; chill.

In another microwave-safe bowl, melt candy coating. Cut a hole in another pastry bag. Insert round tip #3 and fill with candy coating. Fill in chocolate outline. Chill until set. Use as a garnish for desserts. **Yield:** 16 Pots o' Gold.

Editor's Note: Pots o' Gold can be made a week in advance. When set, use a spatula to remove them from the waxed paper and place in a single layer in an airtight container. Store in a cool dry place.

MAKING POTS O' GOLD

SPOON the melted chocolate into a pastry or plastic bag fitted with a #3 round tip. Pipe the chocolate onto the waxed paper, using the outline on the paper beneath as your guide. Chill, then fill with melted candy coating as directed.

Brunch Celebrates the Season

FLOWING dresses, pretty hats, fun-filled baskets, delicate daffodils…there's just something about Easter that signals the arrival of spring. Now is the time to put aside the heavy fare you served all winter and bring out a sunnier selection perfect for warmer weather.

To celebrate this season with family and friends, why not host a bright late-morning brunch featuring Swedish Pancakes, Fruit Salad with Poppy Seed Dressing and Crab-Spinach Egg Casserole?

In addition to these cheerful choices, the following pages are blooming with a host of other innovative Easter brunch ideas… from egg dishes, salads and breads to pancakes, waffles, French toast and more.

RISE 'N' SHINE SELECTION

(Clockwise from top right)

Crab-Spinach Egg Casserole (p. 20)

Swedish Pancakes (p. 21)

Fruit Salad with Poppy Seed Dressing (p. 18)

Fruit Salad with Poppy Seed Dressing

(Pictured on opposite page and on page 16)

*My family requests this yummy fruit salad every Easter.
The slightly sweet poppy seed dressing served on the side really makes it special.*
—Joni Kingsley, Redlands, California

POPPY SEED DRESSING:
 1/3 cup red wine vinegar
 3/4 cup sugar
 1 teaspoon ground mustard
 3/4 teaspoon salt
 3/4 cup vegetable oil
 1 tablespoon poppy seeds
SALAD:
 2 cups pineapple chunks
 2 cups green grapes
 2 medium firm bananas, sliced
 2 cups sliced fresh strawberries
Floral Ice Bowl (opposite page)
Lettuce *or* lemon leaves, optional

In a blender or food processor, combine the vinegar, sugar, mustard and salt. While processing, gradually add the oil in a steady stream. Stir in the poppy seeds.

Just before serving, combine the fruits. Serve with poppy seed dressing in an ice bowl lined with lettuce or lemon leaves if desired. **Yield:** 10 servings.

Editor's Note: If using lemon leaves, properly identify before picking and make sure the tree has not been treated with chemicals.

FAST FRUIT SALAD

TO SAVE TIME on the day of your brunch, you can prepare the dressing for Fruit Salad with Poppy Seed Dressing the night before and store it in a covered container at room temperature.

Also, cut up the pineapple and strawberries and measure the grapes; store in separate containers in the refrigerator. Just before guests arrive, slice the bananas and combine all the fruit.

Apricot Casserole

*This sweet fruit dish is a terrific complement to salty ham on Easter morning.
Apricot is a tasty change from the more common pineapple.*
—Janice Montiverdi, Sugar Land, Texas

 2 cans (15 ounces *each*) apricot halves
 1/2 cup plus 2 tablespoons butter, *divided*
 1 cup packed brown sugar
 1/4 cup all-purpose flour
1-1/3 cups crushed butter-flavored crackers (about 36 crackers)

Drain apricots, reserving 3/4 cup juice. Place apricots in a greased 11-in. x 7-in. x 2-in. baking dish. Melt 1/2 cup butter; add the brown sugar, flour and reserved juice. Pour over apricots.

Bake, uncovered, at 350° for 20 minutes. Melt remaining butter; toss with cracker crumbs. Sprinkle over top. Bake 15-20 minutes longer or until golden brown. **Yield:** 6-8 servings.

Floral Ice Bowl

(Pictured at right)

Bowl folks over at your Easter gathering with this frozen serving bowl from our Test Kitchen. It can be made days in advance and kept frozen until ready to use.

Assorted herbs and edible flowers such as mint, chamomile, pansies, nasturtiums, etc. *or* colorful silk flowers and leaves
1-quart and 2-1/2-quart freezer-proof glass bowls
Ice cubes
Freezer tape
Wooden skewer

If you are using herbs and edible flowers, wash blossoms and leaves and pat dry. If you are using silk flowers and leaves, wash them gently in warm sudsy water, rinse and let air-dry.

Fill the 2-1/2-qt. bowl half full with water. Arrange herbs and flowers or silk flowers and leaves to completely cover surface of the water. Place the 1-qt. bowl on top of flowers so there is about 1 in. of space between the bowls. Fill the 1-qt. bowl with ice cubes. Place freezer tape across both bowls to hold them in place.

Place the taped bowls in the freezer for 30 minutes or until ice crystals form on top of the water.

Using a wooden skewer, place additional herbs or leaves and flowers between the sides of the bowls. Return bowls to the freezer.

Checking periodically on the bowls, continue to add and reposition flow-ers as the water freezes. Freeze overnight.

Remove freezer tape and ice cubes. Fill the 1-qt. bowl with lukewarm water, then remove it. Dip the 2-1/2-qt. bowl in warm water and twist to loosen. Remove the ice bowl and return to the freezer until ready to use. **Yield:** 1 floral ice bowl (6 inches in diameter and 3 inches high).

MAKING A FLORAL ICE BOWL

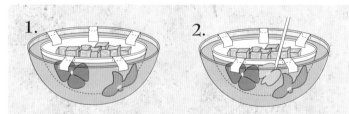

1. Place the 1-qt. bowl on top of the flowers in the 2-1/2-qt. bowl; fill the 1-qt. bowl with ice cubes. Place freezer tape across both bowls to hold them in place.

2. After freezing the bowls for about 30 minutes, place additional herbs or leaves and flowers between the sides of the bowls with a wooden skewer.

Crab-Spinach Egg Casserole

(Pictured on page 17)

*I've developed a strong interest in cooking over the years. As a matter of fact, I came up with
this casserole as a special breakfast for our daughter when she was home for a visit.*
—Steve Heaton, Deltona, Florida

8 eggs
2 cups half-and-half cream
2 cans (6 ounces *each*)
 crabmeat, drained
1 package (10 ounces) frozen
 chopped spinach, thawed and
 squeezed dry
1 cup dry bread crumbs
1 cup (4 ounces) shredded
 Swiss cheese
1/2 teaspoon salt
1/4 teaspoon pepper
1/4 teaspoon ground nutmeg
2 celery ribs, chopped

1/2 cup chopped onion
1/2 cup chopped sweet red pepper
 3 medium fresh mushrooms, chopped
 2 tablespoons butter

In a bowl, beat eggs and cream. Stir in the crab, spinach,
bread crumbs, cheese, salt, pepper and nutmeg; set aside. In
a skillet, saute the celery, onion, red pepper and mushrooms
in butter until tender. Add to the spinach mixture.

Transfer to a greased shallow 2-1/2-qt. baking dish. Bake,
uncovered, at 375° for 30-35 minutes or until golden brown
around the edges and center is set. Let stand for 10 minutes before serving. **Yield:** 12-16 servings.

Apple Pie Sandwiches

*I created this recipe one autumn when we had an abundant apple crop.
We enjoy these sandwiches for breakfast and dessert all year long.*
—Gloria Jarrett, Loveland, Ohio

2 cups diced peeled tart apples
1 cup water
1/2 cup plus 1 tablespoon sugar,
 divided
5 teaspoons cornstarch
1/2 teaspoon ground cinnamon
1/4 teaspoon ground nutmeg
2 teaspoons lemon juice
12 slices day-old bread
3 eggs
2/3 cup milk
2 teaspoons vanilla extract
Confectioners' sugar, optional

In a saucepan, cook apples and water over medium heat
for 10 minutes or until apples are tender. Combine 1/2 cup
sugar, cornstarch, cinnamon and nutmeg; stir into apple
mixture. Bring to a boil; cook and stir for 2 minutes or until thickened. Remove from the heat; stir in lemon juice.
Spread six slices of bread with 1/3 cup filling each; top
with remaining bread.

In a shallow bowl, beat the eggs, milk, vanilla and remaining sugar. Dip sandwiches in egg mixture. Cook on a
lightly greased hot griddle until golden brown on both sides.
Dust with confectioners' sugar if desired. **Yield:** 6 servings.

Swedish Pancakes

(Pictured at right and on page 17)

When we spend the night at my mother-in-law's house, our kids beg her to make these crepe-like pancakes for breakfast. They're a little lighter than traditional pancakes, so my family can eat a lot!
—Susan Johnson, Lyons, Kansas

   2 cups milk
   4 eggs
   1 tablespoon vegetable oil
1-1/2 cups all-purpose flour
   3 tablespoons sugar
   1/4 teaspoon salt
Lingonberries *or* raspberries
Seedless raspberry jam *or* fruit
   spread, warmed
Whipped topping

In a blender, combine the first six ingredients. Cover and process until blended. Heat a lightly greased 8-in. nonstick skillet; pour 1/4 cup batter into center of skillet. Lift and tilt pan to evenly coat bottom. Cook until top appears dry; turn and cook 15-20 seconds longer. Repeat with remaining batter, adding oil to skillet as needed. Stack pancakes with waxed paper or paper towels in between. Reheat in the microwave if desired.

Fold pancakes into quarters; serve with berries, raspberry jam and whipped topping. **Yield:** 20 pancakes.

EARLY EASTER EGGS

IN 3000 B.C., Persians began using colored eggs to herald the arrival of spring. Thirteenth-century Macedonians were the first Christians on record to use colored eggs in Easter celebrations.

Cinnamon Pecan Braids

*Whenever there's a bake sale, I make these braids. They're so eye-catching
that most of the loaves get snapped up by the people working the sale!*
—Connie Dahmer, Marion, Illinois

1 package (1/4 ounce) active
  dry yeast
1 cup warm water (110°
  to 115°), *divided*
3 eggs, beaten
5 cups all-purpose flour
1/2 cup sugar
1/2 teaspoon salt
1 cup cold butter
FILLING:
1 cup butter, softened
1 cup packed brown sugar
1 cup chopped pecans
1 tablespoon ground cinnamon
GLAZE:
1-1/2 cups confectioners' sugar
1 tablespoon butter, melted
1/2 teaspoon vanilla extract
1 to 2 tablespoons milk

In a mixing bowl, dissolve yeast in 1/4 cup warm water. Add eggs and remaining water; mix well. In another bowl, combine the flour, sugar and salt. Cut in butter until crumbly. Beat into yeast mixture (do not knead). Cover and refrigerate overnight.

For filling, in a small mixing bowl, cream butter and brown sugar. Stir in pecans and cinnamon; set aside.

Turn dough onto a lightly floured surface; divide into four portions. Roll each into a 12-in. x 9-in. rectangle on a greased baking sheet. Spread filling lengthwise down center third of each rectangle.

On each long side, cut 3/4-in.-wide strips to the center to within 1/2 in. of the filling. Starting at one end, fold alternating strips at an angle across filling. Pinch ends to seal and tuck under. Cover and let rise in a warm place for 1 hour (dough will not double).

Bake at 350° for 18-20 minutes or until golden brown. Cool slightly before removing from pans to wire racks. Combine glaze ingredients; drizzle over cooled braids. **Yield:** 4 loaves.

Date Crumb Cake

*This recipe makes a big pan perfect for holiday entertaining. Guests always
comment on this cake's wonderful old-fashioned flavor.*
—Shelly Korell, Bayard, Nebraska

2 cups all-purpose flour
1 cup sugar
3/4 cup shortening
2 eggs, lightly beaten
1 cup buttermilk
1 teaspoon baking powder
1 teaspoon baking soda
3/4 cup chopped dates
1/2 cup chopped walnuts

In a mixing bowl, combine flour and sugar. Cut in shortening until mixture resembles coarse crumbs; set aside 1 cup for topping. To the remaining crumb mixture, add eggs, buttermilk, baking powder and baking soda; beat until smooth. Fold in dates and walnuts.

Transfer to a greased 13-in. x 9-in. x 2-in. baking pan; sprinkle with reserved crumb mixture. Bake at 350° for 25-30 minutes or until a toothpick inserted near the center comes out clean. Cool on a wire rack. **Yield:** 12-15 servings.

Asparagus Hollandaise Puff

(Pictured at right)

This impressive puff earns many oohs and aahs from brunch guests. It's relatively easy to make, so I don't mind serving it often.
—Leslie Cunnian, Peterborough, Ontario

1 cup water
1/2 cup butter
1/2 teaspoon salt
1/8 teaspoon white pepper
1 cup all-purpose flour
1 cup (4 ounces) shredded
   Swiss cheese
4 eggs
1 envelope hollandaise
   sauce mix
3/4 pound fresh asparagus
   (about 18 spears), trimmed
4 ounces thinly sliced ham,
   julienned

In a large saucepan, bring water, butter, salt and pepper to a boil. Add flour and cheese; stir until a smooth ball forms. Remove from the heat; let stand for 5 minutes. Add eggs, one at a time, beating well after each addition. Continue beating until mixture is smooth and shiny.

Spread dough over the bottom of a greased 10-in. quiche pan or pie plate, forming a shell by pushing dough from center toward the edges. Bake, uncovered, at 375° for 30 minutes or until puffed around the edges and golden brown.

Meanwhile, prepare hollandaise sauce according to package directions. Add 1/2 in. of water to a large skillet; add asparagus and bring to a boil. Reduce heat; cover and simmer until crisp-tender, about 4 minutes. Drain and keep warm.

Arrange ham and asparagus in center of puff. Drizzle with hollandaise sauce. Serve immediately. **Yield:** 8 servings.

Cheddar Pancakes

*This is our favorite special-occasion breakfast. I usually
double the recipe and freeze leftovers for a quick midweek morning meal.*
—*Virginia Mae Folsom, Agincourt, Ontario*

1 cup all-purpose flour
2 tablespoons sugar
2 teaspoons baking powder
1/2 teaspoon salt
1/4 teaspoon ground nutmeg
1 egg
1 cup milk
2 tablespoons vegetable oil
1 teaspoon vanilla extract
1 cup (4 ounces) shredded sharp
  cheddar cheese
Applesauce, warmed, optional

In a bowl, combine the flour, sugar, baking powder, salt and nutmeg. Combine the egg, milk, oil and vanilla; stir into dry ingredients just until moistened. Stir in cheese.

Pour batter by 1/4 cupfuls onto a lightly greased hot griddle; turn when bubbles form on top of pancakes. Cook until second side is golden brown. Serve with applesauce if desired. **Yield:** 8-10 pancakes.

French Toast Strata

*I'm always on the lookout for different breakfast and brunch ideas. I like to serve
this easy make-ahead casserole when we have out-of-town guests.*
—*Jill Middleton, Baldwinsville, New York*

1 loaf (1 pound) cinnamon
  bread, cubed
1 package (8 ounces) cream
  cheese, cubed
8 eggs
2-1/2 cups milk
6 tablespoons butter, melted
1/4 cup maple syrup
CIDER SYRUP:
1/2 cup sugar
4 teaspoons cornstarch
1/2 teaspoon ground cinnamon
1 cup apple cider
1 tablespoon lemon juice
2 tablespoons butter

Arrange half of the bread cubes in a greased 13-in. x 9-in. x 2-in. baking dish. Top with cream cheese and remaining bread. In a blender, combine eggs, milk, butter and maple syrup; cover and process until smooth. Pour over bread. Cover and refrigerate overnight.

Remove from the refrigerator 30 minutes before baking. Bake, uncovered, at 350° for 35-40 minutes or until a knife inserted near the center comes out clean and a thermometer reads at least 160°. Let stand for 10 minutes before serving.

For syrup, in a saucepan, combine sugar, cornstarch and cinnamon. Gradually whisk in cider and lemon juice. Bring to a boil; cook and stir for 2 minutes or until thickened. Stir in butter until melted. Serve warm with strata. **Yield:** 8 servings (1 cup syrup).

Holiday Ham

(Pictured at right)

When I was a young girl, ham made appearances at all of our holiday dinners. The old-fashioned flavor reminds folks of Grandma's kitchen.
—Betty Butler, Union Bridge, Maryland

  1 **can (20 ounces) sliced**
     pineapple
1/2 **spiral-sliced fully cooked**
     bone-in ham (8 to 10 pounds)
2/3 **cup maraschino cherries**
1-1/2 **cups packed brown sugar**
1/2 **teaspoon seasoned salt**

Drain pineapple, reserving juice. Place ham on a rack in a shallow roasting pan. Secure pineapple and cherries to ham with toothpicks. Combine brown sugar and seasoned salt; rub over ham. Gently pour pineapple juice over ham.

Bake, uncovered, at 325° for 1-1/2 to 2 hours or until a meat thermometer reads 140° and ham is heated through. Baste frequently with brown sugar mixture. **Yield:** about 18-20 servings.

Strawberry Syrup

This recipe is a spin-off of my dad's homemade syrup. Our son requests it with fluffy pancakes whenever he and his family come to visit.
—Nancy Dunaway, Springfield, Illinois

  1 **cup sugar**
  1 **cup water**
1-1/2 **cups mashed unsweetened**
     strawberries

In a saucepan, bring sugar and water to a boil. Gradually add strawberries; return to a boil. Reduce heat; simmer, uncovered, for 10 minutes, stirring occasionally. Serve over pancakes, waffles or ice cream. **Yield:** about 2-1/2 cups.

Minty Pineapple Punch

(Pictured on opposite page)

People are surprised to learn that tea is an ingredient in this pleasant beverage.
It's a nice change from punch recipes that call for soda.
—Margaret McNeil, Memphis, Tennessee

3 medium lemons, halved
6 cups water
2 cups sugar
1-1/2 teaspoons vanilla extract
1-1/2 teaspoons almond extract
4 individual tea bags
4 cups boiling water
2 cans (46 ounces *each*)
   pineapple juice
Fresh mint, optional

Squeeze juice from lemons; set juice aside. Place lemon halves in a large saucepan; add water and sugar. Bring to a boil; boil for 5 minutes. Remove from the heat and discard lemons. Stir in extracts and reserved lemon juice.

Steep tea in boiling water for 5 minutes; discard tea bags. Stir tea and pineapple juice into lemon mixture. Chill. Serve over ice. Garnish with mint if desired. **Yield:** 5 quarts.

Sausage Mushroom Manicotti

If you're tired of pasta with tomato sauce, try this version instead.
A creamy sauce covering sausage-filled noodles makes it hard to resist.
—Kathy Taipale, Iron River, Wisconsin

1 pound bulk Italian sausage
1/2 cup thinly sliced green onions
1 garlic clove, minced
2 tablespoons butter
1 jar (4-1/2 ounces) sliced
   mushrooms, drained
1 can (10-3/4 ounces) condensed
   cream of mushroom soup,
   undiluted
1/2 cup sour cream
1/4 teaspoon pepper
1 package (8 ounces) manicotti
   shells, cooked and drained
SAUCE:
1 can (5 ounces) evaporated milk
1 jar (4-1/2 ounces) sliced
   mushrooms, drained

1 tablespoon minced fresh parsley
2 cups (8 ounces) shredded mozzarella cheese,
   divided

In a skillet, cook sausage over medium heat until no longer pink; drain and set aside. In the same skillet, saute onions and garlic in butter until tender. Add mushrooms; heat through. Transfer to a bowl; stir in the sausage, soup, sour cream and pepper. Stuff into manicotti shells. Place in a greased 13-in. x 9-in. x 2-in. baking dish.

In a saucepan, heat milk, mushrooms and parsley. Remove from the heat; stir in 1-1/2 cups cheese until melted. Pour over stuffed shells.

Cover and bake at 350° for 25 minutes. Uncover; sprinkle with remaining cheese. Bake 5-10 minutes longer or until cheese is melted. **Yield:** 7 servings.

Tangy Fruit Salsa with Cinnamon Chips

(Pictured at right)

Paired with sweet cinnamon chips, this fruit salsa is quickly gobbled up by friends and family. It makes a nice addition to a brunch buffet. Plus it's a great snack.
—Margaret McNeil
Memphis, Tennessee

1 tablespoon sugar
1/4 teaspoon ground cinnamon
4 flour tortillas (7 inches)
SALSA:
  1 can (15 ounces) sliced peaches, drained and chopped
  2 kiwifruit, peeled and chopped
  1 cup sliced unsweetened strawberries
  2 teaspoons lime juice
  1 teaspoon sugar
  1 teaspoon grated lime peel

Combine sugar and cinnamon. Spritz tortillas with nonstick cooking spray; sprinkle with cinnamon-sugar. Cut each tortilla into eight wedges; place in a single layer in an ungreased 15-in. x 10-in. x 1-in. baking pan. Bake at 400° for 8-10 minutes or until lightly browned. Remove to a wire rack to cool.

In a bowl, combine the salsa ingredients; mix gently. Serve with cinnamon chips. **Yield:** 2-1/4 cups salsa (32 chips).

Fluffy Bacon-Cheese Frittata

My four best friends and I frequently rely on this recipe. Alongside English muffins and fresh fruit, this frittata makes a hearty, wholesome breakfast.
—Sheryl Holsten, Alexandria, Minnesota

  6 bacon strips, diced
1/3 cup chopped onion
  5 eggs, *separated*
1-1/4 cups milk
  3 tablespoons all-purpose flour
1/4 teaspoon paprika
1-1/2 cups (6 ounces) shredded Swiss cheese
1/4 to 1/2 teaspoon salt
  1 cup (4 ounces) shredded sharp cheddar cheese
  1 tablespoon minced fresh parsley

In a skillet, cook bacon over medium heat until crisp; remove to paper towels. Drain, reserving 1 tablespoon drippings. In the drippings, saute onion until tender. Remove from the heat; set aside.

In a large mixing bowl, beat egg yolks, milk, flour and paprika until smooth. Add Swiss cheese. In a small mixing bowl, beat egg whites and salt until stiff peaks form. Fold into cheese mixture.

Pour over onion in skillet; cover and cook on medium-low heat for 12-15 minutes or until almost set. Sprinkle with cheddar cheese and bacon. Cover and cook 5 minutes longer or until cheese is melted. Sprinkle with parsley. **Yield:** 6 servings.

Creamy Asparagus Soup

This is my version of a recipe I tasted while on vacation. When we got home, I tinkered around with ingredients until I came up with a winning combination.
—Lisa Hagdohl, Walbridge, Ohio

  1 medium potato, peeled and diced
  1 medium onion, chopped
  5 green onions, chopped
  1 medium carrot, chopped
  1 celery rib, chopped
1/4 cup butter
1/4 cup all-purpose flour
  1 teaspoon salt
1/4 teaspoon pepper
  1 can (49-1/2 ounces) chicken broth
  1 pound fresh asparagus, trimmed and cut into 2-inch pieces
1/2 cup half-and-half cream
  1 cup (8 ounces) sour cream

  2 bacon strips, cooked and crumbled
Additional sour cream
Asparagus tips, optional

In a Dutch oven or soup kettle, saute potato, onions, carrot and celery in butter until onions and celery are tender. Stir in flour, salt and pepper until blended. Gradually add broth. Bring to a boil; cook and stir for 2 minutes.

Add asparagus; reduce heat. Cover and simmer for 20-25 minutes or until vegetables are tender. Cool to lukewarm.

In a blender, puree vegetable mixture in small batches until smooth. Pour into a large bowl; stir in cream and sour cream until smooth.

Serve warm, or cover and refrigerate for at least 2 hours and serve chilled. Garnish with bacon, sour cream and asparagus tips if desired. **Yield:** 8-10 servings.

Peach Praline Muffins

(Pictured at right)

We eat a lot of muffins around our house. The kids love to nibble on them around the clock. This is a favorite.
— Paula Wiersma
Eastampton, New Jersey

1-2/3 cups all-purpose flour
   2 teaspoons baking powder
1/4 teaspoon salt
1/2 cup packed brown sugar
1/2 cup milk
1/3 cup vegetable oil
   1 egg
   1 teaspoon vanilla extract
   1 cup chopped fresh *or* frozen
     peaches, thawed and drained
1/2 cup chopped pecans
TOPPING:
1/4 cup packed brown sugar
1/4 cup chopped pecans
   1 tablespoon cold butter

In a large bowl, combine the flour, baking powder and salt. In another bowl, combine the brown sugar, milk, oil, egg and vanilla. Stir into dry ingredients just until moistened. Fold in peaches and pecans. Fill greased or paper-lined muffin cups two-thirds full.

   Combine topping ingredients until crumbly; sprinkle over batter. Bake at 400° for 15-18 minutes or until a toothpick comes out clean. Cool for 5 minutes before removing from pan to a wire rack. **Yield:** 1 dozen.

PEACH POINTERS

PURCHASE peaches that have an intense fragrance and that give slightly to palm pressure. Avoid those that are hard or have soft spots. A half pound will yield about 1 cup chopped peaches.

   Store ripe peaches in a plastic bag in the refrigerator for up to 5 days. To ripen peaches, place in a brown paper bag and store at room temperature for about 2 days.

   To easily remove the pit, cut the fruit from stem to stem all the way around. Twist the peach halves in opposite directions and lift out the pit.

Ham 'n' Swiss Strudel

You just can't beat this strudel stuffed with ham, cheese and rice when you want to serve a special breakfast or brunch. Fresh fruit rounds out the meal.
—Sally Coffey, Hilton, New York

1-1/2 **cups chicken broth**
  3/4 **cup uncooked long grain rice**
    1 **cup finely chopped onion**
    1 **tablespoon plus 1/2 cup butter,** *divided*
  12 **sheets phyllo dough (18 inches x 14 inches)**
    4 **ounces thinly sliced deli ham, julienned**
    2 **cups (8 ounces) shredded Swiss cheese**
    1 **teaspoon paprika**

In a saucepan, bring broth to a boil; add rice. Reduce heat; cover and simmer for 15 minutes or until rice is tender and liquid is absorbed. In another saucepan, saute onion in 1 tablespoon butter until tender; add to rice.

Melt remaining butter. Place one sheet of phyllo dough on a work surface; brush with butter. Layer with remaining phyllo and butter (keep dough covered with waxed paper until ready to use). Spoon rice mixture over dough to within 1 in. of edges. Sprinkle with ham, cheese and paprika.

Fold short sides 1 in. over filling. Roll up jelly-roll style, starting with a long side. Brush with remaining butter. Place seam side down on a greased baking sheet. Bake at 375° for 25-30 minutes or until golden brown. Cool for 5 minutes before slicing. **Yield:** 10-12 servings.

AVOID A BRUNCH CRUNCH

YOU DON'T have to crack under the pressure of hosting an Easter breakfast or brunch. The key is selecting a good assortment of foods and getting a lot done the night before.

- When selecting recipes to serve, look for some make-ahead choices as well as some last-minute dishes. If children are part of the guest list, you may want to offer them the old standby of cereal and milk…they'll likely prefer it to some of your more "fancy" foods.
- The day before, iron tablecloths and napkins and set the table. Put out the serving dishes and utensils.
- Put condiments that are stored in the fridge (such as butter, jam, cream cheese, etc.) on the same shelf so you can quickly reach for them the next morning. Condiments stored at room temperature (like syrup and honey) can be poured into their serving pitchers and covered with plastic wrap.
- Get a head start on as many dishes as possible by chopping, slicing and dicing the night before.
- Measure the coffee the night before. Then make it in the morning and transfer it to a thermal carafe for serving. Make and refrigerate the juice. In the morning, transfer it to a pretty pitcher.
- Review your menu and make a list of what needs to be done in the morning before your guests arrive.

Scrambled Egg Brunch Bread

(Pictured at right)

This attractive bread is brimming with eggs, ham and cheese, making it a real meal in one. By using refrigerated crescent rolls, it's a snap to prepare.
—Julie Deal
China Grove, North Carolina

- 2 tubes (8 ounces *each*) refrigerated crescent rolls
- 4 ounces thinly sliced deli ham, julienned
- 4 ounces cream cheese, softened
- 1/2 cup milk
- 8 eggs
- 1/4 teaspoon salt
- Dash pepper
- 1/4 cup chopped sweet red pepper
- 2 tablespoons chopped green onion
- 1 teaspoon butter
- 1/2 cup shredded cheddar cheese

Unroll each tube of crescent dough (do not separate rectangles). Place side by side on a greased baking sheet with long sides touching; seal seams and perforations. Arrange ham lengthwise down center third of rectangle.

In a mixing bowl, beat cream cheese and milk. Separate one egg; set egg white aside. Add the egg yolk, remaining eggs, salt and pepper to cream cheese mixture; mix well. Add red pepper and onion.

In a large skillet, melt butter; add egg mixture. Cook and stir over medium heat just until set. Remove from the heat. Spoon scrambled eggs over ham. Sprinkle with cheese.

On each long side of dough, cut 1-in.-wide strips to the center to within 1/2 in. of filling. Starting at one end, fold alternating strips at an angle across filling. Pinch ends to seal and tuck under. Beat reserved egg white; brush over dough. Bake at 375° for 25-28 minutes or until golden brown. **Yield:** 6 servings.

Easter Feast Features Ham

THE WONDERFUL AROMA of a ham baking in the oven can take you back in taste and time to special occasions spent in Grandma's kitchen.

And nothing signals Easter and the arrival of spring in such a mouth-watering way!

Family and friends will be called to the kitchen by the sweet and tangy aroma of Plum-Glazed Gingered Ham. No one will be able to resist nibbling!

A medley of meal mates includes creamy Mustard Potatoes Au Gratin and eye-catching Vegetable Bundles.

For dessert, lighter-than-air Lemon Clouds with Custard won't weigh anyone down after dinner.

MEMORABLE MEAL
(Clockwise from bottom left)

Lemon Clouds with Custard (p. 39)

Plum-Glazed Gingered Ham (p. 36)

Vegetable Bundles (p. 35)

Mustard Potatoes Au Gratin (p. 34)

EASTER DINNER TIMELINE

A Few Weeks Before:

- Order a 5- to 7-pound bone-in fully cooked ham from your butcher.
- Prepare two grocery lists—one for non-perishable items to purchase now and one for perishable items to purchase a few days before Easter.
- Look for a vase and ribbon for the Carrot and Daisy Bouquet (see page 38).

Two Days Before:

- Buy ham and remaining grocery items.

The Day Before:

- Set the table.
- Buy carrots and flowers for the Carrot and Daisy Bouquet. Place flowers in water and refrigerate carrots until ready to assemble.
- Prepare and refrigerate glaze for Plum-Glazed Gingered Ham.
- Assemble and refrigerate Mustard Potatoes Au Gratin.

- Make the custard for Lemon Clouds; refrigerate.
- Bake Poppy Seed Easter Cake; let cool. Assemble and decorate as directed; chill.

Easter Day:

- In the morning, make the Carrot and Daisy Bouquet. Assemble the Spring Vegetable Bundles; refrigerate.
- Make the "clouds" for Lemon Clouds with Custard; chill for 2 hours.
- Bake the Plum-Glazed Gingered Ham.
- Remove the Mustard Potatoes Au Gratin from the refrigerator 30 minutes before baking; bake as directed.
- Cook the Spring Vegetable Bundles as directed.
- When the ham is done, prepare the gravy.
- For dessert, assemble Lemon Clouds with Custard and serve alongside Poppy Seed Easter Cake.

Mustard Potatoes Au Gratin

(Pictured on page 33)

These rich and creamy potatoes taste great with a variety of meats.
— Tangee Thaler, Silver Lake, Ohio

1/3 cup finely chopped green onions
3 tablespoons butter, *divided*
2 cups heavy whipping cream
1/2 cup Dijon mustard

1 cup (4 ounces) shredded Swiss *or* Gruyere cheese, *divided*
8 medium potatoes, peeled and thinly sliced

In a small saucepan, cook onions in 1 tablespoon butter for 2 minutes or until tender. Stir in the cream, mustard and remaining butter. Bring to a boil. Reduce heat; simmer, uncovered, for 5 minutes.

Reduce heat to low; stir in half of the cheese until melted. Remove from the heat. In a greased shallow 2-1/2-qt. baking dish, layer a third of the potatoes; top with a third of the sauce. Repeat layers twice; sprinkle with remaining cheese.

Bake, uncovered, at 400° for 30 minutes. Cover and bake 25-30 minutes longer or until potatoes are tender. Let stand for 5 minutes before serving. **Yield:** 12 servings.

Vegetable Bundles

(Pictured at right and on page 33)

You can assemble these bundles from our Test Kitchen before guests arrive, then cook them in mere minutes. To keep them warm while serving, place the serving platter on a heating tray.

4 to 6 green onions
1 cup water
1 pound thin asparagus, trimmed
1 medium sweet red pepper, julienned
1 medium sweet yellow pepper, julienned
2 medium carrots, julienned
12 thyme sprigs
1-1/3 cups white wine *or* 1 cup chicken broth
3 tablespoons butter

Trim both ends of onions; cut the green tops into 7-in. lengths. In a saucepan, bring water to a boil. Add onion tops; boil for 1 minute or until softened. Drain and immediately place onion tops in ice water. Drain and pat dry. Chop white portion of onions and set aside.

Divide asparagus, peppers and carrots into 12 bundles. Top each with a thyme sprig. Tie each bundle with a blanched onion top.

In a large skillet, place wine or broth, chopped onions and vegetable bundles. Bring to a boil. Cook, uncovered, for 5-7 minutes or until vegetables are tender and liquid is reduced by two-thirds. Carefully remove bundles with a slotted spoon to a serving plate. Add butter to skillet; cook and stir until melted. Spoon over bundles. **Yield:** 12 bundles.

Editor's Note: Use asparagus spears that are 1/4 inch in diameter. Larger asparagus should be cut lengthwise in half.

Plum-Glazed Gingered Ham

(Pictured at right and on page 32)

Our Test Kitchen home economists created a slightly sweet ham glaze that gets a little kick from ginger and mustard.

2 jars (12 ounces *each*) plum preserves
2 tablespoons lime juice
1 tablespoon grated lime peel
1 tablespoon Dijon mustard
2 tablespoons grated fresh gingerroot
3/4 teaspoon pepper
1 bone-in fully cooked ham (5 to 7 pounds)

3 tablespoons all-purpose flour
1-1/4 cups water, *divided*

For glaze, combine the first six ingredients in a saucepan; bring to a boil, stirring constantly. Remove from the heat; set aside. Place ham on a rack in a shallow roasting pan. Score surface of the ham, making diamond shapes 1/2 in. deep. Spoon half of the glaze over ham. Cover and bake at 325° for 1-1/2 hours.

Remove drippings from pan and set aside. Return ham to pan. Bake, uncovered, 30 minutes longer or until a meat thermometer reads 140°, basting twice with remaining glaze.

Skim fat from ham drippings. In a saucepan, combine flour and 1/4 cup water until smooth. Stir in 3/4 cup drippings and remaining water (discard any remaining drippings). Bring to a boil; cook and stir for 2 minutes or until thickened. **Yield:** 8-10 servings (2 cups gravy).

Poppy Seed Easter Cake

(Pictured at right)

A few years ago, this cake became our traditional Easter dinner dessert. It's so much fun to decorate...and so delicious to eat!
— Gena Aschleman
West Columbia, South Carolina

1-1/4 cups butter, softened
1-1/2 cups sugar
    4 eggs
    2 cups (16 ounces) sour cream
1/4 cup milk
    2 tablespoons lemon juice
    1 to 2 tablespoons grated lemon
      peel
    1 teaspoon vanilla extract
    3 cups all-purpose flour
    2 teaspoons baking powder
    2 teaspoons baking soda
1/4 teaspoon salt
1/4 cup poppy seeds
FROSTING:
    2 packages (8 ounces *each*)
      cream cheese, softened
    1 cup butter, softened
    8 cups confectioners' sugar
    2 to 3 tablespoons milk, *divided*
Green food coloring
1/2 cup jelly beans

In a large mixing bowl, cream butter and sugar. Add eggs, one at a time, beating well after each addition. Combine the sour cream, milk, lemon juice, peel and vanilla; add to creamed mixture. Combine the flour, baking powder, baking soda and salt; add to the creamed mixture and beat just until combined. Stir in poppy seeds (batter will be thick).

Transfer to three greased and floured 9-in. round baking pans. Bake at 350° for 25-30 minutes or until a toothpick inserted near the center comes out clean. Cool for 10 minutes before removing from pans to wire racks.

For frosting, in a mixing bowl, beat cream cheese and butter until light and fluffy. Gradually beat in sugar. Beat in 2 tablespoons milk. Place 1 cup of frosting in a small bowl and tint pale green; set aside.

To assemble, place one cake layer on a serving plate; frost top with white frosting. Repeat. Top with remaining cake layer. Frost top and sides of cake with remaining frosting.

Cut a small hole in the corner of a pastry or plastic bag; insert round tip No. 3. Fill bag with green frosting. Write "Happy Easter" on top of cake. With multi-opening or grass tip No. 233, pipe green frosting on top of cake to resemble a bird's nest. Pipe green frosting around top edge of cake. Place jelly beans in nest. Store in the refrigerator. **Yield:** 14-16 servings.

Editor's Note: A coupler and round tip No. 2 may be used in place of multi-opening tip No. 233.

Carrot and Daisy Bouquet

(Pictured at right and on page 33)

Folks will root for the hostess when they catch sight of this whimsical spring centerpiece. Be sure to order extra flowers to tuck into the Pocket Napkin Fold.

Fresh carrots with greens
Clear glass vase
White gerbera daisies *or* other
   flowers of choice
Additional greens, optional
Coordinating wired ribbon

Cut off the greens from the carrots, leaving a bit of greens on the carrot tops. Immediately place the removed greens in water. Place the carrots, narrow ends down, inside the vase, filling it completely. The carrots should be tight and stand upright.

Fill the vase with water. Insert the daisies between carrots so the carrot tops are covered. Fill in with carrot greens and other greens if desired.

Tie a loose knot in the center of a length of ribbon. Place a strip of double-stick tape around the vase where the ribbon will be. Wrap the ribbon around the vase with the knot in front. Tie a loose knot in the ribbon on the other side of the vase; trim ribbon ends close to the knot.

POCKET NAPKIN FOLD

THE DECORATIVE DESIGN of the Pocket Napkin Fold (pictured at left) creates a pretty place in which you can tuck in flowers, eating utensils or small party favors. Start with a cloth napkin folded into a square. (If using a patterned napkin, make sure the design is the same on both sides.)

1. Fold down the open point of the top layer so it aligns with the closed point. Fold down the open point of the next layer until it's a short distance from the previous point. Repeat with the last layer, placing the open point a short distance from the previous point.

2. Carefully turn over the napkin. Fold the side corners toward the center so they overlap. Carefully turn over the napkin. Set it on a plate; tuck the stem of a single flower in the pocket.

Lemon Clouds with Custard

(Pictured on page 32)

Cool custard on a cloud of fluffy egg whites is the perfect ending to a heavy meal.
—Jessica Wallace, Fort Worth, Texas

11 tablespoons sugar, *divided*
3 tablespoons cornstarch
2 teaspoons grated lemon peel
1-1/3 cups plus 1 tablespoon cold water, *divided*
1/3 cup lemon juice
3 egg whites
1/8 teaspoon cream of tartar
CUSTARD SAUCE:
3 tablespoons sugar
1 tablespoon cornstarch
1-3/4 cups cold milk
3 egg yolks, lightly beaten
1/2 teaspoon vanilla extract

In a heavy saucepan, combine 5 tablespoons sugar, cornstarch and lemon peel. Gradually stir in 1-1/3 cups water until blended. Bring to a boil; cook and stir for 1-2 minutes or until thickened. Remove from the heat; stir in lemon juice. Set aside.

In another heavy saucepan, combine the egg whites, cream of tartar and remaining sugar and water. With a portable mixer, beat on low speed over low heat for 1 minute. Continue beating until mixture reaches 160°. Pour into a large mixing bowl. Beat on high speed until stiff peaks form. Fold into lemon syrup. Cover and refrigerate for at least 2 hours.

For sauce, in a small saucepan, combine sugar and cornstarch. Gradually stir in milk until smooth. Bring to a boil; cook and stir for 2 minutes or until thickened. Remove from the heat. Stir a small amount of hot milk mixture into egg yolks; return all to pan, stirring constantly. Bring to a gentle boil; cook and stir for 2 minutes. Remove from the heat; stir in vanilla. Cover and refrigerate until chilled. Spoon lemon meringue into dessert cups; top with custard sauce. **Yield:** 5-6 servings.

Editor's Note: A stand mixer is recommended for beating the egg whites after they reach 160°.

Old-Fashioned Easter Egg Hunt

THE THOUGHT of spring conjures up images of Easter bonnets, shiny new shoes, brightly colored clothes and most importantly …more time spent outdoors!

So if you have a case of spring fever, hatch a plan to host an old-fashioned Easter egg hunt.

Your brood will happily perch upon their seats to sample Bacon 'n' Egg Bundles.

Bring a bit of sunshine to the buffet table by serving a dish brimming with Marinated Fruit Salad.

For those youngsters who just can't sit still, French Toast Sticks and Meringue Bunnies are easy to eat on the fly.

A MEAL WITH KID APPEAL
(Clockwise from top)

Meringue Bunnies (p.43)

French Toast Sticks (p.42)

Bacon 'n' Egg Bundles (p.44)

Marinated Fruit Salad (p.43)

French Toast Sticks

(Pictured on page 41)

These French toast sticks from our Test Kitchen are handy to have in the freezer for a hearty breakfast in an instant. They're great for buffets because they can be eaten on the go.

6 slices day-old Texas Toast
4 eggs
1 cup milk
2 tablespoons sugar
1 teaspoon vanilla extract
1/4 to 1/2 teaspoon ground
   cinnamon
1 cup crushed cornflakes,
   optional
Confectioners' sugar, optional
Maple syrup

Cut each piece of bread into thirds; place in an ungreased 13-in. x 9-in. x 2-in. dish. In a large bowl, whisk the eggs, milk, sugar, vanilla and cinnamon. Pour over bread; soak for 2 minutes, turning once. If desired, coat bread with cornflake crumbs on all sides. Place in a greased 15-in. x 10-in. x 1-in. baking pan. Freeze until firm, about 45 minutes. Transfer to an airtight container or resealable freezer bag and store in the freezer.

To bake, place desired number of frozen French toast sticks on a greased baking sheet. Bake at 425° for 8 minutes. Turn; bake 10-12 minutes longer or until golden brown. Sprinkle with confectioners' sugar if desired. Serve with syrup. **Yield:** 1-1/2 dozen.

Bird's Nests

To celebrate the arrival of spring, our Test Kitchen shaped chocolate-coated chow mein noodles into nests, then filled them with jelly bean "eggs." You may want to make a double batch because they're bound to fly off your table!

1 package (11-1/2 ounces) milk
   chocolate chips
1 tablespoon shortening
1 can (5 ounces) chow mein
   noodles
2/3 cup flaked coconut
45 to 60 jelly beans

In a saucepan, melt the chocolate chips and shortening over low heat; stir until smooth. Remove from the heat. Stir in the chow mein noodles and coconut until well coated.

Divide into 15 mounds on a waxed paper-lined baking sheet. Shape into nests; press an indentation in the center. Place three or four jelly beans in each nest. Cool. Store in an airtight container. **Yield:** 15 servings.

Meringue Bunnies

(Pictured at right and on page 40)

These cute cookies created by our home economists are a great addition to your table when entertaining at Easter. Enlist the kids to help shape the bunnies.

- **2 egg whites**
- **1/8 teaspoon cream of tartar**
- **1/2 cup sugar**
- **1/4 cup pink candy coating disks**
- **36 heart-shaped red decorating sprinkles**

In a mixing bowl, beat the egg whites and cream of tartar on medium speed until soft peaks form. Gradually add sugar, 1 tablespoon at a time, beating on high until stiff peaks form. Transfer to a pastry or plastic bag; cut a small hole in a corner of the bag. On parchment-lined baking sheets, pipe the meringue into 4-3/4-in. bunny shapes. Bake at 225° for 1-1/2 hours or until firm. Remove to wire racks.

In a microwave, melt candy coating; stir until smooth. Place in a pastry or plastic bag; cut a small hole in a corner of the bag. Pipe ears, whiskers and mouths on bunnies. Attach hearts for eyes and nose with melted candy coating. **Yield:** 1 dozen.

Marinated Fruit Salad

(Pictured on page 40)

Juice adds refreshing flavor to this make-ahead fruit salad from our home economists. For added color, sprinkle some strawberries or raspberries on top just before serving.

- **2 cups cubed cantaloupe**
- **2 cups cubed honeydew**
- **2 medium kiwifruit, peeled, halved and sliced**
- **1/4 cup orange peach mango juice concentrate *or* orange pineapple juice concentrate, undiluted**

In a bowl, combine the cantaloupe, honeydew and kiwi. Add juice concentrate; toss to coat. Refrigerate for at least 2 hours, stirring occasionally. Serve with a slotted spoon. **Yield:** 6-8 servings.

Editor's Note: This recipe was tested with Dole frozen juice concentrate.

Bacon 'n' Egg Bundles

(Pictured on page 40)

This is a fun way to serve bacon and eggs all in one bite!
The recipe can easily be doubled for a larger group.
—Edith Landinger, Longview, Texas

1 teaspoon butter
12 to 18 bacon strips
6 eggs
Fresh parsley sprigs

Lightly grease six muffin cups with the butter. In a large skillet, cook the bacon over medium heat until cooked but not crisp. Drain on paper towels.

Cut six bacon strips in half widthwise; line the bottom of each muffin cup with two bacon pieces. Line the sides of each muffin cup with one or two bacon strips. Break an egg into each cup. Bake, uncovered, at 325° for 12-18 minutes or until whites are completely set and yolks begin to thicken but are not firm. Transfer to a serving plate; surround with parsley. **Yield:** 6 servings.

BUYING AND STORING BACON

ALWAYS check the date stamp on packages of vacuum-sealed bacon to make sure it's fresh. The date reflects the last date of sale.

Once the package is opened, bacon should be used within a week. For long-term storage, freeze bacon for up to 1 month.

Springtime Strawberry Bars

Warmer weather calls for a lighter dessert like these fruity bars.
The recipe makes a big batch, so it's perfect for company.
—Marna Heitz, Farley, Iowa

1 cup butter, softened
1-1/2 cups sugar
2 eggs
1 teaspoon grated lemon peel
3-1/4 cups all-purpose flour, *divided*
3/4 cup slivered almonds, chopped
1 teaspoon baking powder
1/2 teaspoon salt
1 jar (12 ounces) strawberry preserves

In a large mixing bowl, cream the butter and sugar. Add eggs, one at a time, beating well after each addition. Beat in lemon peel. Combine 3 cups flour, almonds, baking powder and salt; gradually add to the creamed mixture until mixture resembles coarse crumbs (do not overmix).

Set aside 1 cup of dough. Press the remaining dough into a greased 15-in. x 10-in. x 1-in. baking pan. Spread preserves to within 1/4 in. of edges. Combine the reserved dough with the remaining flour; sprinkle over preserves. Bake at 350° for 25-30 minutes or until lightly browned. Cool on a wire rack. Cut into bars. **Yield:** about 3 dozen.

Ham 'n' Cheese Egg Bake

(Pictured at right)

This make-ahead egg casserole is just the thing when entertaining in the morning. It's loaded with ham, cheese and mushrooms.
—Susan Miller
North Andover, Massachusetts

1-1/2 cups (6 ounces) shredded cheddar cheese
1-1/2 cups (6 ounces) shredded mozzarella cheese
1/2 pound fresh mushrooms, sliced
6 green onions, sliced
1 medium sweet red pepper, chopped
2 tablespoons butter
1-3/4 cups cubed fully cooked ham
1/4 cup all-purpose flour
8 eggs
1-3/4 cups milk
Salt and pepper to taste

Combine the cheeses; sprinkle into a greased 13-in. x 9-in. x 2-in. baking dish. In a large skillet, saute the mushrooms, onions and red pepper in butter; stir in ham. Spoon over the cheese. In a bowl, combine the flour, eggs, milk, salt and pepper. Pour over ham mixture; cover and refrigerate overnight.

Remove from the refrigerator 30 minutes before baking. Bake, uncovered, at 350° for 35-45 minutes or until a knife inserted near the center comes out clean. Let stand for 5 minutes before serving. **Yield:** 8-10 servings.

Fast Fruit Punch

This family recipe is featured at all of our special events. The pink punch is so pretty on the table.
—Joanne Stark, Wabamun, Alberta

1/2 cup orange breakfast
    drink mix
4 cups water
1 can (12 ounces) frozen pink
    lemonade concentrate,
    thawed
1 can (12 ounces) frozen
    white grape raspberry juice
    concentrate, thawed
1 can (12 ounces) frozen orange
    juice concentrate, thawed

2 cups chilled cranberry juice
2 cups chilled pineapple juice
2 bottles (2 liters *each*) lemon-lime soda, chilled
Lemon, lime and orange slices

In a large container or punch bowl, dissolve drink mix in water. Stir in the next five ingredients. Add soda and sliced fruit. Serve immediately. **Yield:** 40 servings (7-3/4 quarts).

Buttermilk Potato Doughnut Holes

Having worked in a school cafeteria for more than 10 years, I've seen my share of recipes.
Everyone loves the comforting flavor of these old-fashioned doughnuts.
—Linda Lam, Mt. Sidney, Virginia

2 cups sugar
3 eggs
1/3 cup shortening
1-1/2 cups hot mashed potatoes
    (prepared without milk and
    butter)
1 cup buttermilk
1 teaspoon vanilla extract
5-1/2 cups all-purpose flour
4 teaspoons baking powder
1 teaspoon salt
1 teaspoon ground nutmeg
Oil for deep-fat frying
Additional sugar

In a mixing bowl, beat sugar, eggs and shortening. Add the potatoes, buttermilk and vanilla. Combine the dry ingredients; add to potato mixture. Cover and refrigerate for 1 hour.

In an electric skillet or deep-fat fryer, heat oil to 375°. Drop rounded teaspoonfuls of batter, a few at a time, into hot oil. Fry for 1-1/2 minutes on each side or until golden brown. Drain on paper towels; roll in additional sugar while warm. **Yield:** about 9-1/2 dozen.

POTATO POINTERS

WHEN BUYING potatoes, look for those that are firm, well shaped and free of blemishes. Avoid potatoes that are wrinkled, cracked or sprouting.

If kept in a cool, dark, well-ventilated place, most potatoes will keep for up to 2 weeks. However, new potatoes should be used within 4 days of purchase.

One pound of russet potatoes—about 3 medium potatoes—equals approximately 3-1/2 cups chopped or 2 to 3 cups mashed.

Easter Egg Candies

(Pictured at right)

Our home economists prove that candy-making can be easy! Have kids help roll the candies in sprinkles, colored sugar or jimmies.

  1 package (10 to 12 ounces) vanilla *or* white chips
  1 package (3 ounces) cream cheese, cubed
  1 teaspoon water
1/2 teaspoon vanilla extract
Colored sprinkles, colored sugar *and/or* jimmies

In a microwave-safe bowl, melt the chips at 50% power. Add the cream cheese, water and vanilla; stir until blended. Chill for 1 hour or until easy to handle. Quickly shape into 1-1/4-in. eggs. Roll in sprinkles, colored sugar or jimmies. Store in an airtight container in the refrigerator. **Yield:** about 4 dozen (1-1/2 pounds).

Italian Veggie Turkey Pitas

One day I took the recipe for a favorite dip and added vegetables and turkey to create this flavorful sandwich filling. Pitas are a nice change from ordinary bread.
—Elaine Hollenbach, Milton, Wisconsin

  1 cup mayonnaise
1/2 cup sour cream
  1 envelope Italian salad dressing mix
1/2 teaspoon hot pepper sauce
  2 cups diced cooked turkey
  1 cup chopped cauliflowerets
  1 cup chopped broccoli florets
  1 cup shredded red cabbage
  1 celery rib, julienned
  1 small carrot, julienned
1/2 medium green pepper, julienned
  1 green onion, chopped
  5 pita breads (6 inches), halved
Lettuce leaves, optional

In a large bowl, combine the mayonnaise, sour cream, salad dressing mix and hot pepper sauce. Stir in the turkey, cauliflower, broccoli, cabbage, celery, carrot, green pepper and onion. Spoon into pita breads lined with lettuce if desired. **Yield:** 5 servings.

Blueberry-Rhubarb Refrigerator Jam

I think the best recipes come from good friends…that's where I got this jam recipe.
It's a great way to use an abundant supply of rhubarb.
—Arloia Lutz, Sebewaing, Michigan

5 cups chopped fresh *or* frozen rhubarb, thawed
1/2 cup water
5 cups sugar
1 can (21 ounces) blueberry pie filling
2 cups fresh *or* frozen blueberries
3 tablespoons lemon juice
2 packages (3 ounces *each*) raspberry gelatin

In a large kettle, cook rhubarb and water over medium-high heat for 3-5 minutes or until rhubarb is tender. Add sugar. Bring to a boil; boil for 2 minutes. Stir in pie filling, blueberries and lemon juice. Return to a boil. Reduce heat; cook and stir for 10 minutes. Remove from the heat; stir in gelatin until dissolved. Cool slightly. Pour into refrigerator containers. Cool to room temperature. Cover and refrigerate. **Yield:** 4-1/2 pints.

Asparagus Rice Salad

Fresh asparagus makes this salad special. It's one of my favorite salads to serve in spring.
—Adrene Schmidt, Waldersee, Manitoba

1 can (14-1/2 ounces) chicken broth
1/4 cup water
1 cup uncooked long grain rice
2 cups cut fresh asparagus (2-inch pieces)
3/4 cup frozen peas, thawed
3 green onions, sliced
1/3 cup pecan halves
2 to 4 tablespoons minced fresh cilantro
1/4 cup olive oil
3 tablespoons lemon juice
3 tablespoons sour cream
1/2 teaspoon grated lemon peel
1/4 teaspoon salt
1/4 teaspoon white pepper
4 cups fresh spinach

In a saucepan, bring broth and water to a boil. Stir in rice. Reduce heat; cover and simmer for 15 minutes or until tender. Place 1 in. of water and asparagus in a skillet; bring to a boil. Reduce heat; cover and simmer for 2 minutes. Add peas; return to a boil. Reduce heat; cover and simmer for 2-3 minutes or until crisp-tender. Drain.

In a large bowl, combine the rice, asparagus mixture, onions, pecans and cilantro; mix well. In a bowl, whisk the oil, lemon juice, sour cream, lemon peel, salt and pepper. Pour over rice mixture; toss to coat. Cover and refrigerate for 1-2 hours.

Just before serving, line a serving platter with 1 cup of spinach. Tear remaining spinach; arrange over spinach leaves. Top with rice mixture. **Yield:** 6 servings.

Rabbit Rolls

(Pictured at right)

To create these cute rolls that depict the back view of a bunny, our home economists twisted a rope of dough to form the ears, then used a ball of dough for the tail.

  4 to 4-1/2 cups all-purpose flour
1/2 cup sugar
  2 packages (1/4 ounce *each*)
     active dry yeast
1-1/2 teaspoons salt
  1 cup plus 1/2 teaspoon water,
     divided
  6 tablespoons butter, cubed
  1 egg, *separated*
  1 egg

In a mixing bowl, combine 1 cup flour, sugar, yeast and salt. In a saucepan, heat 1 cup water and butter to 120°-130°. Add to dry ingredients; beat for 2 minutes. Cover and refrigerate egg white. Add egg yolk, egg and 1 cup flour to yeast mixture; beat until smooth. Stir in enough remaining flour to form a firm dough.

Turn onto a lightly floured surface; knead until smooth and elastic, about 6-8 minutes. Place in a greased bowl, turning once to grease top. Cover and let rise in a warm place until doubled, about 1 hour.

Turn dough onto a lightly floured surface; divide into 20 pieces. Shape 18 pieces into 10-in.-long ropes. Fold in half; twist top half twice to form ears. Place 2 in. apart on greased baking sheets. Shape remaining dough into 18 balls. Place one on the loop end of each roll to form tail; press into dough. Cover and let rise until doubled, about 30 minutes.

Whisk the reserved egg white with remaining water; brush over rolls. Bake at 375° for 12-15 minutes or until golden brown. Cool on wire racks. **Yield:** 1-1/2 dozen.

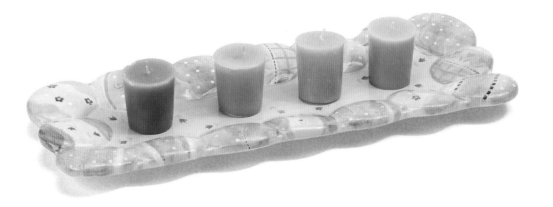

Chocolate Chip Coffee Cake

*The irresistible aromas of chocolate, cinnamon and nutmeg waft through the house
as this tasty coffee cake bakes. Before long, my family is clamoring for a generous slice!*
—*Kathy Dunn, Yorktown, Virginia*

1 cup butter, softened
1-1/4 cups sugar
2 eggs
1-1/4 cups sour cream
1 teaspoon vanilla extract
2-1/2 cups all-purpose flour
1 teaspoon baking powder
1 teaspoon ground nutmeg
1/2 teaspoon baking soda
FILLING/TOPPING:
   3/4 cup chopped pecans
   3/4 cup miniature semisweet
     chocolate chips
   1/3 cup sugar
   1/3 cup packed brown sugar

1-1/2 teaspoons ground cinnamon
1/2 teaspoon ground nutmeg

In a large mixing bowl, cream butter and sugar. Add eggs, one at a time, beating well after each addition. Add sour cream and vanilla; mix well. Combine the flour, baking powder, nutmeg and baking soda; add to creamed mixture just until combined (batter will be stiff). Place half of the batter in a greased 13-in. x 9-in. x 2-in. baking pan.

Combine the filling/topping ingredients. Sprinkle half over batter. Spread remaining batter over top. Sprinkle with remaining filling/topping. Bake at 325° for 40-45 minutes or until golden brown. Cool on a wire rack. **Yield:** 12-15 servings.

HOW YOUR EASTER EGG HUNT CAN BE A HIT

PLANNING an Easter egg hunt is a wonderful excuse to squelch spring fever. Throwing the party is a breeze if you keep these tips in mind:

- Since most folks have plans on Easter Sunday, schedule the party a week or two earlier on a Saturday or Sunday morning.
- If you don't want the expense of buying every guest an Easter basket, ask each child to bring a basket from home. You may want to have a few extra baskets (or some lunch bags) on hand the day of the party just in case someone forgot to bring their own.
- Keep the event casual by serving a buffet-style brunch and offer foods that appeal to old and young alike.
- There's no need to go all out on your decorating. Simply set out a vase brimming with tulips, fill an assortment of Easter baskets with decorated eggs or sprinkle colorful jelly beans on the buffet table.
- For food safety purposes, it's best not to use real eggs for the hunt. Instead, rely on colored plastic eggs, which can be found in a variety of stores. To be fair to all guests, plan on having each child look for the same number of eggs.
- In addition to filling the eggs with candy, surprise the children with stickers, Silly Putty, jacks or even a certificate for a book or puzzle that they can "cash in" with you.
- For the younger children, "hide" the eggs in open areas, but get a little more creative for the older kids. Before starting the hunt, instruct the children that they all need to look for the number of eggs you specify.

Easter Egg Invitation

(Pictured at right)

THINK outside the box when creating the invitations for your Easter egg hunt. Why not make your own invitations and send them off in a fun way?

Look in variety or craft stores for paper in the shape of a bunny, chick or egg. (We traced a chick cookie cutter onto yellow paper to make our invitation shown at right.)

Tuck the invitation inside a colored plastic egg. Then rest the egg on a bed of Easter grass in a small box. Close the box, secure with tape and adhere a mailing sticker. Take the boxed invitations to the post office for mailing.

Or if your guests live nearby, tuck the ends of a ribbon inside the plastic egg, then seal. Drive to your guests' homes and hang an egg invitation on their front door.

Deviled Egg Bunnies

These eggs are a must at our traditional Easter dinner. With nine grandchildren, there are never any leftovers.
— Bernice Martinoni, Petaluma, California

- 8 hard-cooked eggs
- 6 tablespoons mayonnaise
- 1 tablespoon sweet pickle relish
- 1/4 teaspoon salt
- Dash pepper
- 8 baby carrots
- 32 dried currants
- 8 mini marshmallows, halved

Slice eggs in half lengthwise; remove yolks and set whites aside. In a small bowl, mash yolks. Add the mayonnaise, pickle relish, salt and pepper; mix well.

Pipe into the egg whites, creating a mound at the pointed end of the white for the bunny's head. For the ears, cut each carrot lengthwise into four slices; place two slices upright on bunny's head. Press currants into eggs for eyes; add marshmallow pieces for tails. Cover and refrigerate until serving. **Yield:** 16 servings.

SPRING Celebrations

Exciting Ideas for Hard-Cooked Eggs!

EASTER just wouldn't be the same without colorful baskets brimming with beautifully decorated hard-cooked eggs.

But what do you do with all of those Grade A goodies after the Easter Bunny has hopped away?

If your family doesn't think dozens of leftover hard-cooked eggs are all they're cracked up to be, turn to this chapter, where fellow cooks—and our own home economists—shell out some "eggs-citing" new recipes.

Molded Egg Salad, Ham 'n' Potato Casserole and Three-Cheese Deviled Eggs are just a sample of the innovative ideas you'll find on the following pages.

LIVELY LEFTOVERS
(Clockwise from top left)

Molded Egg Salad (p.55)

Ham 'n' Potato Casserole (p.54)

Three-Cheese Deviled Eggs (p.56)

Hard-Cooked Eggs

Our home economists share this recipe for hard-cooked eggs
that can be eaten plain or used in various recipes.

12 eggs
Cold water

Place eggs in a single layer in a large saucepan; add enough cold water to cover by 1 in. Cover and quickly bring to a boil. Remove from the heat. Let stand for 15 minutes for large eggs (18 minutes for extra-large eggs and 12 minutes for medium eggs). Rinse eggs in cold water and place in ice water until completely cooled. Drain; refrigerate. **Yield:** 12 servings.

Ham 'n' Potato Casserole

(Pictured on page 53)

Sour cream and cheese give this hearty casserole an irresistible richness.
Paired with fresh fruit, it is a filling breakfast, lunch or dinner.
—*Rosetta Miller, Middlebury, Indiana*

    1/4 cup butter
    1/4 cup all-purpose flour
      1 teaspoon salt
    1/4 teaspoon pepper
1-1/2 cups (12 ounces) sour cream
      4 ounces process cheese
        (Velveeta), cubed
      1 cup (4 ounces) shredded
        Colby cheese
      8 hard-cooked eggs, chopped
      3 cups cubed cooked potatoes
      2 cups cubed fully cooked ham
      2 tablespoons dried minced
        onion
      2 tablespoons minced fresh
        parsley

In a large saucepan over medium heat, melt butter. Stir in flour, salt and pepper until smooth. Cook and stir for 1-2 minutes. Remove from the heat; stir in sour cream and cheeses. Cook and stir over low heat just until cheese is melted (mixture will be thick). Remove from the heat. Stir in the eggs, potatoes, ham, onion and parsley.

Transfer to a greased 2-qt. baking dish. Bake, uncovered, at 350° for 30-35 minutes or until bubbly and edges are golden brown. **Yield:** 6 servings.

Family Traditions

When I was a youngster, we celebrated Easter by "eppering." These were contests to see who had the hardest egg. To play, you cupped your egg in your fist so that only a small portion of each end was showing. Your opponent would tap it with his egg, trying to crack yours. Then you got a chance to tap your opponent's egg. If you cracked your opponent's egg at both ends, you got to keep it.
—*Robert Braker, Boynton Beach, Florida*

Molded Egg Salad

(Pictured at right and on page 52)

This pretty mold is an attractive way to display egg salad. My family enjoys hearty helpings on crackers for a snack or on bread for lunch.
—Joann Erbe, Hobart, Indiana

12 hard-cooked eggs, finely chopped
2 cups mayonnaise
1-1/2 cups finely chopped celery
1/4 cup finely chopped green pepper
1/4 cup sweet pickle relish
2 tablespoons lemon juice
1/2 teaspoon salt
2 envelopes unflavored gelatin
1/2 cup cold water

In a bowl, combine the eggs, mayonnaise, celery, green pepper, pickle relish, lemon juice and salt; set aside. In a saucepan, sprinkle gelatin over water; let stand for 1 minute. Cook and stir over low heat until dissolved. Immediately drizzle over egg mixture; mix well. Quickly transfer to a 7-cup mold coated with nonstick cooking spray. Cover and refrigerate for 8 hours or overnight. Unmold; serve with crackers or bread. **Yield:** 6 cups.

GARNISHING SALAD MOLDS

MAKE YOUR salad mold the center of attention by adding some garnishes to the middle.

In the Molded Egg Salad picture (above), we rolled up thin slices of salami and tucked them in the center, along with a few celery leaves. Not only does it add interest and color, the garnishes are edible, too!

You can also roll up thin slices of ham or use bunches of red and green grapes.

(For another idea, see the Red Radish Rosettes used to garnish the Potato Salad Mold on page 109.)

Three-Cheese Deviled Eggs

(Pictured on page 52)

Our home economists enhanced ordinary deviled eggs by stirring in three different kinds of cheese.
A dash of paprika and sprinkle of chives on top add a little color.

6 hard-cooked eggs
3/4 cup mayonnaise
2 tablespoons finely shredded
    Monterey Jack cheese
2 tablespoons finely shredded
    Swiss cheese
2 tablespoons minced chives,
    divided
1/8 teaspoon ground mustard
1/8 teaspoon pepper

2 ounces process cheese (Velveeta), cubed
Dash paprika

Cut eggs in half lengthwise. Remove yolks; set whites aside. In a bowl, mash the yolks. Add the mayonnaise, shredded cheeses, 1 tablespoon chives, mustard and pepper. In a microwave-safe bowl, melt the process cheese on high for 1-2 minutes; stir until smooth. Stir into yolk mixture. Pipe or spoon into egg whites. Sprinkle with paprika and remaining chives. Refrigerate until serving. **Yield:** 1 dozen.

Egg Bake with Sausage Biscuits

When I want to treat my family to a delicious down-home breakfast,
this is the recipe I rely on. Sausage biscuits are a perfect partner for the egg and cheese casserole.
— Penny Bridge, Lebanon, Indiana

6 tablespoons butter, *divided*
1/4 cup all-purpose flour
1-1/2 cups milk
1 cup heavy whipping cream
1/4 cup minced fresh parsley
1/4 teaspoon *each* dried basil,
    marjoram and thyme
3 cups (12 ounces) shredded
    cheddar cheese
12 hard-cooked eggs, thinly
    sliced
1 pound sliced bacon, cooked
    and crumbled
1/2 cup dry bread crumbs
SAUSAGE BISCUITS:
    2 cups biscuit/baking mix
    2/3 cup milk

3/4 pound bulk pork sausage, cooked and
    crumbled

In a large saucepan, melt 4 tablespoons butter. Stir in flour until smooth. Gradually whisk in milk and cream. Add the parsley, basil, marjoram and thyme. Bring to a boil; cook and stir for 1-2 minutes or until thickened and bubbly. Remove from the heat; stir in cheese until melted.

In a greased shallow 2-1/2-qt. baking dish, layer a third of the egg slices, a third of the bacon and about 1 cup cheese sauce. Repeat layers twice. Melt remaining butter; toss with bread crumbs. Sprinkle over the top. Bake, uncovered, at 400° for 25-30 minutes or until bubbly and golden brown.

In a bowl, combine biscuit mix and milk. Stir in sausage. Shape into 1-1/2-in. balls. Place 2 in. apart on an ungreased baking sheet. Bake at 400° for 13-15 minutes or until lightly browned. Serve with casserole. **Yield:** 10-12 servings.

Swiss 'n' Asparagus Egg Salad

(Pictured at right)

Whether served alone or on bread, this egg salad from our Test Kitchen will satisfy your hunger. Asparagus, Swiss cheese and ham give ordinary egg salad a tasty twist.

8 fresh asparagus spears, cut
   into 1/4-inch pieces
6 hard-cooked eggs, chopped
1 cup (4 ounces) shredded
   Swiss cheese
1/2 cup cubed fully cooked ham
3/4 cup mayonnaise
1 teaspoon Dijon mustard
Salt to taste
10 slices rye bread

Place 1 in. of water and asparagus in a saucepan. Bring to a boil; simmer, uncovered, for 5 minutes or until crisp-tender. Drain and cool. In a bowl, combine the asparagus, eggs, cheese, ham, mayonnaise, mustard and salt. Spread on five slices of bread, about 1/2 cup on each; top with the remaining bread. **Yield:** 5 servings.

STORING HARD-COOKED EASTER EGGS

TO SAFELY enjoy leftover hard-cooked eggs in a variety of ways, keep these helpful hints in mind:

• After making hard-cooked eggs, refrigerate them as soon as the ice water has cooled them. Keep them refrigerated until you're ready for coloring, then chill as soon as you're done.

• Don't let hard-cooked eggs stand at room temperature for more than 2 hours. If you plan on using hard-cooked eggs as a centerpiece, cook extra eggs for eating and discard the eggs on display.

• Don't eat any colored eggs that have cracked. Either throw them out immediately or use them for display and then discard.

• Unpeeled hard-cooked eggs will stay fresh in the refrigerator for up to 1 week. Once shelled, the eggs should be used right away.

Egg and Spinach Side Dish

With four young children, I'm always on the lookout for fast and flavorful recipes.
This speedy side dish is a nice complement to chicken or steak dinners.
—Jeanne Prendergast, Clearwater, Florida

2 packages (10 ounces *each*) frozen chopped spinach, thawed and squeezed dry
1-1/2 cups mayonnaise
5 hard-cooked eggs, coarsely chopped
1/4 cup shredded Parmesan cheese
1/4 to 1/2 teaspoon crushed red pepper flakes
1/2 teaspoon garlic salt

In a large bowl, combine all of the ingredients. Spoon into a greased 1-1/2-qt. microwave-safe dish. Microwave, uncovered, on high for 3-4 minutes or until bubbly and heated through. **Yield:** 4-6 servings.

Editor's Note: This recipe was tested in an 850-watt microwave. Reduced-fat or fat-free mayonnaise is not recommended for this recipe.

Breakfast Burritos

Instead of making breakfast burritos with scrambled eggs, our home economists
created this version as a way to use extra hard-cooked Easter eggs.
Green chilies and pepper Jack cheese add a little zip.

1/2 pound bulk pork sausage
1/4 cup chopped sweet red pepper
1/4 cup chopped green onions
1 package (3 ounces) cream cheese, cubed
1 can (4 ounces) chopped green chilies
3 hard-cooked eggs, chopped
1 cup (4 ounces) shredded pepper Jack cheese
4 flour tortillas (8 inches)
Salsa, sour cream and sliced ripe olives, optional

In a large skillet, cook the sausage, red pepper and onions over medium heat until meat is no longer pink; drain. Add the cream cheese; cook and stir until cheese is melted. Add the chilies, eggs and cheese. Spoon 1/2 cup filling off center on each tortilla; fold ends and sides over filling and roll up. Serve with salsa, sour cream and olives if desired. **Yield:** 4 servings.

German-Style Pickled Eggs

(Pictured at right)

I make these pickled eggs and refrigerate them in a glass gallon jar for my husband to sell at his tavern. The customers love them! I found the recipe in an old cookbook years ago.
—Marjorie Hennig, Seymour, Indiana

2 cups cider vinegar
1 cup sugar
1/2 cup water
2 tablespoons prepared mustard
1 tablespoon salt
1 tablespoon celery seed
1 tablespoon mustard seed
6 whole cloves
2 medium onions, thinly sliced
12 hard-cooked eggs, peeled

In a large saucepan, combine the first eight ingredients. Bring to a boil. Reduce heat; cover and simmer for 10 minutes. Cool completely. Place onions and eggs in a large jar; add enough vinegar mixture to completely cover. Cover and refrigerate for at least 8 hours or overnight. Use a clean spoon each time you remove eggs for serving. May be refrigerated for up to 1 week. **Yield:** 12 servings.

CHOPPING HARD-COOKED EGGS

MY MOM and I are always looking for ways to cut preparation time in the kitchen. A few years ago, I discovered a real time-saver for chopping hard-cooked eggs.

Instead of cutting each egg individually, I put the shelled eggs in a bowl and break them apart with my pastry cutter. It works perfectly! —*Jory Stiffarm Fort Wayne, Indiana*

Cinco de Mayo Fiesta

THE HOLIDAY of Cinco de Mayo (the fifth of May) commemorates the victory of a band of Mexicans over the French army at the battle of Puebla in 1862. (It is not Mexico's Independence Day, which is actually September 16.)

Celebrate this occasion in style with a scrumptious spread of food from south of the border.

Greet guests with a cool glass of Refreshing Lime Slush. Then turn up the heat and serve Southwest Rib Roast with Salsa.

Creamy Cheesy Green Chili Rice is an appropriate accompaniment to the spicy entree.

For dessert, scoop up Cinnamon Chocolate Chip Ice Cream and pass a bowl brimming with traditional Sopaipillas. (All recipes shown at right.)

Mmm-Mexican Meal

(Clockwise from top right)

Refreshing Lime Slush (p. 63)

Cheesy Green Chili Rice (p. 63)

Cinnamon Chocolate Chip Ice Cream (p. 64)

Sopaipillas (p. 64)

Southwest Rib Roast With Salsa (p. 62)

Southwest Rib Roast with Salsa

(Pictured on page 60)

After purchasing a steer at a local 4-H fair, we were looking for tasty new beef recipes.
A blend of seasonings makes this tender cut of meat even more succulent.
—*Darlene King, Estevan, Saskatchewan*

2 tablespoons chili powder
2 teaspoons salt
2 teaspoons ground cumin
1 teaspoon cayenne pepper
1 beef rib roast (8 to 10 pounds)
2 cans (15 ounces *each*) black beans, rinsed and drained
2 medium tomatoes, seeded and chopped
1 medium red onion, chopped
1/3 cup minced fresh cilantro

In a bowl, combine the chili powder, salt, cumin and cayenne. Set aside 2 teaspoons for salsa. Rub the remaining seasoning mixture over roast. Place roast fat side up in a shallow roasting pan.

Bake, uncovered, at 325° for 2-1/2 to 3 hours or until meat reaches desired doneness (for rare, a meat thermometer should read 140°; medium, 160°; well-done, 170°). Transfer to serving platter. Let stand for 15 minutes before carving.

For salsa, combine the beans, tomatoes, onion, cilantro and reserved seasoning mixture in a bowl; mix well. Serve with roast. **Yield:** 12-16 servings.

Nana's Chilies Rellenos

This zesty dish is not for the faint of heart. My family has been enjoying it
for three generations…and will be doing so for years to come!
—*Peta-Maree Lamb, Poulsbo, Washington*

1 can (27 ounces) whole green chilies, drained
4 cups (16 ounces) shredded sharp cheddar cheese
4 eggs
1 can (12 ounces) evaporated milk
1/4 cup all-purpose flour
1 can (29 ounces) tomato sauce
1 envelope taco seasoning
8 ounces sharp cheddar cheese, cut into 1-inch cubes

Slice chilies in half and remove seeds. Arrange half of the chilies in a greased 13-in. x 9-in. x 2-in. baking dish. Sprinkle with shredded cheese. Cover with remaining chilies. In a small mixing bowl, beat eggs, milk and flour until smooth; pour over cheese. Bake, uncovered, at 350° for 30 minutes.

Whisk tomato sauce and taco seasoning until blended; pour over casserole. Carefully place cheese cubes on top in a checkerboard pattern; bake 10-15 minutes longer or until top is set. Let stand for 10 minutes before serving. **Yield:** 8-10 servings.

Editor's Note: When cutting or seeding hot peppers, use rubber or plastic gloves to protect your hands. Avoid touching your face.

Refreshing Lime Slush

(Pictured at right and on page 61)

Nothing quenches my thirst on a hot summer day quite like this slush with a subtle lime flavor. When warm weather arrives, a batch will be chilling in my freezer.
—Karen Bourne, Magrath, Alberta

11 cups water
3 cups sugar
3/4 cup limeade concentrate
2 liters lemon-lime soda, chilled
Lime slices, optional

In a 4-qt. freezer container, combine the water, sugar and limeade concentrate until sugar is dissolved; cover and freeze. Remove from the freezer several hours before serving. Chop mixture until slushy. Add soda just before serving. Garnish with lime slices if desired. **Yield:** 5-1/2 quarts (30 servings).

Cheesy Green Chili Rice

(Pictured on page 61)

This creamy rice dish is a nice addition to a spicy meal. When I first tried it at a church potluck, I knew I had to have the recipe.
—Laurie Fisher, Greeley, Colorado

1 large onion, chopped
2 tablespoons butter
4 cups hot cooked long grain rice
2 cups (16 ounces) sour cream
1 cup small-curd cottage cheese
1/2 teaspoon salt
1/8 teaspoon pepper
2 cans (4 ounces *each*) chopped green chilies, drained
2 cups (8 ounces) shredded cheddar cheese

In a large skillet, cook onion in butter until tender. Remove from the heat. Stir in the rice, sour cream, cottage cheese, salt and pepper. Spoon half of the mixture into a greased 11-in. x 7-in. x 2-in. baking dish. Top with half of the chilies and cheese. Repeat layers. Bake, uncovered, at 375° for 20-25 minutes or until heated through and bubbly. **Yield:** 6-8 servings.

Sopaipillas

(Pictured on page 60)

These deep-fried breads were a hit when I made them for our
daughter's birthday party. They're a fun way to round out a Mexican-theme meal.
—Glenda Jarboe, Oroville, California

1-3/4 cups all-purpose flour
   2 teaspoons baking powder
   1 teaspoon salt
   2 tablespoons shortening
2/3 cup water
Oil for deep-fat frying
Honey

In a bowl, combine the dry ingredients; cut in shortening until crumbly. Gradually add water, tossing with a fork until mixture holds together. On a lightly floured surface, knead dough for 1-2 minutes or until smooth. Cover and let stand for 5 minutes. Roll out to 1/4-in. thickness. Cut with a 2-1/2-in. star cookie cutter or into 2-1/2-in. triangles.

In an electric skillet or deep-fat fryer, heat oil to 375°. Fry sopaipillas for 1-2 minutes on each side or until golden brown and puffed. Drain on paper towels. Serve immediately with honey. **Yield:** 1 dozen.

Cinnamon Chocolate Chip Ice Cream

(Pictured on page 61)

I was first served this creamy, soft-set ice cream at a friend's house.
A hint of cinnamon is the secret ingredient.
—Gloria Heidner, Elk River, Minnesota

   2 cups heavy whipping cream
   2 cups half-and-half cream
   1 cup sugar
1/2 cup chocolate syrup
1-1/2 teaspoons vanilla extract
1/4 teaspoon ground cinnamon
Pinch salt
1/2 cup miniature semisweet
   chocolate chips
Additional miniature semisweet
  chocolate chips

In a bowl, combine the first seven ingredients; stir until the sugar is dissolved. Fill cylinder of ice cream freezer two-thirds full; freeze according to manufacturer's directions. Stir in chocolate chips. Refrigerate remaining mixture until ready to freeze. Allow to ripen in ice cream freezer or firm up in your refrigerator freezer 2-4 hours before serving. Sprinkle with additional chips. **Yield:** about 2 quarts.

Black Bean Chicken Tacos

(Pictured at right)

While growing up, I developed a love of cooking from scratch. Friends and family are delighted when I present my homemade tortillas so they can assemble these tasty tacos.
— *Teresa Obsnuk, Berwyn, Illinois*

2 cups all-purpose flour
1 teaspoon baking powder
1-1/2 teaspoons ground cumin, *divided*
2 tablespoons shortening
1/2 cup plus 1 tablespoon warm water
1 pound boneless skinless chicken breasts, cubed
2 cups salsa
1 can (15 ounces) black beans, rinsed and drained
1 teaspoon onion powder
1/2 teaspoon chili powder

Shredded lettuce, shredded cheddar cheese, chopped ripe olives, sour cream and additional salsa, optional

In a bowl, combine the flour, baking powder and 1/2 teaspoon cumin. Cut in shortening until crumbly. Stir in enough water for mixture to form a ball. Knead on a floured surface for 1 minute. Cover and let rest for 20 minutes.

Meanwhile, in a large skillet, combine the chicken, salsa, beans, onion powder, chili powder and remaining cumin. Cover and simmer for 15-20 minutes or until chicken juices run clear.

For tortillas, divide dough into eight balls; roll each ball into an 8-in. circle. In an ungreased skillet, cook tortillas, one at a time, until lightly browned, about 30 seconds on each side. Layer between pieces of waxed paper or paper towel; keep warm. Spoon chicken mixture over half of each tortilla and fold over. Serve with lettuce, cheese, olives, sour cream and salsa if desired. **Yield:** 4-6 servings.

MAKING HOMEMADE TORTILLAS

1. Roll out each ball of dough into an 8-inch circle (dough will be very thin).

2. Cook tortillas, one at a time, in an ungreased skillet for about 30 seconds on each side or until lightly browned.

Three Milk Cake

With a large Hispanic population here, I have found the best recipes for Mexican food.
This traditional Tres Leches Cake is a cross between cake and pudding.
—*Janice Montiverdi, Sugar Land, Texas*

6 eggs, *separated*
1-1/2 cups sugar
2 cups all-purpose flour
2 teaspoons baking powder
1/2 teaspoon baking soda
1/2 teaspoon salt
1-1/2 cups water
1 teaspoon almond extract
TOPPING:
1 can (14 ounces) sweetened condensed milk
2 cups heavy whipping cream
1/2 cup light corn syrup
7 tablespoons evaporated milk
2 teaspoons vanilla extract
ICING:
1/2 cup heavy whipping cream
1/2 cup sugar
1 teaspoon vanilla extract
1 cup (8 ounces) sour cream

2 tablespoons confectioners' sugar
1 teaspoon almond extract

In a large mixing bowl, beat egg whites until soft peaks form. Gradually beat in sugar until stiff peaks form. Add yolks, one at a time, beating until combined. Combine the flour, baking powder, baking soda and salt; add to egg mixture alternately with water. Stir in extract. Pour into a greased 13-in. x 9-in. x 2-in. baking dish. Bake at 350° for 35-45 minutes or until a toothpick comes out clean. Cool on a wire rack. Poke holes in cake with a fork. Chill overnight.

In a saucepan, combine condensed milk, cream, corn syrup and evaporated milk. Bring to a boil over medium heat, stirring constantly; cook and stir for 2 minutes. Remove from the heat; stir in vanilla. Slowly pour over cold cake, letting milk absorb into cake. Cover and refrigerate.

In a mixing bowl, beat cream until soft peaks form. Gradually beat in sugar until stiff peaks form. Stir in vanilla. In a bowl, combine the sour cream, confectioners' sugar and extract. Fold in whipped cream. Spread over topping. Refrigerate until serving. **Yield:** 12-15 servings.

Creamy Chicken Enchiladas

I adapted the recipe for these rich and creamy enchiladas from a cooking class I had a while back.
—*Janice Montiverdi, Sugar Land, Texas*

1 small onion, chopped
1 small green pepper, chopped
1 jalapeno pepper, seeded and chopped
1 tablespoon vegetable oil
5-1/2 cups cubed cooked chicken
1/4 cup butter
1/4 cup all-purpose flour

3 cups chicken broth
1 to 2 tablespoons ground cumin
1 teaspoon garlic powder
1 teaspoon salt
1/2 teaspoon white pepper
1 cup (8 ounces) sour cream
12 flour tortillas (8 inches)
1-1/2 cups (12 ounces) shredded Monterey Jack cheese

In a large skillet, saute onion, green pepper and jalapeno in oil until onion is tender. Stir in chicken. Remove from the heat; set aside.

For sauce, melt butter in a saucepan. Stir in flour until smooth. Add broth, cumin, garlic powder, salt and pepper. Bring to a boil; cook and stir for 2 minutes or until thickened and bubbly. Remove from the heat; stir in sour cream.

Add 1 cup of the sauce to chicken mixture. Spoon 1/2 cup chicken mixture on each tortilla; roll up and place seam side down in a greased 13-in. x 9-in. x 2-in. baking dish. Pour remaining sauce over enchiladas.

Bake, uncovered, at 350° for 15 minutes or until sauce is bubbly. Sprinkle with cheese. Bake 5-10 minutes longer. **Yield:** 6 servings.

Editor's Note: When cutting or seeding hot peppers, use rubber or plastic gloves to protect your hands. Avoid touching your face.

Cheese-Stuffed Jalapenos
(Pictured at right)

A few years ago, I saw a man in the grocery store buying a big bag full of jalapeno peppers. I asked him what he intended to do with them, and he shared this recipe with me right there in the store!
—Janice Montiverdi, Sugar Land, Texas

    25 medium fresh jalapeno
       peppers
     1 package (8 ounces) cream
       cheese, softened
     3 cups (12 ounces) finely
       shredded cheddar cheese
 1-1/2 teaspoons Worcestershire
       sauce
     4 bacon strips, cooked and
       crumbled

Cut jalapenos in half lengthwise; remove seeds and membranes. In a large saucepan, boil peppers in water for 5-10 minutes (the longer you boil the peppers, the milder they become). Drain and rinse in cold water; set aside.

In a small mixing bowl, beat the cream cheese, cheddar cheese and Worcestershire sauce. Spoon 2 teaspoonfuls into each jalapeno half; sprinkle with bacon. Place on a greased baking sheet. Bake at 400° for 5-10 minutes or until cheese is melted. Serve warm. **Yield:** about 4 dozen.

Editor's Note: When cutting or seeding hot peppers, use rubber or plastic gloves to protect your hands. Avoid touching your face.

Chicken Tortilla Soup

This soup is as good as (if not better than) any kind I've had in a restaurant.
I get so many compliments on it...I know you will, too!
—Laura Johnson, Largo, Florida

1 large onion, chopped
2 tablespoons olive oil
1 can (4 ounces) chopped green chilies
2 garlic cloves, minced
1 jalapeno pepper, seeded and chopped
1 teaspoon ground cumin
5 cups chicken broth
1 can (15 ounces) tomato sauce
1 can (14-1/2 ounces) diced tomatoes with garlic and onion, undrained
3 cans (5 ounces *each*) white chicken, drained
1/4 cup minced fresh cilantro
2 teaspoons lime juice
Salt and pepper to taste
Crushed tortilla chips
Shredded Monterey Jack *or* cheddar cheese

In a large saucepan, saute onion in oil; add the chilies, garlic, jalapeno and cumin. Stir in the broth, tomato sauce and tomatoes. Bring to a boil. Reduce heat; stir in chicken. Simmer, uncovered, for 10 minutes. Add the cilantro, lime juice, salt and pepper. Top with chips and cheese. **Yield:** 7 servings.

Editor's Note: When cutting or seeding hot peppers, use rubber or plastic gloves to protect your hands. Avoid touching your face.

LEARN ABOUT CILANTRO

WITH its slightly sharp flavor, cilantro—also known as Chinese parsley—gives a distinctive taste to Mexican, Latin American and Oriental dishes. (The spice coriander comes from the seed of the cilantro plant.)

Like all other fresh herbs, cilantro should be used as soon as possible. For short-term storage, immerse the freshly cut stems in water about 2 inches deep. Cover leaves loosely with a plastic bag and refrigerate for several days. Wash just before using.

Chili Pepper Place Card

(Pictured at right)

Pepper-shaped place cards add the perfect touch to a Mexican meal. You can make them a week in advance and store them in an airtight container. Attach the raffia and name tag just before using.

**1 sun-dried tomato *or* spinach
   flour tortilla (8 to 10 inches)
Chili pepper cookie cutter (3-1/2
   inches x 1-1/2 inches)
Nonstick cooking spray**

Warm tortilla in the microwave for 10 seconds. With cookie cutter, cut out pepper shapes from tortilla. (The warmer the tortilla is, the easier it will be to cut.) If necessary, use a paring knife to assist with the cutting. Using the end of a straw, make a hole in the stem of the pepper. Place on a baking sheet; lightly coat with nonstick cooking spray. Bake at 350° for 7-8 minutes or until slightly crisp. Remove to a wire rack to cool.

Loop raffia or string through the hole; attach a name tag and tie. **Yield:** 6 to 7 place cards.

WATER GOBLET NAPKIN BOUQUET

BRING a burst of color to your table by taking two napkins in different colors and making this napkin bouquet.

1. Layer one napkin on top of the other so that each corner is offset a bit.

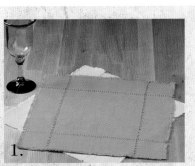
1.

2.

3.

2. Grab the napkins in the center and pull up.

3. With the edges pointing up, place napkins in a water goblet and fluff.

Backyard Memorial Day Party

WHEN YOU GATHER with family and friends to remember those who lost their lives defending their country, proudly display your patriotism with this tried-and-true menu.

Family and friends will be in their glory when you tap into the merry mood and make a Flag Cake.

Add to the spirited celebration by serving Orange Fruit Dip with an assortment of red, white and blue produce.

For many people, Memorial Day marks the beginning of summer. Herald the arrival of warmer weather with pleasing picnic fare like Herb Burgers and Potato Chip Chicken Strips.

STARS AND STRIPES SUPPER
(Clockwise from top right)

Herb Burgers (p. 72)

Orange Fruit Dip (p. 76)

Potato Chip Chicken Strips (p. 74)

Flag Cake (p. 73)

Herb Burgers

(Pictured on page 71)

These tasty burgers have lots of flavor! My dear Uncle Mickey shared the recipe with me years ago.
—Brenda Sorrow, Kannapolis, North Carolina

1 egg, lightly beaten
1 medium onion, chopped
2 teaspoons ketchup
2 garlic cloves, minced
1 teaspoon salt
1 teaspoon Worcestershire
sauce
1/2 teaspoon pepper
1/4 teaspoon dried oregano
1/4 teaspoon dried parsley flakes
1/4 teaspoon rubbed sage

1/8 to 1/4 teaspoon hot pepper sauce
2 pounds ground beef
8 hamburger buns, split
Mayonnaise, lettuce leaves, and sliced tomatoes
and red onion

In a bowl, combine the first 11 ingredients. Crumble beef over mixture and mix well. Shape into eight patties. Grill, uncovered, over medium heat for 5-6 minutes on each side or until meat is no longer pink. Serve on buns with mayonnaise, lettuce, tomatoes and onion. **Yield:** 8 servings.

Deli-Style Pasta Salad

This salad is wonderful for a crowd. Men love the robust flavor, women enjoy the
colorful vegetables and kids gobble up the tender pasta.
—Lana Boyd, Laredo, Texas

1 package (1 pound)
ziti, penne, bow tie *or*
tricolor spiral pasta
2 large cucumbers, peeled,
seeded and chopped
2 large red onions, sliced into
thin strips
2 large green peppers, chopped
2 large tomatoes, chopped
1 bottle (16 ounces) Italian
salad dressing
1 container (2.62 ounces) Salad
Supreme Seasoning

Cook pasta according to package directions; drain and rinse with cold water. In a large bowl, combine the pasta, cucumbers, onions, green peppers and tomatoes. In a small bowl, whisk the salad dressing and seasoning. Drizzle over pasta mixture and toss to coat. Cover and refrigerate for at least 1 hour. Gently toss just before serving. **Yield:** 20-24 servings.

Editor's Note: This recipe was tested with McCormick's Salad Supreme Seasoning. Look for it in the spice aisle of your grocery store.

Flag Cake

(Pictured at right and on page 70)

This impressive cake makes for a pretty presentation on a Memorial Day table. It conveniently starts with a boxed cake mix, then is topped with a sweet homemade frosting.
—*Glenda Jarboe, Oroville, California*

1 package (18-1/4 ounces) white cake mix
1 cup shortening
1 package (2 pounds) confectioners' sugar
1/2 cup water
1/2 teaspoon salt
1/2 teaspoon vanilla extract
Blue and red food coloring

Prepare and bake cake according to package directions, using two greased 9-in. round baking pans. Cool for 10 minutes before removing from pans to wire racks.

For frosting, in a mixing bowl, com-

bine the shortening, sugar, water, salt and vanilla. Beat on medium speed for 5-8 minutes or until fluffy. Place one cake on a serving plate; spread with 2/3 cup frosting. Top with remaining cake.

In a small bowl, combine 2/3 cup frosting and blue food coloring. In another bowl, combine 1-1/2 cups frosting and red food coloring. Fill a pastry or plastic bag with 1/4 cup white frosting; cut a small hole in the corner of the bag and set aside.

Frost cake top and sides with remaining white frosting. With blue frosting, frost a 3-in. section in the upper left corner of the cake. Pipe white stars over blue frosting. Fill another pastry or plastic bag with red frosting; cut a large hole in the corner of the bag. Pipe stripes across top of cake. **Yield:** 12-14 servings.

Potato Chip Chicken Strips

(Pictured on page 70)

This novel recipe is a fast and tasty change from fried chicken.
—Sister Judith LaBrozzi, Canton, Ohio

1 cup (8 ounces) sour cream
1/8 teaspoon garlic salt
1/8 teaspoon onion salt
1/8 teaspoon paprika
1 package (12 ounces) potato chips, crushed
2 pounds boneless skinless chicken breasts, cut into 1-inch strips

1/4 cup butter, melted
Salsa, barbecue sauce *or* sweet-and-sour sauce

In a shallow bowl, combine sour cream and seasonings. Place crushed potato chips in another shallow bowl. Dip chicken strips in sour cream mixture, then coat with potato chips. Place in a greased 15-in. x 10-in. x 1-in. baking pan. Drizzle with butter. Bake at 400° for 20-22 minutes or until chicken is no longer pink. Serve with salsa or sauce. **Yield:** 6 main-dish or 10 appetizer servings.

Berry Sour Cream Cake

Add this delightful dessert from our Test Kitchen to your Memorial Day menu. The moist white cake is laden with colorful raspberries and blueberries and drizzled with a sweet glaze.

1 cup butter, softened
1-1/4 cups sugar
2 eggs
1 cup (8 ounces) sour cream
1 teaspoon vanilla extract
2 cups all-purpose flour
1 teaspoon baking powder
1/2 teaspoon baking soda
2 cups fresh raspberries
1 cup fresh blueberries
GLAZE:
2 cups confectioners' sugar
1/4 cup butter, melted
1/2 teaspoon vanilla extract
2 to 3 tablespoons milk

In a mixing bowl, cream butter and sugar. Add the eggs, sour cream and vanilla; mix well. Combine the flour, baking powder and baking soda; gradually add to creamed mixture. Spread into a greased 13-in. x 9-in. x 2-in. baking dish. Sprinkle with raspberries and blueberries. Bake at 325° for 40-45 minutes or until a toothpick inserted near the center comes out clean.

For glaze, in a mixing bowl, beat confectioners' sugar, butter, vanilla and enough milk to achieve drizzling consistency. Drizzle over warm cake. Cool on a wire rack before cutting. **Yield:** 12-15 servings.

Rhubarb Terrine with Raspberry Sauce

(Pictured at right)

I'm a retired home economist who loves to make desserts and share them with family and friends. To easily cut this dessert, first dip a sharp knife in warm water, dry it, then slice.
—Lucile Cline, Wichita, Kansas

1-1/4 pounds fresh rhubarb, cut
    into 1-inch pieces
1-1/2 cups sugar, *divided*
   1 cup heavy whipping cream
  1/2 teaspoon vanilla extract
  1/2 teaspoon grated fresh
    gingerroot
   3 cups vanilla ice cream,
    softened
   3 packages (10 ounces *each*)
    frozen sweetened raspberries,
    thawed

Line a 9-in. x 5-in. x 3-in. loaf pan with plastic wrap; set aside. In a large saucepan, bring rhubarb and 1 cup sugar to a boil. Reduce heat; simmer, uncovered, for 12-14 minutes or until thickened and rhubarb is tender, stirring several times. Remove from the heat. Cool completely, about 25 minutes, stirring several times to break apart rhubarb.

In a small mixing bowl, combine the heavy whipping cream, 2 tablespoons of sugar and vanilla; beat until soft peaks form. Fold into rhubarb mixture. Transfer half to prepared pan. Cover and freeze for 1 hour. Cover and refrigerate remaining rhubarb mixture.

Stir ginger into ice cream; spread 1-1/2 cups over rhubarb layer. Cover and freeze for 30 minutes. Refrigerate remaining ice cream mixture. Spread remaining rhubarb mixture over the ice cream layer. Cover and freeze for 1 hour. Spread with remaining ice cream mixture. Freeze until firm.

For sauce, drain raspberries, reserving juice. In a blender, combine raspberries and 2 tablespoons of juice; cover and process until pureed. Press through a fine sieve; discard seeds and pulp. Stir remaining sugar into raspberry mixture. Add enough of the remaining juice to measure 1-1/2 cups.

Remove terrine from the freezer 15 minutes before cutting. Serve with raspberry sauce. **Yield:** 10-12 servings.

BERRY BEAUTIFUL CENTERPIECE

TABLE TOPPERS don't have to take a lot of thought or effort. A patriotic bowl brimming with red raspberries and blueberries (as shown in the photo above) is a simple Memorial Day centerpiece you can produce in minutes!

Orange Fruit Dip

(Pictured on page 71)

This refreshing dip is the perfect complement to fresh summer fruit.
Folks just can't seem to get enough of it...the bowl is always scraped clean!
— *Tiffany Anderson-Taylor, Gulfport, Florida*

1 cup sugar
2 tablespoons plus 1 teaspoon
   cornstarch
1/4 teaspoon salt
1 cup orange juice
1/2 cup water
1/4 cup lemon juice
1/2 teaspoon grated orange peel
1/2 teaspoon grated lemon peel
Assorted fresh fruit

In a small saucepan, combine the sugar, cornstarch and salt; stir in the orange juice, water, lemon juice, and orange and lemon peel until blended. Bring to a boil; cook and stir or 2 minutes or until thickened. Cover and refrigerate until chilled. Serve with fruit. **Yield:** 2 cups.

Chilled Blueberry Soup

With 100 blueberry bushes in my garden, I'm always looking for recipes calling for this
sweet-tart fruit. So I was delighted when my granddaughter shared this one with me.
— *Edith Richardson, Jasper, Alabama*

1/2 cup sugar
2 tablespoons cornstarch
2-3/4 cups water
2 cups fresh *or* frozen
   blueberries
1 cinnamon stick (3 inches)
1 can (6 ounces) frozen orange
   juice concentrate
Sour cream, optional

In a large saucepan, combine sugar and cornstarch. Gradually stir in water until smooth. Bring to a boil over medium heat; cook and stir for 2 minutes or until thickened. Add blueberries and cinnamon stick; return to a boil. Remove from the heat. Stir in orange juice concentrate until melted. Cover and refrigerate for at least 1 hour. Discard cinnamon stick. Garnish with sour cream if desired. **Yield:** 4 servings.

Patriotic Taco Salad

(Pictured at right)

One year, my daughter decided to celebrate her birthday with a patriotic theme. This colorful and refreshing salad was the main dish on the menu. The kids gobbled it up!
—*Glenda Jarboe, Oroville, California*

  1 pound ground beef
  1 medium onion, chopped
1-1/2 cups water
  1 can (6 ounces) tomato paste
  1 envelope taco seasoning
  6 cups tortilla *or* corn chips
  4 to 5 cups shredded lettuce
  9 to 10 pitted large ripe olives, sliced lengthwise
  2 cups (8 ounces) shredded cheddar cheese
  2 cups cherry tomatoes, halved

In a large skillet over medium heat, cook beef and onion until meat is no longer pink; drain. Stir in the water, tomato paste and taco seasoning. Bring to a boil. Reduce heat; simmer, uncovered, for 20 minutes.

Place chips in an ungreased 13-in. x 9-in. x 2-in. dish. Spread beef mixture evenly over the top. Cover with lettuce. For each star, arrange five olive slices together in the upper left corner. To form stripes, add cheese and tomatoes in alternating rows. Serve immediately. **Yield:** 8 servings.

Editor's Note: If you wish to prepare this salad in advance, omit the layer of chips and serve them with the salad.

Summertime Fruit Tea

Pineapple-orange juice gives ordinary iced tea a refreshing citrus flavor. It never lasts long, so I keep plenty of these ingredients on hand.
—*Rosalee Dixon, Sardis, Mississippi*

12 cups water, *divided*
1-1/2 cups sugar
  9 individual tea bags
  1 can (12 ounces) frozen lemonade concentrate, thawed
  1 can (12 ounces) frozen pineapple-orange juice concentrate, thawed

In a Dutch oven, bring 4 cups water to a boil. Stir in sugar until dissolved. Remove from the heat; add tea bags. Steep for 5-8 minutes. Discard tea bags. Stir in juice concentrates and remaining water. Serve over ice. **Yield:** 3-1/2 quarts.

Strawberry Cookies

My family finds these fruity cookies to be a light treat in summer.
I sometimes use lemon cake mix in place of the strawberry.
—Nancy Shelton, Boaz, Kentucky

1 package (18-1/4 ounces)
   strawberry cake mix
1 egg, lightly beaten
1 carton (8 ounces) frozen
   whipped topping, thawed
2 cups confectioners' sugar

In a mixing bowl, combine the cake mix, egg and whipped topping until well combined. Place confectioners' sugar in a shallow dish. Drop dough by tablespoonfuls into sugar; turn to coat. Place 2 in. apart on greased baking sheets. Bake at 350° for 10-12 minutes or until lightly browned around the edges. Remove to wire racks to cool. **Yield:** about 5 dozen.

German Chocolate Cupcakes

These cupcakes disappear in a dash when I take them to the school where I teach.
Pecans, coconut and brown sugar dress up the topping nicely.
—Lettice Charmasson, San Diego, California

1 package (18-1/4 ounces)
   German chocolate cake mix
1 cup water
3 eggs
1/2 cup vegetable oil
3 tablespoons chopped pecans
3 tablespoons flaked coconut
3 tablespoons brown sugar

In a large mixing bowl, combine the cake mix, water, eggs and oil. Beat on medium speed for 2 minutes. Fill paper-lined muffin cups three-fourths full. Combine pecans, coconut and brown sugar; sprinkle over batter.

Bake at 400° for 15-20 minutes or until a toothpick inserted into a cupcake comes out clean. Cool for 5 minutes before removing from pans to wire racks. **Yield:** about 2 dozen.

Patriotic Picnic Table

(Pictured above)

WHEN DINING OUTDOORS on Memorial Day, show your patriotic colors with this red, white and blue table trim.

First, cover your picnic or patio table with a white tablecloth, allowing it to hang over the sides of the table. You can use cloth if you choose, but disposable paper tablecloths are less expensive and require no laundering afterward. They can be found at variety and party supply stores.

Next, gather red and blue ribbon in assorted widths. Cut lengths of ribbon equal to the length of the tablecloth. Center the widest ribbon down the length of the table. Place a bit of double-stick tape on the underside of

the ribbon at each edge of the table. Add additional ribbons on each side of the wide ribbon, and tape as before. Trim the ribbons even with the tablecloth.

Now cut lengths of ribbon equal to the width of the table. Place them across the width of the table between each place setting, weaving them through the lengthwise ribbons, and tape as before. Trim ribbons even with the tablecloth.

Place red and white geraniums in a patriotic container on the center of the table. Wrap tableware in a festive napkin; tie in a bow with a contrasting ribbon.

SUMMER
Celebrations

A Special Day for Dad 82-89

Festive Fare for July Fourth 90-101

Fourth of July Burger Bar 102-113

Sweet Summer Brownies 114-121

Family Reunion Picnic 122-133

A Special Day for Dad

TO SHOW Pop he's tops, head to the great outdoors for a tried-and-true barbecue!

The selection of stick-to-your-ribs fare in this chapter will surely satisfy Dad's big appetite.

Hot pepper sauce, salsa and taco sauce turn up the heat on Zesty Grilled Pork Medallions. It's bound to be a surefire success at your family gathering.

To round out this manly meal, pair the meaty entree with generous slices of Peppered Corn Bread and hearty helpings of Simple Cabbage Slaw.

Packed with oats and candy bar pieces, the recipe for Championship Cookies will become a prized possession in your kitchen.

FATHER'S DAY FARE
(Clockwise from top left)

Championship Cookies (p. 86)

Peppered Corn Bread (p. 87)

Zesty Grilled Pork Medallions (p. 85)

Simple Cabbage Slaw (p. 87)

Tangy Sirloin Strips

My love of cooking started when I was trying to earn my Girl Scout cooking badge.
My family savors the sweet sauce on these skewers.
—Joanne Haldeman, Bainbridge, Pennsylvania

1/4 cup vegetable oil
2 tablespoons Worcestershire
  sauce
1 garlic clove, minced
1/2 teaspoon onion powder
1/2 teaspoon salt
1/4 teaspoon pepper
1 pound boneless sirloin steak
  (1 inch thick)
4 bacon strips
Lemon-pepper seasoning
GLAZE:
1/2 cup barbecue sauce
1/2 cup steak sauce
1/2 cup honey
1 tablespoon molasses

In a large resealable plastic bag, combine the first six ingredients. Cut steak into four wide strips; add to the marinade. Seal bag and turn to coat; refrigerate for 2-3 hours or overnight, turning once.

Drain and discard marinade. Wrap a bacon strip around each steak piece; secure with a toothpick. Sprinkle with lemon-pepper. Coat grill rack with nonstick cooking spray before starting the grill.

Grill steak, covered, over medium-low heat for 10-15 minutes, turning occasionally, until meat reaches desired doneness (for rare, a meat thermometer should read 140°; medium, 160°; well-done, 170°). Combine the glaze ingredients; brush over steak. Grill until glaze is heated. Discard toothpicks. **Yield:** 4 servings.

GREAT GRILLING TIPS

GRILLING is a wonderful way to get summer suppers sizzling. Before you head to your backyard for some fun outdoor cooking, refresh your grilling skills with these tips:

- Before grilling meats, trim excess fat to avoid flare-ups.
- Marinades can be used to add flavor to meat and vegetables or to tenderize less-tender cuts of meat. Always marinate in the refrigerator in a glass container or resealable plastic bag.

  In general, do not reuse marinades. If a marinade is also used as a basting or dipping sauce, reserve a portion before adding the uncooked foods, or bring it to a rolling boil after removing the raw meat.

- Bring foods to a cool room temperature before grilling. Cold foods may burn on the outside before the interior is cooked.
- Use tongs to turn meat instead of a meat fork to avoid piercing and losing juices. Also, salting meats after cooking helps retain juices.
- Brush on thick or sweet sauces during the last 10 to 15 minutes of cooking. Baste and turn every few minutes to prevent burning.
- Use a meat or instant-read thermometer to check the internal temperature of meat and poultry before the recommended cooking time is up.

Zesty Grilled Pork Medallions

(Pictured at right and on page 82)

Some of our friends made up this marinade but weren't able to give me exact measurements. I experimented until I came up with this recipe, which tastes as good as theirs.
— Patty Collins, Morgantown, Indiana

2 cups salsa
1/4 cup sugar
4-1/2 teaspoons sweet-and-sour sauce
1 tablespoon vegetable oil
1 tablespoon green taco sauce
2 teaspoons balsamic vinegar
Dash hot pepper sauce
2 pork tenderloins (about 1 pound *each*)

In a bowl, combine the first seven ingredients; mix well. Set aside 1 cup for dipping; cover and refrigerate. Pour remaining marinade into a large resealable plastic bag; add the pork. Seal bag and turn to coat; refrigerate overnight.

Drain and discard marinade. Grill pork, covered, over indirect medium heat for 30-40 minutes or until a meat thermometer reads 160°. Warm the dipping sauce; serve with sliced pork. **Yield:** 6-8 servings.

Peanut Butter Ice Cream Pie

This recipe has been a family favorite for nearly 30 years. I often have a pie handy in the freezer to serve unexpected guests.
— Sharon Mensing, Greenfield, Iowa

1-1/2 cups chocolate wafer crumbs, *divided*
1/4 cup sugar
1/2 cup butter, melted
1 quart vanilla ice cream, softened
1/2 cup chunky peanut butter
1 cup whipped topping
Peanuts, optional

Set aside 1 tablespoon of wafer crumbs for garnish. In a bowl, combine the sugar and remaining crumbs. Stir in butter. Press onto the bottom and up the sides of greased 9-in. pie plate. Refrigerate for 1 hour or until set.

In a bowl, combine ice cream and peanut butter. Fold in whipped topping. Pour into pie shell. Top with reserved crumbs and peanuts if desired. Cover and freeze for at least 2 hours. Remove from the freezer 15 minutes before cutting. **Yield:** 6-8 servings.

Championship Cookies

(Pictured on page 82)

I got this recipe from a friend who baked at a conference center.
Snickers candy bar pieces make them irresistible.
—*Patricia Miller, North Fork, California*

2/3 cup shortening
1-1/4 cups packed brown sugar
1 egg
1 teaspoon vanilla extract
1-1/2 cups all-purpose flour
1 teaspoon baking powder
1 teaspoon baking soda
1/2 teaspoon ground cinnamon
1/4 teaspoon salt
2 Snickers candy bars (2.07 ounces *each*), chopped
1/2 cup quick-cooking oats

In a mixing bowl, cream shortening and brown sugar. Beat in egg and vanilla. Combine the flour, baking powder, baking soda, cinnamon and salt; gradually add to the creamed mixture. Stir in chopped candy bars and oats.

Drop by rounded tablespoonfuls 2 in. apart onto greased or parchment-lined baking sheets. Bake at 350° for 10-12 minutes or until lightly browned. Remove to wire racks to cool. **Yield:** about 5 dozen.

Hot Wings

For parties, I like to make these wings in advance and keep them warm
in a slow cooker. The mild sauce is finger-licking good!
—*Tracie Calkin, Casper, Wyoming*

20 whole chicken wings (about 4 pounds)
Vegetable oil for deep-fat frying
1/2 cup butter
1-1/2 teaspoons brown sugar
1 teaspoon lemon juice
1 garlic clove, minced
2 to 3 tablespoons Louisiana hot sauce
3 to 4 teaspoons hot pepper sauce
Celery and carrot sticks
Ranch *or* blue cheese salad dressing

Cut chicken wings into three sections; discard wing tips. In an electric skillet or deep-fat fryer, heat oil to 375°. Fry chicken wings, a few at a time, until juices run clear. Drain on paper towels.

In a large skillet, melt butter. Stir in the brown sugar, lemon juice, garlic and hot sauces; bring just to a boil. Add chicken wings; turn to coat. Cook and turn for 5-10 minutes or until well coated. Serve with celery and carrot sticks and salad dressing for dipping. **Yield:** 10 servings.

Editor's Note: 4 pounds of uncooked chicken wing sections may be substituted for the whole chicken wings. Omit the first step of the recipe.

Peppered Corn Bread

(Pictured at right and on page 83)

Pretty flecks of jalapeno and red peppers peek out from this golden corn bread. It has a mild flavor, which appeals to all palates.
—Ila Bray, Pelham, North Carolina

1-1/2 cups cornmeal
   1 tablespoon all-purpose flour
   1 tablespoon sugar
2-1/4 teaspoons baking powder
  3/4 teaspoon salt
  1/2 teaspoon baking soda
   2 eggs, beaten
   1 can (8-3/4 ounces) cream-style corn
   1 cup buttermilk
  2/3 cup vegetable oil
   2 cups (8 ounces) shredded cheddar cheese
   1 medium sweet red pepper, chopped
   2 jalapeno peppers, seeded and diced
   4 to 5 green onions, chopped

In a bowl, combine the cornmeal, flour, sugar, baking powder, salt and baking soda; set aside. Combine the eggs, corn, buttermilk and oil; stir into the dry ingredients just until blended. Fold in the cheese, peppers and onions. Pour into a greased 13-in. x 9-in. x 2-in. baking dish. Bake at 350° for 30-35 minutes or until a toothpick comes out clean. Cut into squares; serve warm. **Yield:** 12-16 servings.

Editor's Note: When cutting or seeding hot peppers, use rubber or plastic gloves to protect your hands. Avoid touching your face.

Simple Cabbage Slaw

(Pictured on page 82)

When I was growing up, my father would make this salad as part of our Sunday dinner. Now I carry on the tradition with my own family.
—Sandra Lampe, Muscatine, Iowa

   4 cups coleslaw mix
   1 medium sweet red *or* green pepper, finely chopped
   5 tablespoons sugar
   5 tablespoons cider vinegar
  1/4 cup water
  1/4 teaspoon salt
  1/8 teaspoon pepper

In a large bowl, combine all ingredients and toss to coat. Cover and refrigerate for at least 4 hours or overnight. **Yield:** 6 servings.

Skewered Potatoes

Here's a unique way to prepare red potatoes. Cooking them in the microwave ensures they're tender inside, while grilling gives them a crisp outside.
—Sarah Steinacher, Geneva, Nebraska

2 **pounds small red potatoes, quartered**
1/3 **cup cold water**
1/2 **cup mayonnaise**
1/4 **cup dry white wine** *or* **chicken broth**
2 **teaspoons dried rosemary, crushed**
1 **teaspoon garlic powder**

Place potatoes and water in a 2-qt. microwave-safe dish. Cover and cook on high for 10-15 minutes or until tender, stirring halfway through; drain. In a large bowl, combine the remaining ingredients. Add potatoes; stir gently to coat. Cover and refrigerate for 1 hour.

Drain, reserving marinade. Thread potatoes on metal or soaked wooden skewers. Grill, covered, over hot heat for 6-8 minutes or until potatoes are golden brown. Turn and brush occasionally with reserved marinade. **Yield:** 6-8 servings.

Editor's Note: This recipe was tested in an 850-watt microwave.

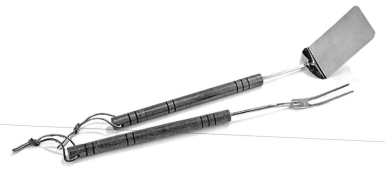

Saucy Orange Shrimp

On a trip to New Orleans, my husband picked up some fresh Gulf shrimp. The wife of the shrimp boat captain sent this recipe along with him. It's our favorite way to prepare shrimp.
—Gloria Jarrett, Loveland, Ohio

4 **pounds uncooked large shrimp in the shell**
2 **cups butter**
2 **medium navel oranges, peeled and thinly sliced**
1 **cup orange juice concentrate**
2 **tablespoons Worcestershire sauce**

1 **teaspoon** *each* **lemon-pepper seasoning, paprika, dried parsley flakes, garlic powder, onion powder and barbecue** *or* **hickory seasoning**
Dash cayenne pepper

Place shrimp in two 13-in. x 9-in. x 2-in. baking dishes. In a saucepan, melt butter. Add orange slices; cook and stir until oranges fall apart. Stir in the remaining ingredients; heat through. Pour over the shrimp. Bake, uncovered, at 375° for 15-20 minutes or until shrimp turn pink. **Yield:** 8-10 servings.

Peach Streusel Pie

(Pictured at right)

Dad will want to save room for dessert when this peach pie from our Test Kitchen is on the menu. Serve each warm juicy slice with a scoop of vanilla ice cream.

Pastry for single-crust pie
  (9 inches)
  1/4 cup sugar
    2 tablespoons cornstarch
    2 tablespoons lemon juice
    5 cups sliced fresh *or* frozen
      peaches, thawed
TOPPING:
  2/3 cup packed brown sugar
  1/2 cup granola cereal (without
    raisins)
  1/4 cup all-purpose flour
    1 teaspoon ground cinnamon
  1/4 cup cold butter
Vanilla ice cream

Line a 9-in. pie plate with pastry; flute edges. Line the pastry shell with a double thickness of heavy-duty foil. Bake at 450° for 5 minutes. Remove foil; bake 5 minutes longer. Cool on a wire rack.

In a bowl, combine the sugar, cornstarch, lemon juice and peaches. Spoon into pastry shell. In another bowl, combine the brown sugar, granola, flour and cinnamon; cut in butter until crumbly. Sprinkle over filling. Bake at 375° for 35-40 minutes or until filling is bubbly. Cool on a wire rack. Serve warm with ice cream. **Yield:** 6-8 servings.

Grilled Corn with Chive Butter

When our son was young, corn was the only vegetable he'd eat. My husband and I soon got bored with the simple salt and butter topping, so I stirred in some lemon juice and chives.
—Sue Kirsch, Eden Prairie, Minnesota

  6 medium ears sweet corn
    in husks
1/2 cup butter, melted
  2 tablespoons snipped chives
  1 tablespoon sugar
1-1/2 teaspoons lemon juice
Salt and pepper to taste

Soak corn in cold water for 1 hour. In a small bowl, combine the butter, chives, sugar, lemon juice, salt and pepper. Carefully peel back corn husks to within 1 in. of bottom; remove silk. Brush with butter mixture. Rewrap corn in husks and secure with kitchen string. Grill corn, uncovered, over medium heat for 25-30 minutes, turning occasionally. **Yield:** 6 servings.

Festive Fare For July Fourth

IF YOU are in charge of the Fourth of July festivities this year, why not try a revolutionary idea and forgo ordinary hamburgers and hot dogs?

Instead, add some sizzle to your menu with on-the-grill goodies such as Sesame Chicken Kabobs and Sweet 'n' Spicy Grilled Pork Chops. Then pay tribute to the finest summer produce with Picnic Potato Salad and Melon with Minted Lime Dip. For the finale, Lemon Nut Star Cookies will trigger many oohs and aahs from your flag-waving family.

So, when planning a patriotic picnic, spark your creativity by turning to the true-blue favorites in this chapter.

BACKYARD BARBECUE
(Clockwise from top right)

Picnic Potato Salad (p. 98)

Sesame Chicken Kabobs (p. 94)

Lemon Nut Star Cookies (p. 93)

Sweet 'n' Spicy
Grilled Pork Chops (p. 92)

Melon with Minted Lime Dip (p. 96)

Sweet 'n' Spicy Grilled Pork Chops

(Pictured on page 90)

This started out as a mild sauce that I decided to "spice up." You'll find it's easy to adjust the seasonings to suit your family's taste. I also like to use the sauce on boneless skinless chicken breasts.
—Gladys Peterson, Beaumont, Texas

1 can (14-1/2 ounces) diced
   tomatoes, drained
1 can (10 ounces) diced
   tomatoes with chilies,
   undrained
1/2 cup raisins
1/4 cup currant jelly
4-1/2 teaspoons cider vinegar
1/4 teaspoon *each* garlic powder,
   salt and crushed red pepper
   flakes
12 boneless pork chops (3/4
   inch thick)

In a blender, combine the tomatoes, raisins, jelly, vinegar and seasonings; cover and process until smooth. Pour into a 1-qt. saucepan; bring to a boil. Reduce heat; simmer, uncovered, for 20 minutes or until thickened. Set aside 3/4 cup for serving.

Coat grill rack with nonstick cooking spray before starting grill. Grill pork chops, uncovered, over medium heat, for 4 minutes. Turn; brush with sauce. Grill 4-6 minutes longer or until meat juices run clear. Serve with reserved sauce. **Yield:** 12 servings.

FOOD SAFETY TIPS FOR SUMMER

SUMMER is prime time for memorable picnics and cookouts with friends and family. But the last thing you want to bring home from these fun-filled outings is food poisoning, so follow these precautions. (Also see Properly Packing a Cooler on page 98.)

- When packing the cooler or picnic basket, wrap raw meat, poultry and fish separately from cooked foods in airtight plastic containers or resealable plastic bags.
- It's a good idea to have two sets of cutting boards, grilling utensils and platters—one for uncooked foods and one for cooked items.
- Pack a meat thermometer to ensure you're grilling meat and poultry to the proper temperature.
- Prevent the spread of bacteria by washing fruits and vegetables before putting in the basket or cooler.
- Pack clean foil, plastic wrap and resealable plastic bags to store leftovers.
- If you won't have access to soap and water at the picnic, bring along moist towelettes, antibacterial soap that doesn't require water or a spray bottle with soapy water.
- Hot foods should be eaten within 2 hours of being made.
- Remove foods from the cooler just before cooking or serving.
- Food should not stand out longer than 2 hours. (On days above 85°, 1 hour is the maximum.) Promptly store hot and cold leftovers in an ice-filled cooler. If no ice remains in the cooler when you get home, play it safe and discard the food.

Lemon Nut Star Cookies

(Pictured at right and on page 90)

Family and friends will say "Hooray!" when they see these star-spangled cookies from our Test Kitchen. Make these treats throughout the year by using different cookie cutters and food coloring.

```
    1 cup butter, softened
    2 cups confectioners' sugar
    2 eggs
    2 tablespoons lemon juice
    4 teaspoons half-and-half cream
    2 teaspoons grated lemon peel
3-1/4 cups all-purpose flour
  1/2 cup ground almonds
  1/2 teaspoon baking soda
  1/8 teaspoon salt
GLAZE:
    2 cups confectioners' sugar
  1/4 cup light corn syrup
    2 tablespoons lemon juice
Red and blue food coloring
```

In a mixing bowl, cream butter and confectioners' sugar. Add eggs, one at a time, beating well after each addition. Beat in the lemon juice, cream and lemon peel. Combine the flour, almonds, baking soda and salt; gradually add to creamed mixture. Cover and refrigerate for 2 hours or until easy to handle.

On a lightly floured surface, roll out dough to 1/8-in. thickness. Cut with a floured star-shaped cookie cutter. Place 1 in. apart on ungreased baking sheets. Bake at 350° for 8-10 minutes or until lightly browned. Remove to wire racks to cool.

For glaze, combine confectioners' sugar, corn syrup and lemon juice until smooth. Divide into three bowls. Tint one portion red and one portion blue; leave the third portion plain. Spread over cookies; let stand overnight for glaze to harden. **Yield:** about 5-1/2 dozen.

Sesame Chicken Kabobs

(Pictured on page 91)

This colorful dish is a favorite of mine for entertaining. I marinate the chicken and cut up the peppers the night before. Then the next day, I just assemble the kabobs and grill.
—Cindy Novak, Antioch, California

1/3 cup sherry *or* chicken broth
1/3 cup soy sauce
2 green onions, chopped
3 tablespoons apricot preserves
1 tablespoon vegetable oil
2 garlic cloves, minced
2 teaspoons minced fresh gingerroot
1/2 teaspoon hot pepper sauce
3 teaspoons sesame seeds, toasted, *divided*
1-1/2 pounds boneless skinless chicken breasts, cut into 1-inch cubes

1 medium sweet red pepper, cut into 1-inch pieces
1 medium sweet yellow pepper, cut into 1-inch pieces

In a bowl, combine the sherry or broth, soy sauce, onions, preserves, oil, garlic, ginger, hot pepper sauce and 1-1/2 teaspoons sesame seeds. Pour 1/3 cup into another bowl for basting; cover and refrigerate. Pour remaining marinade into a large resealable plastic bag; add chicken. Seal bag and turn to coat; refrigerate for 2-3 hours or overnight, turning occasionally.

Drain and discard marinade. On metal or soaked wooden skewers, alternately thread chicken and peppers. Grill, uncovered, over medium heat for 6 minutes, turning once. Baste with reserved marinade. Grill 5-10 minutes longer or until meat juices run clear, turning and basting frequently. Sprinkle with remaining sesame seeds. **Yield:** 6 servings.

Zucchini Salad

My husband and I have a big garden and grow a variety of vegetables, including lots of zucchini. That abundant summer produce stars in this simple salad.
—Shirley Smith, Wichita, Kansas

4 medium zucchini, sliced (about 5 cups)
1 can (14 ounces) water-packed artichoke hearts, drained and chopped
2 jars (4-1/2 ounces *each*) sliced mushrooms, drained
1 can (2-1/4 ounces) sliced ripe olives

1 can (8 ounces) sliced water chestnuts, drained
1 envelope ranch salad dressing mix
1 cup Italian salad dressing
Leaf lettuce, optional

In a bowl, combine the zucchini, artichokes, mushrooms, olives and water chestnuts. Combine the ranch dressing mix and Italian dressing; pour over vegetables and toss to coat. Cover and refrigerate for several hours or overnight. Drain; serve in a lettuce-lined bowl if desired. **Yield:** 8 servings.

Caesar Chicken Potato Salad

(Pictured at right)

Here in Texas, we seem to have summer year-round. So quick-to-fix dishes like this that get you in and out of the kitchen are popular.
—Sarita Johnston, San Antonio, Texas

  4 **cups quartered small white** *or* **red potatoes**
3/4 **pound boneless skinless chicken breasts, cubed**
  1 **tablespoon vegetable oil**
  1 **package (10 ounces) mixed salad greens**
  1 **small red onion, sliced and separated into rings**
3/4 **cup Caesar salad dressing**
1/3 **cup croutons**
  2 **tablespoons shredded Parmesan cheese**

Place potatoes in a large saucepan and cover with water. Cover and bring to a boil over medium-high heat; cook for 15-20 minutes or until tender. Meanwhile, in a skillet, saute chicken in oil for 5-10 minutes or until juices run clear. Drain potatoes; add to chicken.

Place greens and onion in a serving bowl. Top with chicken mixture. Drizzle with dressing; sprinkle with croutons and Parmesan cheese. Serve immediately. **Yield:** 4 servings.

Family Traditions

JULY FOURTH was truly kids' day in the little Arkansas town where I reared my children. We bought small flags and yards of crepe-paper streamers to decorate wagons, tricycles, bicycles—anything with wheels. All the local kids would then participate in the town parade, each hoping to win the grand prize.
—*Mary Lewis*
Memphis, Tennessee

Melon with Minted Lime Dip

(Pictured on page 90)

For a refreshing summer side dish for any meal, our Test Kitchen recommends these marinated melon balls with a cool, creamy dip. You can also serve this fruity treat as a light dessert.

1/4 cup sugar
1/4 cup water
  6 tablespoons lime juice
  2 tablespoons minced fresh mint
  2 teaspoons grated lime peel
  2 tablespoons grated fresh gingerroot
  8 cups melon balls *or* cubes

MINTED LIME DIP:
  1 cup (8 ounces) sour cream
  2 tablespoons sugar
  1 tablespoon lime juice
  2 teaspoons grated lime peel

In a bowl, combine the sugar, water, lime juice, mint, lime peel and ginger. Add melon balls. Cover and refrigerate for 1-6 hours. Thread melon onto wooden skewers or toothpicks. In a bowl, combine dip ingredients. Serve with melon. **Yield:** 8 cups fruit (1 cup dip).

CHILLING DIP AT PICNICS

WHEN serving dip on a hot day, it's important to keep it cool. If you don't have a ceramic dip set (shown on page 90 with the Minted Lime Dip), use what you have on hand.

Fill a large glass or plastic serving bowl with ice cubes, crushed ice or ice packs. Fill a smaller bowl with dip and set on top of the ice. Replace the ice as it melts.

If you're taking the dip to an outing, put the dip in a small bowl (plastic is best for traveling because it won't break), cover with plastic wrap and put in a cooler. Assemble the ice-filled serving bowl when you get to the picnic.

Patriotic Fruit Pizza

(Pictured at right)

When strawberry season arrives, folks who know me anticipate this flavorful fruity dessert. It's very pretty and always gets lots of compliments wherever I take it.

—Amy Murdoch
Union Grove, Wisconsin

1-1/2 cups all-purpose flour
1/4 cup confectioners' sugar
1 cup cold butter
1 package (4-3/4 ounces) strawberry Danish dessert
FILLING:
1 package (8 ounces) cream cheese, softened
1 cup sugar
1/4 teaspoon vanilla extract
3 cups sliced fresh strawberries
1 cup fresh blueberries

In a bowl, combine the flour and confectioners' sugar. Cut in butter until mixture begins to hold together. Press into a 12-in. tart or pizza pan; build up edges slightly. Bake at 350° for 10 minutes or until golden brown. Cool for 15 minutes. Cook Danish dessert according to package directions for pie glaze; cool to room temperature.

In a mixing bowl, beat cream cheese, sugar and vanilla. Spread over crust. Arrange strawberries in an 8- to 10-in. circle in center of pizza. Sprinkle blueberries around strawberries. Pour half of the Danish dessert over strawberries (save remaining glaze for another use). Refrigerate until serving. Cut into wedges. **Yield:** 8-10 servings.

Editor's Note: Look for strawberry Danish dessert in the gelatin aisle of your grocery store.

Strawberry Sherbet

When our boys were young and always hungry, we'd head to our strawberry patch and gather fruit for this sherbet. This treat was a must for company.
—Ruth Guse, Stillwater, Minnesota

4 quarts fresh strawberries, sliced
4 cups sugar
2-2/3 cups milk
2/3 cup orange juice
1/8 teaspoon ground cinnamon, optional

In a large bowl, combine strawberries and sugar; let stand for 1-1/2 to 2 hours or until very juicy. Process in small batches in a blender until pureed. Strain seeds; pour strawberry juice into a bowl. Stir in milk, orange juice and cinnamon if desired.

Freeze in batches in an ice cream freezer according to manufacturer's directions. Refrigerate remaining mixture until it can be frozen. **Yield:** about 4 quarts.

Picnic Potato Salad

(Pictured on page 91)

What would a picnic be without potato salad? In this recipe, mint adds a tasty twist on the traditional. Because it contains oil instead of mayonnaise, it travels well to picnics.
—Sheri Neiswanger, Ravenna, Ohio

10 medium red potatoes, cubed
2/3 cup vegetable oil
2 tablespoons cider vinegar
4 teaspoons honey
1 teaspoon dried basil
1 teaspoon ground mustard
1/2 teaspoon salt
1/2 teaspoon dried thyme
1/4 teaspoon dried marjoram

1/4 teaspoon dried mint
Dash cayenne pepper

Place potatoes in a large saucepan and cover with water. Cover and bring to a boil over medium-high heat; cook for 15-20 minutes or until tender. Drain and place in a large bowl. Combine the remaining ingredients; pour over potatoes and toss to coat. Cool to room temperature. Cover and refrigerate until serving. **Yield:** 12 servings.

PROPERLY PACKING A COOLER

COOLERS serve as portable refrigerators when going on picnics. These tips will help your coolers—and the items inside—stay well-chilled for the duration of your outing.

- Cold foods (especially those containing mayonnaise) and beverages should be thoroughly chilled before being put in insulated coolers.
- Beverage coolers tend to be opened frequently during a picnic. So use one cooler for beverages and one for cold food.
- Transport hot food in a separate insulated cooler. Wrap the hot items in newspapers or dish towels, then pack the dishes tightly in a cooler lined with dish towels.
- Prechill coolers by placing a few ice cubes inside and closing the lid about an hour before filling.
- Right before you leave for the picnic, pack the cooler in the opposite order of how you'll be using the items. That means the

foods you need first should be on top, so they're easily accessible.

- Put blocks of ice or ice packs on the bottom of the cooler. Layer with food or beverages, then top with ice cubes or crushed ice.
- A full cooler will stay colder longer than a partially filled one, so pick the right size cooler. If your food or beverages don't fill the cooler, add more ice.
- Don't put coolers in a hot trunk, especially if traveling quite a distance. Put them in the backseat of your air-conditioned car. Surround with blankets, sleeping bags and clothes to insulate even more.
- While at the picnic, keep coolers in the shade, cover with blankets and keep the lids closed as much as you can.
- If possible, replenish the ice as it melts. If you don't have access to more ice, don't drain the cold water from the cooler…it keeps things cold almost as well as ice.

Red, White And Blue Chili

(Pictured at right)

Instead of the usual picnic fare, I surprised family and guests with this mild-flavored dish one Independence Day. They were delighted with the blue tortilla chips and colorful chili.
—Dotty Parker, Christmas Valley, Oregon

1 medium green pepper, diced
1/4 cup diced onion
2 garlic cloves, minced
1 tablespoon vegetable oil
2 cans (14-1/2 ounces *each*)
   Mexican diced tomatoes,
   undrained
2 cans (14-1/2 ounces *each*)
   chicken broth
2 cups shredded cooked chicken
2 cans (15-1/2 ounces *each*)
   great northern beans, rinsed
   and drained
1 can (16 ounces) kidney beans,
   rinsed and drained
1 envelope chili seasoning
1 tablespoon brown sugar
1 teaspoon salt
1/4 teaspoon pepper
Blue tortilla chips

In a Dutch oven or soup kettle, saute the green pepper, onion and garlic in oil until tender. Stir in the tomatoes, broth, chicken, beans, chili seasoning, brown sugar, salt and pepper. Bring to a boil. Reduce heat; cover and simmer for 45 minutes. Serve with tortilla chips. **Yield:** 8 servings (about 2 quarts).

Summertime Salsa

*My friends and I make batches of this salsa every year. We tuck a few jars away
so we can enjoy the flavor of summer when the weather turns cooler.*
—*Pat Shearer, Coutts, Alberta*

10 cups chopped seeded peeled
    tomatoes (about 6 pounds)
5 cups chopped onions
3-1/2 cups chopped green peppers
    (about 1-1/2 pounds)
1-1/2 cups chopped sweet red
    peppers (about 3/4 pound)
1-1/4 cups white vinegar
6 jalapeno peppers, seeded and
    finely chopped
3 garlic cloves, minced
3 teaspoons salt
1-1/2 teaspoons crushed red pepper
    flakes

1/2 teaspoon sugar
1/2 teaspoon mustard seed
1/2 teaspoon chili powder
1/4 teaspoon pepper

Combine all ingredients in a large kettle; bring to a boil. Reduce heat; simmer, uncovered, for 1-3/4 hours or until mixture reaches desired thickness. Pour hot mixture into hot jars, leaving 1/4-in. headspace. Adjust caps. Process in a boiling-water bath for 15 minutes. **Yield:** about 6 pints.

Editor's Note: When cutting or seeding hot peppers, use rubber or plastic gloves to protect your hands. Avoid touching your face.

Honey-Ginger Barbecued Ribs

*Grilling season just wouldn't be the same without these tender, finger-licking-good ribs.
My family loves how ginger enhances the slightly sweet marinade.*
—*Linda Tuchband, Overland Park, Kansas*

4 to 5 pounds pork spareribs
2 cups chicken broth
1 cup soy sauce
3/4 cup ketchup
1/2 cup pineapple juice
1/2 cup honey
1 garlic clove, minced
1/2 teaspoon pepper
1 teaspoon minced fresh
    gingerroot
GLAZE:
2/3 cup honey

2 tablespoons soy sauce
1 teaspoon minced fresh gingerroot

Place ribs on a rack in a shallow baking pan; cover with foil. Bake at 325° for 1-1/2 hours; cool. In a bowl, combine the broth, soy sauce, ketchup, pineapple juice, honey, garlic, pepper and ginger. Place ribs in a gallon-size resealable plastic bag; add marinade. Seal bag; refrigerate overnight, turning occasionally.

Drain and discard marinade. In a small bowl, combine glaze ingredients; set aside. Grill ribs, uncovered, over medium heat for 20-25 minutes or until heated through, brushing with glaze during the last 10 minutes. **Yield:** 4-6 servings.

Fourth of July Ice Cream Cake

(Pictured at right)

This eye-catching dessert is actually easy to prepare and keeps well in the freezer for days. It's nice to be able to serve cake and ice cream in one slice.
—*Anne Scholovich*
Waukesha, Wisconsin

1 prepared angel food cake (10 inches)
2 quarts strawberry ice cream, softened
1 quart vanilla ice cream, softened
2-1/2 cups heavy whipping cream
2 tablespoons confectioners' sugar
Decorative mini paper flags, optional

Cut cake horizontally into four equal layers. Place bottom layer on a serving plate; spread with half of the strawberry ice cream. Immediately place in freezer. Spread second cake layer with vanilla ice cream; place over strawberry layer in freezer. Spread third cake layer with remaining strawberry ice cream; place over vanilla layer in freezer. Top with remaining cake layer.

In a mixing bowl, beat cream until soft peaks form. Add sugar; beat until stiff peaks form. Frost top and sides of cake. Freeze until serving. Decorate with mini flags if desired. **Yield:** 12-14 servings.

Fourth of July Burger Bar

FOLKS from sea to shining sea agree that no food is more American than a juicy hamburger.

So when you and your family gather to salute the Stars and Stripes on the Fourth of July, fire up the grill and bring on the burgers!

Add a little spark to your patriotic picnic with meaty All-American Hamburgers and Tortilla Burgers.

Don't forget to include an appealing assortment of side dishes and desserts, like Old-Fashioned Lemonade and Sherbet Watermelon.

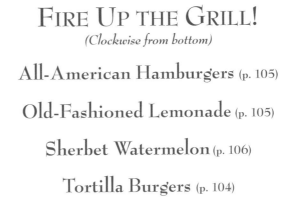

FIRE UP THE GRILL!
(Clockwise from bottom)

All-American Hamburgers (p. 105)

Old-Fashioned Lemonade (p. 105)

Sherbet Watermelon (p. 106)

Tortilla Burgers (p. 104)

Tortilla Burgers

(Pictured on page 103)

With pork instead of ground beef and tortillas in place of buns,
these Southwestern-style burgers stand out from all others.
— Katie Koziolek, Hartland, Minnesota

1 teaspoon ground cumin
1/2 teaspoon dried oregano
1/2 teaspoon crushed red pepper
    flakes
1/4 teaspoon seasoned salt
1 pound ground pork
4 flour *or* corn tortillas
    (6 inches), warmed
Salsa, sour cream and shredded
  cheese, optional

In a bowl, combine the first four ingredients. Crumble pork over seasonings and mix well. Shape into four oval patties. Grill, covered, over medium heat for 6-7 minutes on each side or until meat is no longer pink. Serve on tortillas with salsa, sour cream and cheese if desired. **Yield:** 4 servings.

HINTS FOR MAKING HAMBURGERS

HAMBURGERS are one of the easiest entrees to prepare. And with a few timeless tips, your burgers will turn out tasty every time!

- To keep hamburgers moist, first combine the filling ingredients, then add the meat and mix just until combined. Overmixing can cause the burgers to be dense and heavy.
- If you don't like getting your hands messy when mixing the meat mixture, put the ingredients in a large resealable plastic bag, then mix.

    Or if you do use your hands, first dampen them with water and nothing will stick.

- The leaner the ground beef, the drier the cooked burger will be. Ground sirloin makes the leanest burgers, then ground round, ground chuck and, lastly, ground beef.
- Keep in mind that the more fat there is in the meat, the more shrinkage there is during cooking. So if you're making burgers out of regular ground beef, shape the patties to be slightly larger than the bun.
- Don't use a metal spatula to flatten the burgers while cooking...you'll squeeze out all of the succulent juices.
- Always cook ground beef hamburgers until a meat thermometer reads 160°.

All-American Hamburgers

(Pictured at right and on page 102)

We do a lot of camping and outdoor cooking. Hamburgers are on our menu more than any other food.
— *Diane Hixon, Niceville, Florida*

2 tablespoons diced onion
2 tablespoons chili sauce
2 teaspoons Worcestershire sauce
2 teaspoons prepared mustard
1 pound ground beef
4 slices American *or* cheddar cheese, halved diagonally
2 slices Swiss cheese, halved diagonally
4 hamburger buns, split and toasted
Lettuce leaves, sliced tomato and onion, cooked bacon, ketchup and mustard, optional

In a bowl, combine the first four ingredients. Crumble beef over mixture and mix well. Shape into four patties. Grill, covered, over medium heat for 6 minutes on each side or until meat is no longer pink.

During the last minute of cooking, top each patty with two triangles of American cheese and one triangle of Swiss cheese. Serve on buns with lettuce, tomato, onion, bacon, ketchup and mustard if desired. **Yield:** 4 servings.

Old-Fashioned Lemonade

(Pictured on page 102)

This sweet-tart lemonade is a traditional part of my Memorial Day and Fourth of July menus. Folks can't get enough of the fresh-squeezed flavor.
— *Tammi Simpson, Greensburg, Kentucky*

6 medium lemons
2 to 2-1/2 cups sugar
5 cups water, *divided*
1 tablespoon grated lemon peel

Squeeze juice from the lemons (juice should measure about 1-3/4 cups); set aside. In a large saucepan, combine the sugar, 1 cup water and lemon peel. Cook and stir over medium heat until sugar is dissolved, about 4 minutes. Remove from the heat. Stir in reserved lemon juice and remaining water. Pour into a pitcher and refrigerate until chilled. Serve over ice. **Yield:** 2 quarts.

Sherbet Watermelon

(Pictured on page 103)

I usually double this recipe so I can have one dessert on hand for family and friends who stop by unexpectedly in summer. Each refreshing wedge comes complete with chocolate chip "seeds."
—*Margaret Hanson-Maddox, Montpelier, Indiana*

About 1 pint lime sherbet, slightly
  softened
About 1 pint pineapple sherbet,
  slightly softened
About 1-1/2 pints raspberry
  sherbet, slightly softened
1/4 cup miniature semisweet
  chocolate chips

Line a 1-1/2-qt. round metal bowl with plastic wrap. Press a thin layer of lime sherbet against the bottom and sides of bowl. Freeze, uncovered, until firm. Spread a thin layer of pineapple sherbet evenly over lime sherbet layer. Freeze until firm. Pack raspberry sherbet into center of sherbet-lined bowl. Smooth the top to resemble a cut watermelon. Cover and freeze until firm, about 8 hours.

Just before serving, remove bowl from the freezer and uncover. Invert onto a serving plate. Remove bowl and plastic wrap. Cut into wedges; press a few chocolate chips into the raspberry sherbet section of each wedge to resemble watermelon seeds. **Yield:** 8 servings.

Dilly Turkey Burgers

This recipe originally called for ground lamb, but my family prefers turkey instead.
Dill is a great herb to enhance the flavor of turkey.
—*Andrea Ros, Moon Township, Pennsylvania*

1 egg, lightly beaten
1/2 cup soft bread crumbs
2 tablespoons lemon juice
1 to 2 tablespoons snipped fresh
  dill *or* 1 to 2 teaspoons dill
  weed
1 garlic clove, minced
1/2 teaspoon salt
1/2 teaspoon dried oregano
1/4 teaspoon pepper
1 pound ground turkey
4 hamburger buns, split
Lettuce leaves
2 tablespoons mayonnaise,
  optional

In a large bowl, combine the first eight ingredients. Crumble turkey over mixture and mix well. Shape into four patties. Grill, covered, over medium heat or broil 4 in. from the heat for 4-5 minutes on each side or until a meat thermometer reads 165°. Serve on buns with lettuce and mayonnaise if desired. **Yield:** 4 servings.

Burger Bar Topping Tray

(Pictured above)

WHEN serving a burger bar at your barbecue, set out a large platter loaded with an assortment of condiments and toppings.

Traditional additions include lettuce (leaves or shredded), shredded and sliced cheese, dill pickles, pickle relish and tomato and onion slices.

Ketchup and mustard are reliable standbys, but don't forget mayonnaise, butter and even sour cream. For folks who want to add a little zip to their burger, you could also offer salsa, pickled jalapeno slices and guacamole.

Looking for a few hot additions? Consider sauteed mushrooms, warmed process cheese sauce (Mexican or plain) or a can of heated chili, with or without beans.

There's no limit to what you can use to top hot-off-the-grill burgers!

Chili Burgers

Here's our attempt at re-creating an open-faced burger we enjoyed in a restaurant.
The chili can also be served over hot dogs.
—Jesse and Anne Foust, Bluefield, West Virginia

CHILI:
- 1 pound ground beef
- 1 large onion, chopped
- 1 can (16 ounces) kidney beans, rinsed and drained
- 1 can (14-1/2 ounces) diced tomatoes, undrained
- 1 can (14-1/2 ounces) beef broth
- 1 can (8 ounces) tomato sauce
- 1 tablespoon chili powder
- 1/2 teaspoon garlic powder
- 1/2 teaspoon dried basil

BURGERS:
- 1 egg
- 1/2 cup soft bread crumbs
- 1 teaspoon salt
- 1/2 teaspoon ground cumin
- 1/4 teaspoon pepper
- 1 pound ground beef
- 4 hamburger buns

Chopped onion and shredded cheddar cheese

In a Dutch oven, cook beef and onion over medium heat until meat is no longer pink; drain. Stir in the remaining chili ingredients. Bring to a boil; reduce heat. Simmer, uncovered, for 1 hour.

In a large bowl, combine the egg, crumbs, salt, cumin and pepper. Crumble beef over mixture; mix well. Shape into four patties. Grill, covered, over medium heat for 4-5 minutes on each side or until meat is no longer pink. Serve on buns with chili. Top with onion and cheese. Refrigerate or freeze remaining chili. **Yield:** 4 servings.

Wagon Wheel Pasta Salad

Summertime gatherings aren't complete without a refreshing pasta salad.
This tasty version features a mayonnaise and picante dressing.
—Kathryn Donahey, Oil City, Pennsylvania

- 3 cups uncooked wagon wheel pasta *or* elbow macaroni
- 1 can (16 ounces) kidney beans, rinsed and drained
- 1 cup cubed cheddar cheese
- 1 cup halved cherry tomatoes
- 1 small green pepper, julienned
- 1 small sweet red pepper, julienned
- 1/2 cup thinly sliced green onions
- 2 cups mayonnaise
- 1 cup picante sauce
- 1 teaspoon salt
- 1 teaspoon ground cumin

Cook pasta according to package directions; drain and rinse in cold water. In a large bowl, combine the pasta, beans, cheese, tomatoes, peppers and onions; mix well. Combine the mayonnaise, picante sauce, salt and cumin; pour over salad and toss to coat. Cover and refrigerate for 2 hours before serving. **Yield:** 16 servings.

Potato Salad Mold

(Pictured at right)

This potato salad is the result of my combining several recipes through the years. Using a mold makes for a pretty presentation.
— Linda Murray
Allenstown, New Hampshire

**4 cups sliced peeled cooked
  red potatoes**
1/4 cup chopped celery
1/4 cup sliced green onions
1/4 cup sliced radishes
  1 cup (8 ounces) sour cream
  2 tablespoons cider vinegar
  **1 envelope zesty Italian salad
    dressing mix**
1/8 teaspoon pepper
Red Radish Rosettes, optional

In a large bowl, combine the potatoes, celery, onions and radishes. Combine the sour cream, vinegar, salad dressing mix and pepper; pour over potato mixture and toss gently. Press into a 5-cup ring mold coated with nonstick cooking spray. Cover with plastic wrap. Refrigerate for 2-3 hours.

Run a knife around edges of mold to loosen. Invert onto a serving plate. Garnish with Red Radish Rosettes if desired. **Yield:** 6 servings.

MAKING RED RADISH ROSETTES

1. With a small paring knife, slice off the stem so the radish rests on the cutting board with its root standing straight up. Cut a V into the top of the radish, removing the root. Cut two more V's into the top of the radish, positioning them like an X over the first V. You should end up with six pointed peaks.

2. Carefully cut an inverted V under each of the pointed peaks. Soak radishes in cold water for at least 8 hours, allowing petals to open.

Blue Cheese Burgers

Instead of topping your burgers with the usual cheddar or Swiss cheeses,
stuff them with blue cheese. We've been serving these for many years.
—Jesse and Anne Foust, Bluefield, West Virginia

1 pound ground beef
Salt and pepper to taste
2 ounces crumbled blue cheese
2 hamburger buns, split and toasted
2 thin slices red onion
Tomato slices and lettuce leaves, optional

Shape beef into four thin patties. Grill, covered, over medium heat for 6 minutes on each side or until meat is no longer pink. Season with salt and pepper. Press blue cheese into the center of two patties; top with remaining patties. Serve on buns with onion, tomato and lettuce if desired. **Yield:** 2 servings.

Pepperoncini Firecrackers

My youngest daughter and I enjoy time in the kitchen together making these attractive
appetizers. The "firecrackers" burst with chicken, cheese and pepperoncinis.
—Virginia Perkins, Columbiana, Ohio

1 jar (32 ounces) pepperoncinis
1/2 pound boneless skinless chicken breasts, cooked and cut into 24 pieces
24 thin strips Monterey Jack *or* pepper Jack cheese (about 1-1/2 inches x 1/4 inch x 1/8 inch)
24 sheets phyllo dough
Refrigerated butter-flavored spray
Melted butter
48 fresh chives

Remove 24 pepperoncinis from jar; remove and discard stems and seeds. Drain peppers on paper towels. Stuff each with a piece of chicken and a cheese strip (cheese may need to be cut to fit in some peppers).

Place one sheet of phyllo dough on a work surface (keep remaining dough covered with waxed paper to avoid drying out). Spritz dough with butter-flavored spray. Repeat three times; stack sprayed phyllo dough. Cut stack into four pieces, about 6-1/2 in. x 4-1/4 in. each.

Center one stuffed pepper on one long side of each phyllo stack; roll up and twist the ends to seal. Repeat with remaining peppers and dough. Place on ungreased baking sheets. Drizzle butter over center of firecrackers. Bake at 375° for 18-22 minutes or until golden brown. Tie ends with chives. **Yield:** 2 dozen.

Editor's Note: Look for pepperoncinis (pickled peppers) in the pickle and olive section of your grocery store. This recipe was tested with I Can't Believe It's Not Butter Spray. When cutting or seeding hot peppers, use rubber or plastic gloves to protect your hands. Avoid touching your face.

Berries 'n' Cream Torte

(Pictured at right)

It's easy to see why this fruity dessert always impresses dinner guests. I sometimes substitute the berries with sliced bananas.
— *Tina Sawchuk, Ardmore, Alberta*

1 cup butter, softened
1 cup sugar
2 eggs
2 cups all-purpose flour
2 teaspoons baking powder
1/2 teaspoon salt

FILLING:
1/2 cup sugar
4-1/2 teaspoons confectioners' sugar
4-1/2 teaspoons cornstarch
3 cups heavy whipping cream
4 cups sliced fresh strawberries
2 cups fresh blueberries
2 cups fresh raspberries

In a large mixing bowl, cream butter and sugar. Add eggs, one at a time, beating well after each addition. Combine the flour, baking powder and salt; gradually add to creamed mixture.

Line two baking sheets with parchment paper or greased aluminum foil; draw a 9-3/4-in. circle on each. Spoon a fourth of the batter onto each circle; spread evenly with a spoon to within 1/4 in. of edge. Bake at 350° for 8-10 minutes or until edges are golden brown. Remove to wire racks to cool completely.

Combine the sugar, confectioners' sugar and cornstarch. In a large mixing bowl, beat cream and sugar mixture until stiff peaks form. To assemble, place one cookie layer on a large serving plate. Top with 1-1/2 cups whipped cream mixture and 2 cups of mixed berries. Repeat layers twice. Top with remaining cookie layer and whipped cream mixture. Arrange remaining berries on top. Cover and refrigerate for 4 hours. **Yield:** 12 servings.

Nacho Popcorn

When I allow myself to indulge in a snack, I make this spicy popcorn. One batch doesn't last long at our house. You can add more or less red pepper flakes to suit your family's taste.
—*Kay Young, Flushing, Michigan*

 10 cups popped popcorn
1/4 cup butter, melted
  1 teaspoon paprika
1/2 teaspoon ground cumin
1/4 to 1/2 teaspoon crushed red
    pepper flakes
1/3 cup grated Parmesan cheese

Place popcorn in large bowl. In a small bowl, combine butter, paprika, cumin and red pepper flakes. Pour over popcorn and toss to coat. Sprinkle with Parmesan cheese and toss again. **Yield:** 10 servings.

Chewy Chocolate Cookies

These on-the-go goodies are great to take along to the beach, for a picnic or on vacation. They have the great flavor and texture of brownies in a cookie shape.
—*Mary Fravel, Langhorne, Pennsylvania*

1-1/4 cups butter, softened
   2 cups sugar
   2 eggs
   2 teaspoons vanilla extract
   2 cups all-purpose flour
 3/4 cup baking cocoa
   1 teaspoon baking soda
 1/2 teaspoon salt

In a large mixing bowl, cream butter and sugar. Add eggs and vanilla; mix well. Combine the flour, cocoa, baking soda and salt; gradually add to creamed mixture. Drop by rounded tablespoonfuls 2 in. apart onto ungreased baking sheets.

Bake at 350° for 8-10 minutes or until edges are set and centers are puffed and cracked. Cool for 2 minutes before removing from pans to wire racks (cookies will flatten as they cool). **Yield:** about 5 dozen.

Soda Bottle Flower Vases

(Pictured above and on page 103)

DURING the dog days of summer, it's fun to take a break from formal entertaining. Casual summer get-togethers call for easy-to-prepare foods and effortless decorating ideas.

After you and your family enjoy some ice-cold soda pop, wash and save the bottles to use as homespun vases for the single-stem flower arrangements shown above. For best results, use flowers with long stems, such as daisies, gerberas, cosmos and carnations.

These charming table toppers can be grouped in an old-fashioned soda crate and displayed together on the buffet table. Or you can use them as individual centerpieces on picnic or patio tables.

They're so simple to put together that you can enlist older kids to help cut the flowers and fill the bottles while you're preparing the food.

SUMMER Celebrations

Sweet Summer Brownies

WHEN the kids settle down after a day of fun in the sun, re-energize them with a sweet selection of brownies.

Chewy, gooey, sometimes nutty and always good, scrumptious squares are prepared in one pan and usually bake in a flash. So they're great when you want to offer a sweet summer treat but don't want to spend hours in a hot kitchen making cookies.

You'll find this classic dessert in a flavorful assortment of variations, such as Ice Cream Brownie Mountain, Cinnamon Brownies and Brownie Pizza.

So set out a plate piled high with irresistible brownies—don't forget the cold milk!—and watch them disappear.

BROWNIE BONANZA
(Top to bottom)

Ice Cream Brownie
Mountain (p. 117)

Brownie Pizza (p. 119)

Cinnamon Brownies (p. 116)

Cinnamon Brownies

(Pictured on page 114)

No frosting is needed on top of these chewy, fudge-like brownies.
This nice, basic bar has a burst of cinnamon in every bite.
—*Christopher Wolf, Belvidere, Illinois*

1-2/3 cups sugar
  3/4 cup butter, melted
    2 tablespoons strong brewed
      coffee
    2 eggs
    2 teaspoons vanilla extract
1-1/3 cups all-purpose flour
  3/4 cup baking cocoa
    1 tablespoon ground cinnamon
  1/2 teaspoon baking powder
  1/4 teaspoon salt

    1 cup chopped walnuts
Confectioners' sugar

In a mixing bowl, beat the sugar, butter and coffee. Add eggs and vanilla. Combine the flour, cocoa, cinnamon, baking powder and salt; gradually add to the sugar mixture and mix well. Stir in walnuts.

Spread into a greased 13-in. x 9-in. x 2-in. baking pan. Bake at 350° for 18-22 minutes or until a toothpick inserted near the center comes out clean (do not overbake). Cool on a wire rack. Dust with confectioners' sugar. **Yield:** 2 dozen.

Almond Macaroon Brownies

Even when we were in the middle of remodeling our old farmhouse, I made time to bake at least
three times a week. This is a slightly fancier brownie that's great for guests.
—*Jayme Goffin, Crown Point, Indiana*

    6 squares (1 ounce *each*)
      semisweet chocolate
  1/2 cup butter
  2/3 cup sugar
    2 eggs
    1 teaspoon vanilla extract
    1 cup all-purpose flour
  1/3 cup chopped almonds
TOPPING:
    1 package (3 ounces) cream
      cheese, softened
  1/3 cup sugar
    1 egg
    1 tablespoon all-purpose flour
    1 cup flaked coconut

  1/3 cup chopped almonds
  16 whole almonds
    1 square (1 ounce) semisweet chocolate, melted

In a microwave-safe bowl, heat chocolate and butter until melted; stir until smooth. Whisk in sugar, eggs and vanilla until smooth. Add flour and chopped almonds; mix well. Spread into a greased 8-in. square baking pan.

In a mixing bowl, combine cream cheese, sugar, egg and flour; beat until smooth. Stir in coconut and chopped almonds. Spread over brownie layer. Evenly place whole almonds over topping. Bake at 350° for 35-40 minutes until a toothpick inserted near the center comes out with moist crumbs (do not overbake). Cool on a wire rack. Drizzle with melted chocolate. **Yield:** 16 brownies.

Ice Cream Brownie Mountain

(Pictured at right and on page 115)

If you like ice cream cake as my family does, you'll love this easy-to-make version. It's a fun, festive dessert for birthdays and other occasions, especially in summer.
—*Mirien Church, Aurora, Colorado*

4 eggs
2 cups sugar
1/2 cup vegetable oil
1-1/2 cups all-purpose flour
2/3 cup baking cocoa
1 teaspoon baking powder
1/2 teaspoon salt
1/2 cup chopped peanuts
1 quart vanilla ice cream, softened
1 carton (8 ounces) frozen whipped topping, thawed
2 tablespoons chocolate syrup
Colored nonpareils and chopped peanuts, optional

In a mixing bowl, beat the eggs, sugar and oil. Combine flour, cocoa, baking powder and salt; gradually add to sugar mixture and mix well. Stir in peanuts. Spread into a greased 13-in. x 9-in. x 2-in. baking pan. Bake at 350° for 25-28 minutes or until a toothpick inserted near the center comes out with moist crumbs (do not overbake). Cool on a wire rack.

Line a 2-1/2-qt. bowl with a double layer of plastic wrap. Break brownies into pieces about 2 in. square; set aside a third of the pieces. Line the bottom and sides of prepared bowl with remaining brownie pieces, pressing firmly to completely cover to within 1 in. of rim. Fill brownie-lined bowl with ice cream, pressing down firmly. Top with reserved brownie pieces, covering ice cream completely. Cover and freeze overnight.

To serve, uncover and invert onto a serving plate. Let stand for 10 minutes before removing bowl and plastic wrap. Spread whipped topping over top and sides of dessert; drizzle with chocolate syrup. Garnish with nonpareils and peanuts if desired. Cut into wedges with a sharp knife. **Yield:** 10-12 servings.

Frosted Brownies

You can't go wrong with this traditional treat. These fudgy frosted squares travel well
to potlucks and picnics and are sure to be one of the first desserts to disappear.
—*Pat Yaeger, Naples, Florida*

4 squares (1 ounce *each*)
   unsweetened chocolate
1 cup vegetable oil
2 cups sugar
4 eggs
1 teaspoon vanilla extract
1 cup all-purpose flour
1/4 teaspoon salt
1 cup chopped walnuts
FROSTING:
   2 tablespoons butter
   2 squares (1 ounce *each*)
      unsweetened chocolate
2-1/2 cups confectioners' sugar
   1/4 cup milk
   1 teaspoon vanilla extract

In a large microwave-safe bowl, heat chocolate until melted; cool for 10 minutes. Add oil and sugar; mix well. Stir in eggs and vanilla. Add flour and salt; mix well. Stir in the nuts. Pour into a greased 13-in. x 9-in. x 2-in. baking pan. Bake at 350° for 25-30 minutes or until a toothpick inserted near the center comes out with moist crumbs (do not overbake). Cool on a wire rack.

For frosting, melt butter and chocolate; stir until smooth. Cool to room temperature. In a mixing bowl, combine the chocolate mixture, sugar, milk and vanilla until smooth. Frost brownies. **Yield:** 2-1/2 dozen.

FAST FROSTING

AFTER removing a pan of brownies from the oven, sprinkle with chocolate chips. Let stand until the chocolate melts. Spread with a rubber spatula.

Caramel Macadamia Nut Brownies

One bite and you'll agree this is the most delectable brownie you'll ever sink your teeth into.
Eat it with a fork to enjoy every last morsel of chocolate, caramel and nuts.
—*Jamie Bursell, Juneau, Alaska*

1 teaspoon plus 3/4 cup butter,
   divided
3 squares (1 ounce *each*)
   unsweetened chocolate
3 eggs
1-1/2 cups packed brown sugar
2 teaspoons vanilla extract
3/4 cup all-purpose flour
1/4 teaspoon baking soda

CARAMEL LAYER:
   3/4 cup sugar
   3 tablespoons water
   1/4 cup heavy whipping cream
   2 tablespoons butter
TOPPING:
1-1/2 cups semisweet chocolate chips
   1 cup milk chocolate chips
   1 jar (3-1/2 ounces) macadamia nuts, coarsely
      chopped

Line a 9-in. square baking pan with foil; grease the foil with 1 teaspoon butter and set aside. In a microwave-safe bowl, heat chocolate and remaining butter until melted; cool for 10 minutes. In a mixing bowl, beat eggs and brown sugar; stir in chocolate mixture and vanilla. Combine flour and baking soda; add to chocolate mixture.

Pour into prepared pan. Bake at 325° for 40 minutes or until a toothpick inserted near the center comes out with moist crumbs (do not overbake). Cool on a wire rack.

In a heavy saucepan, combine sugar and water. Cook and stir over medium heat for 4-5 minutes or until sugar is dissolved. Cook over medium-high heat without stirring until syrup is golden, about 5 minutes; remove from the heat.

In a small saucepan, heat cream over low heat until small bubbles form around edge of pan. Gradually stir cream into syrup (mixture will boil up). Cook and stir over low heat until blended. Stir in butter until melted. Remove from the heat; cool slightly.

Pour over brownies to within 1/4 in. of edges. Sprinkle with chips and nuts. Bake at 325° for 5 minutes (do not let chips melt completely). Cool completely on a wire rack. Refrigerate for 4 hours. Lift out of the pan; remove foil. Cut into bars. **Yield:** 20 brownies.

Brownie Pizza

(Pictured at right and on page 114)

Kids of all ages will find this a delightfully different way to serve brownies. Use whatever toppings you like to suit your family's tastes.
—*Loretta Wohlenhaus*
Cumberland, Iowa

3/4 cup butter, softened
1 cup sugar
1 egg
1 teaspoon vanilla extract
1-1/2 cups all-purpose flour
1/4 cup baking cocoa
1/2 teaspoon baking powder
1/4 teaspoon salt
3/4 cup milk chocolate M&M's, *divided*
1/2 cup chopped walnuts, *divided*
1/4 cup miniature marshmallows
1/4 cup flaked coconut

In a mixing bowl, cream butter and sugar. Beat in egg and vanilla. Combine the flour, cocoa, baking powder and salt; gradually add to creamed mixture and mix well. Stir in 1/2 cup M&M's and 1/4 cup walnuts.

Spread onto a greased 14-in. pizza pan to within 1/2 in. of edges. Sprinkle with remaining M&M's and walnuts. Top with marshmallows and coconut. Bake at 350° for 15-20 minutes or until a toothpick inserted near the center comes out clean. Cool on a wire rack. Cut into wedges. **Yield:** 10-12 servings.

Butterscotch Pecan Brownies

Starting with my mother's basic brownie, I made up this version as I went along.
It tastes just like candy, so you'll want to cut it into small squares.
—Donna Hampton, Warr Acres, Oklahoma

2 squares (1 ounce *each*)
    unsweetened chocolate
1/3 cup shortening
2 eggs
1 cup sugar
3/4 cup all-purpose flour
1/2 teaspoon baking powder
1/2 teaspoon salt
1/2 cup chopped pecans
FILLING:
  1/4 cup butter
  1/2 cup sugar
  1/4 cup evaporated milk
  3/4 cup marshmallow creme
  1/2 teaspoon vanilla extract
  1/4 cup chopped pecans
CARAMEL LAYER:
  24 caramels
  1/4 cup heavy whipping cream
TOPPING:
  1 cup semisweet chocolate chips
  1/4 cup butterscotch chips
  1/4 cup chopped pecans

In a microwave-safe bowl, melt chocolate and shortening; stir until smooth. Cool slightly. In a mixing bowl, beat eggs and sugar; stir in chocolate mixture. Combine flour, baking powder and salt; gradually stir into chocolate mixture. Stir in pecans. Spread into a greased 13-in. x 9-in. x 2-in. baking pan. Bake at 350° for 18-20 minutes or until a toothpick inserted near the center comes out clean. Cool on a wire rack.

For filling, melt butter in a heavy saucepan over medium heat. Add sugar and milk; bring to a gentle boil. Reduce heat to medium-low; boil and stir for 5 minutes. Remove from the heat; stir in marshmallow creme and vanilla. Add pecans. Spread over top of brownies. Refrigerate until set.

Combine the caramels and cream in a saucepan. Cook and stir over low heat until melted and smooth; cook and stir 4 minutes longer. Spread over filling. Refrigerate until set.

Melt the chocolate and butterscotch chips; stir until smooth. Stir in pecans; spread over caramel layer. Refrigerate for at least 4 hours or overnight. Remove from the refrigerator 20 minutes before cutting. Cut into 1-in. squares. **Yield:** about 8 dozen.

FOILED AGAIN!

TO EASILY cut brownies, line the baking pan with foil, leaving 3 inches hanging over each end. Grease the foil if the recipe instructs. After the baked brownies have cooled, use the foil to lift them out. Cut into bars and discard the foil. This not only makes it easier to cut the bars but saves cleanup time and prevents your pans from getting scratched.

Decadent Brownie Pie

(Pictured at right)

I guarantee this will be the richest, fudge-like brownie you've ever tasted. Slices can be dressed up or down with an assortment of toppings.
—Stephanie Vozzo, Belvidere, New Jersey

2/3 cup butter, softened
1-1/4 cups sugar
1/2 cup light corn syrup
2 eggs
1-1/4 cups all-purpose flour
1/2 cup baking cocoa
1/2 teaspoon salt
3 tablespoons milk
2 cups chopped walnuts
GANACHE:
1 cup heavy whipping cream
8 squares (1 ounce *each*) semisweet chocolate, chopped
Optional toppings—mint Andes candies, raspberries and fresh mint, caramel ice cream topping and whipped cream

In a mixing bowl, cream butter and sugar. Add corn syrup; mix well. Add eggs, one at a time, beating well after each addition. Combine the flour, cocoa and salt; add to creamed mixture alternately with milk. Fold in walnuts. Spread into a greased 10-in. springform pan. Bake at 325° for 55-60 minutes or until a toothpick inserted 1 in. from side of pan comes out clean. Cool on a wire rack.

For ganache, in a saucepan, bring cream to a boil. Remove from the heat; stir in chocolate until melted. Cool completely.

Remove sides of springform pan. Place a wire rack over waxed paper; set brownie on rack. Pour ganache over the brownie; spread over top and let drip down sides. Let stand until set. Cut into wedges; garnish with desired toppings. Store in the refrigerator. **Yield:** 10-12 servings.

Family Reunion Picnic

SUMMER is the perfect time for relatives from near and far to come together for a reunion picnic in the park.

Such a grand gathering isn't complete without those treasured recipes that have been in the family for generations.

In addition, branch out and make some new memories with Grilled Picnic Chicken, Southwestern Pasta Salad, Summer Sub Sandwich, Brownies in a Cone, Root Beer Cookies and Marinated Vegetable Salad.

Every recipe in this chapter is a tried-and-true favorite of a family just like yours and is perfectly portioned for larger groups.

COOKING FOR A CROWD

(Clockwise from top center)

Grilled Picnic Chicken (p. 125)

Southwestern Pasta Salad (p. 128)

Summer Sub Sandwich (p. 125)

Brownies in a Cone (p. 126)

Root Beer Cookies (p. 127)

Marinated Vegetable Salad (p. 124)

Marinated Vegetable Salad

(Pictured on page 122)

This recipe is so versatile because you can use whatever vegetables your family prefers.
It's a nice change from typical mayonnaise-based salads.
—*Rita Wagers, Emporia, Kansas*

3 cups broccoli florets
2 cups cauliflowerets
1-1/2 cups sliced baby carrots
2 celery ribs, cut into 1/2-inch pieces
1 medium zucchini, sliced
1 can (14 ounces) water-packed artichoke hearts, drained and quartered
1 can (6 ounces) pitted ripe olives, drained
1 jar (4-1/2 ounces) whole mushrooms, drained

DRESSING:
3/4 cup vegetable oil
1/3 cup cider vinegar
1 teaspoon garlic salt
3/4 teaspoon sugar
1/2 teaspoon salt
1/2 teaspoon lemon-pepper seasoning

In a large salad bowl, combine the first eight ingredients. In a jar with a tight-fitting lid, combine the dressing ingredients; shake well. Pour over the vegetable mixture and toss to coat. Cover and refrigerate for 8 hours or overnight, stirring occasionally. **Yield:** 14 servings.

FOOD QUANTITIES FOR A CROWD

WHEN PLANNING a buffet, use this guide to estimate how much you'll need per person.

Keep in mind, if you offer more than one item from each category, the less you'll need per serving.

Beverages
3/4 cup of coffee or tea
24 ounces of soft drinks, juices, lemonade or bottled water
1 cup of milk

Breads
1 to 2 slices of bread
1 biscuit, roll or muffin

Salads
1 cup of green salads
1/2 cup of fruit, potato or pasta salads

Condiments
3 to 4 pickle slices or 1 pickle spear

3 olives
1 ounce of ketchup, mustard and pickle relish

Dairy
1 teaspoon (1 pat) of butter or margarine for bread and rolls
1 ounce of sliced cheese for sandwiches
2 tablespoons of cream for coffee

Desserts
1/2 cup of ice cream or frozen yogurt
1 portion of cake or pie

Meats
4 to 6 ounces of meat, fish or poultry
2 hot dogs
1 to 2 ounces of sliced luncheon meat

Miscellaneous
1 ounce of potato or corn chips
3 to 4 ounces of ice for beverages

Summer Sub Sandwich

(Pictured at right and on page 123)

*When I cook for a large group,
I turn to this super sandwich.
It can be assembled in minutes.*
*—Laverne Renneberg
Chelan, Saskatchewan*

1 package (3 ounces) cream
   cheese, softened
1 loaf (20 inches) unsliced
   French bread, halved
   lengthwise
6 slices deli ham
6 slices provolone cheese
1 jar (4-1/2 ounces) sliced
   mushrooms, drained
2 medium tomatoes, thinly
   sliced, optional

1 small onion, thinly sliced
2 banana peppers, thinly sliced
2 cups shredded lettuce

Spread cream cheese on bottom half of bread. Layer with the ham, cheese, mushrooms, tomatoes if desired, onion, peppers and lettuce. Replace top. Cut into 1-1/2-in. slices. **Yield:** 10-15 servings.

Grilled Picnic Chicken

(Pictured on page 123)

This tasty chicken marinates overnight. The next day, I just pop it on the grill for dinner in no time.
—Cindy DeRoos, Iroquois, Ontario

1-1/2 cups white vinegar
  3/4 cup vegetable oil
    6 tablespoons water
4-1/2 teaspoons salt
1-1/2 teaspoons poultry seasoning
  3/4 teaspoon garlic powder
  3/4 teaspoon pepper
    3 broiler/fryer chickens (3 to 4
      pounds *each*), quartered
      or cut up

In a bowl, combine the first seven ingredients. Remove 1 cup for basting; cover and refrigerate. Pour remaining marinade into a gallon-size resealable plastic bag; add chicken. Seal bag and turn to coat; refrigerate for 4 hours or overnight, turning once or twice.

Drain and discard marinade. Grill chicken, uncovered, over medium heat for 30 minutes, turning once. Baste with the reserved marinade. Grill 10-20 minutes longer or until the juices run clear, turning and basting several times. **Yield:** 12 servings.

Brownies in a Cone

(Pictured at right and on page 123)

These brownie-filled ice cream cones are a fun addition to any summer gathering. They appeal to the child in everyone.
—Mitzi Sentiff, Greenville, North Carolina

1 package fudge brownie mix
   (13-inch x 9-inch pan size)
17 ice cream cake cones
   (about 2-3/4-inches tall)
1 cup (6 ounces) semisweet
   chocolate chips
1 tablespoon shortening
Colored sprinkles

Prepare brownie batter according to package directions, using 3 eggs. Place the ice cream cones in muffin cups; spoon about 3 tablespoons batter into each cone. Bake at 350° for 25-30 minutes or until a toothpick comes out clean and top is dry (do not overbake). Cool completely.

In a microwave, melt chocolate chips and shortening; stir until smooth. Dip tops of brownies in melted chocolate; decorate with sprinkles. **Yield:** 17 servings.

Editor's Note: This recipe was tested with Keebler ice cream cups. These brownie cones are best served the day they're prepared.

Olive Potato Salad

My mother shared this recipe with me at my bridal shower more than 45 years ago.
—Margaret Matson, Metamora, Illinois

10 hard-cooked eggs
10 medium potatoes, cooked,
   peeled and cubed
2 celery ribs, chopped
2 cans (2-1/4 ounces *each*) sliced
   ripe olives, drained
1 tablespoon minced fresh
   parsley
1-1/2 teaspoons salt
1/4 teaspoon pepper
DRESSING:
1/4 cup sugar
1-1/2 teaspoons all-purpose flour
1/4 to 1/2 teaspoon salt
1/4 teaspoon ground mustard
4 egg yolks, lightly beaten
6 tablespoons white vinegar

6 tablespoons water
1-1/2 teaspoons butter
Paprika

Chop six hard-cooked eggs; set aside. Slice remaining hard-cooked eggs and refrigerate. In a large serving bowl, combine the chopped eggs, potatoes, celery, olives, parsley, salt and pepper; refrigerate.

For dressing, combine the sugar, flour, salt and mustard in a saucepan. Combine the egg yolks, vinegar and water; gradually whisk into saucepan. Add butter. Bring to a boil, stirring constantly. Cook and stir for 1-2 minutes or until thickened. Cool to room temperature, stirring several times. Pour over potato mixture; gently stir to coat. Cover and refrigerate for at least 2 hours. Top with sliced eggs; sprinkle with paprika. **Yield:** 12-14 servings.

Root Beer Cookies

(Pictured at right and on page 122)

Since it's too difficult to take along root beer floats on a picnic, take these cookies instead! I've found the flavor is even better the next day. The hard part is convincing my family to wait that long before sampling them.
— *Violette Bawden*
West Valley City, Utah

1 cup butter, softened
2 cups packed brown sugar
2 eggs
1 cup buttermilk
3/4 teaspoon root beer
    concentrate *or* extract
4 cups all-purpose flour
1 teaspoon baking soda
1 teaspoon salt
1-1/2 cups chopped pecans
FROSTING:
3-1/2 cups confectioners' sugar
3/4 cup butter, softened
3 tablespoons water
1-1/4 teaspoons root beer
    concentrate *or* extract

In a mixing bowl, cream butter and brown sugar. Add eggs, one at a time, beating well after each addition. Beat in buttermilk and root beer concentrate. Combine the flour, baking soda and salt; gradually add to creamed mixture. Stir in pecans.

Drop by tablespoonfuls 3 in. apart onto ungreased baking sheets. Bake at 375° for 10-12 minutes or until lightly browned. Remove to wire racks to cool. In a mixing bowl, combine frosting ingredients; beat until smooth. Frost cooled cookies. **Yield:** about 6 dozen.

Southwestern Pasta Salad

(Pictured on page 123)

*This satisfying salad has a nice blend of textures and flavors. I appreciate
its make-ahead convenience when I'm entertaining.*
—Ann Brown, Bolivar, Missouri

1 package (1 pound) small
   shell pasta
2/3 cup cider vinegar
2 celery ribs, chopped
6 green onions, thinly sliced
1/2 cup chopped green pepper
1 can (15-1/2 ounces)
   black-eyed peas, rinsed
   and drained
1 can (11 ounces) whole kernel
   corn, drained
1 can (2-1/4 ounces) sliced ripe
   olives, drained
1/2 cup sliced stuffed olives

3 tablespoons diced pimientos
1/3 cup mayonnaise
1/4 cup vegetable oil
1 to 2 teaspoons chili powder
1 teaspoon salt
1/4 teaspoon Worcestershire sauce
1/8 to 1/4 teaspoon hot pepper sauce

Cook pasta according to package directions; drain and rinse
with cold water. Place in a large bowl; add the vinegar and
toss to combine. Stir in the celery, onions, green pepper,
peas, corn, olives and pimientos. In a small bowl, combine
the remaining ingredients; stir into pasta mixture. Cover and
refrigerate overnight. **Yield:** 10-12 servings.

Apple Broccoli Salad

*I came up with this recipe in an attempt to combine the flavors of Waldorf salad
and my favorite broccoli salad. It appeals to family and friends.*
—Brenda Sue Huntington, Clemons, New York

6 medium tart apples, chopped
3 cups broccoli florets
1 small onion, chopped
1/2 cup raisins
1-1/2 cups mayonnaise
2 tablespoons white vinegar
1-1/2 teaspoons sugar
1/2 teaspoon lemon juice
1/2 teaspoon salt
10 bacon strips, cooked and
   crumbled
1/2 cup coarsely chopped walnuts

In a large bowl, combine the apples, broccoli, onion and
raisins. In a small bowl, combine the mayonnaise, vinegar,
sugar, lemon juice and salt; pour over apple mixture and toss
to coat. Cover and chill for at least 2 hours. Just before serving, stir in the bacon and walnuts. **Yield:** 10-12 servings.

Tropical Fruit Salad

(Pictured at right)

Flavored whipped cream makes each bite of this salad taste like candy. The bowl always empties quickly.
—Carol Gillespie
Chambersburg, Pennsylvania

2 large bananas, cut
  into 1/4-inch slices
4 teaspoons lemon juice
2 large cantaloupe melons, cut
  into cubes *or* balls
5 cups cubed fresh pineapple
3 cups halved fresh
  strawberries
1 cup heavy whipping cream
1/2 cup confectioners' sugar
1 teaspoon rum extract,
  optional

1/2 cup flaked coconut, toasted
2 tablespoons slivered almonds, toasted

In a 4-qt. serving bowl, toss the bananas and lemon juice. Stir in the cantaloupe, pineapple and strawberries. In a small mixing bowl, beat cream until it begins to thicken. Add sugar and extract if desired; beat until soft peaks form. Spoon over fruit. Sprinkle with coconut and almonds. Serve immediately. **Yield:** 16-20 servings.

Family-Style Baked Beans

My mother has been making these baked beans for more than 30 years.
Whenever I serve them at cookouts or family gatherings, I receive many compliments.
—Cathy Weidner, Cincinnati, Ohio

3 cans (16 ounces *each*) pork
  and beans
1-1/2 cups ketchup
1 large onion, chopped
3 tablespoons brown sugar
3 tablespoons Worcestershire
  sauce

1 tablespoon white vinegar
3/4 teaspoon chili powder
1/4 to 1/2 teaspoon hot pepper sauce

In a large bowl, combine all ingredients. Transfer to an ungreased 2-1/2-qt. baking dish or bean pot. Cover and bake at 350° for 30-35 minutes or until bubbly. **Yield:** 10 servings.

Cheddar Pan Rolls

Cheddar cheese gives these rich rolls golden color and fabulous flavor.
—Esther Current, Kitchener, Ontario

4-1/2 cups all-purpose flour
   2 tablespoons sugar
   1 tablespoon salt
   1 package (1/4 ounce) active
     dry yeast
   2 cups milk
   1 tablespoon butter
   2 cups (8 ounces) shredded
     cheddar cheese
   1 egg white, beaten

In a large mixing bowl, combine 2 cups flour, sugar, salt and yeast. In a saucepan, heat milk and butter to 120°-130°. Add to dry ingredients; beat until smooth. Stir in cheese and enough remaining flour to make a soft dough. Do not knead. Cover and let rise in a warm place until doubled, about 45 minutes (dough will be soft).

Punch dough down; divide into three portions. Shape each portion into 12 balls. Place in three greased 9-in. round baking pans. Cover and let rise in a warm place until nearly doubled, about 30 minutes. Brush with egg white. Bake at 350° for 20-25 minutes or until golden brown. Serve warm. **Yield:** 3 dozen.

Potluck Strawberry Trifle

This recipe is a great way to serve dessert to a crowd. Frozen pound cake, strawberries and whipped topping add to the ease of preparation for this trifle, which is made in a jelly roll pan.
—Celia Clark, New Tazewell, Tennessee

2 packages (3 ounces *each*)
   cook-and-serve vanilla
   pudding mix
2 packages (3 ounces *each*)
   strawberry gelatin
1 package (10-3/4 ounces)
   frozen pound cake, thawed
1 package (20 ounces)
   unsweetened frozen
   strawberries, thawed and
   halved
1 carton (8 ounces) frozen
   whipped topping, thawed

Prepare pudding according to package directions; cool. Prepare gelatin according to package directions; refrigerate until partially set. Meanwhile, slice the pound cake into 26 pieces. Place in an ungreased 15-in. x 10-in. x 1-in. baking pan. Top with strawberries. Spoon gelatin over strawberries. Refrigerate until set.

Carefully spread cooled pudding over gelatin (pan will be full). Carefully spread with whipped topping. Refrigerate until serving. **Yield:** 24-30 servings.

Fiesta Chili Dogs

(Pictured at right)

*These hot dogs are a hit with
my grandchildren.*
—*Marion Lowery, Medford, Oregon*

  3 cans (15 ounces *each*) chili
     without beans
  2 cans (10-3/4 ounces *each*)
     condensed cheddar cheese
     soup, undiluted
1/2 cup minced fresh cilantro,
     divided
  1 jalapeno pepper, seeded and
     minced
  2 garlic cloves, minced
 24 hot dogs
 24 hot dog buns, split and
     toasted
  2 cans (4 ounces *each*) sliced
     ripe olives, drained
  1 medium onion, chopped
  3 cups crushed corn chips

In a large saucepan, combine the chili and soup; stir in 1/4 cup cilantro, jalapeno and garlic. Add hot dogs. Bring to a boil. Reduce heat; cover and simmer for 35-40 minutes, stirring occasionally. Stir in the remaining cilantro. To assemble, place hot dogs in buns; top with chili sauce, olives, onion and chips. **Yield:** 24 servings.

   Editor's Note: When cutting or seeding hot peppers, use rubber or plastic gloves to protect your hands. Avoid touching your face.

Crisp Onion Relish

*I take this relish to picnics for people to use as a condiment on
hamburgers and hot dogs. It adds a special zip!*
—*Marie Patkau, Hanley, Saskatchewan*

  4 medium sweet onions, halved
     and thinly sliced
1/2 cup sugar
1/3 cup water
1/3 cup cider vinegar
  1 cup mayonnaise
  1 teaspoon celery seed

Place onions in a large bowl. In a small bowl, combine the sugar, water and vinegar; stir until sugar is dissolved. Pour over onions. Cover and refrigerate for at least 3 hours. Drain. Combine mayonnaise and celery seed; add to onions and mix well. Store in the refrigerator. **Yield:** about 6 cups.

Barbecued Pork Sandwiches

Although my cooking experience is limited, I can prepare these sandwiches successfully every time.
—*Pat Lemmer, Greenville, Ohio*

1 pork shoulder *or* butt roast
   (3 to 4 pounds)
2 tablespoons vegetable oil
1-1/2 cups water
2 cans (14-1/2 ounces *each*)
   beef broth
2 cans (10-3/4 ounces *each*)
   condensed tomato soup,
   undiluted
1 large onion, chopped
3/4 cup steak sauce
3 tablespoons Worcestershire
   sauce
2 tablespoons sugar
2 tablespoons cider vinegar

1/2 teaspoon salt
1/2 teaspoon pepper
1/8 teaspoon hot pepper sauce
12 to 14 sandwich buns, split

In a Dutch oven over medium heat, brown roast in oil; drain. Add water; bring to a boil. Reduce heat; cover and simmer for 2-1/2 to 3 hours or until meat is tender. Remove meat; discard cooking juices or save for another use. Cool meat; shred and refrigerate.

In a large saucepan over medium heat, combine the next 10 ingredients; bring to a boil. Reduce heat; simmer, uncovered, for 1-1/2 to 2 hours or until thickened. Add shredded pork; simmer, uncovered, for 30 minutes or until heated through. Serve on buns. **Yield:** 12-14 servings.

Smoky Barbecue Sauce

My mother has been relying on this recipe for years. We especially enjoy it on a beef brisket.
—*Carla Holland, Oktaha, Oklahoma*

2-1/2 cups ketchup
1/4 cup packed brown sugar
1/4 cup chopped onion
2 tablespoons Worcestershire
   sauce
2 to 3 teaspoons Liquid Smoke,
   optional
1 teaspoon garlic powder
1 teaspoon hot pepper sauce
1/2 teaspoon pepper

In a large saucepan, combine all ingredients. Bring to a boil over medium heat,

stirring often. Reduce heat; simmer, uncovered, for 10-15 minutes or until heated through. **Yield:** 2-1/2 cups.

THE HISTORY OF WORCESTERSHIRE SAUCE

IN 1835, Englishman Lord Sandys commissioned two chemists from Worcestershire, John Lea and William Perrins, to duplicate a sauce he had acquired during his travels in India. The pungent batch proved disappointing and wound up in the cellar. When the pair stumbled upon the aged concoction 2 years later, they tasted it and were pleasantly surprised by its wonderfully unique taste.

Mandarin Pasta Salad

(Pictured at right)

I developed this recipe when I was asked to bring a salad to a birthday party for my husband's grandfather. Guests raved about my creative dish!
—Kathleen Dougherty
Williamsville, Illinois

1 package (1 pound) angel hair pasta *or* thin spaghetti, broken into thirds
1 pound boneless skinless chicken breasts, cut into 1-inch cubes
2 garlic cloves, minced
2 tablespoons butter
1-1/2 teaspoons seasoned salt
1 can (8 ounces) sliced water chestnuts, drained
2 cans (11 ounces *each*) mandarin oranges
1 package (6 ounces) frozen snow peas, thawed and drained
2 cups sliced fresh mushrooms
2 cups shredded carrots
2 bunches green onions, sliced

DRESSING:
2/3 cup vegetable oil
1/2 cup white wine vinegar
3 tablespoons soy sauce
1 garlic clove, minced
1 tablespoon sugar
1 tablespoon honey
1/2 teaspoon ground ginger
3 tablespoons sesame seeds, toasted

Cook pasta according to package directions. Drain and rinse with cold water; set aside. In a large skillet, saute chicken and garlic in butter until chicken juices run clear; sprinkle with seasoned salt. Remove with a slotted spoon; set aside.

In the same skillet, saute water chestnuts for 2-3 minutes. Drain oranges, reserving 1/2 cup juice. In a large serving bowl, combine oranges, pasta, chicken, water chestnuts, peas, mushrooms, carrots and onions.

In a jar with a tight-fitting lid, combine the oil, vinegar, soy sauce, garlic, sugar, honey, ginger and reserved mandarin orange juice; shake well. Pour over pasta mixture and toss. Sprinkle with sesame seeds. Refrigerate until serving. **Yield:** 20-25 servings.

FALL
Celebrations

Halloween "Spooktacular" 136-143

A Haunting Halloween 144-153

Traditional Turkey Dinner 154-159

A Thanksgiving Gala with Goose ..160-167

A Bounty of Side Dishes 168-177

Pleasing Thanksgiving Pies 178-187

Fitting Fall Finales 188-195

Give a Lift to Leftovers! 196-205

FALL Celebrations

Halloween "Spooktacular"

AS THE clock ticks closer to the witching hour of Halloween, don't be haunted by the headaches of hosting a frighteningly fun party for the youngsters in your family.

Entertaining can be eerily easy! The trick lies in offering an awesome assortment of kid-approved snacks and beverages.

Little ghosts and goblins will have a smashing good time at your Halloween bash when they spy a spooky spread of Orange Witches' Brew Punch, Bewitching Ice Cream Cones, Marshmallow Ghosts, Frightening Fingers and Black Cat Cookies.

All of the ghoulish goodies on the following pages will get you and your guests into the spirit of this magical holiday!

SPINE-TINGLING TREATS

(Clockwise from top left)

Black Cat Cookies (p. 141)

Orange Witches'
Brew Punch (p. 142)

Bewitching
Ice Cream Cones (p. 139)

Marshmallow Ghosts (p. 138)

Frightening Fingers (p. 138)

Marshmallow Ghosts

(Pictured on page 136)

Kids of all ages can help prepare these easy-to-make treats. With just three ingredients that I often keep on hand, they can be put together at a moment's notice.
—Nancy Foust, Stoneboro, Pennsylvania

12 ounces white candy coating
1-1/2 cups miniature marshmallows
Chocolate decorating gel *or*
assorted candies

In a microwave, melt candy coating; stir until smooth. Cool slightly. Stir in marshmallows until coated. Drop by heaping tablespoonfuls onto waxed paper; smooth and flatten into ghost shapes. Decorate with gel or candies for eyes. Cool completely. Store in an airtight container. **Yield:** about 15 servings.

Frightening Fingers

(Pictured on opposite page and page 136)

These cookies have become somewhat famous at the school our children attend. One year, I made more than 150 of these "fingers" for their classroom Halloween parties.
—Natalie Hyde, Cambridge, Ontario

1 cup butter, softened
1 cup confectioners' sugar
1 egg
1 teaspoon vanilla extract
1 teaspoon almond extract
2-3/4 cups all-purpose flour
1 teaspoon baking powder

1 teaspoon salt
Red decorating gel
1/2 cup sliced almonds

In a mixing bowl, cream butter and sugar. Beat in the egg and extracts. Combine the flour, baking powder and salt; gradually add to the creamed mixture. Divide dough into fourths. Cover and refrigerate for 30 minutes or until easy to handle.

Working with one piece of dough at a time, roll into 1-in. balls. Shape balls into 3-in. x 1/2-in. fingers. Using the flat tip of a table knife, make an indentation on one end of each for fingernail. With a knife, make three slashes in the middle of each finger for knuckle.

Place 2 in. apart on lightly greased baking sheets. Bake at 325° for 20-25 minutes or until lightly browned. Cool for 3 minutes. Squeeze a small amount of red gel on nail bed; press a sliced almond over gel for nail, allowing gel to ooze around nail. Remove to wire racks to cool. **Yield:** about 5 dozen cookies.

Bewitching Ice Cream Cones

(Pictured at right and on page 137)

Both young and old members of my family request these frozen treats every Halloween. It's been a fun tradition around here for many years.
—Edie DeSpain, Logan, Utah

8 chocolate sugar ice cream cones
1 tube chocolate decorating gel
8 thin round chocolate wafers (2-1/4-inch diameter)
1 quart pistachio, mint *or* ice cream of your choice
Black shoestring licorice
16 semisweet chocolate chips
8 candy corn candies
Red decorating gel

Coat edge of ice cream cones with decorating gel; press chocolate wafer against gel to make brim of hat. Set aside.

Drop eight scoops of ice cream onto a waxed paper-lined baking sheet. Cut licorice into strips for hair; press into ice cream. Add chocolate chips for eyes and candy corn for noses. Pipe red gel for mouths.

Flatten scoops slightly to hold hats in place; position hats over heads. Freeze for at least 2 hours or until hats are set. Wrap each in plastic wrap after solidly frozen. **Yield:** 8 servings.

DEVILISH DECORATIONS

A SLEW of simple spooky decorations can set a spirited mood at your Halloween party. In addition to pumpkins and balloons, try these tricks.

- With a black marker, draw ghostly eyes and mouths on old white sheets. Drape over the bristle ends of brooms and prop up against walls.
- Cut out shapes of bats from black construction paper and suspend them from the ceiling with black thread and tape.
- For an eerie glow, replace some of your regular lightbulbs with green or orange bulbs, which can be found at hardware and party supply stores.
- Greet guests with spooky sounds from a purchased cassette or compact disc.
- Pick up a bag of spider webbing from a party supply store. Place in corners throughout the house and attach black plastic spiders. Also scatter spiders on tables, mantels and counters.

Candy Corn Clay Pot

(Pictured on opposite page)

Instead of omitting a centerpiece for a children's Halloween party, create one that will give the youngsters "paws." Just paint a clean clay pot, then fill it with candy corn and Black Cat Cookies. The kids can dip into this clever container for snacks. Or keep the display intact and use it as a door prize.

Ruler and pencil
New 6-inch clay pot
Two wide flat rubber bands
Sponge brush
Acrylic craft paints—white, yellow
  and orange
Craft knife
Candy corn
Black Cat Cookies (recipe on
  opposite page)

Use ruler and pencil to measure and lightly mark a line around clay pot 2 inches from the top rim of the pot and 1-1/2 inches from the bottom of the pot. Center a rubber band over each marked line.

With sponge brush and white paint, basecoat bottom and top sections of clay pot, taking care not to allow paint to puddle along edges of rubber bands. Also basecoat inside of rim. Let dry. Add an additional coat of white paint to bottom section only. Let dry. Paint outside top section and inside of rim yellow. Let dry.

When paint is thoroughly dry, use craft knife to score paint along painted edges of the rubber bands to break any paint seal that might have formed.

Position edge of bottom rubber band along the white painted edge and top rubber band along the yellow painted edge for painting guides. Paint center section orange. Let dry. Carefully remove rubber bands as before. Line the pot with plastic wrap; fill with candy corn and cookies.

MAKING A CANDY CORN CLAY POT

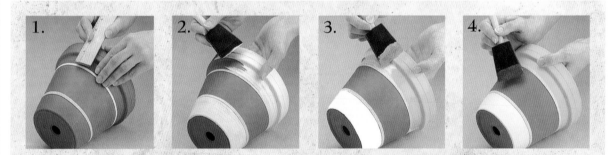

1. With a ruler and pencil, mark a line 2 inches from top rim and 1-1/2 inches from bottom of pot. Center rubber bands over each line.

2. Basecoat bottom and top sections and inside of rim with white paint. Let dry. Add a second coat of white paint to the bottom section. Let dry.

3. Paint the outside top section and inside rim yellow. Let dry.

4. Reposition rubber bands. Paint the center section orange. Let dry. Carefully remove rubber bands. Line the pot with plastic wrap before filling.

Black Cat Cookies

(Pictured at right and on page 136)

Our children look forward to helping me bake these cute cat cookies each year. They've become experts at making the faces with candy corn and red-hots.
—Kathy Stock, Levasy, Missouri

1 cup butter, softened
2 cups sugar
2 eggs
3 teaspoons vanilla extract
3 cups all-purpose flour
1 cup baking cocoa
1/2 teaspoon baking powder
1/2 teaspoon baking soda
1/2 teaspoon salt
24 wooden craft *or* Popsicle sticks
48 candy corn candies
24 red-hot candies

In a mixing bowl, cream butter and sugar. Beat in eggs and vanilla. Combine the flour, cocoa, baking powder, baking soda and salt; gradually add to the creamed mixture. Roll dough into 1-1/2-in. balls. Place 3 in. apart on lightly greased baking sheets.

Insert a wooden stick into each cookie. Flatten with a glass dipped in sugar. Pinch top of cookie to form ears. For whiskers, press a fork twice into each cookie. Bake at 350° for 10-12 minutes or until cookies are set. Remove from the oven; immediately press on candy corn for eyes and red-hots for noses. Remove to wire racks to cool. **Yield:** 2 dozen.

Orange Witches' Brew Punch

(Pictured on page 137)

This slushy punch requires no ice ring to keep it cold. It's not too sweet, so it appeals to everyone. Use this refreshing beverage for any celebration.
—Susan Johnson, Lyons, Kansas

1 package (6 ounces) orange gelatin
1/2 to 1 cup sugar
2 cups boiling water
1 can (46 ounces) apricot nectar
1 can (46 ounces) pineapple juice
3/4 cup lemon juice
4 liters ginger ale, chilled

In a large bowl, dissolve gelatin and sugar in water. Stir in the apricot nectar, pineapple juice and lemon juice.

Freeze in two 2-qt. freezer containers. Remove from the freezer 2-3 hours before serving. Place contents of one container in a punch bowl; mash with potato masher. Stir in ginger ale just before serving. Repeat. **Yield:** about 8 quarts.

Three-in-One Popcorn Crunch

Folks with a sweet tooth will dig into these bite-size snacks. Candy corn is a colorful addition, so this mouth-watering mix is suitable for any autumn event.
—Carma Blosser, Livermore, Colorado

4 quarts popped popcorn
2 cups dry roasted peanuts
1-1/3 cups sugar
1-1/3 cups packed brown sugar
1 cup dark corn syrup
1/2 cup water
1/2 cup butter
1/2 teaspoon salt
1-1/2 cups candy corn

Place popcorn and peanuts in large buttered heatproof containers or bowls; set aside. In a large heavy saucepan, combine the sugars, corn syrup, water, butter and salt. Cook over medium heat until a candy thermometer reads 285° (soft-crack stage), stirring occasionally.

Pour over popcorn mixture; stir gently to coat. Stir in candy corn. Drop into bite-size pieces onto waxed paper. Cool completely. Store in an airtight container. **Yield:** 6 quarts.

Editor's Note: We recommend that you test your candy thermometer before each use by bringing water to a boil; the thermometer should read 212°. Adjust your recipe temperature up or down based on your test.

Witch Hat Treats

(Pictured at right)

Here's a clever twist on ordinary marshmallow cereal treats. They add to the festive feeling around Halloween.
—Nancy Foust, Stoneboro, Pennsylvania

   3 tablespoons butter
   1 package (10 ounces) large
      marshmallows
  1/2 cup peanut butter
   6 cups crisp rice cereal
1-1/2 cups milk chocolate
      chips
   1 teaspoon shortening
Orange frosting
Chocolate jimmies
Black rope licorice

In a large microwave-safe bowl, melt butter on high for about 45 seconds. Add marshmallows; stir to coat. Microwave on high for 45 seconds; stir. Microwave 45 seconds longer or until smooth. Stir in peanut butter. Immediately add cereal; stir gently until coated. Press into a greased 13-in. x 9-in. x 2-in. pan.

In a small microwave-safe bowl, heat chocolate chips and shortening on 70% power for 1 minute. Heat in 10- to 20-second intervals until melted; stir until smooth. Spread over cereal mixture. Cool completely.

Cut into 2-1/2-in. x 2-in. triangles with a thin base on bottom of triangle for hat brim. Decorate with frosting, jimmies for the buckle and licorice for the brim. **Yield:** 2 dozen.

Editor's Note: This recipe was tested in an 850-watt microwave.

CREEPY CAULDRON

TO CREATE the spooky scene shown at right and on page 136, purchase dry ice from your local grocery store's seafood department or ice supplier. Using tongs or thick gloves, place the dry ice in a watertight container; cover with water. Warm water will create more smoke, but it will disappear quickly. Cooler water will produce less dense smoke, but it will last longer. If the amount of smoke decreases during your party, add more dry ice and water.

Editor's Note: Do not handle dry ice with your bare hands. Use tongs or thick gloves. Keep dry ice out of the reach of children.

A Haunting Halloween

WHO SAYS Halloween is just for kids? The young at heart will have a ghoulishly good time when presented with this spooky yet scrumptious spread of grown-up goodies.

As guests arrive at your haunt, offer steaming mugs of Hot Apple Cider to chase away autumn chills.

Loaded with beef and vegetables, Pumpkin Stew will thrill every hungry ghoul and goblin attending your bewitching bash.

Put a spin on the traditional and pass a basket of breadsticks shaped like Witches' Broomsticks. Then toss some salad greens with Favorite French Dressing.

Getting into the Halloween spirit will be a snap when you serve Spiderweb Pumpkin Cheesecake.

SPOOKY SPREAD
(Clockwise from top left)

Witches' Broomsticks (p. 148)

Favorite French Dressing (p. 151)

Pumpkin Stew (p. 146)

Hot Apple Cider (p. 150)

Spiderweb Pumpkin Cheesecake (p. 147)

Pumpkin Stew

(Pictured on page 145)

After our kids carve their Halloween pumpkins, I use the discarded pieces in this savory stew. My family eagerly looks forward to it every year.
—Christine Bauer, Durand, Wisconsin

1/2 cup all-purpose flour
1/2 teaspoon salt
1/2 teaspoon pepper, *divided*
  2 **pounds beef stew meat, cut into 1-inch cubes**
  2 **tablespoons vegetable oil**
  2 **tablespoons butter**
  1 **large onion, chopped**
  2 **to 3 garlic cloves, minced**
  3 **medium carrots, thinly sliced**
  2 **celery ribs, thinly sliced**
  4 **cups water**
  1 **to 2 bay leaves**
  1 **to 2 teaspoons beef bouillon granules**
  1 **to 1-1/2 teaspoons dried thyme**
  3 **cups cubed peeled pumpkin**

In a large resealable plastic bag, combine the flour, salt and 1/4 teaspoon pepper. Add meat, a few pieces at a time, and shake to coat. In a Dutch oven, brown meat in oil and butter. Add onion and garlic; cook and stir for 2-3 minutes. Stir in the carrots, celery, water, bay leaves, bouillon, thyme and remaining pepper. Bring to a boil. Reduce heat; cover and simmer for 1-1/4 hours.

Stir in pumpkin. Return to a boil. Reduce heat; cover and simmer for 20-25 minutes or until meat and pumpkin are tender. Discard bay leaves. **Yield:** 9 servings.

Spinning a Spiderweb Garnish

1. Carefully drizzle syrup over outlines in the pattern of a web. Cool completely.

2. Pipe 1-inch spiders onto parchment paper or foil; cool. Attach spiders to webs with remaining melted chocolate.

Spiderweb Pumpkin Cheesecake

(Pictured at right and on page 144)

This spiced cheesecake makes an appearance on my Halloween table every year. Folks get a kick out of the candy web and chocolate spiders.
—*Bev Kotowich, Winnipeg, Manitoba*

**1-3/4 cups chocolate wafer crumbs
(about 28 wafers)**
1/4 cup butter, melted
FILLING:
 **3 packages (8 ounces *each*)
cream cheese, softened**
3/4 cup sugar
1/2 cup packed brown sugar
 3 eggs
 **1 can (15 ounces) solid-pack
pumpkin**
 2 tablespoons cornstarch
 3 teaspoons vanilla extract
1-1/2 teaspoons pumpkin pie spice
TOPPING:
 2 cups (16 ounces) sour cream
 3 tablespoons sugar
 2 teaspoons vanilla extract
SPIDERWEB GARNISH:
 1 cup sugar
1/8 teaspoon cream of tartar
1/3 cup water
 **4 squares (1 ounce *each*)
semisweet chocolate, melted**

Combine wafer crumbs and butter; press onto the bottom and 1 in. up the sides of a greased 10-in. springform pan. Set aside. In a mixing bowl, beat cream cheese and sugars until smooth. Add eggs; beat on low speed just until combined. Whisk in pumpkin, cornstarch, vanilla and pumpkin pie spice just until blended. Pour into crust. Place pan on a baking sheet. Bake at 350° for 60-65 minutes or until center is almost set. Cool on a wire rack for 10 minutes.

Combine topping ingredients; spread over filling. Bake at 350° for 6 minutes. Cool on a wire rack for 10 minutes. Carefully run a knife around edge of pan to loosen; cool 1 hour longer. Refrigerate overnight. Remove sides of pan; set aside.

For spiderwebs, draw six 3-in. x 2-in. half circles on two sheets of parchment paper. Place another sheet of parchment paper on top; tape both securely to work surface. In a saucepan, bring the sugar, cream of tartar and water to a boil over medium heat. Boil, without stirring, until mixture turns a light amber color and a candy thermometer reads 350°. Immediately remove from the heat and stir. Cool, stirring occasionally, for 10-15 minutes or until hot sugar mixture falls off a metal spoon in a fine thread.

Using a spoon or meat fork, carefully drizzle syrup over half-circle outlines and inside the outlines to form spiderwebs; reheat syrup if needed. Cool completely. Place melted chocolate in a resealable plastic bag; cut a small hole in a corner of bag. Pipe 1-in. spiders onto parchment or foil; cool completely. With remaining melted chocolate, pipe two or three dots on each web; attach spiders.

Remove sides of springform pan. Cut cheesecake; place a web on top of each slice and remaining spiders on the side. Refrigerate leftovers. **Yield:** 12 servings.

Editor's Note: We recommend that you test your candy thermometer before each use by bringing water to a boil; the thermometer should read 212°. Adjust your recipe temperature up or down based on your test. Webs and spiders can be made in advance and stored at room temperature in an airtight container.

Witches' Broomsticks

(Pictured on page 144)

My family loves bread, so I try to serve some with every meal.
Halloween isn't the same without these oh-so-good breadsticks.
—Nicole Clayton, Las Vegas, Nevada

2-1/3 cups biscuit/baking mix
2/3 cup milk
1 teaspoon Italian seasoning
3 tablespoons butter, melted
1/4 cup grated Parmesan cheese

In a bowl, combine biscuit mix, milk and Italian seasoning. Turn onto a lightly floured surface; knead 10 times. Divide into 30 portions; set half aside.

Roll the remaining 15 pieces into 7-in. ropes for broom handles; fold in half and twist. Place on ungreased baking sheets.

Shape reserved pieces into 2-1/2-in. circles; cut with scissors to form a bundle of broom twigs. Place below each broom handle; pinch edges to seal. Brush with butter; sprinkle with Parmesan cheese. Bake at 450° for 10-12 minutes or until lightly browned. Serve warm or cool on a wire rack. **Yield:** 15 servings.

Sweet 'n' Spicy Halloween Munch

(Pictured on opposite page)

Kids of all ages love the sweet and salty blend in this fast-to-fix snack mix.
—Shana Reiley, Theresa, New York

1 pound spiced gumdrops
1 pound candy corn
1 can (16 ounces) salted peanuts

In a bowl, combine the gumdrops, candy corn and peanuts. Store in an airtight container. **Yield:** 2 quarts.

SNACK MIX SERVING SUGGESTION

INSTEAD of simply setting out bowls of Sweet 'n' Spicy Halloween Munch, place individual servings in edible containers like waffle cones and set them in a bowl filled with candy corn (as shown at right). This way guests will be able to munch as they mingle.

Or, instead of waffle cones, make paper cones (as in the photo on the opposite page). Take heavy-duty paper (we used origami paper) and roll it to make a cone shape. Secure with tape and fill with snack mix.

Jumbo Jack-O'-Lantern Cookies

(Pictured at right)

Every Halloween, I'd have a batch of these cookies waiting for my kids when they came home from school so they could decorate their own. Eventually, they started bringing friends home to join in the fun.
—Marlene Kuiper, Oostburg, Wisconsin

1 cup butter, softened
1 cup sugar
1 cup packed brown sugar
1 egg
1 teaspoon vanilla extract
2 cups all-purpose flour
1 cup quick-cooking oats
1 teaspoon baking soda
1 teaspoon ground cinnamon
1/2 teaspoon salt
1 cup canned pumpkin
1 cup (6 ounces) semisweet chocolate chips
Orange and green decorating icing *or* vanilla frosting and orange and green gel food coloring

In a large mixing bowl, cream the butter and sugars; add the egg and vanilla. Combine the flour, oats, baking soda, cinnamon and salt; add to the creamed mixture alternately with pumpkin. Stir in the chocolate chips.

Drop by 1/4 cupfuls onto ungreased baking sheets. Spread into 3-1/2-in. pumpkin shapes. Drop 1/2 teaspoon of dough at the top of each for stem. Bake at 350° for 15-18 minutes or until edges are golden brown. Cool for 1 minute before removing to wire racks to cool completely. Create jack-o'-lantern faces on cookies with decorating icing or tinted frosting. **Yield:** 1-1/2 dozen.

Hot Apple Cider

(Pictured on page 145)

A hot beverage like this is savored here when chilly weather returns after summer.
The clove-studded orange slices are so attractive.
—Sue Gronholz, Beaver Dam, Wisconsin

1 medium navel orange, cut
   into 1/2-inch slices
50 to 60 whole cloves
6 cups apple cider *or* juice
1 cinnamon stick (4 inches)
2-1/4 cups unsweetened pineapple
   juice
1/4 cup honey
3 tablespoons lemon juice
1 teaspoon grated lemon peel
1/4 teaspoon ground nutmeg
Additional cinnamon sticks,
   optional

Cut orange slices in half. Using a wooden toothpick, poke holes in the peel of each orange slice at 1/2-in. intervals. Insert a clove into each hole; set aside.

In a large saucepan, bring apple juice and cinnamon stick to a boil. Reduce heat; cover and simmer for 5 minutes. Stir in the pineapple juice, honey, lemon juice and peel and nutmeg; return to a boil. Reduce heat; cover and simmer for 5 minutes. Discard cinnamon stick. Garnish with orange slices. Serve warm with additional cinnamon sticks for stirrers if desired. **Yield:** 8-10 servings.

Pumpkin-Face Ice Cream Sandwiches

These friendly faces will elicit smiles from friends and family.
You can use homemade or purchased sugar cookies in this recipe.
—Pattie Ann Forssberg, Logan, Kansas

3 tablespoons butter, softened
1-1/2 cups confectioners' sugar
1/2 teaspoon vanilla extract
1 to 2 tablespoons milk
Red and yellow liquid food coloring
48 round sugar cookies
72 raisins
Red and green decorating icing
1 quart vanilla ice cream,
   softened

In a small mixing bowl, combine the butter, confectioners' sugar, vanilla and enough milk to achieve spreading consistency. Tint orange with red and yellow food coloring. Frost the tops of 24 sugar cookies. Make pumpkin faces, using raisins for eyes and nose. Add a smile with red icing and stem with green icing. Let dry completely.

Spoon ice cream onto bottom of plain cookies; top with frosted cookies. Place in individual plastic bags; seal. Freeze until serving. **Yield:** 2 dozen.

Eyeball Soup

(Pictured at right)

My family has fun serving this creamy soup to unsuspecting guests and watching their reaction when they stir up an onion "eyeball." You can make the soup a day ahead and reheat it in the slow cooker.
—*Aleta Clegg, Pleasant Grove, Utah*

1/4 cup butter
1/4 cup all-purpose flour
1 teaspoon salt
1/2 to 1 teaspoon coarsely ground
  pepper
5 cups milk
1 can (46 ounces) V8 juice *or* 4
  cans (11-1/2 ounces *each*)
  picante V8 juice
1 cup frozen pearl *or* small
  whole onions, thawed

In a large saucepan, melt butter. Stir in the flour, salt and pepper until blended. Gradually whisk in milk. Bring to a boil; cook and stir for 1-2 minutes or until thickened. In another saucepan, bring V8 to a boil. Reduce heat; gradually whisk in white sauce. Add onions; heat through. **Yield:** 10 servings (about 2-3/4 quarts).

   Editor's Note: If a smoother soup is desired, cool and puree in batches in a blender before adding the onions.

Favorite French Dressing

(Pictured on page 144)

This was the house dressing at a small restaurant near our home. When it closed, the owner graciously shared the recipe with me. It's fast to whip up on short notice.
—*Connie Knolles, Huntersville, North Carolina*

1 can (10-3/4 ounces) condensed
  tomato soup, undiluted
1 cup sugar
3/4 cup cider vinegar
3/4 cup vegetable oil
1 teaspoon salt
1 teaspoon pepper
1 teaspoon paprika

1 teaspoon ground mustard
1 teaspoon Worcestershire sauce
1 garlic clove
Salad greens and vegetables of your choice

Place the first 10 ingredients in a blender; cover and process until smooth and creamy. Serve with salad. Store in the refrigerator. **Yield:** 3-1/4 cups.

Black Widow Bites

Our home economists add even more fun to Halloween with these candy spiders resting on a chocolate cookie web. Little goblins will be delighted with these sweet treats.

Black shoestring licorice
  12 grape Jujubes
   1 cup vanilla *or* white chips
  24 red nonpareils
  12 chocolate wafers

Cut licorice into 96 pieces, about 1/2 in. long. Using a toothpick, poke one licorice piece about 1/8 in. into a candy. Repeat seven times to make eight spider legs. Repeat with remaining licorice pieces and candy.

Melt chips in a microwave or heavy saucepan; stir until smooth. Transfer to a heavy-duty resealable plastic bag; cut a small hole in a corner of bag. Pipe two small dots on one candy and immediately place one nonpareil on each dot to create eyes. Repeat with remaining candies.

Pipe a web on each chocolate wafer. Pipe a dot of melted vanilla chips onto the bottom of the spider and attach to wafer. **Yield:** 1 dozen.

COOKIE-CUTTER PUMPKIN CARVING

BEFORE YOU BEGIN, carefully cut a circle around the pumpkin stem, lift off the lid and remove the seeds from the lid and inside the pumpkin.

1. Place a cookie cutter on the pumpkin and tap firmly with a rubber mallet until at least half of the cutter has pierced the pumpkin's shell. (If the pumpkin shell is thin, the cutter may be pounded all the way through the shell.)

2. Remove the cookie cutter, using a needle-nose pliers if needed.

3. With a small serrated knife (or the serrated saw from a pumpkin carving kit), follow the pattern made from the cookie cutter to cut out the image, making sure to cut all the way through the shell.

4. With one hand inside the pumpkin, push out cookie cutter image from the pumpkin and discard.

Spine-Tingling Table Topper

(Pictured above and on page 144)

JACK-O'-LANTERNS glowing in a darkened room are a natural choice when decorating for Halloween. But instead of carving pumpkins in the same old way, use cookie cutters!

For an eerie evening effect, we used an assortment of star and moon cookie cutters. You could also use cutters with a fall theme, like leaves and pumpkins.

You may want to purchase an inexpensive pumpkin carving kit, which can be found at craft, hardware and variety stores during the Halloween season. Instead of a kitchen knife, we used the small serrated saw from the kit to cut out the cookie cutter image. The kit's plastic drill came in handy to create small circles on some of the pumpkins.

To make your pumpkins look their best for your party, cut them the day before. Rub a little petroleum jelly on the edges of the cutouts and refrigerate. The day of the party, place a tea light candle in each pumpkin.

Set the jack-o'-lanterns on the table along with your other decorations. We used a felt witch's hat, dried leaves, Indian corn and tree branches. Just before guests arrive, dim the lights, light the candles in the pumpkins and have a "spooktacular" Halloween!

Traditional Turkey Dinner

"IF IT'S NOT broken, don't fix it." That's the popular motto Edie DeSpain lives by in her Logan, Utah kitchen.

So it's no wonder that each Thanksgiving Day, this mother of three and grandmother of seven relies on the tried-and-true menu of Turkey with Apple Stuffing, Maple-Glazed Carrots, Peachy Sweet Potato Bake and Pumpkin Shortbread Dessert.

Other staples in this special dinner include brussels sprouts, a cranberry gelatin salad, mashed potatoes and fresh-baked rolls.

"A few years ago, I tried to start a new tradition of having my daughters make a recipe they like. But they both ended up bringing the same dishes I was already making!" she laughs.

Why not try one of Edie's delicious recipes and start a new tradition in your home this holiday season?

ALL THE FIXINGS
(Clockwise from top left)

Turkey with Apple Stuffing (p. 157)

Maple-Glazed Carrots (p. 158)

Peachy Sweet Potato Bake (p. 156)

Pumpkin Shortbread Dessert (p. 158)

Peachy Sweet Potato Bake

(Pictured on page 155)

With canned sweet potatoes and peaches, this side dish can be put together in a hurry.

1/2 cup packed brown sugar
   3 tablespoons all-purpose flour
1/2 teaspoon ground nutmeg
   2 tablespoons cold butter
1/2 cup chopped pecans
   4 cans (17 ounces *each*) cut-up sweet potatoes, drained
   2 cans (16 ounces *each*) sliced peaches, drained
   1 to 1-1/2 cups miniature marshmallows

In a bowl, combine brown sugar, flour and nutmeg; cut in butter until the mixture resembles coarse crumbs. Stir in pecans. Place sweet potatoes and peaches in a shallow 2-qt. broiler-proof baking dish. Sprinkle with pecan mixture.

Bake, uncovered, at 350° for 35 minutes. Sprinkle with marshmallows. Broil 4-6 in. from the heat until marshmallows are golden brown. **Yield:** 10-12 servings.

THANKSGIVING DAY DINNER TIMELINE

A Few Weeks Before:
- Make Harvest Centerpiece on page 159.
- Prepare two grocery lists—one for non-perishable items to purchase now, and one for perishable items to purchase a few days before Thanksgiving.
- Order a fresh turkey or buy and freeze a frozen turkey.

Four to Five Days Before:
- Thaw frozen turkey in a pan in the refrigerator. (Allow 24 hours of thawing for every 5 pounds.)

Two Days Before:
- Buy remaining grocery items, including the fresh turkey if you ordered one.

The Day Before:
- Set the table.
- Prepare and refrigerate the Pumpkin Shortbread Dessert.
- For the Apple Stuffing, chop onion and celery; refrigerate in an airtight container. Cube bread; store in an airtight container.

Thanksgiving Day:
- Make stuffing, stuff turkey and bake.
- Make the Peachy Sweet Potato Bake and Maple-Glazed Carrots.
- Let cooked turkey stand for 20 minutes. Meanwhile, make the gravy. Remove the stuffing and carve the turkey.
- Serve Pumpkin Shortbread Dessert.

Turkey with Apple Stuffing

(Pictured at right and on page 154)

The accompanying foolproof gravy recipe is one I created in an attempt to copy my mom's own rich gravy.

4 cups chopped peeled tart apples
3 cups sliced almonds
1-1/2 cups chopped onion
1-1/2 cups chopped celery
1/2 cup butter
2 teaspoons salt
2 teaspoons ground cinnamon
2 teaspoons poultry seasoning
12 cups cubed whole wheat bread
2 cups raisins
1 cup apple cider *or* juice
1/2 cup egg substitute
1 turkey (15 to 20 pounds)
1-1/2 cups water

BASIC BRUSSELS SPROUTS

TO MAKE boiled buttered brussels sprouts as shown on page 155, remove any yellow outer leaves and trim stem ends. Cut an X in the core of back.

Add 1 inch of water to saucepan; add brussels sprouts. Bring to a boil. Reduce heat; cover and simmer for 10 to 12 minutes or until crisp-tender. Drain. Top with melted butter.

GRAVY:
2 teaspoons chicken bouillon granules
1/2 teaspoon poultry seasoning
1/4 teaspoon pepper
1/2 cup all-purpose flour
1 cup milk

In a large skillet, saute apples, almonds, onion and celery in butter for 5 minutes. Remove from the heat. Stir in salt, cinnamon and poultry seasoning. In a large bowl, combine bread cubes, raisins and apple mixture. Add cider and egg substitute; toss to mix.

Just before baking, loosely stuff turkey with half of the stuffing. Place remaining stuffing in a greased 2-qt. baking dish; refrigerate until ready to bake. Skewer turkey opening; tie drumsticks together. Place breast side up on a rack in a roasting pan. Pour water into pan.

Bake, uncovered, at 325° for 4-1/2 to 5 hours or until a meat thermometer reads 180° for the turkey and 165° for the stuffing, basting occasionally with pan drippings. (Cover loosely with foil if turkey browns too quickly.)

Bake additional stuffing, covered, for 30-40 minutes. Uncover; bake 10 minutes longer or until lightly browned. Cover turkey and let stand for 20 minutes before removing stuffing and carving.

For gravy, pour pan drippings into a 4-cup measuring cup; skim off fat. Add enough water to measure 4 cups. Pour into a saucepan. Stir in bouillon, poultry seasoning and pepper. Bring to a boil. In a bowl, combine flour and milk until smooth; whisk into boiling broth. Cook and stir for 2 minutes or until thickened and bubbly. Serve with turkey and stuffing. **Yield:** 15-18 servings (12 cups stuffing and 3 cups gravy).

Pumpkin Shortbread Dessert

(Pictured on page 154)

My family prefers this to traditional pumpkin pie, which is just fine with me.
It feeds a crowd, so I only need to make one dessert instead of several pies.

1-3/4 cups sugar, *divided*
1-1/2 cups all-purpose flour
  1/2 cup cold butter
    4 eggs, lightly beaten
    1 can (29 ounces) solid-pack
      pumpkin
    1 teaspoon salt
    1 teaspoon ground cinnamon
    1 teaspoon ground ginger
  1/2 teaspoon ground cloves
    2 cans (12 ounces *each*)
      evaporated milk
Whipped cream and additional
  ground cinnamon, optional

In a bowl, combine 1/4 cup sugar and flour; cut in butter until the mixture resembles coarse crumbs. Press into an ungreased 13-in. x 9-in. x 2-in. baking pan. In a bowl, combine the eggs, pumpkin, salt, spices and remaining sugar. Stir in milk. Pour over crust.

Bake at 425° for 15 minutes. Reduce heat to 350°; bake 50-55 minutes longer or until filling is set. Cool on a wire rack. Cover and refrigerate overnight.

Cut into squares. Top with whipped cream and sprinkle with cinnamon if desired. **Yield:** 15-18 servings.

Maple-Glazed Carrots

(Pictured on page 154)

Carrots are my favorite vegetable, so I'm always searching for different ways to prepare them. This
festive dish is quick to make and nicely complements the turkey.

12 medium carrots, peeled and
    julienned
  2 tablespoons cornstarch
2/3 cup orange juice
  5 tablespoons maple syrup
  5 tablespoons butter, melted
  1 tablespoon grated orange peel
3/4 teaspoon ground nutmeg
1/2 teaspoon salt

Add 1 in. of water to a large saucepan; add carrots. Bring to a boil. Reduce heat; cover and simmer for 3-5 minutes or until crisp-tender.

Meanwhile, in another saucepan, combine the cornstarch and orange juice until smooth. Stir in the remaining ingredients. Bring to a boil; cook and stir for 2 minutes or until thickened and heated through.

Drain carrots; top with glaze and toss to coat. **Yield:** 6-8 servings.

Editor's Note: Two 10-ounce packages of shredded carrots can be substituted for julienned carrots.

Harvest Centerpiece

(Pictured at right)

There's no need to call your local florist and order a centerpiece for this autumn gathering. With a few easy-to-find and inexpensive items—like a simple basket, rustic candles and seasonal natural materials—you can quickly create your own festive table decoration that captures the warm and rustic feel of fall.

Divided container such as a cutlery tray *or* drawer divider
Candles of various sizes, shapes and colors
Jute string, optional
Assorted natural materials such as Indian corn kernels, dried apple slices, bark *or* small stones, strawflowers and small pinecones

Select a divided container to coordinate with your tableware and linens (we used a rattan drawer divider). Place candles into compartments as desired, varying the height for added interest. (If needed, place smaller candles on a sturdy base to add height.) Tie jute string around the larger candles if desired. Fill remaining partitions with a variety of natural materials.

MAKING THE HARVEST CENTERPIECE

1. Place candles of different shapes and heights into selected compartments of a divided container.

2. Fill compartments with assorted natural materials.

A Thanksgiving Gala With Goose

FOR FOLKS looking to add a little twist to their traditional Thanksgiving table, this special supper showcasing succulent Goose with Corn Bread Stuffing is just the thing!

(If you think your family will cry "Foul!" when they don't find turkey on the table, we've also provided a recipe for Herb 'n' Spice Turkey Breast.)

For side dishes, you can't go wrong with Orange Whipped Sweet Potatoes, Cranberry Fruit Mold, Thyme Green Beans with Almonds and Butterfluff Rolls.

Pumpkin Cheesecake Dessert blends the wonderful flavors of pumpkin pie and cheesecake into an unforgettable finale.

FLAVORFUL FALL FARE
(Clockwise from top right)

Goose with Corn Bread Stuffing (p. 163)

Orange Whipped Sweet Potatoes (p. 165)

Thyme Green Beans with Almonds (p. 162)

Cranberry Fruit Mold (p. 165)

Pumpkin Cheesecake Dessert (p. 164)

Thyme Green Beans with Almonds

(Pictured on page 160)

*Thyme is a nice addition to this classic vegetable side dish.
It's a snap to make for family, yet special enough to serve guests.
—Kenna Baber, Rochester, Minnesota*

2 **pounds fresh green beans**
2 **tablespoons butter**
1 **tablespoon minced fresh
    thyme** *or* **1 teaspoon dried
    thyme**
1/2 **teaspoon salt**
1/2 **teaspoon pepper**
1/3 **cup slivered almonds, toasted**

Place beans in a steamer basket. Place in a saucepan over 1 in. of water; bring to a boil. Cover and steam for 10-12 minutes or until crisp-tender.

In a large skillet, melt butter; add the beans, thyme, salt and pepper. Cook and stir for 5 minutes or until heated through. Sprinkle with almonds. **Yield:** 8 servings.

THANKSGIVING DINNER AGENDA

A Few Weeks Before:
- Order a 10- to 12-pound domestic goose from your butcher.
- Buy a fresh or frozen 4-1/4- to 6-pound bone-in turkey breast; freeze.
- Prepare two grocery lists—one for nonperishable items to purchase now and one for perishable items to purchase a few days before Thanksgiving.

A Few Days Before:
- Buy goose and any remaining groceries.
- Thaw frozen turkey breast in a pan in the refrigerator. (Allow about 24 hours for a 6-pound turkey breast.)

The Day Before:
- Set the table.
- Clean and trim the fresh beans for Thyme Green Beans with Almonds.
- Make the Pumpkin Cheesecake Dessert; refrigerate.
- Prepare the Cranberry Fruit Mold; cover and refrigerate.
- For the Corn Bread Stuffing, bake corn bread as directed. Cool; store in an airtight container at room temperature. Prepare vegetables; refrigerate in airtight containers.

Thanksgiving Day:
- In the morning, peel and cube sweet potatoes for Orange Whipped Sweet Potatoes; cover with cold water and let stand at room temperature.
- Bake the Butterfluff Rolls. Cool and store in an airtight container at room temperature.
- Make the Corn Bread Stuffing; stuff goose and bake.
- Bake Herb 'n' Spice Turkey Breast.
- Make Orange Whipped Sweet Potatoes.
- Let the cooked turkey breast stand for 20 minutes before carving. Let the cooked goose stand for 10 to 15 minutes; remove the stuffing and carve.
- Make the Thyme Green Beans with Almonds.
- Set out the Cranberry Fruit Mold.
- Serve Pumpkin Cheesecake Dessert.

Goose with Corn Bread Stuffing

(Pictured at right and on page 161)

I've been making this special entree ever since my husband and I were first married many years ago. The dressing pairs well with the moist meat.

—Patsy Faye Steenbock
Riverton, Wyoming

1 package (8-1/2 ounces) corn bread/muffin mix
1 domestic goose (10 to 12 pounds)
Salt
1-2/3 cups chopped onions
2 cups sliced fresh mushrooms
2 cups sliced celery
6 tablespoons butter
1-1/2 cups grated peeled apples
1 cup chopped pecans
3/4 cup shredded carrots
2 tablespoons minced fresh parsley
3/4 teaspoon *each* dried thyme, marjoram and rubbed sage
1/4 teaspoon pepper
1 cup chicken broth
3 medium carrots, cut into chunks
1 medium onion, cut into 6 wedges
3 garlic cloves, minced
1/2 cup white wine *or* additional chicken broth

Prepare corn bread according to package directions; cool on a wire rack. Rub inside of goose cavity with salt. Prick skin well; set aside. Cut corn bread into cubes; place on a baking sheet. Bake at 350° for 15-20 minutes or until lightly browned. Place in a large bowl. In a skillet, saute chopped onions, mushrooms and celery in butter; add to corn bread cubes. Gently stir in apples, pecans, shredded carrots, parsley, herbs and pepper. Add broth; toss gently. Stuff the goose body and neck cavities; truss opening.

Place carrot chunks, onion wedges and garlic in a shallow roasting pan. Place goose breast side up over vegetables. Pour wine or additional broth over goose. Bake, uncovered, at 350° for 3-1/2 to 4 hours or until a meat thermometer reads 180° (cover with foil during the last hour to prevent overbrowning). Cover and let stand for 10-15 minutes before carving. **Yield:** 10-12 servings.

VERSATILE STUFFING

THE CORN BREAD STUFFING recipe (above) yields about 8 cups of stuffing and is also ideal for a 10- to 12-pound turkey. Just before baking, loosely stuff the turkey and bake at 325° for 3 to 3-1/2 hours or until a meat thermometer reads 180° in the thigh and 160° in the stuffing.

The stuffing can also be baked in a greased 2-1/2-quart baking dish. Cover and bake at 325° for 1 hour. Uncover and bake 10 to 15 minutes longer or until heated through.

Pumpkin Cheesecake Dessert

(Pictured on page 160)

*My family requests this dessert each Thanksgiving. For a change of pace,
I sometimes use cinnamon graham crackers instead of plain ones.*
—*Melissa Davies, Clermont, Florida*

3/4 cup finely chopped walnuts
3/4 cup graham cracker crumbs
   (about 12 squares)
1/4 cup sugar
1/4 teaspoon ground cinnamon
1/4 teaspoon ground ginger
1/8 teaspoon ground cloves
1/4 cup butter, melted
FILLING:
  2 packages (8 ounces *each*)
   cream cheese, softened
3/4 cup sugar
  2 eggs
  1 cup canned pumpkin

1/2 teaspoon ground cinnamon, *divided*
  2 tablespoons chopped walnuts

In a bowl, combine the first six ingredients; stir in butter. Press onto the bottom of an ungreased 10-in. tart pan with a removable bottom.

In a mixing bowl, beat cream cheese and sugar until smooth. Add eggs, beating just until blended. Add pumpkin and 1/4 teaspoon cinnamon; beat on low speed just until combined. Pour into crust; sprinkle with walnuts and remaining cinnamon.

Bake at 350° for 35-40 minutes or until center is almost set. Cool on a wire rack for 1-1/2 hours. Refrigerate until serving. **Yield:** 9-12 servings.

Herb 'n' Spice Turkey Breast

*This nicely seasoned turkey breast from our Test Kitchen is a great
accompaniment to goose at Thanksgiving. Or prepare it throughout the
year for a delicious dinner on its own.*

3 tablespoons vegetable oil
1 tablespoon brown sugar
1 teaspoon salt
1/2 teaspoon rubbed sage
1/2 teaspoon dried thyme
1/2 teaspoon dried rosemary,
   crushed
1/4 teaspoon pepper
1/8 to 1/4 teaspoon ground
   allspice
1 bone-in turkey breast
   (4-1/4 to 6 pounds)

In a small bowl, combine the oil, brown sugar, salt, sage, thyme, rosemary, pepper and allspice. Carefully loosen the skin from the turkey. Rub herb mixture under the skin; rub remaining herb mixture over the skin.

Place turkey breast side up on a rack in a roasting pan. Bake, uncovered, at 325° for 1-1/2 to 2-1/4 hours or until a meat thermometer reads 170° (cover loosely with foil if turkey browns too quickly). Cover and let stand for 20 minutes before carving. **Yield:** 10-14 servings.

Cranberry Fruit Mold

(Pictured at right and on page 160)

This special gelatin salad takes the place of ordinary cranberry sauce on my Thanksgiving table. Grapes and mandarin oranges make it deliciously different.
—Kristy Duncan
Smithfield, North Carolina

1 package (3 ounces) cranberry gelatin
1 package (3 ounces) raspberry gelatin
1 cup boiling water
1-1/2 cups ginger ale, chilled
2 cups halved seedless red *or* green grapes
1 can (11 ounces) mandarin oranges, drained

In a bowl, dissolve gelatins in boiling water. Gently stir in ginger ale. Refrigerate until slightly thickened, about 1-1/2 hours. Stir in grapes and oranges. Transfer to a 5-cup mold coated with nonstick cooking spray. Cover and refrigerate until firm. Invert onto a serving plate. **Yield:** 10-12 servings.

Orange Whipped Sweet Potatoes

(Pictured on page 161)

Orange juice adds a tantalizing twist to mashed sweet potatoes. The color and flavor are incredible!
—Shirley Bedzis, San Diego, California

3 pounds sweet potatoes, peeled and cubed
2-2/3 cups orange juice, *divided*
1/4 cup packed brown sugar
2 tablespoons butter
1/4 teaspoon salt
1/4 teaspoon ground nutmeg
1/4 teaspoon ground ginger

Place sweet potatoes and 2-1/3 cups orange juice in a large saucepan or Dutch oven. Cover and bring to a boil. Boil for 35-45 minutes or just until potatoes are tender. Drain and place in a large mixing bowl. Mash potatoes with the brown sugar, butter, salt, nutmeg, ginger and remaining orange juice. **Yield:** 6-8 servings.

Butterfluff Rolls

(Pictured at right)

In my house, a meal isn't complete unless a basket of rolls is passed around. Just one rising time makes these fluffy rolls easy to prepare.
—*Harriet Stichter, Milford, Indiana*

1 package (1/4 ounce) active
  dry yeast
1/4 cup warm water (110°
  to 115°)
1 cup warm buttermilk (110°
  to 115°)
1/4 cup sugar
1/4 cup shortening
2 eggs
1-1/2 teaspoons salt
1/2 teaspoon baking soda
4 to 4-1/2 cups all-purpose flour
GLAZE:
1 egg
1 tablespoon water

In a mixing bowl, dissolve yeast in warm water. Add buttermilk, sugar, shortening, eggs, salt, baking soda and 2 cups flour; beat until blended. Stir in enough remaining flour to form a soft dough. Turn onto a floured surface; knead until smooth and elastic, about 6-8 minutes. Divide into 18 pieces. Roll each into a 9-in. rope; coil the ends of each rope toward center in opposite directions to form an S shape. Place 3 in. apart on greased baking sheets. Cover and let rise in a warm place until doubled, about 40 minutes.

In a small bowl, beat egg and water; brush over rolls. Bake at 350° for 15-20 minutes or until golden brown. Remove from pans to wire racks to cool. **Yield:** 1-1/2 dozen.

Editor's Note: Warmed buttermilk will appear curdled.

Simply Elegant Thanksgiving Table

(Pictured above)

WHEN you're hosting a Thanksgiving meal at your house, the last thing you want to do is spend time worrying about how to decorate your table.

You don't need an elaborate centerpiece to make your table attractive. Simply top your table with a crisp white or ivory linen tablecloth, then run an eye-catching autumn garland down the center.

In the table setting shown above, we chose a silk garland that can be used from year to year. You can find a great selection of garlands at craft and variety stores.

For a natural look, try tucking in pinecones, gourds or Indian corn. Or replace the silk garland with boughs of dried bittersweet or fresh holly.

Thin white or ivory pillar candles placed on both sides of the garland are a simple yet striking addition. Feel free to use pillar, votive or tea light candles...or a combination of all three. If you use colored candles, make sure they pair well with your garland, linens and dishes.

Instead of traditional place mats, we added a little elegance by setting napkins matching our tablecloth on a diagonal, draping them off the side of the table and topping with plates.

For the fast finishing touch, fold a napkin into a rectangle, roll it up lengthwise and tie with a ribbon. Tuck a sprig of the garland under the ribbon and place the napkin on the plate.

FALL Celebrations

A Bounty of Side Dishes

THANKSGIVING dinner with all the fixings is often the year's most memorable meal for families—and one they eagerly look forward to. In addition to the traditional succulent turkey, a variety of side dishes round out this special feast.

From delectable dressings and seasonal vegetables to fresh tossed salads and sweet sauces or fruits, this harvest of holiday dishes provides many mouth-watering options you can take to your Thanksgiving table year after year.

For a surefire way to receive a bushel of compliments, you'll want to try Oat 'n' Rye Bread Dressing, Tangy Baked Apples and Roasted Root Vegetables.

CORNUCOPIA!
(Clockwise from top left)

Oat 'n' Rye
Bread Dressing (p. 170)

Tangy Baked Apples (p. 171)

Roasted Root
Vegetables (p. 173)

Oat 'n' Rye Bread Dressing

(Pictured on page 168)

Two kinds of bread, spinach, green pepper and cranberries make this an outstanding dressing for special occasions. The flavor of sage really shines through.
—*Judith Toubes, Tamarac, Florida*

3 cups cubed day-old oatmeal
   bread
3 cups cubed day-old rye bread
1 cup chopped fresh spinach
1 cup chopped green pepper
1 cup dried cranberries
2 tablespoons chopped onion
2 teaspoons rubbed sage
1 cup chicken broth
2 eggs, lightly beaten *or* 1/2 cup
   egg substitute

In a large bowl, combine the bread cubes, spinach, green pepper, cranberries, onion and sage. Stir in broth and eggs until well combined. Spoon into a greased 2-qt. baking dish. Cover and bake at 350° for 45 minutes. Uncover; bake 10-15 minutes longer or until lightly browned. **Yield:** 6 servings.

Editor's Note: This recipe makes enough to stuff a 6-pound roasting chicken. It can easily be doubled for a 12-pound turkey.

TURKEY AND STUFFING TIPS

ANY DRESSING can be used to stuff a turkey. For food safety reasons, review these pointers before cooking your Thanksgiving turkey and stuffing.

- Use egg substitute in place of eggs for dressing that is stuffed into the turkey.
- Stuff the turkey just before baking—not beforehand. Loosely spoon the stuffing into the neck and body cavities to allow for expansion as it cooks.
- To be sure the stuffing is done, a meat thermometer at the center of the stuffing inside the bird should reach 165°.
- Always remove all of the stuffing before carving the bird. Never leave stuffing in cooked turkey when storing in the refrigerator.
- Don't let cooked turkey and stuffing stand at room temperature longer than 2 hours.

Maple Cranberry Sauce

My mother insists I bring this simple cranberry sauce every Thanksgiving. Maple syrup adds a pleasant sweetness people don't expect.
—*Mathilda Navias, Tiffin, Ohio*

1 package (12 ounces) fresh *or*
   frozen cranberries
1-1/2 cups maple syrup
1/3 cup water

In a large saucepan, combine all ingredients. Bring to a boil. Reduce heat; simmer, uncovered, for 20 minutes, stirring occasionally. Cool. Cover and refrigerate until ready to serve. **Yield:** 2-1/2 cups.

Tangy Baked Apples

(Pictured at right and on page 169)

*When the weather turns cooler in fall,
these baked apples from my mom
are sure to warm you up. Our family
enjoys them with turkey, pork...even
meat loaf. My husband and I like to add
a bit more horseradish for extra zip.*
— Dee Poppie, Gilman, Illinois

3 medium tart apples, cored
2 teaspoons lemon juice,
   divided
1/3 cup packed brown sugar
1/3 cup ketchup
2 tablespoons butter, softened
2 tablespoons prepared
   horseradish
1/4 cup water

Cut apples in half; brush with 1 teaspoon lemon juice. Place in an ungreased 11-in. x 7-in. x 2-in. baking dish. Combine the brown sugar, ketchup, butter, horseradish and remaining lemon juice. Top each apple half with 2 tablespoons ketchup mixture. Pour water around apples.

Bake, uncovered, at 325° for 30 minutes or until apples are tender. Serve warm. **Yield:** 6 servings.

Sausage Potato Dressing

*Mashed potatoes and sausage are the deliciously different ingredients in this moist dressing.
I've been using this recipe since the 1960s with no complaints from my family.*
— Germaine Stank, Pound, Wisconsin

1 large onion, chopped
1/2 cup butter, melted
3 cups hot mashed potatoes
   (prepared with milk and
   butter)
8 slices bread, toasted and
   cubed
1/2 pound bulk pork sausage,
   cooked and drained
2 eggs, lightly beaten *or* 1/2 cup
   egg substitute

1 teaspoon rubbed sage
1/2 teaspoon salt
1/2 teaspoon pepper

In a large skillet, saute onion in butter until tender. Remove from the heat. Add the remaining ingredients; mix well. Transfer to a greased 2-1/2-qt. baking dish. Cover and bake at 325° for 35 minutes. Uncover; bake 10 minutes longer or until golden brown. **Yield:** 8-10 servings.

Editor's Note: This recipe makes enough to stuff a 10- to 12-pound turkey.

Two-Cheese Spinach Bake

*My family will eat spinach on Thanksgiving and throughout the year if it's in
this rich, cheesy side dish loaded with flavor. It also makes
a great meatless meal with a tossed salad.*
—*Chris Barila, Pisgah Forest, North Carolina*

1 cup all-purpose flour
2 eggs, lightly beaten
1 cup milk
1/4 cup butter, melted
1/2 small onion, chopped
2 tablespoons grated
   Parmesan cheese
2 garlic cloves, minced
1/2 teaspoon salt
1/8 teaspoon cayenne
   pepper

1 package (10 ounces) frozen chopped spinach,
   thawed and squeezed dry
2 cups (8 ounces) shredded Monterey Jack cheese

In a large bowl, whisk the flour, eggs, milk, butter, onion, Parmesan cheese, garlic, salt and cayenne until combined. Fold in spinach and Monterey Jack cheese. Transfer to a greased 1-1/2-qt. baking dish.

   Bake, uncovered, at 350° for 40-45 minutes or until a knife inserted near the center comes out clean. Serve immediately. **Yield:** 6 servings.

Artichoke-Red Pepper Tossed Salad

*During college, I lived in France, where I learned to make vinaigrette.
My host family served the dressing with artichoke hearts. That inspired me to add
them to my basic tossed salad when I returned home.*
—*Rachel Hinz, St. James, Minnesota*

1 head iceberg lettuce, torn
1 bunch romaine, torn
1 can (14 ounces) water-packed
   artichoke hearts, drained and
   chopped
2 medium sweet red peppers,
   julienned
1/2 cup thinly sliced red onion
1/2 cup olive oil
1/2 cup red wine vinegar

2 tablespoons Dijon mustard
2 teaspoons sugar
1 teaspoon seasoned salt
1/2 cup shredded Parmesan cheese

In a large bowl, combine the first five ingredients. In a jar with a tight-fitting lid, combine the oil, vinegar, mustard, sugar and seasoned salt; shake well. Drizzle over the salad and toss to coat. Sprinkle with the Parmesan cheese. **Yield:** 20-25 servings.

Roasted Root Vegetables

(Pictured at right and on page 168)

This dish's pretty harvest colors make it an eye-catching addition to the Thanksgiving table. It's a fix-it-and-forget-it favorite of mine.
—Cathryn White, Newark, Delaware

2 cups pearl onions
2 pounds red potatoes, cut into 1/2-inch pieces
1 large rutabaga, peeled and cut into 1/2-inch pieces
1 pound parsnips, peeled and cut into 1/2-inch pieces
1 pound carrots, cut into 1/2-inch pieces
3 tablespoons butter, melted
3 tablespoons olive oil
4-1/2 teaspoons dried thyme
1-1/2 teaspoons salt
3/4 teaspoon coarsely ground pepper
2 packages (10 ounces *each*) frozen brussels sprouts, thawed
3 to 4 garlic cloves, minced

In a Dutch oven or large kettle, bring 6 cups water to a boil. Add the pearl onions; boil for 3 minutes. Drain and rinse with cold water; peel.

In a large roasting pan, combine the onions, potatoes, rutabaga, parsnips and carrots. Drizzle with butter and oil. Sprinkle with thyme, salt and pepper; toss to coat. Cut an X in the core of each brussels sprout.

Cover and bake at 425° for 30 minutes. Uncover; stir in brussels sprouts and garlic. Bake, uncovered, for 50-60 minutes or until vegetables are tender and begin to brown, stirring occasionally. **Yield:** 16-18 servings.

Family Traditions

INSTEAD of simply saying grace at our Thanksgiving dinner, each person around the table takes a turn to state what they're thankful for. Even the little ones pipe in and express their appreciation for something they cherish. More often than not, our eyes fill with tears as we take the time to remember what's truly important in life. We hope the kids carry on this touching tradition.
—*Suzanne Davidsz, Oak Creek, Wisconsin*

Sweet Potato Casserole

*Pineapple, sugar and marshmallows lend a super sweetness to sweet potatoes.
I've been making this casserole for years, both for special occasions at home and for casual dinners.*
—*Ruth Leach, Shreveport, Louisiana*

6 medium sweet potatoes
1/2 cup butter, cubed
3/4 cup sugar
1 can (20 ounces) crushed
   pineapple, drained
2 eggs, beaten
1 teaspoon vanilla extract
1/2 teaspoon ground nutmeg
1/2 teaspoon salt
15 large marshmallows

Place sweet potatoes in a large kettle and cover with water; bring to a boil. Boil gently until potatoes can easily be pierced with the tip of a sharp knife, about 30-45 minutes. Drain; cool slightly. Peel potatoes and place in a large bowl; mash. Stir in butter and sugar until butter is melted. Add pineapple, eggs, vanilla, nutmeg and salt.

Spoon into a greased 2-qt. baking dish. Top with marshmallows. Bake, uncovered, at 350° for 40-45 minutes. **Yield:** 8 servings.

SWEET POTATO SECRETS

SELECT sweet potatoes that are firm with no cracks or bruises. If stored in a cool, dark and well-ventilated place, they'll remain fresh for about 2 weeks. If the temperature is above 60°, they'll sprout sooner or become woody. Once cooked, sweet potatoes can be stored for up to 1 week in the refrigerator.

Frosty Cranberry Salad Cups

*Instead of traditional cranberry sauce, consider these individual fruit salads.
They're a make-ahead treat terrific for potlucks.*
—*Bernadine Bolte, St. Louis, Missouri*

1 can (16 ounces) jellied
   cranberry sauce
1 can (8 ounces) crushed
   pineapple, drained
1 cup (8 ounces) sour cream
1/4 cup confectioners' sugar
3/4 cup miniature marshmallows
Red food coloring, optional

In a bowl, combine all ingredients. Fill foil- or paper-lined muffin cups two-thirds full. Cover and freeze until firm, about 3 hours. **Yield:** 16 servings.

Dilly Bread Ring

(Pictured at right)

I made this bread when my boyfriend came to meet my family for the first time. It obviously made an impression on him, because we eventually got married! This batter bread requires no kneading, so even novice bakers will find it easy.
—Natercia Yailaian
Somerville, Massachusetts

2 packages (1/4 ounce *each*)
   active dry yeast
1/3 cup warm water (110°
   to 115°)
1/3 cup warm milk (110°
   to 115°)
6 tablespoons butter, softened
1/3 cup sugar
2 eggs
1 cup (8 ounces) sour cream
2 tablespoons minced fresh
   parsley
1 to 2 tablespoons dill weed
2 teaspoons salt
1-1/2 teaspoons minced chives
4-1/2 cups all-purpose flour

In a mixing bowl, dissolve yeast in warm water. Add milk, butter, sugar, eggs, sour cream, seasonings and 3 cups flour. Beat on low speed for 30 seconds. Beat on high for 3 minutes. Stir in remaining flour (batter will be sticky). Do not knead. Cover and let rise in a warm place until doubled, about 1 hour.

Stir dough down. Spoon into a greased 10-in. tube or fluted tube pan. Cover and let rise until nearly doubled, about 45 minutes. Bake at 375° for 30-35 minutes or until golden brown (cover loosely with foil if top browns too quickly). Cool for 10 minutes before removing from pan to a wire rack. **Yield:** 1 loaf.

After-Thanksgiving Turkey Soup

As much as my family loves Thanksgiving, they look forward to this cream soup using leftover turkey even more. It makes a big batch that we can enjoy for days.
—*Valorie Walker, Bradley, South Carolina*

1 leftover turkey carcass (from a 12- to 14-pound turkey)
3 medium onions, chopped
2 large carrots, diced
2 celery ribs, diced
1 cup butter
1 cup all-purpose flour
2 cups half-and-half cream
1 cup uncooked long grain rice
2 teaspoons salt
1 teaspoon chicken bouillon granules
3/4 teaspoon pepper

Place turkey carcass in a soup kettle or Dutch oven and cover with water. Bring to a boil. Reduce heat; cover and simmer for 1 hour. Remove carcass; cool. Set aside 3 qts. broth. Remove turkey from bones and cut into bite-size pieces; set aside.

In a soup kettle or Dutch oven, saute the onions, carrots and celery in butter until tender. Reduce heat; stir in flour until blended. Gradually add 1 qt. of reserved broth. Bring to a boil; cook and stir for 2 minutes or until thickened.

Add cream, rice, salt, bouillon, pepper, remaining broth and reserved turkey. Reduce heat; cover and simmer for 30-35 minutes or until rice is tender. **Yield:** 16 servings (about 4 quarts).

Winter Squash Souffle

My large family gets together quite often. To make it easy on the host, everyone brings a dish to pass, and we often swap recipes. I've shared this one many times.
—*Colleen Birchill, Spokane, Washington*

3 cups mashed cooked winter squash
1/4 cup shredded Swiss cheese
2 tablespoons butter, melted
2 tablespoons heavy whipping cream
3/4 teaspoon salt
1/4 teaspoon pepper
1/4 teaspoon dried thyme
3 eggs, *separated*

In a large bowl, combine the squash, cheese, butter, cream, salt, pepper and thyme. Beat egg yolks; add to squash mixture. In a small mixing bowl, beat egg whites until stiff peaks form. Fold into squash mixture. Transfer to a greased 2-qt. baking dish.

Bake, uncovered, at 375° for 45-50 minutes or until a knife inserted near the center comes out clean. Serve immediately. **Yield:** 6-8 servings.

BAKING A WINTER SQUASH

TO BAKE winter squash for mashing, cut the squash in half; scoop out and discard seeds. Place cut side down in a greased baking dish. Bake, uncovered, at 350° for 45 to 60 minutes or until tender. Cool slightly. Scoop squash out of shell; mash. A 1-pound squash will yield about 2 cups mashed squash.

Almond-Cranberry Squash Bake

(Pictured at right)

When my husband and I visit family in North Dakota, I bring along the ingredients to make this casserole. It gets rave reviews every time I make it.
—*Ronica Skarphol Brownson*
Madison, Wisconsin

4 cups hot mashed butternut
    squash
4 tablespoons butter, softened,
    divided
1/2 teaspoon salt
1/2 teaspoon ground cinnamon
1/4 teaspoon ground allspice
1/4 teaspoon ground nutmeg
1 can (16 ounces) whole-berry
    cranberry sauce
1/2 cup sliced almonds
1/4 cup packed brown sugar

In a large bowl, combine the squash, 2 tablespoons butter, salt, cinnamon, allspice and nutmeg; mix well. Transfer to a greased 2-qt. baking dish. Stir cranberry sauce until softened; spoon over squash.

Combine almonds, brown sugar and remaining butter; mix well. Sprinkle over cranberry sauce. Bake, uncovered, at 350° for 50-60 minutes or until golden brown and bubbly. **Yield:** 8 servings.

Crunchy Apple Salad

This old-fashioned salad is part of my favorite meal that Mom used to make. Crunchy apples, celery and walnuts blend well with the creamy mayonnaise.
—*Julie Pearsall, Union Springs, New York*

4 large red apples, diced
1 cup chopped celery
1 cup raisins
1 cup chopped walnuts
1/2 cup mayonnaise

In a large bowl, combine the apples, celery, raisins and walnuts. Blend in mayonnaise. Cover and refrigerate until serving. **Yield:** 16 servings.

FALL
Celebrations

Pleasing Thanksgiving Pies

EVEN AFTER a big turkey dinner with all the fixin's, who can resist a slice of pie?

From fruit-filled favorites and creamy custard creations to cool refrigerator treats and magnificent meringues, an assortment of homemade pies provides the perfect finishing touch on Thanksgiving Day.

So gather your guests around the dessert table to sample a wonderful wedge of Spiced Pumpkin Pie, Rustic Pear Tart or Cherry Meringue Pie...or maybe even a sliver of each!

A SLICE OF HEAVEN

(Clockwise from top)

Cherry Meringue Pie (p. 182)

Spiced Pumpkin Pie (p. 181)

Rustic Pear Tart (p. 180)

Rustic Pear Tart

(Pictured on page 178)

*In this delightful pie from our Test Kitchen, the pastry makes a
"pouch" for a pleasant pear filling. For even more flavor, top the tart with
a powdered sugar glaze and toasted slivered almonds.*

1-1/3 cups all-purpose flour
   3 tablespoons sugar
  1/4 teaspoon salt
   7 tablespoons cold butter,
     cubed
   2 to 3 tablespoons cold water
FILLING:
  3/4 cup sugar
  1/4 cup slivered almonds,
     toasted
  1/4 cup all-purpose flour
1-1/2 teaspoons grated lemon peel
  1/2 to 3/4 teaspoon ground
     cinnamon
   4 medium ripe pears, peeled
     and sliced
   1 tablespoon butter

GLAZE (optional):
  1/4 cup confectioners' sugar
1-1/2 teaspoons milk
  1/4 teaspoon vanilla extract
  1/4 cup slivered almonds, toasted

In a bowl, combine the flour, sugar and salt; cut in butter until crumbly. Gradually add water, tossing with a fork until dough forms a ball. Roll out to a 14-in. circle. Transfer pastry to a 14-in. pizza pan. In a bowl, combine the sugar, almonds, flour, lemon peel and cinnamon. Add pears; toss to coat. Spoon over the pastry to within 2 in. of edges; dot with butter. Fold edges of pastry over pears. Bake at 375° for 45-50 minutes or until golden brown.

For glaze, combine the confectioners' sugar, milk and vanilla. Pour over warm tart. Sprinkle with almonds. Cool on a wire rack. **Yield:** 8-10 servings.

Sour Cream Raisin Pie

*For my family, this pie is as essential for Thanksgiving dinner as turkey, dressing and
mashed potatoes! I've been told this recipe's been in the family since the 1860s.*
— Trish Rempe, Superior, Nebraska

Pastry for double-crust pie
  (9 inches)
   2 eggs
   1 cup (8 ounces) sour cream
  3/4 cup sugar
   2 tablespoons cider vinegar
   1 teaspoon ground cinnamon
  1/2 teaspoon ground cloves
  1/8 teaspoon salt
   1 cup raisins

Line a 9-in. pie plate with bottom pastry; trim even with edge of plate. In a mixing bowl, beat eggs on medium speed for 1 minute. Add sour cream, sugar, vinegar, cinnamon, cloves and salt; mix well. Stir in raisins. Pour into pastry shell. Roll out remaining pastry to fit top of pie. Place over filling; trim, seal and flute edges. Cut slits in pastry.

Cover edges loosely with foil. Bake at 400° for 10 minutes. Reduce heat to 350° and remove foil. Bake 40-45 minutes longer or until golden brown. Cool on a wire rack. Refrigerate leftovers. **Yield:** 6-8 servings.

Spiced Pumpkin Pie

(Pictured at right and on page 179)

What would Thanksgiving be without a traditional pumpkin pie like this? The smooth and creamy filling features a wonderful blend of spices.
—*Pat Marken, Hansville, Washington*

 3 eggs
 1 cup milk
 1/2 cup sugar
 1/2 cup packed brown sugar
 1 teaspoon ground cinnamon
 3/4 teaspoon ground nutmeg
 1/2 teaspoon salt
 1/2 teaspoon ground ginger
 1/2 teaspoon ground cloves
 1 can (15 ounces) solid-pack
  pumpkin
 1 unbaked pastry shell (9 inches)
**Whipped topping and additional
 ground cinnamon**

In a bowl, lightly beat eggs. Add the milk, sugars, cinnamon, nutmeg, salt, ginger and cloves; mix well. Stir in the pumpkin just until blended. Pour into pastry shell. Bake at 350° for 50-60 minutes or until a knife inserted near the center comes out clean. Cool on a wire rack. Chill until serving. Garnish with whipped topping sprinkled with cinnamon. Refrigerate leftovers. **Yield:** 6-8 servings.

DECORATING PIE WITH PASTRY CUTOUTS

PASTRY CUTOUTS (pictured above on the Spiced Pumpkin Pie) are a fast, festive way to dress up plain single-crust pies.

To make cutouts, roll out dough to 1/8-inch thickness. Cut out with 1/2- or 1-inch cookie cutters of desired shape. If desired, score designs on cutouts with sharp knife.

Bake cutouts on an ungreased baking sheet at 400° for 6-8 minutes or until golden brown. Remove to a wire rack to cool. Arrange cutouts over the cooled filling on the baked pie.

Cutouts can also be used on double-crust pies. Brush the bottom of each unbaked cutout with water and place on top of an unbaked pie. Press lightly to secure. Bake pie according to the recipe.

Cherry Meringue Pie

(Pictured on page 178)

People are surprised to hear this pie's meringue crust features saltines.
The cream cheese and cherry pie filling make this dessert extra special.
—Susan Card, Franklin, New Jersey

3 egg whites
1 teaspoon white vinegar
1 cup sugar
1/2 cup crushed saltines (about 12 crackers)
1/2 cup finely chopped pecans
1 teaspoon baking powder
1 teaspoon vanilla extract
TOPPING:
1 package (3 ounces) cream cheese, softened
1/2 cup confectioners' sugar
1 teaspoon vanilla extract
1/2 cup heavy whipping cream, whipped
1 can (21 ounces) cherry pie filling

In a mixing bowl, beat egg whites and vinegar on medium speed until soft peaks form. Gradually beat in sugar, 1 tablespoon at a time, on high until stiff glossy peaks form and sugar is dissolved. Fold in the cracker crumbs, pecans, baking powder and vanilla. Spread onto the bottom and up the sides of a greased deep-dish 9-in. pie plate.

Bake at 350° for 14-18 minutes or until the meringue is lightly browned. Cool on a wire rack (meringue shell will fall in center).

In a small mixing bowl, beat the cream cheese, confectioners' sugar and vanilla until fluffy. Fold in the whipped cream. Spoon into meringue shell. Top with pie filling. Chill for at least 2 hours before serving. **Yield:** 8-10 servings.

White Chocolate Banana Pie

I developed this recipe based on a popular pie served at an Atlanta restaurant.
Everyone looks forward to this dessert at the annual Christmas party we host on our farm.
Chocolate curls as a garnish are a nice contrast to the creamy white pie.
—Mary Ann Morgan, Cedartown, Georgia

2 cups heavy whipping cream
6 squares (1 ounce *each*) white baking chocolate
3 teaspoons vanilla extract
2 medium firm bananas, sliced
Lemon juice
1 pastry shell (9 inches), baked

In a saucepan, cook and stir the cream and chocolate over low heat until chocolate is melted. Remove from the heat; stir in vanilla. Transfer to a mixing bowl. Cover and refrigerate for 6 hours or until thickened, stirring occasionally.

Beat on high speed until light and fluffy, about 4 minutes (do not overbeat). Dip banana slices in lemon juice. Pour half of the cream mixture into pastry shell. Top with bananas. Cover with remaining cream mixture. Refrigerate until serving. **Yield:** 6-8 servings.

Citrus Cranberry Pie

(Pictured at right)

To showcase abundant fall cranberries, our home economists developed the recipe for this lattice-topped pie. A dollop of orange cream complements the slightly tart flavor.

Pastry for double-crust pie
  (9 inches)
3-1/2 cups fresh *or* frozen
    cranberries
  1 small navel orange, peeled,
    sectioned and chopped
  1 cup sugar
  2 tablespoons butter, melted
4-1/2 teaspoons all-purpose flour
  2 teaspoons grated lemon peel
  1 teaspoon grated orange peel
1/4 teaspoon salt
  1 egg, lightly beaten
Additional sugar
ORANGE CREAM:
  1 cup heavy whipping cream
  1 tablespoon sugar
  2 teaspoons grated orange peel
  1 teaspoon orange extract

Line a 9-in. pie plate with bottom pastry; trim pastry even with edge of plate. In a bowl, combine the cranberries, orange, sugar, butter, flour, lemon and orange peel and salt. Pour into pastry shell. Roll out remaining pastry; make a lattice crust. Trim, seal and flute edges. Brush lattice crust with egg. Sprinkle with additional sugar. Cover edges loosely with foil. Bake at 450° for 10 minutes. Reduce heat to 350° and remove foil. Bake 40-45 minutes longer or until golden brown.

Meanwhile, in a mixing bowl, beat cream until it begins to thicken. Add the sugar, orange peel and extract; beat until stiff peaks form. Cover and refrigerate. Serve with warm pie. **Yield:** 6-8 servings.

Family Traditions

The night before Thanksgiving, our church holds a pie fest, where those attending are asked to bring a presliced pie to share. After the service, we head to the hall and find tables laden with slices of scrumptious pie for all to sample. It's a wonderful social before the busy preparations for Thanksgiving Day begin. —*Sue Jurack, Mequon, Wisconsin*

Caramel Chocolate Mousse Pie

Busy cooks will love the make-ahead convenience of this no-bake pie.
I prepare it the night before I'm expecting company, then garnish just before serving.
—*Carol Steig, Butte, North Dakota*

1/2 cup chopped pecans, toasted
1 graham cracker crust
  (9 inches)
7 ounces caramels (about 25)
1/4 cup evaporated milk
1/2 cup milk
20 large marshmallows
1 cup (6 ounces) semisweet
  chocolate chips
3 tablespoons butter, cubed
1 teaspoon vanilla extract
1 carton (8 ounces) frozen
  whipped topping, thawed

Additional whipped topping, toasted pecan halves and chocolate curls, optional

Place pecans in crust. In a heavy saucepan over medium heat, cook and stir caramels and evaporated milk until caramels are melted and mixture is smooth. Cool for 10 minutes, stirring several times. Pour over pecans; refrigerate.

In a heavy saucepan, combine the milk, marshmallows, chocolate chips and butter; cook and stir over low heat until marshmallows are melted and mixture is smooth. Remove from the heat; stir in vanilla. Cool to room temperature, stirring several times. Fold in whipped topping. Pour over caramel layer. Cover and refrigerate overnight. Garnish with additional whipped topping, pecans and chocolate curls if desired. **Yield:** 6-8 servings.

Apple Butter Pumpkin Pie

The addition of apple butter gives this pumpkin pie a slightly fruity flavor.
I'm always happy to share reliable recipes like this.
—*Edna Hoffman, Hebron, Indiana*

3 eggs
1 cup canned pumpkin
1 cup prepared apple butter
3/4 cup packed brown sugar
1 can (5 ounces) evaporated
  milk
1/3 cup milk
1 teaspoon vanilla extract
1/2 teaspoon salt
1/2 teaspoon ground cinnamon
1/8 teaspoon *each* ground ginger,
  cloves and nutmeg

1 unbaked pastry shell (9 inches)
Whipped cream, optional

In a bowl, combine the first seven ingredients. Add the salt, cinnamon, ginger, cloves and nutmeg; whisk until well blended. Pour into pastry shell. Bake at 400° for 50-55 minutes or until a knife inserted near the center comes out clean. Cover edges loosely with foil during the last 20 minutes if necessary. Cool on a wire rack. Garnish with whipped cream if desired. Refrigerate leftovers. **Yield:** 6-8 servings.

Editor's Note: This recipe was tested with commercially prepared apple butter.

Creamy Apple Pie

(Pictured at right)

Like my mother, I have a reputation for making great pies…thanks to wonderfully unique recipes like this. After the pie is baked, a cream sauce is poured inside. It's irresistible!
—Wanda Stuart, Kapaa, Hawaii

2-1/4 cups all-purpose flour
  3/4 teaspoon salt
  3/4 cup cold butter
    6 tablespoons cold water
FILLING:
    6 cups sliced peeled tart apples
    1 tablespoon lemon juice
  3/4 cup sugar
    2 tablespoons all-purpose flour
    1 teaspoon grated lemon peel
  1/2 teaspoon ground cinnamon
  1/4 teaspoon salt
    2 tablespoons butter
CREAM SAUCE:
    1 egg
    2 tablespoons sugar
    1 tablespoon lemon juice
    3 tablespoons cream cheese, softened
  1/4 cup sour cream

In a bowl, combine flour and salt; cut in butter until mixture resembles course crumbs. Gradually add water, tossing with a fork until dough forms a ball. Divide dough in half. Roll out one portion. Line a 9-in. pie plate with bottom pastry; trim pastry even with edge of plate. Set aside.

In a large bowl, toss apples with lemon juice. Combine the sugar, flour, lemon peel, cinnamon and salt; add to apples and gently toss. Mound apples in pastry shell so center is higher than edges; dot with butter. Roll out remaining pastry to fit top of pie; cut a hole in the center about the size of a quarter. Place over filling; trim, seal and flute edges. Cut slits in pastry. Add decorative cutouts if desired.

Cover edges loosely with foil. Bake at 450° for 10 minutes. Reduce heat to 375° and remove foil. Bake 35-40 minutes longer or until crust is golden brown and filling is bubbly. Cool on a wire rack for 10 minutes.

Meanwhile, in a small saucepan, beat the egg, sugar and lemon juice. Cook and stir over low heat until mixture is thickened and reaches 160°. Remove from the heat; stir in cream cheese and sour cream until smooth. Slowly pour into center of pie. Cool on a wire rack for 1 hour. Cover and refrigerate until serving. **Yield:** 6-8 servings.

Pastry for Single-Crust Pie

*If you want to try your hand at making pie pastry from scratch,
give this traditional recipe from our Test Kitchen a try.*

1-1/4 cups all-purpose flour
1/2 teaspoon salt
1/3 cup shortening
4 to 5 tablespoons cold water

In a bowl, combine flour and salt; cut in shortening until crumbly. Gradually add water, tossing with a fork until dough forms a ball. Roll out to fit a 9-in. or 10-in. pie plate. Transfer pastry to pie plate. Trim pastry to 1/2 in. beyond edge of plate; flute edges. Fill or bake shell according to recipe directions. **Yield:** 1 pastry shell (9 or 10 inches).

Pastry for Double-Crust Pie

*Use this recipe from our Test Kitchen when you need pastry
for a double-crust or lattice-topped pie.*

2 cups all-purpose flour
3/4 teaspoon salt
2/3 cup shortening
6 to 7 tablespoons cold water

In a bowl, combine flour and salt; cut in shortening until crumbly. Gradually add water, tossing with a fork until dough forms a ball. Divide dough in half so one ball is slightly larger than the other.

Roll out the larger ball to fit a 9-in. or 10-in. pie plate. Transfer pastry to pie plate. Trim pastry even with edge of plate. Pour desired filling into crust.

Roll out second ball; cut slits in pastry. Position over filling. Trim pastry to 1 in. beyond edge of pie plate. Fold top crust over bottom crust. Flute edges. Bake according to recipe directions. **Yield:** pastry for 1 double-crust or lattice-topped pie (9 or 10 inches).

MAKING AND SHAPING SINGLE- AND DOUBLE-CRUST PIE PASTRY

1. Combine flour and salt in a bowl. With a pastry blender or two knives, cut in shortening until the mixture is the size of small peas.

2. Sprinkle a tablespoon of cold water at a time over the mixture and gently mix with a fork. Repeat until all the dough is moist, using only as much water as necessary to moisten the flour.

3. Shape into a ball. (For a double-crust pie, divide dough in half so that one ball is slightly larger than the other.) On a floured surface or floured pastry cloth, flatten the ball (the larger one, if making a double-crust pie) into a circle, pressing together any cracks or breaks.

4. Roll with a floured rolling pin from the center of the dough to the edges, forming a circle 2 inches larger than the pie plate. The dough should be about 1/8 inch thick.

5. To move pastry to the pie plate, roll up onto the rolling pin. Position over the edge of pie plate and unroll, letting the pastry ease into the plate. Do not stretch the pastry to fit.

   For a single-crust pie, trim pastry with a kitchen shears to 1/2 inch beyond plate edge; turn under and flute as in step 8.

   For a double-crust pie, trim pastry even with plate edge. For a lattice-crust pie, trim pastry to 1 inch beyond plate edge. Either bake the shell or fill according to recipe directions.

6. For a double-crust pie, roll out second ball into a 12-inch circle about 1/8 inch thick. With a knife, cut slits in dough to allow steam to escape while baking. Roll up onto the rolling pin; position over filling.

7. With kitchen shears, trim top crust to 1 inch beyond plate edge. Fold top crust over bottom crust.

8. To flute the edge as shown above right, place your thumb on the inside of the crust and your other thumb and index finger on the outside of the crust. Press the dough to seal.

Fitting Fall Finales

PUMPKIN PIE topped with whipped cream is likely a sweet standby on every family's Thanksgiving table.

But don't limit your dessert tray to the traditional when there's a bounty of other awesome autumn choices.

Sweet and creamy Gingersnap Dip is a tasty complement to nicely spiced cookies.

Slices of Cranberry Bundt Cake are bursting with tart and tangy berries, while Frozen Pumpkin Dessert features a fun ice cream filling.

Family and friends are guaranteed to fall for these tempting desserts. And who knows? You may even start a delicious new family tradition!

SWEET TREATS
(Clockwise from top right)

Gingersnap Dip (p. 191)

Frozen Pumpkin Dessert (p. 192)

Cranberry Bundt Cake (p. 190)

Cranberry Bundt Cake

(Pictured on page 188)

Cranberry sauce gives this moist cake its pretty swirled look.
Serve slices for dessert after dinner or as coffee cake for brunch.
—*Lucile Cline, Wichita, Kansas*

3/4 cup butter, softened
1-1/2 cups sugar
3 eggs
1-1/2 teaspoons almond extract
3 cups all-purpose flour
1-1/2 teaspoons baking powder
1-1/2 teaspoons baking soda
1/2 teaspoon salt
1-1/2 cups (12 ounces) sour cream
1 can (16 ounces) whole-berry
cranberry sauce
1/2 cup finely chopped pecans
ICING:
3/4 cup confectioners' sugar
4-1/2 teaspoons water
1/2 teaspoon almond extract

In a large mixing bowl, cream butter and sugar. Add eggs, one at a time, beating well after each addition. Stir in extract. Combine the flour, baking powder, baking soda and salt; add to the creamed mixture alternately with sour cream, beating well after each addition.

Spoon a third of the batter into a greased and floured 10-in. fluted tube pan. Top with a third of the cranberry sauce. Repeat layers twice. Sprinkle with pecans.

Bake at 350° for 65-70 minutes or until a toothpick inserted near the center comes out clean. Cool for 10 minutes before removing from pan to a wire rack. Combine icing ingredients until smooth; drizzle over warm cake. **Yield:** 12-16 servings.

Apple Cranberry Crumble

When I first took this fruity dessert to my family's Thanksgiving dinner, it quickly became a
tradition. We enjoy it for breakfast, lunch, dinner and snack time!
—*Teri Roberts, Hilliard, Ohio*

3 cups chopped peeled apples
2 cups fresh *or* frozen
cranberries
3/4 cup sugar
1 cup old-fashioned *or*
quick-cooking oats
3/4 cup packed brown sugar
1/3 cup all-purpose flour
1/2 cup butter, melted
1/2 cup chopped pecans, optional

In a greased 8-in. square baking dish, combine apples and cranberries; sprinkle with sugar. In another bowl, combine the oats, brown sugar, flour and butter; sprinkle over cranberry mixture. Top with pecans if desired. Bake, uncovered, at 350° for 55-60 minutes or until browned and bubbly. Serve warm. **Yield:** 6-8 servings.

Gingersnap Dip

(Pictured at right and on page 189)

I serve this dip in a clean plastic pumpkin at all of our fall church gatherings. It's a nice way to dress up packaged gingersnaps.
— *Tessie Hughes, Marion, Virginia*

1 package (8 ounces) cream cheese, softened
1 cup confectioners' sugar
2 teaspoons pumpkin pie spice
1 carton (8 ounces) frozen whipped topping, thawed
1 package (16 ounces) gingersnaps

In a small mixing bowl, combine the cream cheese, confectioners' sugar and pumpkin pie spice. Beat in whipped topping until blended. Refrigerate until serving. **Yield:** 3 cups.

HOMEMADE PUMPKIN PIE SPICE

IF YOU RARELY use pumpkin pie spice in your cooking, you may want to make your own instead of buying it. Combine 4 teaspoons ground cinnamon, 2 teaspoons ground ginger, 1 teaspoon ground cloves and 1/2 teaspoon ground nutmeg. Store in an airtight container. Substitute for store-bought pumpkin pie spice in any recipe. **Yield:** 7-1/2 teaspoons.

Frozen Pumpkin Dessert

(Pictured on page 189)

This ice cream dessert can be prepared and frozen weeks in advance.
I've found it has more mass appeal than traditional pumpkin pie.
—*Susan Bennett, Edmond, Oklahoma*

1 can (15 ounces) solid-pack
  pumpkin
3/4 cup sugar
1 teaspoon vanilla extract
1/2 teaspoon salt
1/4 teaspoon ground ginger
1/4 teaspoon ground nutmeg
1/8 to 1/4 teaspoon ground
  cloves

2 quarts vanilla ice cream, softened
1 cup finely chopped walnuts

In a large mixing bowl, combine the pumpkin, sugar, vanilla, salt, ginger, nutmeg and cloves. Fold in ice cream. Transfer to a greased 13-in. x 9-in. x 2-in. dish. Sprinkle with walnuts. Cover and freeze overnight. Remove from the freezer 10 minutes before serving. Cut into squares. **Yield:** 16-20 servings.

Apple Pound Cake

An apple cider glaze makes each slice of this rich pound cake nice
and sweet. It's a favorite fall treat at our house.
—*Mary Martin, Madison, North Carolina*

2 cups sugar
1-1/2 cups vegetable oil
3 eggs
2 teaspoons vanilla extract
3 cups all-purpose flour
1 teaspoon baking soda
1 teaspoon salt
1/2 teaspoon ground cinnamon
1/2 teaspoon ground nutmeg
2 cups chopped peeled tart
  apples
1 cup chopped almonds
1/2 cup raisins

APPLE CIDER GLAZE:
1/2 cup apple cider *or* juice
1/2 cup packed brown sugar
2 tablespoons butter

In a mixing bowl, combine sugar, oil, eggs and vanilla; mix well. Combine the flour, baking soda, salt, cinnamon and nutmeg; add to egg mixture and mix well. Stir in apples, almonds and raisins. Pour into a greased and floured 10-in. fluted tube pan.

Bake at 350° for 1-1/4 to 1-1/2 hours or until a toothpick comes out clean. Cool for 15 minutes before removing from pan to a wire rack to cool completely.

In a saucepan, combine glaze ingredients; cook over low heat until sugar is dissolved. Prick top of cake with a fork; drizzle with glaze. **Yield:** 16 servings.

Pumpkin Baked Alaska

(Pictured at right)

For years, I was a flop at making pumpkin pies. So I pulled out this recipe, which I got at a cooking class. It's been a success ever since.
—Linda Sanner, Portage, Wisconsin

> 1 quart vanilla ice cream, softened
> 2 teaspoons pumpkin pie spice
> 2 eggs
> 1-1/4 cups sugar, *divided*
> 3 tablespoons plus 5 teaspoons water, *divided*
> 1/2 teaspoon vanilla extract
> 2/3 cup cake flour
> 1/2 teaspoon baking powder
> 1/8 teaspoon salt
> 5 egg whites
> 1/2 teaspoon cream of tartar
> 1 teaspoon rum extract
> 2 tablespoon sliced almonds, toasted

In a bowl, combine the ice cream and pumpkin pie spice. Transfer to a 1-1/2-qt. bowl lined with plastic wrap; freeze until set.

Line a greased 9-in. round baking pan with waxed paper; grease the paper and set aside. Place a clean kitchen towel over a wire rack; dust towel with confectioners' sugar; set aside.

In a mixing bowl, beat eggs, 1/2 cup sugar, 3 tablespoons water and vanilla until thick and lemon-colored. Combine the flour, baking powder and salt; fold into egg mixture. Pour into prepared pan. Bake at 375° for 12-14 minutes or until cake springs back when lightly touched. Immediately run a knife around the edge of the pan; invert onto prepared kitchen towel. Gently peel off waxed paper; cool completely.

Place cake on an ungreased freezer-to-oven-safe platter or foil-lined baking sheet. Unmold ice cream onto cake; remove plastic wrap. Return to freezer.

In a heavy saucepan or double boiler, combine the egg whites, cream of tartar and remaining sugar and water; beat on low speed with a portable mixer for 1 minute. Continue beating over low heat until mixture reaches 160°, about 10 minutes. Remove from the heat. Add extract; beat until stiff peaks form, about 4 minutes. Spread meringue over frozen ice cream and cake, sealing meringue to the platter; sprinkle with almonds. Freeze until ready to serve, up to 24 hours.

Just before serving, broil on lowest oven rack position for 3-5 minutes or until meringue is light browned. Serve immediately. **Yield:** 12 servings.

Pecan Carrot Pie

After moving from New York to Georgia, I had many opportunities to make pecan pie.
This recipe stuns the Southerners when I tell them carrots are the secret ingredient!
—*Susan Elise Jansen, Smyrna, Georgia*

2 cups sliced carrots
1 cup water
1 cup half-and-half cream
1/4 cup butter, softened
1/2 cup packed brown sugar
2 eggs
1/2 teaspoon ground nutmeg
1/2 teaspoon ground cinnamon
1/4 teaspoon salt
1/8 teaspoon ground ginger
1 unbaked pastry shell
   (9 inches)
PECAN TOPPING:
   2 tablespoons butter
   1 tablespoon brown sugar
   1 cup chopped pecans

In a saucepan, simmer carrots in water for 20 minutes or until tender; drain. Place carrots and cream in a blender; cover and process until smooth.

In a mixing bowl, cream butter and brown sugar. Add eggs, nutmeg, cinnamon, salt, ginger and carrots; mix well. Pour into pastry shell. Bake at 450° for 15 minutes.

For topping, melt butter in a small saucepan. Stir in brown sugar until dissolved. Add pecans; stir until coated, about 2 minutes. Spoon over carrot filling.

Reduce heat to 325°; bake 35-40 minutes longer or until a knife inserted near the center comes out clean. Cool completely. Store in the refrigerator. **Yield:** 8-10 servings.

Baked Stuffed Pears

This simple dessert is a tasty ending to our Thanksgiving meal of roast turkey or pork.
Pears are a yummy change from the typical apples.
—*Marie Labanowski, New Hampton, New York*

4 medium ripe pears (about 2
   pounds)
2 tablespoons lemon juice
1/3 cup coarsely chopped walnuts
1/4 cup golden raisins
2 tablespoons maple syrup
2 teaspoons brown sugar
1 teaspoon grated lemon peel
1/8 teaspoon ground cinnamon
1 tablespoon butter
2/3 cup apple juice

Core pears and peel 1 in. down from the top on each. Brush peeled portion with some of the lemon juice. Place in a greased 1-qt. baking dish.

In a bowl, combine walnuts, raisins, syrup, brown sugar, lemon peel, cinnamon and remaining lemon juice. Spoon into pears. Dot with butter. Pour apple juice around pears. Bake, uncovered, at 350° for 30-40 minutes or until pears are tender, basting several times. **Yield:** 4 servings.

Bread Pudding Pumpkin

(Pictured at right)

When doing my fall decorating, I'm certain to set aside a few pumpkins for this unique dessert. It adds a festive touch to our Thanksgiving table.
—Darlene Markel, Mt. Hood, Oregon

2 medium pie pumpkins
  (about 3 pounds *each*)
4 eggs, lightly beaten
1 can (14 ounces) sweetened
  condensed milk
1/2 cup packed brown sugar
1 teaspoon salt
1 teaspoon ground cinnamon
1 teaspoon vanilla extract
3/4 teaspoon ground nutmeg
6 cups cubed crustless day-old
  bread
1 can (8 ounces) crushed
  pineapple, drained
1 cup chopped walnuts
1 cup raisins

Wash pumpkins; cut off tops and discard. Scoop out seeds and loose fibers (save seeds for another use if desired). In a large bowl, whisk the eggs, milk, brown sugar, salt, cinnamon, vanilla and nutmeg. Stir in bread cubes, pineapple, walnuts and raisins. Spoon into pumpkin shells.

Place on a greased 15-in. x 10-in. x 1-in. baking pan. Loosely cover tops with foil. Bake at 350° for 1-1/4 hours. Uncover; bake 15-30 minutes longer or until pumpkin is soft and a knife inserted near the center of bread pudding comes out clean. To serve, scoop bread pudding and cooked pumpkin into dessert dishes. **Yield:** 6-8 servings.

TOASTING PUMPKIN SEEDS

DON'T TOSS OUT the pumpkin seeds from a freshly cut pumpkin. Instead, toast them for a tasty snack.

Wash and dry the pumpkin seeds. In a skillet, saute 1 cup seeds in 2 tablespoons vegetable oil for 5 minutes or until lightly browned. Using a slotted spoon, transfer seeds to an ungreased 15-in. x 10-in. x 1-in. baking pan. Sprinkle with salt or garlic salt; stir to coat. Spread in a single layer.

Bake at 325° for 15-20 minutes or until crisp. Remove to paper towels to cool completely. Store in an airtight container for up to 3 weeks.

Give a Lift to Leftovers!

FOR MOST FAMILIES, the joy of Thanksgiving extends to the days following and the anticipation of wonderful leftovers.

Instead of simply serving those extra goodies the same old way, why not try one of this chapter's delectable second-time-around recipes? Each is sure to give a mouth-watering boost to leftover turkey, stuffing, potatoes, cranberry sauce and more.

Family and friends will clamor for second helpings of Fruited Turkey Salad, Hot 'n' Spicy Cranberry Dip and Turkey Divan Pizza.

Even folks who typically turn up their noses at leftovers will be pleasantly surprised when you dress up the food in a deliciously different disguise!

TWICE AS NICE
(Clockwise from top left)

Fruited Turkey Salad (p. 198)

Hot 'n' Spicy
Cranberry Dip (p. 201)

Turkey Divan Pizza (p. 199)

Fruited Turkey Salad

(Pictured on page 196)

A subtle tarragon flavor adds a different twist to this well-dressed turkey salad.
With cranberry sauce and a dinner roll, it's a hearty lunch or dinner.
—Donna Nole, Skokie, Illinois

6 cups cubed cooked turkey
2 cups chopped celery
1 cup green grapes
3/4 cup sour cream
3/4 cup mayonnaise
1-1/2 teaspoons dried tarragon
1 teaspoon salt
1/8 teaspoon pepper
1/2 cup chopped walnuts, toasted
Leaf lettuce

In a bowl, combine the turkey, celery and grapes. In a small bowl, combine the sour cream, mayonnaise, tarragon, salt and pepper. Add to turkey mixture and toss to coat. Cover and refrigerate for at least 5 hours. Just before serving, stir in walnuts. Serve in a lettuce-lined bowl. **Yield:** 8 servings.

SAFELY STORING THANKSGIVING LEFTOVERS

FOLLOW these guidelines to ensure that the leftovers you keep will be safe to eat.

"When in doubt, throw it out" is a good rule of thumb, whether you're questioning the safety of food you're about to store or of food you're taking out of the refrigerator or freezer to eat.

- Stock up on plastic storage bags and containers so you're prepared to store leftovers soon after the meal. Having storage supplies at the ready also makes it easy for others to help out in the kitchen.
- Immediately after cooking, remove stuffing from the turkey, chicken, duck or goose. Within 2 hours, carve all meat off the bones. Place the meat and stuffing in separate containers and refrigerate. For faster cooling, don't stack the containers.
- Leftover turkey, stuffing and pumpkin pie can be refrigerated for 3 to 4 days.
- Meat combined with gravy and gravy by itself should be used within 1 to 2 days.
- Cranberry sauce and relish can be stored in the refrigerator for 5 to 7 days.
- Cooked vegetables should be eaten within 3 to 5 days.
- Freeze any leftovers you won't eat within 3 days. Frozen cooked meat and gravy should be used within 2 to 3 months.
- When reheating leftovers, bring gravy to a full rolling boil and all others foods to a temperature of 165°.

Glazed Cranberry Carrots

(Pictured at right)

Although this is a wonderful way to use leftover carrots and cranberry sauce, I often find myself making it specifically for Thanksgiving dinner.
—Mary Ann Gilbert, Cincinnati, Ohio

      2 pounds fresh baby carrots
  1/2 cup jellied cranberry sauce
  1/4 cup butter
  1/4 cup packed brown sugar
      1 tablespoon lemon juice
  1/2 teaspoon salt

Place 1 in. of water in a large saucepan; add carrots. Bring to a boil. Reduce heat; cover and simmer for 10-12 minutes or until tender. Drain and set aside.

In the same pan, combine the cranberry sauce, butter, brown sugar, lemon juice and salt. Cook and stir until cranberry sauce is melted and mixture is smooth. Add carrots; stir to coat. Heat through. **Yield:** 6 servings.

Turkey Divan Pizza

(Pictured on page 196)

Kids who are typically picky eaters will gobble up slice after slice of this savory pizza. I often have frozen cubed cooked turkey on hand to make this meal in a moment's notice.
—Charlotte Smith, Pittsburgh, Pennsylvania

      1 prebaked Italian bread shell
          crust (16 ounces)
      2 teaspoons olive oil
  1/2 to 1 teaspoon garlic salt
      2 cups fresh broccoli florets
  1-1/2 cups cubed cooked turkey
      1 can (10-3/4 ounces) condensed
          broccoli cheese soup,
          undiluted
  1/3 cup milk
  1/2 cup shredded cheddar cheese
      2 tablespoons dry bread crumbs
      1 tablespoon butter, melted

Place pizza crust on a baking sheet. Brush with oil; sprinkle with garlic salt. Top with broccoli and turkey. Combine soup and milk; spread over broccoli and turkey. Sprinkle with cheddar cheese. Toss bread crumbs and butter; sprinkle over the top. Bake at 400° for 13-15 minutes or until cheese is melted and broccoli is crisp-tender. **Yield:** 6-8 servings.

Thanksgiving Turkey Sandwich

I created this recipe after sampling a similar sandwich at a nearby restaurant.
At first, my husband turned up his nose. But after one bite, he was converted!
—*Jeanne Imbrigiotta, Pennington, New Jersey*

2 tablespoons cream cheese,
  softened
2 slices multigrain bread
1 tablespoon hot pepper jelly
3 slices thinly sliced deli *or*
  cooked turkey

Spread cream cheese on both slices of bread; spread jelly over cream cheese. Place turkey on one slice; cover with remaining slice. **Yield:** 1 sandwich.

Cranberry Turkey Salad

This recipe is most treasured because it's from my husband's grandmother. A savory turkey salad
is cleverly topped with cranberry-raspberry gelatin for an eye-catching dish.
—*Kim Kirven, Wadsworth, Ohio*

1 package (3 ounces) lemon
  gelatin
2 cups boiling water, *divided*
2 cups cubed cooked turkey
  or chicken
4 celery ribs, chopped
8 ounces process cheese
  (Velveeta), cubed
1 cup chopped almonds
3 hard-cooked eggs, chopped,
  optional
1 cup mayonnaise
1 cup heavy whipping cream,
  whipped
1/2 teaspoon salt

1/2 teaspoon onion salt
1 package (3 ounces) raspberry gelatin
1 can (16 ounces) whole-berry cranberry sauce

In a mixing bowl, dissolve lemon gelatin in 1 cup of boiling water; refrigerate for 1 hour or until slightly thickened. Beat for 1 minute on high speed. Stir in turkey, celery, cheese, almonds, eggs if desired, mayonnaise, cream, salt and onion salt. Spread evenly into a 13-in. x 9-in. x 2-in. dish. Cover and refrigerate until firm, about 2 hours.

Dissolve the raspberry gelatin in remaining boiling water; stir in cranberry sauce until melted and blended. Spoon over turkey mixture. Refrigerate for 2 hours or until set. Cut into squares. **Yield:** 12-15 servings.

Hot 'n' Spicy Cranberry Dip

(Pictured at right and on page 197)

When I want to make this as an
appetizer on Christmas or New Year's,
I double the recipe, using one
16-ounce can of cranberry sauce.
—*Marian Platt, Sequim, Washington*

3/4 cup jellied cranberry sauce
  1 to 2 tablespoons prepared
    horseradish
  1 tablespoon honey
1-1/2 teaspoons lemon juice
1-1/2 teaspoons Worcestershire
    sauce
  1/8 to 1/4 teaspoon cayenne
    pepper
  1 garlic clove, minced
Miniature hot dogs *or* smoked
  sausage links, warmed
Sliced apples *or* pears

In a small saucepan, combine the first seven ingredients; bring to a boil, stirring constantly. Reduce heat. Cover and simmer for 5 minutes, stirring occasionally. Serve warm with sausage and/or fruit. **Yield:** 3/4 cup.

STAR FRUIT FACTS

CARAMBOLA is nicknamed star fruit because when it's cut crosswise, the slices are shaped like stars (see garnish on Hot 'n' Spicy Cranberry Dip above right). The more golden-colored the fruit is, the sweeter it will be. There's no need to peel the shiny skin, but you may want to remove the brown fibers from the ridges before slicing. Refrigerate completely yellow fruit in a plastic bag for 1 week.

Hearty Alfredo Potatoes

With turkey and broccoli, this special scalloped potato dish is a meal in itself.
Using a jar of Alfredo sauce makes the preparation time minimal.
—Lissa Hutson, Phelan, California

1 jar (16 ounces) Alfredo sauce
1 cup milk
1 teaspoon garlic powder
3 pounds potatoes, peeled and
   thinly sliced
5 tablespoons grated Parmesan
   cheese, *divided*
Salt and pepper to taste
2 to 3 cups diced cooked turkey
1 package (10 ounces) frozen
   chopped broccoli, thawed
2 cups (8 ounces) shredded
   Swiss cheese, *divided*

In a bowl, combine Alfredo sauce, milk and garlic powder; pour a fourth of the mixture into a greased 13-in. x 9-in. x 2-in. baking dish. Layer with a fourth of the potatoes; sprinkle with 1 tablespoon Parmesan cheese, salt and pepper.

In a bowl, combine the turkey, broccoli and 1-1/2 cups Swiss cheese; spoon a third over potatoes. Repeat layers twice. Top with remaining potatoes. Cover with remaining Swiss and Parmesan cheeses. Spread with remaining Alfredo sauce mixture.

Cover and bake at 400° for 45 minutes. Reduce heat to 350°. Bake, uncovered, 30 minutes longer or until potatoes are tender. Let stand for 15 minutes before serving. **Yield:** 6-8 servings.

PREPPING POTATOES

TO SAVE TIME, you can peel the potatoes for Hearty Alfredo Potatoes up to 2 hours in advance. Rinse and place in a bowl of cold water. Drain and thinly slice just before preparing the recipe.

Turkey Shepherd's Pie

We live way out in the country, and the nearest grocery store is 25 miles away.
So I've become quite skilled at turning leftovers into second-time-around successes like this.
—Linda Howe, Jackman, Maine

2 cups cubed cooked turkey
3/4 cup turkey gravy
1 cup shredded carrots
2 cups prepared stuffing
1 can (15-1/4 ounces) whole
   kernel corn, drained
2 cups warm mashed potatoes

In a greased 2-qt. baking dish, layer the turkey, gravy, carrots, stuffing and corn. Top with potatoes. Bake, uncovered, at 325° for 45-50 minutes or until edges of potatoes are browned. **Yield:** 4-5 servings.

All-American Turkey Potpie

(Pictured at right)

Ever since my sister-in-law shared this recipe with me, I haven't made any other kind of potpie. The crust is very easy to work with.
—Laureen Naylor
Factoryville, Pennsylvania

2 cups all-purpose flour
1/2 teaspoon salt
1/2 cup finely shredded cheddar cheese
2/3 cup shortening
2 tablespoons cold butter
3 to 4 tablespoons cold water
FILLING:
1 cup diced peeled potatoes
1/2 cup thinly sliced carrots
1/3 cup chopped celery
1/4 cup chopped onion
1 garlic clove, minced
1 tablespoon butter
1 cup chicken *or* turkey broth
2 tablespoons all-purpose flour
1/2 cup milk
1-1/2 cups cubed cooked turkey
1/2 cup frozen peas, thawed
1/2 cup frozen corn, thawed
1/2 teaspoon salt
1/4 teaspoon dried tarragon
1/4 teaspoon pepper

In a food processor, combine flour and salt; cover and pulse to blend. Add cheese; pulse until fine crumbs form. Add shortening and butter; pulse until coarse crumbs form. Gradually add water until dough forms a ball. Divide dough in half with one ball slightly larger than the other; wrap in plastic wrap. Refrigerate for 30 minutes.

For filling, in a large saucepan, saute potatoes, carrots, celery, onion and garlic in butter for 5-6 minutes. Add broth; cover and cook for 10 minutes or until vegetables are tender. In a small bowl, combine flour and milk until smooth. Gradually add to vegetable mixture. Bring to a boil; cook and stir for 2 minutes or until thickened. Add the remaining ingredients; simmer 5 minutes longer.

Roll out larger pastry ball to fit a 9-in. pie plate; transfer to pie plate. Trim pastry even with edge. Pour hot turkey filling into crust. Roll out remaining pastry to fit top of pie; place over filling. Trim, seal and flute edges. Cut slits in top or make decorative cutouts in pastry. Bake at 350° for 35-45 minutes or until crust is light golden brown. Serve immediately. **Yield:** 6-8 servings.

Country Potato Dressing

My family can't get enough dressing around the holidays. With this recipe,
I use up leftover mashed potatoes to create a tasty new dish.
—Lauren Buckner, Greenville, South Carolina

1	large onion, chopped
3/4	cup chopped celery
1/4	cup butter
1/4	cup turkey *or* chicken broth
8	slices day-old white bread, crusts removed and cubed
3	cups mashed potatoes
1	egg, beaten
1-1/2	teaspoons poultry seasoning
1	teaspoon salt
1/4	teaspoon pepper
1/4	teaspoon ground nutmeg

In a small skillet, saute onion and celery in butter until tender. Remove from the heat; stir in broth. In a large bowl, combine bread cubes, potatoes, egg and seasonings. Stir in onion mixture. Transfer to a greased 2-qt. baking dish. Cover and bake at 325° for 50-60 minutes or until a meat thermometer reads 160°. **Yield:** 6-8 servings.

Broccoli Souffle

This recipe is from my mom's fabulous collection. Without fail, I serve it every holiday
and the dish gets emptied every time. It's a clever way to get kids to eat broccoli.
—Marilyn Rockwell, Lynden, Washington

6	eggs
2	teaspoons dry bread crumbs
1/2	cup butter
1/2	cup all-purpose flour
1/2	teaspoon salt
1/4	teaspoon pepper
2	cups milk
4	cups cooked chopped broccoli, patted dry
2	tablespoons chopped onion
1	cup mayonnaise
1/2	cup shredded cheddar cheese, optional

Separate the eggs. Let yolks and whites stand at room temperature for up to 30 minutes. Grease a 2-1/2-qt. souffle dish and dust with bread crumbs; set aside.

In a saucepan, melt butter. Stir in the flour, salt and pepper until smooth. Gradually add milk. Bring to a boil; cook and stir for 2 minutes or until thickened. Stir in broccoli and onion. Remove from the heat; stir in egg yolks until combined. Cool slightly. Stir in mayonnaise.

In a mixing bowl, beat egg whites until stiff peaks form. Stir a fourth of the egg whites into the broccoli mixture. Fold in remaining whites. Transfer to prepared souffle dish. Sprinkle with cheese if desired.

Bake at 325° for 38-42 minutes or until top is golden brown, a toothpick inserted near the side comes out clean and a meat thermometer reads 160°. Serve immediately. **Yield:** 8-10 servings.

Editor's Note: Reduced-fat or fat-free mayonnaise may not be substituted for regular mayonnaise in this recipe.

Lemony Turkey Rice Soup

(Pictured at right)

While growing up in Texas, I spent a lot of time helping my grandma cook. Lemon and cilantro add a deliciously different twist to turkey soup.
—Margarita Cuellar
East Chicago, Indiana

6 cups chicken broth, *divided*
1 can (10-3/4 ounces) condensed cream of chicken soup, undiluted
2 cups cooked rice
2 cups diced cooked turkey
1/4 teaspoon pepper
2 tablespoons cornstarch
1/4 to 1/3 cup lemon juice
1/4 to 1/2 cup minced fresh cilantro

In a large saucepan, combine 5-1/2 cups of broth, soup, rice, turkey and pepper. Bring to a boil; boil for 3 minutes. In a small bowl, combine cornstarch and remaining broth until smooth. Gradually stir into hot soup. Cook and stir for 1-2 minutes or until thickened and heated through. Remove from the heat; stir in lemon juice and cilantro. **Yield:** 8 servings (about 2 quarts).

Swiss Creamed Peas

A creamy cheese sauce turns ordinary peas into a succulent side dish.
I make this quite often for family gatherings, and it's always well received.
—Lin Carr, West Seneca, New York

1 cup chopped green onions
4-1/2 teaspoons butter
1 tablespoon all-purpose flour
1/2 teaspoon salt
1 cup heavy whipping cream
3/4 cup shredded Swiss cheese
3 cups cooked peas

In a large saucepan, saute onions in butter until tender. Stir in flour and salt until blended; gradually add the cream. Bring to a boil; cook and stir for 2 minutes or until thickened. Reduce heat; stir in cheese until melted. Add peas; cook and stir until heated through. **Yield:** 4 servings.

WINTER
Celebrations

Festival of Lights Feast 208-213
Turkey Dinner for Christmas Day 214-221
Feast on Festive Entrees 222-233
Sparkling Yuletide Sides 234-249
Home-Baked Holiday Breads 250-265
Decked Out in Desserts 266-279
Sweet Treats for Santa 280-299
Neighborhood Round-Robin 300-315
A Tree Trimming Get-Together 316-327
Casual New Year's Eve Buffet 328-341
Soups & Breads Warm Up Winter 342-349
Super Bowl Pizza Party 350-357
Valentine's Day Dinner for Two 358-369

Festival of Lights Feast

HANUKKAH ("Festival of Lights") is an 8-day celebration commemorating the victory of the Jews over the Syrians and the rededication of the temple in Jerusalem.

To celebrate this holiday in November or December, our Test Kitchen created a memorable menu featuring traditional foods such as Savory Beef Brisket, Festive Tossed Salad, Latkes (crispy potato pancakes), Challah (braided bread) and Glazed Lebkuchen (honey spice bars).

Tables are typically decorated with the colors of blue, silver and gold, menorahs (candelabra with nine candles, used in Jewish worship) and dreidels (four-sided toy tops marked with Hebrew letters that children play with during Hanukkah).

HIGHLIGHTS OF HANUKKAH
(Clockwise from top right)

Glazed Lebkuchen (p. 212)

Challah (p. 213)

Latkes (p. 211)

Savory Beef Brisket (p. 210)

Festive Tossed Salad (p. 212)

Savory Beef Brisket

(Pictured on page 208)

Caramelized onions give beef and carrots great flavor.
You'll be surprised to see just how easy it is to prepare this fork-tender brisket.

1 fresh beef brisket (5 to 6 pounds)
2 teaspoons all-purpose flour
1/4 to 1/2 teaspoon coarsely ground pepper
1/4 cup vegetable oil
8 small onions, sliced and separated into rings
2 tablespoons tomato paste
1-1/2 teaspoons coarse salt
2 garlic cloves, quartered
2 pounds carrots, cut into 1-inch pieces

Lightly dust brisket with flour; sprinkle with pepper. In a Dutch oven, brown brisket in oil on both sides over medium-high heat. Remove and keep warm. In the drippings, saute onions until golden brown, about 15 minutes. Return meat to pan. Combine tomato paste, salt and garlic; spoon over meat.

Cover and bake at 375° for 1-1/2 hours. Slice meat across the grain; return to pan, overlapping slices. Add carrots. Cover and bake 1-1/4 to 1-3/4 hours longer or until meat is tender. **Yield:** 12-15 servings.

Editor's Note: This is a fresh beef brisket, not corned beef.

TIMETABLE FOR HANUKKAH DINNER

A Few Weeks Before:
- Order a 5- to 6-pound fresh beef brisket from your butcher.
- Prepare two grocery lists—one for nonperishable items that can be purchased now and one for perishable items that need to be purchased a few days before your Hanukkah meal.

The Day Before:
- Buy remaining grocery items, including the beef brisket.
- Set the table.
- For the Festive Tossed Salad, make the dressing; cover and refrigerate. Cut up all the salad ingredients; place in separate airtight containers or resealable plastic bags and refrigerate.
- Bake the Challah and Glazed Lebkuchen; cover and store at room temperature.

The Day of Hanukkah Dinner:
- In the morning, peel the potatoes for the Latkes. Place in a bowl; cover with cold water and refrigerate until ready to grate.
- Make the Savory Beef Brisket and Latkes.
- Remove the salad dressing from the refrigerator. Just before serving, assemble the Festive Tossed Salad; shake the dressing and pour over the salad.
- Set out the Challah.
- Serve the Glazed Lebkuchen for dessert.

Latkes

(Pictured at right and on page 209)

These thin onion and potato pancakes make a tasty accompaniment to any meal. The key to their crispness is draining all the liquid from the grated potatoes and onion before frying.

2 pounds russet potatoes, peeled
1 medium onion
1/2 cup chopped green onions
1 egg, lightly beaten
1 teaspoon salt
1/4 teaspoon pepper
Oil for deep-fat frying
Applesauce

Coarsely grate potatoes and onion; drain any liquid. Place in a bowl; add green onions, egg, salt and pepper. In an electric skillet, heat 1/8 in. of oil to 375°. Drop batter by heaping tablespoonfuls into hot oil. Flatten to form patties. Fry until golden brown; turn and cook the other side. Drain on paper towels. Serve with applesauce. **Yield:** 2 dozen.

DEEP-FAT FRYING FACTS

YOU'LL soon be frying foods like a pro with these timely pointers.

- If you don't have a deep-fat fryer or electric fry pan with a thermostat, you can use a kettle or Dutch oven together with a thermometer so you can accurately regulate the temperature of the oil.
- Always follow the oil temperature recommended in recipes. If the oil is too hot, the foods will brown too fast and not be done in the center. If the oil is below the recommended temperature, the foods will absorb oil and taste greasy.
- To avoid splattering, carefully place foods into the hot oil and never add any liquids to hot oil.
- Don't overload your fryer. You'll have better results if you fry in small batches.
- To keep fried foods warm until the entire recipe is cooked, drain fried foods on paper towel, then place on an ovenproof platter. Cover loosely with foil and place in a 200° oven.

Festive Tossed Salad

(Pictured on page 208)

The light homemade dressing wonderfully coats a colorful combination of salad greens,
vegetables, pickles and olives. This salad has something for everyone.

8 cups torn salad greens
1 medium tomato, cut into wedges
1 cup cubed peeled cucumber
1 medium sweet red pepper, julienned
1 celery rib, sliced
1/4 cup chopped green onions
4 sweet pickles, chopped
1 tablespoon chopped ripe olives

DRESSING:
1/4 cup olive oil
2 tablespoons lemon juice
1 teaspoon salt
1 teaspoon sugar
1/4 teaspoon ground mustard
1/8 teaspoon garlic powder

In a large salad bowl, combine the first eight ingredients. In a jar with a tight-fitting lid, combine the dressing ingredients; shake well. Pour over salad; gently toss to coat. Serve immediately. **Yield:** 12 servings.

Glazed Lebkuchen

(Pictured on page 209)

Honey and spices give great flavor to these cake-like bars topped with a thin sugar glaze.
They're especially popular around the holidays.

3/4 cup honey
1/2 cup sugar
1/4 cup packed brown sugar
2 eggs
2-1/2 cups all-purpose flour
1-1/4 teaspoons ground cinnamon
1 teaspoon baking soda
1/4 teaspoon ground cloves
1/8 teaspoon ground allspice
3/4 cup chopped slivered almonds
1/2 cup finely chopped citron
1/2 cup finely chopped candied lemon peel
FROSTING:
1 cup confectioners' sugar
3 tablespoons hot milk *or* water

1/4 teaspoon vanilla extract
Candied cherries and additional citron

In a saucepan, bring honey to a boil. Remove from the heat; cool to room temperature. In a mixing bowl, combine honey and sugars; mix well. Add eggs, one at a time, beating well after each addition. Combine the flour, cinnamon, baking soda, cloves and allspice; gradually add to honey mixture. Stir in nuts, citron and lemon peel (mixture will be thick).

Press into a greased 15-in. x 10-in. x 1-in. baking pan. Bake at 350° for 20-28 minutes or until top springs back when lightly touched. Meanwhile, combine the confectioners' sugar, milk and vanilla; mix well. Spread over bars while warm. Immediately cut into bars. Decorate with cherries and citron. Cool in pan on a wire rack. **Yield:** about 2 dozen.

Challah

(Pictured at right and on page 209)

Eggs lend to the richness of this traditional braided bread. The attractive golden color and delicious flavor make it hard to resist. For instructions on braiding bread, turn to page 263.

For instructions on braiding bread, turn to page 263.

2 packages (1/4 ounce *each*)
   active dry yeast
1 cup warm water (110°
   to 115°)
1/2 cup vegetable oil
1/3 cup sugar
1 tablespoon salt
5 eggs
6 to 6-1/2 cups all-purpose flour
1 teaspoon cold water
1 tablespoon sesame *or* poppy
   seeds, optional

In a mixing bowl, dissolve yeast in warm water. Add the oil, sugar, salt, 4 eggs and 4 cups of flour. Beat until smooth. Stir in enough remaining flour to form a firm dough. Turn onto a floured surface; knead until smooth and elastic, about 6-8 minutes. Place in a greased bowl, turning once to grease top. Cover and let rise in a warm place until doubled, about 1 hour.

Punch dough down. Turn onto a lightly floured surface; divide in half. Divide each portion into thirds. Shape each piece into a 15-in. rope. Place three ropes on a greased baking sheet and braid; pinch ends to seal and tuck under. Repeat with remaining dough. Cover and let rise until doubled, about 1 hour.

Beat cold water and remaining egg; brush over braids. Sprinkle with sesame or poppy seeds if desired. Bake at 350° for 30-35 minutes or until golden brown. Remove to wire racks to cool. **Yield:** 2 loaves.

WINTER
Celebrations

Turkey Dinner for Christmas Day

FAMILY and friends will sing your praises when they see your Christmas Day dinner table decked out in this feast featuring turkey and all the fixings.

It's no surprise that Turkey with Sausage Stuffing is the festive focal point. The outside roasts to a rich golden brown, while the meat and stuffing remain wonderfully moist.

Trim the table with such satisfying side dishes as Herbed Mashed Potatoes, Beets in Orange Sauce, Dressed-Up Broccoli and Salad with Blue Cheese Dressing.

There's no better way to wrap up this mouth-watering meal than with refreshing servings of Cranberry Ice.

A Very Merry Meal
(Clockwise from top right)

Turkey with Sausage
Stuffing (p. 217)

Herbed Mashed Potatoes (p. 216)

Dressed-Up Broccoli (p. 220)

Cranberry Ice (p. 219)

Herbed Mashed Potatoes

(Pictured on page 215)

*A blend of herbs and garlic makes this an extra-special side dish for the holidays.
My family won't let me prepare mashed potatoes any other way.*
—*Stephanie McKinnon, Salt Lake City, Utah*

6-1/2 cups cubed peeled potatoes
2 garlic cloves, peeled and halved
1/2 cup milk
1/2 cup sour cream
2 tablespoons minced fresh parsley
2 tablespoons minced fresh oregano
1 tablespoon minced fresh thyme

1 tablespoon butter
3/4 teaspoon salt
1/4 teaspoon pepper

Place potatoes and garlic in a large saucepan; cover with water. Bring to a boil over medium-high heat. Cook for 15-20 minutes or until tender; drain. Place potatoes and garlic in a large mixing bowl. Add the remaining ingredients; mash. **Yield:** 6 servings.

TURKEY-CARVING BASICS

AFTER removing the roasted turkey from the oven, cover and let stand for 20 minutes. Remove all stuffing to a warm serving bowl; cover with foil to keep warm. Then carve the turkey following these simple steps:

1. Pull the leg away from the body until the thigh bone pops out of its socket. Cut between the thigh joint and the body to remove the entire leg. Repeat with the other leg. Separate the drumstick and thigh by cutting through the ball joint. Hold each part by the bone and cut off 1/4-inch slices.

2. Hold the turkey with a meat fork and make a deep cut into the breast meat just above the wing area. This marks the end of each breast meat slice.

3. Slice down from the breast into the cut made in Step 2. Slice meat 1/4 inch thick.

Turkey with Sausage Stuffing

(Pictured at right and on page 215)

All year long, my family looks forward to Christmas when I prepare this pretty and pleasing stuffing. Cream-style corn and sausage make every bite moist and delicious.
—Janet Danner, Peebles, Ohio

8 cups cubed day-old bread
1 pound bulk pork sausage, cooked and drained
3 medium onions, chopped
1 can (14-3/4 ounces) cream-style corn
2 tablespoons minced fresh parsley
1-1/2 teaspoons poultry seasoning
1/2 teaspoon salt
1/4 teaspoon pepper
1 turkey (10 to 12 pounds)
Melted butter
2 teaspoons chicken bouillon granules
2 cups boiling water
1/4 to 1/3 cup all-purpose flour

In a large bowl, combine the first eight ingredients. Just before baking, loosely stuff the turkey. Place remaining stuffing in a greased 1-1/2-qt. baking dish; refrigerate. Skewer openings of turkey; tie drumsticks together. Place on a rack in a roasting pan. Brush with butter.

Bake, uncovered, at 325° for 2-3/4 to 3 hours or until a meat thermometer reads 180° for turkey and 165° for stuffing. Bake additional stuffing, covered, for 45-50 minutes or until heated through.

When the turkey begins to brown, baste with drippings; cover loosely with foil if turkey browns too quickly. Cover turkey and let stand for 20 minutes before removing stuffing and carving.

For gravy, dissolve bouillon in water; set aside. Transfer turkey to warm platter. Remove stuffing. Pour 1/4 cup pan drippings into a saucepan; whisk in flour until smooth. Gradually add bouillon mixture. Bring to a boil; cook and stir for 2 minutes or until thickened. Serve with turkey and stuffing. **Yield:** 6-8 servings.

Beets in Orange Sauce

To ensure your family eats their veggies, our Test Kitchen home economists
suggest you top beets with an irresistible orange glaze.

8 medium fresh beets
1/4 cup sugar
2 teaspoons cornstarch
Dash pepper
1 cup orange juice
1 medium navel orange, sliced
  and halved, optional
1/2 teaspoon grated orange peel

Place beets in a large saucepan; cover with water. Bring to a boil. Reduce heat; cover and cook for 25-30 minutes or until tender. Drain and cool slightly. Peel and slice; place in a serving bowl and keep warm.

In a saucepan, combine the sugar, cornstarch and pepper; stir in orange juice until smooth. Bring to a boil; cook and stir for 2 minutes or until thickened. Remove from the heat; stir in orange slices if desired and peel. Pour over beets. **Yield:** 8 servings.

Editor's Note: A 15-ounce can of sliced beets may be substituted for the fresh beets. Drain the canned beets and omit the first step of the recipe.

Salad with Blue Cheese Dressing

This salad is a tradition in my home each Christmas. The chunky blue cheese dressing coats
the lettuce beautifully. Toss in extra vegetables to suit your family's taste.
—Shirley Bedzis, San Diego, California

DRESSING:
1 cup small-curd cottage cheese
1/2 cup crumbled blue cheese,
  divided
1/4 cup mayonnaise
1/4 cup plain yogurt
1/4 cup white wine vinegar
2 garlic cloves, minced
1/4 teaspoon salt
1/4 teaspoon white pepper
SALAD:
12 cups torn Bibb *or*
  Boston lettuce

2 cups cherry tomatoes
1 small red onion, sliced
1 can (2-1/4 ounces) sliced ripe olives, drained
2 cups seasoned salad croutons

In a blender or food processor, place cottage cheese, 1/4 cup blue cheese, mayonnaise, yogurt, vinegar, garlic, salt and pepper. Cover and process until smooth. Pour into a small bowl; stir in the remaining blue cheese. Cover and refrigerate for 2-3 hours. In a large salad bowl, toss lettuce, tomatoes, onion, olives and croutons. Serve with dressing. **Yield:** 14-16 servings.

Cranberry Ice

(Pictured at right and on page 214)

This traditional Christmas dessert was first made in our family by my grandma. She handed the recipe down to my mother, who then shared it with me and my two sisters. The cold tart treat is a wonderful accompaniment to a traditional turkey dinner.
—Carolyn Butterworth
Spirit Lake, Iowa

3 cups fresh *or* frozen
  cranberries
2 cups water
1-1/2 cups sugar
1 teaspoon unflavored gelatin
1/2 cup cold water
1/2 cup lemon juice

In a large saucepan, bring cranberries and water to a boil. Cook over medium heat until the berries pop, about 10 minutes. Remove from the heat; cool slightly. Press mixture through a sieve or food mill, reserving juice and discarding skins and seeds.

In a small bowl, sprinkle gelatin over cold water; set aside. In a saucepan, combine cranberry mixture and sugar; cook and stir until sugar is dissolved and mixture just begins to boil. Remove from the heat. Stir in gelatin mixture until dissolved. Add lemon juice. Transfer to a shallow 1-qt. freezer container. Cover and freeze until ice begins to form around the edges of container, about 1 hour. Freeze until slushy, stirring occasionally. **Yield:** 8 servings.

CRANBERRY BASICS

WITH THEIR ruby color, cranberries are a perfect staple item when cooking around the holidays. Follow these guidelines when storing and using these beautiful berries.

- When stored in a resealable plastic bag and refrigerated, cranberries will remain fresh for 1 month.
- To freeze cranberries, place them in a single layer on a 13-inch x 9-inch baking pan. When frozen, transfer to an airtight container and freeze for up to 1 year. Freezing berries individually allows you to measure only as many as needed.
- Just before using, wash the cranberries and pluck off any stems. There's no need to defrost frozen cranberries first.

CHRISTMAS DINNER COUNTDOWN

A Few Weeks Before:

- Prepare two grocery lists—one for non-perishable items to purchase now and one for perishable items to purchase a few days before Christmas Day.
- Order a fresh 10- to 12-pound turkey or buy and freeze a frozen turkey.

Two to Three Days Before:

- Buy remaining grocery items (including the fresh turkey if you ordered one) and berries and greens for the Cranberries & Boughs Centerpiece (see page 221).
- Thaw frozen turkey in a pan in the refrigerator. (Allow 24 hours of thawing for every 5 pounds.)
- Prepare Cranberry Ice.

Christmas Eve:

- Set the table.
- For the Sausage Stuffing, cube bread and store at room temperature in an airtight container. Cook bulk pork sausage and drain; cover and refrigerate.
- For the Dressed-Up Broccoli, cut broccoli into spears. Store in a large resealable plastic bag; chill.

- Chop onions for the stuffing and broccoli dish; refrigerate in airtight containers.
- Make the Blue Cheese Dressing; cover and chill.

Christmas Day:

- In the morning, assemble the Cranberries & Boughs Centerpiece.
- Peel and cube potatoes for Herbed Mashed Potatoes; cover with cold water and let stand at room temperature.
- Tear lettuce for the tossed salad; place in a resealable plastic bag and chill. Slice the red onion; refrigerate in an airtight container.
- Prepare the stuffing; stuff turkey and bake.
- Make the Beets in Orange Sauce, Dressed-Up Broccoli and Herbed Mashed Potatoes.
- Let cooked turkey stand for 20 minutes. Meanwhile, make the gravy. Remove the stuffing and carve the turkey.
- Assemble the salad ingredients for Salad with Blue Cheese Dressing; serve dressing alongside.
- Serve Cranberry Ice for dessert.

Dressed-Up Broccoli

(Pictured on page 214)

To liven up ordinary broccoli, our Test Kitchen tops the tender spears with a special wine sauce.
The light topping coats the broccoli nicely without being overpowering.
Experiment by sampling the sauce on other vegetables.

1-1/2 pounds fresh broccoli, cut into spears
1 medium onion, chopped
3 garlic cloves, minced
1/2 cup butter, *divided*
3/4 cup white wine *or* chicken broth
2 tablespoons heavy whipping cream

Place 1 in. of water and broccoli in a large saucepan. Bring to a boil. Reduce heat; cover and simmer for 5-8 minutes or until crisp-tender.

Meanwhile, in a small skillet, saute onion and garlic in 1/4 cup butter until golden brown. Add wine or broth; bring to a boil over high heat. Cook until liquid is reduced by half. Remove from the heat. Stir in cream and remaining butter. Drain broccoli and place in a serving bowl; drizzle with sauce. **Yield:** 4-6 servings.

Cranberries & Boughs Centerpiece

(Pictured at right and on page 214)

WHEN CREATING a centerpiece for your Christmas buffet table, look no further than the foods and foliage readily available during the season.

For our stunning arrangement shown at right, we relied on fresh cranberries. The crimson color of this tart berry blends beautifully with such dishes as Beets in Orange Sauce and Cranberry Ice. To carry that hue through, we opted for cranberry-colored napkins instead of the traditional Christmas red.

To fill out the vase, simply snip off some boughs from your Christmas tree or garlands. (We used both juniper and blue spruce branches, but you can use whatever boughs you have available.) Also feel free to tuck in some sprigs of holly or baby's breath and some white roses, lilies or daisies.

For the finishing touch, add a gold cord bow at the top of the vase.

WINTER *Celebrations*

Feast on Festive Entrees

WOULD YOU like to try a new and exciting entree for your next Christmas dinner but are worried your family will scoff?

With this chapter, you can set a new course with confidence. That's because these pages are packed with surefire beef, poultry, pork, seafood and game main dishes to suit casual get-togethers and formal sit-down dinners.

Each and every recipe is guaranteed to please because they've been taste-tested and approved by a finicky family just like yours.

So go ahead…present guests with impressive Stuffed Crown Roast of Pork, Roast Duck with Orange Glaze or Greek-Style Rib Eye Steaks.

Then forever say farewell to skepticism—and ho-hum holiday dinners!

NEWFOUND FAVORITES

(Top to bottom)

**Stuffed Crown
Roast of Pork** (p. 225)

**Roast Duck with
Orange Glaze** (p. 228)

**Greek-Style
Rib Eye Steaks** (p. 226)

Sage Chicken Cordon Bleu

It's nice to surprise the family with special meals like this during the week.
I usually double the recipe so we can enjoy leftovers the next day.
—Martha Stine, Johnstown, Pennsylvania

6 boneless skinless chicken
  breast halves
6 slices thinly sliced deli ham
6 strips mozzarella cheese
  (3 inches x 1-1/2 inches x 1/2
  inch)
1 medium tomato, seeded and
  chopped
3/4 teaspoon dried sage leaves
1/3 cup dry bread crumbs
2 tablespoons grated Parmesan
  cheese
2 tablespoons minced fresh
  parsley
1/4 cup butter, melted

Flatten chicken to 1/8-in. thickness. Place a ham slice, a mozzarella cheese strip, 1 tablespoon tomato and 1/8 teaspoon sage down the center of each chicken breast. Roll up and tuck in ends; secure with toothpicks.

In a shallow bowl, combine bread crumbs, Parmesan cheese and parsley. Dip chicken in butter, then roll in crumb mixture. Place in a greased 9-in. square baking dish. Drizzle with remaining butter.

Bake, uncovered, at 350° for 45 minutes or until chicken juices run clear. Discard toothpicks. **Yield:** 6 servings.

Holiday Pork Roast

This moist and tender pork roast always makes a statement when it appears
on the table. This is my husband's entree of choice for any occasion.
It's a no-fuss favorite because it marinates overnight.
— Teri Lindquist, Gurnee, Illinois

1/2 cup Dijon mustard
2 tablespoons soy sauce
1 tablespoon olive oil
4 garlic cloves, minced
1 teaspoon dried thyme
1 boneless pork loin roast
  (about 4 pounds)
1 teaspoon salt
1/4 teaspoon pepper
1-1/2 cups white wine *or*
  chicken broth

In a bowl, combine the mustard, soy sauce, oil, garlic and thyme; rub over roast. Place in a large resealable bag. Seal bag; refrigerate overnight, turning occasionally.

Place roast on a rack in a shallow roasting pan. Sprinkle with salt and pepper; pour wine or broth into the pan. Bake, uncovered, at 325° for 2-1/2 hours until a meat thermometer reads 160°, basting with pan juices every 30 minutes. Let stand for 10 minutes before slicing. **Yield:** 12-15 servings.

Stuffed Crown Roast Of Pork

(Pictured at right and on page 223)

I make this roast every Christmas, much to the delight of family and friends. The recipe was passed down from my mother, so I've been using it for years. The succulent stuffing is oh-so-tasty!
—Martha Forte, East Setauket, New York

3 tablespoons vegetable oil, *divided*
1 pork crown roast
  (16 ribs and about 8 pounds)
1-1/4 pounds bulk Italian sausage
3 cups finely chopped onions
2 cups finely chopped carrots
2 cups finely chopped celery
2 garlic cloves, minced
4 cups diced cooked peeled potatoes
1/3 cup minced fresh parsley
1 teaspoon fennel seed, crushed
1 teaspoon salt
1/8 teaspoon pepper
Decorative foil *or* paper frills, optional

Rub 1 tablespoon oil over entire roast; place on a rack in a shallow roasting pan. Cover rib ends with aluminum foil. Bake, uncovered, at 325° for 1-3/4 hours.

For stuffing, in a large skillet, cook sausage over medium heat until no longer pink; drain and set aside. In the same skillet, saute the onions, carrots, celery and garlic in remaining oil until tender. Stir in the potatoes, parsley, fennel, salt, pepper and reserved sausage. Carefully spoon into center of roast.

Bake 1 hour longer or until a meat thermometer reads 160° and meat juices run clear. Replace foil with decorative frills if desired. Remove stuffing to a serving bowl; slice roast between ribs. **Yield:** 12-16 servings.

Greek-Style Rib Eye Steaks

(Pictured on page 222)

Because our children are grown, I often cook for just my husband and me.
When I want to serve something special, this is the entree I usually reach for.
Seasonings, black olives and feta cheese give steak great flavor.
—*Ruby Williams, Bogalusa, Louisiana*

1-1/2 teaspoons garlic powder
1-1/2 teaspoons dried oregano
1-1/2 teaspoons dried basil
   1/2 teaspoon salt
   1/8 teaspoon pepper
    2 beef rib eye steaks
      (1-1/2 inches thick)
    1 tablespoon olive oil
    1 tablespoon lemon juice

2 tablespoons crumbled feta cheese
1 tablespoon sliced ripe olives

In a small bowl, combine the garlic powder, oregano, basil, salt and pepper; press into both sides of steaks. In a large skillet, cook steaks in oil for 7-9 minutes on each side or until meat reaches desired doneness. Sprinkle with lemon juice, cheese and olives. Serve immediately. **Yield:** 2 servings.

HOLIDAY MENU SUGGESTIONS

DOES MEAL PLANNING around the holidays have you puzzled? Our Test Kitchen suggests five mouth-watering menus that are wonderful for both fancy get-togethers and casual gatherings. Each meal features an entree from this chapter and side dishes and desserts found in other chapters of this book.

- **Fine Dining.** Instead of traditional turkey, why not try succulent Holiday Pork Roast (page 224)? It makes for a festive meal when paired with Snowcapped Butternut Squash (page 241), green beans, a basket of rolls and Chocolate Truffle Dessert (page 269).

- **Delightful Chicken Dinner.** Entertaining can be easy with the right foods. Honey-Glazed Chicken (page 232) is no-fuss fare because it bakes in the oven, while Broccoli with Ginger-Orange Butter (page 236) cooks in mere minutes. For a make-ahead dessert, turn to Macaroon Cheesecake (page 268).

- **Casual Cooking for Two.** Take a trip for two to the Mediterranean and sample Greek-Style Rib Eye Steaks (above). Dilly Bread Ring (page 175) and a simple green salad are perfect partners for this ethnic entree. Save leftovers of Almond Puff Pastries (page 268) to impress folks at your next social engagement.

- **Convenient Casseroles.** Served alongside oven-baked Dilled Duchess Potatoes (page 245), Asparagus Chicken Divan (page 230) is one dish everyone will enjoy. Then enjoy indulging in decadent Caramel-Chocolate Pecan Pie (page 272).

- **On the Lighter Side.** With all of the rich foods accompanying the holidays, it's nice to offer a little lighter fare. You'll reel in raves with Crispy Orange Roughy (page 228), Curried Rice Pilaf (page 239) and a tossed green salad. Then net compliments with cool and creamy Peppermint Ice Cream (page 270).

Festive Meat Loaf Pinwheel

(Pictured at right)

Most people wouldn't think of serving meat loaf for a holiday gathering, but think again! It's wonderful for a crowd because its hearty, zesty flavor appeals to all.
— Vera Sullivan, Amity, Oregon

3 eggs
1 cup dry bread crumbs
1/2 cup finely chopped onion
1/2 cup finely chopped green pepper
1/4 cup ketchup
2 teaspoons minced fresh parsley
1 teaspoon dried basil
1 teaspoon dried oregano
1 garlic clove, minced
2 teaspoons salt
1/2 teaspoon pepper
5 pounds ground beef
3/4 pound thinly sliced deli ham
3/4 pound thinly sliced Swiss cheese

TOMATO PEPPER SAUCE:
1/2 cup finely chopped onion
2 celery ribs, cut into 1-1/2-inch julienne strips
1/2 medium green pepper, cut into 1-1/2-inch julienne strips
1 garlic clove, minced
1 to 2 tablespoons olive oil
2 cups chopped fresh tomatoes
1 cup beef broth
1 bay leaf
1 teaspoon sugar
1/4 teaspoon salt

1/4 teaspoon dried thyme
1 tablespoon cornstarch
2 tablespoons cold water

In a large bowl, combine the first 11 ingredients. Crumble beef over mixture and mix well. On a piece of heavy-duty foil, pat beef mixture into a 17-in. x 15-in. rectangle. Cover with ham and cheese slices to within 1/2 in. of edges. Roll up tightly jelly-roll style, starting with a short side. Place seam side down in a roasting pan. Bake, uncovered, at 350° for 1-1/4 to 1-1/2 hours or until a meat thermometer reads 160°.

In a saucepan, saute the onion, celery, green pepper and garlic in oil for 3-5 minutes or until tender. Add tomatoes, broth, bay leaf, sugar, salt and thyme. Simmer, uncovered, for 30 minutes. Discard bay leaf. Combine cornstarch and water until smooth; stir into sauce. Bring to a boil; cook and stir for 2 minutes or until thickened. Drain meat loaf; top with sauce. **Yield:** 15-20 servings.

Roast Duck with Orange Glaze

(Pictured on page 222)

This duck is a nice alternative for a festive dinner on holidays.
The meat remains moist and tender, thanks to the fruity glaze and simple stuffing.
—*Jeanne Koelsch, San Rafael, California*

1 **domestic duckling**
　(4 to 6 pounds)
1 **teaspoon caraway seeds**
4 **cups crushed stuffing**
1/2 **medium green pepper,**
　finely chopped
1 **small onion, finely chopped**
1 **celery rib, finely chopped**
1 **tablespoon rubbed sage**
1/2 **teaspoon salt**
1/8 **teaspoon pepper**
Pinch dried thyme
Pinch ground nutmeg
1/2 **cup chicken broth**
ORANGE GLAZE:
1/2 **cup packed brown sugar**
2 **tablespoons plus 1-1/2**
　teaspoons sugar
2 **tablespoons cornstarch**

Pinch salt
1 **cup orange juice**
1 **tablespoon grated orange peel**
1 **drop hot pepper sauce**

Sprinkle inside of duck with caraway seeds; prick skin well. In a bowl, combine stuffing, vegetables, seasonings and broth; mix lightly. Spoon into duck. Place breast side up on a rack in a large shallow roasting pan.

Bake, uncovered, at 350° for 2-1/2 to 3-1/4 hours or until a meat thermometer reads 180° for the duck and 165° for the stuffing (drain fat from pan as it accumulates). Cover and let stand for 20 minutes before removing stuffing and slicing.

Meanwhile, for glaze, combine the sugars, cornstarch and salt in a saucepan. Gradually stir in orange juice, peel and hot pepper sauce until blended. Bring to a boil; cook and stir for 2 minutes or until thickened. Serve with duck. **Yield:** 2-4 servings.

Crispy Orange Roughy

When you're looking for a main course on the lighter side, try this flavorful dish.
The crunchy topping nicely complements the tender fish.
—*Nancy Florian, St. Johnsville, New York*

1/3 **cup lemon juice**
1 **tablespoon olive oil**
2 **teaspoons dried oregano**
1/4 **teaspoon salt**
1/4 **teaspoon pepper**
2 **cups mashed potato flakes**
4 **orange roughy, cod *or***
　haddock fillets (6 ounces *each*)

Line a baking sheet with aluminum foil and spray with non-stick cooking spray; set aside. In a shallow bowl, whisk together the lemon juice, oil, oregano, salt and pepper. Place the potato flakes in another bowl.

Dip fillets in lemon juice mixture, then coat with potato flakes. Place on prepared pan. Bake at 500° for 10 minutes or until fish flakes easily with a fork and is golden brown. **Yield:** 4 servings.

Mushroom Pork Scallopini

(Pictured at right)

Tender pork has fantastic flavor when coated with a buttery sauce seasoned with garlic and herbs. This serves a lot, so I make it often for company.
—Carol Ebner, Fort Dodge, Iowa

3 to 4 pork tenderloins (about 1 pound *each*), cut into 1-inch slices
1 cup all-purpose flour
1/4 cup butter
1/4 cup vegetable oil
1 cup white wine *or* chicken broth
1/2 cup water
1 large onion, chopped
1 to 2 garlic cloves, minced
1/2 teaspoon salt
1/2 teaspoon pepper
1/2 teaspoon *each* dried thyme, oregano and rosemary, crushed
1 pound fresh mushrooms, sliced
Hot cooked fettuccine

Dredge pork slices in flour. In a large skillet, heat butter and oil. Brown pork on both sides in batches; remove and keep warm. Stir wine or broth, water, onion, garlic and seasonings into drippings. Return pork to skillet, layering if necessary. Top with mushrooms.

Cover and cook over low heat for 15-20 minutes or until meat juices run clear. Serve over fettuccine. **Yield:** 8-10 servings.

Family Traditions

ACCORDING to German tradition, children would eagerly head to the tree on Christmas morning to search for the pickle ornament that their parents hid in the green boughs the night before. The children knew whoever found the blown-glass ornament first would receive an extra gift as a reward for being the most observant child.

Asparagus Chicken Divan

I first came across this recipe at a restaurant while living in New York City many years ago.
This makes a delectable dish for lunch or dinner served with a simple tossed salad.
—*Jeanne Koelsch, San Rafael, California*

1 **pound boneless skinless chicken breasts**
2 **pounds fresh asparagus, trimmed**
1 **can (10-3/4 ounces) condensed cream of chicken soup, undiluted**
1 **teaspoon Worcestershire sauce**
1/4 **teaspoon ground nutmeg**
1 **cup grated Parmesan cheese, *divided***
1/2 **cup heavy whipping cream, whipped**
3/4 **cup mayonnaise**

Broil chicken 6 in. from the heat until juices run clear. Meanwhile, in a large skillet, bring 1/2 in. of water to a boil. Add asparagus. Reduce heat; cover and simmer for 3-5 minutes or until crisp-tender. Drain and place in a greased shallow 2-1/2-qt. baking dish. Cut chicken into thin slices.

In a bowl, combine the soup, Worcestershire sauce and nutmeg. Spread half over asparagus. Sprinkle with 1/3 cup Parmesan cheese. Top with chicken. Spread remaining soup mixture over chicken; sprinkle with 1/3 cup Parmesan cheese.

Bake, uncovered, at 400° for 20 minutes. Fold whipped cream into mayonnaise; spread over top. Sprinkle with remaining Parmesan cheese. Broil 4-6 in. from the heat for about 2 minutes or until golden brown. **Yield:** 6-8 servings.

Editor's Note: Reduced-fat or fat-free mayonnaise may not be substituted for regular mayonnaise.

Grilled Rack of Lamb

Whenever my husband and I really want to impress guests, we make this rack of lamb. The
marinade keeps the meat juicy and tender while grilling.
—*Gail Cawsey, Sequim, Washington*

2 **cups apple cider *or* juice**
2/3 **cup cider vinegar**
2/3 **cup thinly sliced green onions**
1/2 **cup vegetable oil**
1/3 **cup honey**
1/4 **cup steak sauce**
2 **teaspoons dried tarragon**
2 **teaspoons salt**
1/2 **teaspoon pepper**
4 **racks of lamb (1-1/2 to 2 pounds *each*)**

In a saucepan, combine the first nine ingredients. Bring to a boil. Reduce heat; simmer, uncovered, for 20 minutes. Remove 1 cup for basting; cover and refrigerate. Pour the remaining marinade into a large resealable plastic bag; add lamb. Seal bag and turn to coat; refrigerate for 2-3 hours or overnight, turning once or twice.

Coat grill rack with nonstick cooking spray before starting the grill. Drain and discard the marinade. Cover rib ends of lamb with foil. Grill, covered, over medium heat for 15 minutes. Baste with reserved marinade. Grill 5-10 minutes longer, basting occasionally, or until meat reaches desired doneness (for rare, a meat thermometer should read 140°; for medium-well, 160°). **Yield:** 4-6 servings.

Shrimp Creole

(Pictured at right)

This seafood dish is perfect for casual holiday gatherings and will reel in rave reviews. I've been using this tried-and-true recipe for more than 30 years.
— Barbara Lindsey, Manvel, Texas

3 medium onions, chopped
1 large green pepper, chopped
2 celery ribs, chopped
6 tablespoons butter, *divided*
1 can (28 ounces) diced tomatoes, undrained
1 can (15 ounces) tomato sauce
1 cup picante sauce
1 tablespoon minced fresh parsley
3 tablespoons all-purpose flour
1 can (14-1/2 ounces) chicken broth
1/2 teaspoon salt
1/4 teaspoon pepper
2 bay leaves
3 pounds cooked medium shrimp, peeled and deveined
1 can (8 ounces) mushroom stems and pieces, drained
1/2 cup chopped stuffed olives
1/2 cup chopped green onions
Hot cooked rice

In a large skillet, saute onions, green pepper and celery in 5 tablespoons butter until tender. Add the tomatoes, tomato sauce, picante sauce and parsley. In a saucepan, melt the remaining butter; stir in flour until smooth. Gradually add the broth, salt, pepper and bay leaves. Stir into vegetable mixture. Bring to a boil. Reduce heat; cover and simmer for 30 minutes.

Add the shrimp, mushrooms, olives and green onions. Cover and cook 10 minutes longer or until heated through. Discard bay leaves. Serve over rice. **Yield:** 12-14 servings.

GREAT GARNISHES

INSTEAD of discarding the unused leaves when chopping celery for Shrimp Creole (pictured above), save them to use as an inexpensive garnish.

Other garnish ideas include a sprig of parsley or additional chopped stuffed olives or green onions. *Never* garnish with bay leaves…they pose a choking hazard.

Stuffed Flank Steak

Family and friends are always impressed when this entree appears on the table,
but it's actually quite easy. I sometimes assemble the steak roll in the morning and refrigerate
before browning. The rich tomato sauce tastes great over mashed potatoes.
—*Nadeen Shrewsberry, Hickory, North Carolina*

1 beef flank steak
   (about 1-1/2 pounds)
1/2 cup chopped onion, *divided*
2 tablespoons vegetable oil,
   divided
2 cups cubed seasoned stuffing
3/4 cup water, *divided*
1/2 teaspoon poultry seasoning
1/2 cup all-purpose flour
1/4 teaspoon salt
1/8 teaspoon pepper
1 can (28 ounces) diced
   tomatoes, undrained
2 tablespoons ketchup
1/4 cup chopped green pepper
1 jar (4-1/2 ounces) sliced
   mushrooms, drained

Flatten steak to 1/4-in. thickness. In a skillet, saute 1/4 cup onion in 1 tablespoon oil until golden brown. Add stuffing, 1/4 cup water and poultry seasoning; cook and stir until water is absorbed. Spoon over steak; roll up tightly jelly-roll style, starting with a long side. Secure with toothpicks or kitchen string.

Combine the flour, salt and pepper. Coat meat with flour mixture. In a Dutch oven, brown meat on all sides in remaining oil. Add the tomatoes, ketchup and remaining water and onion. Bring to a boil. Reduce heat; cover and simmer for 1-1/4 hours.

Add green pepper and mushrooms; cook 15 minutes longer or until meat reaches desired doneness. **Yield:** 4 servings.

Honey-Glazed Chicken

My family can't get enough of this finger-lickin'-good chicken, and I often double the recipe.
The sauce can also be used when grilling chicken.
—*Harriet Lusch, Muncie, Indiana*

2/3 cup soy sauce
2/3 cup sherry *or* apple juice
2/3 cup honey
1/2 cup water
1 small onion, chopped
2 garlic cloves, minced
1/4 teaspoon ground ginger
2 broiler/fryer chickens
   (3 to 4 pounds *each*), cut up

In a large resealable plastic bag, combine the first seven ingredients. Add chicken; seal and turn to coat. Refrigerate for 1-2 hours. Place chicken and marinade in two greased 13-in. x 9-in. x 2-in. baking dishes. Bake, uncovered, at 350° for 1 hour or until juices run clear. Drain marinade and serve with chicken. **Yield:** 8 servings.

Fish Fillets With Citrus-Herb Butter

(Pictured at right)

The staff in our Test Kitchen combined dried herbs to transform ordinary butter into a tasty topping for your favorite fish fillets. Served with wild rice, this is a simply elegant entree.

1 cup butter, softened
1/3 cup mixed dried herbs of your choice (chives, thyme, basil, dill weed)
2 tablespoons grated lemon peel
2 tablespoons grated orange peel
2 tablespoons lemon juice
2 tablespoons orange juice
4 teaspoons confectioners' sugar
1/2 teaspoon salt
1 pound orange roughy, cod *or* haddock fillets

In a small mixing bowl, combine the first eight ingredients; beat until blended. Shape half of the butter mixture into a log; wrap in plastic wrap and freeze. Place remaining mixture in a microwave-safe bowl; heat for 1-2 minutes or until melted.

Place fish fillets in an ungreased 13-in. x 9-in. x 2-in. baking dish. Drizzle with melted butter mixture. Bake, uncovered, at 375° for 10-15 minutes or until fish flakes easily with a fork. Cut butter log into slices; serve with fish. **Yield:** 4 servings.

WINTER
Celebrations

Sparkling Yuletide Sides

IF YOUR FAMILY is like most, they expect your Christmas menu to include many of the same tried-and-true dishes from year to year.

But if you're looking to add a little variety to your table, why not offer one or two deliciously different side dishes alongside the old standbys?

Present holiday guests with the eye-catching color and appealing flavors of Cranberry Sweet Potato Bake, Swiss-Topped Cauliflower Soup, Broccoli with Ginger-Orange Butter, Curried Rice Pilaf and Cinnamon Gelatin Salad.

Or turn the pages for even more mouth-watering vegetables, pasta, rice, soups and salads that are bound to become newfound favorites your family will ask for time and again!

Twists on the Traditional

(Clockwise from top right)

Cranberry Sweet Potato Bake (p. 237)

Swiss-Topped Cauliflower Soup (p. 240)

Broccoli with Ginger-Orange Butter (p. 236)

Curried Rice Pilaf (p. 239)

Cinnamon Gelatin Salad (p. 239)

Broccoli with Ginger-Orange Butter

(Pictured on page 234)

Instead of simply topping steamed broccoli with plain butter, the home economists in our Test Kitchen suggest you try serving it with an easy-to-prepare flavored butter. This is also a tasty topping for sugar snap peas, green beans and carrots.

1 pound fresh broccoli, cut into spears
2 tablespoons orange marmalade
1 tablespoon butter
1/2 teaspoon cider vinegar
1/8 teaspoon ground ginger

Add 1 in. of water to a large saucepan; add broccoli. Bring to a boil. Reduce heat; cover and simmer for 5-8 minutes or until crisp-tender. Meanwhile, in a small saucepan, combine the marmalade, butter, vinegar and ginger. Cook until marmalade and butter are melted. Drain broccoli; drizzle with butter mixture. **Yield:** 6 servings.

Cheddar Cauliflower Quiche

A dear friend shared this recipe one year when we both had an abundance of cauliflower from our gardens. My husband and I enjoy this so much that I make it for breakfast, lunch and dinner!
— Tracy Watson, Hobson, Montana

1 cup all-purpose flour
1/4 teaspoon salt
1/3 cup shortening
3 tablespoons cold milk
4 cups chopped fresh cauliflower, cooked
1/2 cup slivered almonds, toasted
2 eggs
1/2 cup milk
1/2 cup mayonnaise
1-1/2 cups (6 ounces) shredded cheddar cheese, *divided*
1/8 teaspoon ground nutmeg
1/8 teaspoon pepper

In a bowl, combine flour and salt. Cut in shortening until mixture resembles coarse crumbs. Stir in milk until mixture forms a ball. Wrap in plastic wrap; refrigerate for 30 minutes. Unwrap dough. On a floured surface, roll out to fit a 9-in. pie plate. Place in pie plate; flute edges. Line unpricked pastry with a double thickness of foil. Bake at 450° for 5 minutes. Remove foil; bake 5 minutes longer.

Spoon cauliflower into crust; top with almonds. In a blender, combine eggs, milk, mayonnaise, 1-1/4 cups cheese, nutmeg and pepper; cover and process until smooth. Pour over almonds; sprinkle with remaining cheese. Bake at 350° for 30-35 minutes or until a knife inserted near the center comes out clean. Let stand for 10 minutes before cutting. **Yield:** 6-8 servings.

Editor's Note: Reduced-fat or fat-free mayonnaise may not be substituted for regular mayonnaise.

Cranberry Sweet Potato Bake

(Pictured at right and on page 235)

Instead of serving sweet potatoes alone at Christmas, I like to pair them with cranberries. Each bite offers a delicious contrast of sweet and tart flavors.
—Linda Boot
Fort St. John, British Columbia

3-1/2 pounds sweet potatoes
   2 large onions, peeled and halved
   2 teaspoons olive oil
   2 cups halved fresh *or* frozen cranberries
 2/3 cup packed brown sugar
 1/2 cup orange juice
   2 tablespoons butter, melted
   1 tablespoon grated orange peel
 1/2 teaspoon *each* salt, ground ginger, cinnamon and nutmeg

Place sweet potatoes and onions on a baking sheet; brush onions with oil. Bake, uncovered, at 400° for 50-60 minutes or just until tender. When cool enough to handle, peel and cube potatoes and dice onions; place in a large bowl.

Combine the remaining ingredients; mix well. Gently stir into potato mixture. Transfer to a greased 13-in. x 9-in. x 2-in. baking dish. Bake, uncovered, at 350° for 25-30 minutes or until heated through, stirring once. **Yield:** 12-14 servings.

DRESSING UP EVERYDAY VEGETABLES

A SIDE DISH doesn't have to be elaborate. In fact, when serving a variety of flavorful foods, it's nice to include a basic vegetable that's been simply seasoned. Try these tasty toppings for hot cooked vegetables.

- Combine 1/4 cup plain dry bread crumbs, 1-1/2 teaspoons melted butter, 1/2 teaspoon dried parsley flakes and a dash of salt. Sprinkle over cooked vegetables.

- Melt 1/4 cup butter over low heat; stir in 1/2 teaspoon garlic powder, 2 tablespoons lemon juice, 1 tablespoon slivered toasted almonds, 1 tablespoon minced chives *or* 1 tablespoon grated Parmesan cheese. Drizzle over cooked vegetables.

- For extra ease, prepare a packaged white, hollandaise or bernaise sauce mix as directed and serve over your vegetable of choice.

Hearty Meatball Soup

A little bit of this thick and hearty soup goes a long way, so it's terrific to take to potlucks.
My husband, Patrick, and I enjoy this on cold winter nights.
—Janice Thompson, Lansing, Michigan

2 eggs
1 cup soft bread crumbs
1 teaspoon salt
1/2 teaspoon pepper
1 pound ground beef
1 pound ground pork
1/2 pound ground turkey
4 cups beef broth
1 can (46 ounces) tomato juice
2 cans (14-1/2 ounces *each*)
   stewed tomatoes
8 cups shredded cabbage
1 cup thinly sliced celery
1 cup thinly sliced carrots

8 green onions, sliced
3/4 cup uncooked long grain rice
2 teaspoons dried basil
3 tablespoons minced fresh parsley
2 tablespoons soy sauce

In a bowl, combine the eggs, bread crumbs, salt and pepper. Crumble meat over mixture and mix well. Shape into 1-in. balls. In a soup kettle, bring broth to a boil. Carefully add the meatballs. Add the tomato juice, tomatoes, vegetables, rice and basil. Cover and simmer for 30 minutes.

Add the parsley and soy sauce. Simmer, uncovered, for 10 minutes or until meatballs are no longer pink and vegetables are tender. **Yield:** 22-24 servings (5-3/4 quarts).

Supreme Scalloped Potatoes

For a true down-home dinner, serve these creamy potatoes alongside your favorite roast beef.
When I know I have a full day ahead, I'll assemble this casserole the night before.
—Erla Burkholder, Ewing, Illinois

8 medium potatoes (about 3
   pounds), peeled
1-1/2 cups (6 ounces) shredded
   cheddar cheese, *divided*
1/3 cup chopped onion
1 can (10-3/4 ounces)
   condensed cream of chicken
   soup, undiluted
1 cup (8 ounces) sour cream
3/4 cup milk
2 tablespoons butter, melted
1/2 teaspoon salt
1/2 teaspoon pepper

In a Dutch oven or large kettle, cook potatoes in boiling salted water until tender. Cool completely; shred and place in a large bowl. Add 1 cup cheese and onion. Combine remaining ingredients; pour over potato mixture.

Transfer to a greased 2-1/2-qt. baking dish. Sprinkle with remaining cheese. Bake, uncovered, at 350° for 35-40 minutes or until bubbly. **Yield:** 12-14 servings.

Cinnamon Gelatin Salad

(Pictured at right and on page 235)

*Crunchy apples and pecans
contrast nicely with smooth gelatin
in this pretty salad.*
— Denita DeValcourt
Lawrenceburg, Tennessee

1/4 cup red-hot candies
1/4 cup water
  1 package (6 ounces) raspberry
    or cherry gelatin
1-3/4 cups boiling water
1/2 to 1 teaspoon ground
    cinnamon
1-3/4 cups cold water
  1 medium tart apple, peeled
    and chopped
1/4 cup chopped pecans

In a heavy saucepan, cook and stir candies and water until candies are melted. In a bowl, dissolve gelatin in boiling water. Stir in candy mixture and cinnamon. Stir in cold water. Cover and refrigerate until partially set. Fold in apple and pecans. Pour into a 1-1/2-qt. serving bowl. Refrigerate until set. **Yield:** 6 servings.

Curried Rice Pilaf

(Pictured on page 234)

In this baked rice dish, green onions give great color, raisins bring a touch of sweetness and almonds add crunch. I think you'll agree the mild curry flavor pleases all palates.
— Lee Bremson, Kansas City, Missouri

1/2 cup chopped green onions,
    divided
  2 garlic cloves, minced
1/4 cup butter
1-1/2 cups uncooked long grain rice
1/2 teaspoon curry powder
  3 cups chicken broth
1/2 teaspoon salt
1/2 cup golden raisins
1/2 cup chopped almonds, toasted

In a skillet, saute 1/4 cup onions and garlic in butter until tender. Stir in rice and curry. Saute for 2-3 minutes or until rice is lightly browned.

In a saucepan, heat broth and salt. Pour over rice mixture; stir. Cover and simmer for 35-40 minutes or until rice is tender. Remove from the heat; stir in raisins, almonds and remaining onions. **Yield:** 4-6 servings.

Swiss-Topped Cauliflower Soup

(Pictured on page 235)

Since I came across this recipe a few years ago, it's become my husband's favorite soup.
With fresh bread, we enjoy this as a hearty supper in winter.
—*C.C. McKie, Chicago, Illinois*

2 medium onions
4 whole cloves
4 cups water
2 cans (10-1/2 ounces *each*)
   condensed chicken broth,
   undiluted
3 medium leeks (white portion
   only), sliced
3 medium carrots, sliced
1 teaspoon salt
1 teaspoon dried marjoram
1/2 teaspoon celery seed
1/2 teaspoon ground nutmeg
1/4 teaspoon white pepper
1 medium head cauliflower,
   broken into florets and thinly
   sliced (about 6 cups)
1 tablespoon cornstarch
1/2 cup heavy whipping cream
2 egg yolks, beaten
1/2 pound sliced Swiss cheese,
   cut into 4-inch x 1/2-inch
   strips

Quarter one onion; stuff the cloves into the second onion. In a large saucepan, combine water and broth; add onions, leeks, carrots and seasonings. Bring to a boil. Reduce heat; cover and simmer for 15 minutes. Add cauliflower; simmer, uncovered, for 30 minutes or until vegetables are tender. Remove from the heat.

In a bowl, combine cornstarch and cream until smooth. Stir in egg yolks. Stir a small amount of hot soup into cream mixture; return all to the pan, stirring constantly. Simmer, uncovered, for 15 minutes. Discard the whole onion.

Ladle soup into individual ramekins. Top with cheese strips. Broil 4-6 in. from the heat for 3-5 minutes or until cheese is bubbly. Serve immediately. **Yield:** 6-8 servings.

SELECTING SUCCESSFUL SIDE DISHES

TRYING to decide which side dishes to serve for your holiday dinner can be overwhelming. Here are some suggestions to help simplify your selection.

- Variety is key to pleasing all of your guests. So have an assortment of hot and cold foods and offer vegetables along with grains and pasta. For kids and older guests, provide at least one simple, lightly seasoned side dish.
- The entree and side dishes should complement one another. If your entree has intense flavor, pair it with more mild-flavored side dishes and vice versa. If your entree has lots of garlic, onion or nuts, stay away from a side dish that's loaded with any of those same ingredients.
- For ease of preparation, look for an oven-baked side dish that cooks at the same temperature as your oven entree.
- If your oven will be full with the entree and other side dishes, choose another side dish that can be prepared on the stovetop or in a slow cooker. Or for a refreshing break from the hot foods, turn to a tossed salad, an assortment of fresh fruit or a tried-and-true relish tray.
- Recipes that can be prepared ahead (like gelatin salads and overnight casseroles) are a real boon to busy cooks.

Snowcapped Butternut Squash

(Pictured at right)

I first prepared this side dish in my high school home economics class. The cool sour cream sauce makes it irresistible, even to those people who usually don't care for squash.
—Karen Peterson-Johnson
Salt Lake City, Utah

2 pounds butternut squash, peeled, seeded and cubed (about 4 cups)
1 medium onion, halved and thinly sliced
2 tablespoons butter
1 cup (8 ounces) sour cream
1/2 teaspoon salt
1/2 teaspoon dill weed
Dash pepper
Additional dill weed, optional

Place squash in a large saucepan and cover with water; bring to a boil. Reduce heat; cover and simmer for 20-30 minutes or until tender.

In a skillet, saute onion in butter until tender. Remove from the heat. Stir in sour cream, salt, dill and pepper. Drain squash and transfer to a serving bowl; top with sauce. Sprinkle with additional dill if desired. **Yield:** 4-6 servings.

Paprika Mushrooms

I use paprika in much of my cooking. . .it gives food a nice, mild flavor and adds pretty color. These mushrooms are great alongside chicken or beef entrees.
—Rosemarie Kondrk, Old Bridge, New Jersey

2 medium onions, chopped
2 tablespoons vegetable oil
1 tablespoon paprika
1 pound fresh mushrooms, halved
1 cup chicken broth

In a large skillet, saute onions in oil until tender. Stir in paprika. Add mushrooms and broth; bring to a boil. Reduce heat; cover and simmer for 5-10 minutes or until mushrooms are tender. **Yield:** 4 servings.

Slow-Cooked Vegetable Soup

*You just have to try this hearty soup for its unique blend of flavors and
beautiful appearance. With all the rich foods served during the holidays,
it's nice to serve this soup loaded with fiber and vitamins.*
—Christina Till, South Haven, Michigan

3/4 cup chopped onion
1/2 cup chopped celery
1/2 cup chopped green pepper
2 tablespoons olive oil
1 large potato, peeled and diced
1 medium sweet potato, peeled
   and diced
1 to 2 garlic cloves, minced
3 cups chicken broth *or* water
2 medium fresh tomatoes,
   chopped
1 can (16 ounces) kidney beans,
   rinsed and drained
1 can (15 ounces) garbanzo
   beans *or* chickpeas, rinsed and
   drained

2 teaspoons soy sauce
1 teaspoon paprika
1/2 teaspoon dried basil
1/4 teaspoon salt
1/4 teaspoon ground turmeric
1 bay leaf
Dash cayenne pepper

In a large skillet, saute onion, celery and green pepper in
oil until crisp-tender. Add potato, sweet potato and garlic;
saute 3-5 minutes longer. Transfer to a 5-qt. slow cooker. Stir
in the remaining ingredients. Cover and cook on low for 9-
10 hours or until vegetables are tender. Discard bay leaf
before serving. **Yield:** 12 servings (about 3 quarts).

Walnut Broccoli Bake

*A friend shared this recipe with me years ago and it instantly became a family favorite.
When I make it for potluck luncheons, there are no leftovers.*
—Carolyn Bosetti, LaSalle, Ontario

3 packages (10 ounces *each*)
   frozen chopped broccoli
1/2 cup butter, *divided*
1/4 cup all-purpose flour
4-1/2 teaspoons chicken bouillon
   granules
2 cups milk
1/2 cup water
4 cups seasoned stuffing
   croutons
1/2 cup chopped walnuts

Cook broccoli according to package directions; drain and
transfer to a greased 3-qt. baking dish. In a saucepan, melt
1/4 cup butter. Stir in flour and bouillon. Gradually add
milk. Bring to a boil; cook and stir for 2 minutes or until
thickened and bubbly. Pour over broccoli.

In a large saucepan, melt the remaining butter. Add the
water, stuffing and walnuts; mix well. Spoon over the
broccoli. Bake, uncovered, at 375° for 20-25 minutes or
until stuffing is lightly browned. **Yield:** 12 servings.

Chicken Wild Rice Soup

(Pictured at right)

I'm originally from Minnesota, where wild rice grows in abundance and is very popular in recipes. This soup has been part of our Christmas Eve menu for years. To save time, I cook the chicken and wild rice and cut up the vegetables the day before.
— Virginia Montmarquet
Riverside, California

2 quarts chicken broth
1/2 pound fresh mushrooms, chopped
1 cup finely chopped celery
1 cup shredded carrots
1/2 cup finely chopped onion
1 teaspoon chicken bouillon granules
1 teaspoon dried parsley flakes
1/4 teaspoon garlic powder
1/4 teaspoon dried thyme
1/4 cup butter
1/4 cup all-purpose flour
1 can (10-3/4 ounces) condensed cream of mushroom soup, undiluted
1/2 cup dry white wine *or* additional chicken broth
3 cups cooked wild rice
2 cups cubed cooked chicken

In a large saucepan, combine the first nine ingredients. Bring to a boil. Reduce heat; cover and simmer for 30 minutes.

In a soup kettle or Dutch oven, melt butter. Stir in flour until smooth. Gradually whisk in broth mixture. Bring to a boil; cook and stir for 2 minutes or until thickened. Whisk in soup and wine or broth. Add rice and chicken; heat through. **Yield:** 14 servings (3-1/2 quarts).

Family Traditions

WHEN I was growing up in Minnesota, Mom would open our home to many friends and family on Christmas Eve. After having our fill of her steaming Chicken Wild Rice Soup (recipe above), crusty bakery rolls and a sweet assortment of cookies, we'd bundle up and head out for Christmas caroling before attending midnight Mass. The memories of that magical night continue to warm my heart.
— Virginia Montmarquet, Riverside, California

Eggnog Fruit Fluff

I regularly fit a blend of apples, blueberries and other fruit into my December menus.
The eggnog in the dressing suits this sweet salad for Christmas.
— Tami Harrington, West Chicago, Illinois

1 cup eggnog, chilled
1 envelope whipped topping
    mix
1/4 teaspoon ground nutmeg
1 can (20 ounces) pineapple
    tidbits, drained
1 can (16 ounces) sliced
    peaches, drained
2 medium tart apples, chopped
1 cup fresh blueberries
3/4 cup halved maraschino
    cherries
3/4 cup chopped walnuts

In a mixing bowl, beat eggnog, whipped topping mix and nutmeg on high speed until soft peaks form. Combine the remaining ingredients; fold into eggnog mixture. Cover and refrigerate. Gently stir just before serving. **Yield:** 10-12 servings.

Editor's Note: This recipe was tested with commercially prepared eggnog.

Spinach Noodle Casserole

We enjoyed a similar casserole at a friend's house many years ago. She didn't have a recipe but
told me the basic ingredients. I eventually came up with my own version and have shared
the recipe many times since. It goes great with ham but also is filling by itself.
— Doris Tschorn, Levittown, New York

4 cups uncooked egg noodles
1/4 cup butter
1/4 cup all-purpose flour
1 teaspoon salt
1/8 teaspoon pepper
2 cups milk
2 packages (10 ounces *each*)
    frozen chopped spinach,
    thawed and drained
2 cups (8 ounces) shredded
    Swiss cheese
2 cups (8 ounces) shredded
    mozzarella cheese
1/4 cup grated Parmesan cheese
Paprika, optional

Cook noodles according to package directions; drain and rinse in cold water. In a saucepan, melt butter over medium heat. Stir in flour, salt and pepper until smooth. Gradually add milk. Bring to a boil; cook and stir for 2 minutes or until thickened.

Arrange half of the noodles in an ungreased 11-in. x 7-in. x 2-in. baking dish; cover with half of the spinach and half of the Swiss cheese. Spread with half of the white sauce. Repeat layers. Top with mozzarella and Parmesan cheeses. Sprinkle with paprika if desired.

Cover and bake at 350° for 20 minutes. Uncover; bake 20 minutes longer. Let stand for 15 minutes before cutting. **Yield:** 12-14 servings.

Dilled Duchess Potatoes

(Pictured at right)

When you want to impress dinner guests with a splendid side dish, these eye-catching potatoes from our Test Kitchen fill the bill. The appealing flavor of dill really shines through.

9 medium baking potatoes (about 3 pounds), peeled and quartered
3 eggs
3/4 cup butter, softened, *divided*
2 tablespoons snipped fresh dill *or* 2 teaspoons dill weed
1-1/2 teaspoons salt
1/4 teaspoon pepper
3 to 6 tablespoons milk

Place potatoes in a Dutch oven or large kettle and cover with water; bring to a boil. Reduce heat; cover and simmer for 20-25 minutes or until tender. Drain. In a large mixing bowl, mash potatoes. Beat in the eggs, 6 tablespoons of butter, dill, salt, pepper and enough milk to achieve a light fluffy consistency.

Using a pastry bag or heavy-duty resealable plastic bag and a large star tip, pipe potatoes into 12 mounds on two greased baking sheets. Melt remaining butter; drizzle over potatoes. Bake at 400° for 20 minutes or until golden brown. **Yield:** 12 servings.

Hot Fruit Soup

Some fruit soups call for soaking dried fruit overnight. But my fast version conveniently uses canned fruits. This makes a unique ham dinner side dish.
—Rose Kammerling, Sun City, Arizona

1 can (21 ounces) cherry pie filling
1 can (20 ounces) pineapple tidbits, drained
1 can (15-1/4 ounces) apricot halves, drained and halved
1 can (15 ounces) sliced peaches, drained

1 can (15 ounces) sliced pears, drained
1 can (11 ounces) mandarin oranges, drained
1 cup golden raisins

In a large bowl, combine all ingredients; mix well. Pour into an ungreased 2-1/2-qt. baking dish. Bake, uncovered, at 350° for 25-30 minutes or until bubbly. **Yield:** 16-18 servings.

Creamy Vegetable Medley

With its rich, cheesy sauce and golden onion topping, this casserole has broad appeal.
Because of that—and the fact that it's quick to prepare—I frequently prepare it for many functions.
—Pat Waymire, Yellow Springs, Ohio

1 package (16 ounces) frozen broccoli, carrot and cauliflower blend
1 can (10-3/4 ounces) condensed cream of mushroom soup, undiluted
1 cup (4 ounces) shredded Swiss cheese, *divided*
1/3 cup sour cream
1 jar (2 ounces) diced pimientos, drained
1/4 teaspoon salt
1/4 teaspoon pepper
1 can (2.8 ounces) french-fried onions, *divided*

In a bowl, combine the vegetables, soup, 1/2 cup cheese, sour cream, pimientos, salt, pepper and half of the onions. Pour into a greased 1-1/2-qt. baking dish. Cover and bake at 350° for 30-40 minutes or until the edges are browned. Uncover; sprinkle with the remaining cheese and onions. Bake 5 minutes longer or until the cheese is melted. **Yield:** 8 servings.

Slow-Cooked Chowder

The hectic holidays often leave little time for cooking. That's why this slow cooker recipe
is a favorite. I just combine the ingredients, flip a switch and forget it!
—Pam Leonard, Aberdeen, South Dakota

5 cups water
5 teaspoons chicken bouillon granules
8 medium potatoes, cubed
2 medium onions, chopped
1 medium carrot, thinly sliced
1 celery rib, thinly sliced
1/4 cup butter, cubed
1 teaspoon salt
1/4 teaspoon pepper
1 can (12 ounces) evaporated milk
1 tablespoon minced fresh parsley

In a 5-qt. slow cooker, combine the first nine ingredients. Cover and cook on high for 1 hour. Reduce heat to low; cover and cook for 5-6 hours or until vegetables are tender. Stir in milk and parsley; heat through. **Yield:** 12 servings (about 3 quarts).

SIMPLE SOUP GARNISHES

ADDING A GARNISH to soup before serving gives color and adds to the flavor and texture. Easy ideas include: finely chopped green onions or chives, minced fresh parsley, shredded cheddar cheese, grated or shredded Parmesan cheese, a dollop of sour cream and plain or seasoned croutons.

Cauliflower Zucchini Toss

(Pictured at right)

I appreciate make-ahead recipes like this that keep me out of the kitchen.
—Paula Marchesi
Lenhartsville, Pennsylvania

2 cups cauliflowerets
2 cups sliced zucchini
1/2 cup sliced green onions
1/2 cup halved pitted ripe olives
1/3 cup vegetable oil
1/4 cup orange juice
2 tablespoons white wine vinegar
1 teaspoon dried tarragon
1 teaspoon grated orange peel
1/2 teaspoon salt
1/4 to 1/2 teaspoon pepper
8 cups torn salad greens

Add 1 in. of water to a saucepan; add cauliflower. Bring to a boil. Reduce heat; cover and simmer for 5-8 minutes or until crisp-tender. Rinse in cold water; drain and place in a large bowl. Add zucchini, onions and olives; toss.

In a jar with a tight-fitting lid, combine the oil, orange juice, vinegar, tarragon, orange peel, salt and pepper; shake well. Pour over cauliflower mixture and toss to coat. Cover and refrigerate for 2 hours. Just before serving, toss with salad greens. **Yield:** 14-16 servings.

Bacon Wild Rice Bake

This casserole is very special to me. I found the recipe when visiting a friend in Canada, and now my daughter sends me wild rice from Wisconsin. I like to serve this with Cornish game hens.
—Nancy Schlinger, Middleport, New York

2 cups uncooked wild rice
2 small green peppers, chopped
1 large onion, chopped
2 tablespoons butter
2 jars (4-1/2 ounces *each*) sliced mushrooms, drained
1 teaspoon salt
4 to 6 bacon strips, cooked and crumbled

In a large saucepan, cook wild rice according to package directions. Meanwhile, in a skillet, saute green peppers and onion in butter until tender. Add mushrooms and salt; heat through. Stir into wild rice; add bacon.

Transfer to a greased 13-in. x 9-in. x 2-in. baking dish. Cover and bake at 350° for 30 minutes. Uncover; bake 5-10 minutes longer or until heated through. **Yield:** 12-14 servings.

Tangy Red Cabbage

I often make Christmas dinners for the elderly ladies of our church who live alone.
Many are of German descent and look forward to this traditional cabbage dish.
—*Joan Solberg, Ashland, Wisconsin*

1 medium head red cabbage,
  shredded
10 bacon strips, diced
1 cup white vinegar
6 tablespoons sugar
2 teaspoons dill seed
2 teaspoons salt
Minced fresh parsley *or* parsley
  sprigs, optional

Place cabbage in a large bowl; cover with boiling water. Let stand for 5 minutes; drain. In a Dutch oven, cook bacon over medium heat until crisp. Drain, reserving 1/4 cup drippings; set bacon aside. Stir vinegar, sugar, dill seed and salt into drippings until sugar is dissolved.

Stir in cabbage; bring to a boil. Reduce heat; cover and simmer for 1 to 1-1/2 hours or until cabbage is tender. Stir in bacon. Garnish with parsley if desired. **Yield:** 10 servings.

Creamed Pearl Onions

When our children were small, we always celebrated Christmas at our house. This was one of many recipes I relied on that can be prepared a day in advance, which gave me more time to spend with guests. Everyone expected to see this vegetable dish on the table every year.
—*Barbara Caserman, Lake Havasu City, Arizona*

50 pearl onions
1/4 cup butter
1/4 cup all-purpose flour
1/2 teaspoon salt
Dash pepper
1 cup chicken broth
1 cup half-and-half cream
1/4 cup minced fresh parsley
3 tablespoons grated Parmesan
  cheese
Pimiento strips, optional

In a Dutch oven or large kettle, bring 6 cups water to a boil. Add pearl onions; boil for 10-15 minutes or until tender. Drain and rinse in cold water; peel and set aside.

In a saucepan, melt butter. Stir in flour, salt and pepper until smooth. Gradually add broth and cream, stirring constantly. Bring to a boil; cook and stir for 2 minutes or until thickened and bubbly. Stir in parsley, cheese and onions.

Pour into an ungreased 1-qt. baking dish. Cover and refrigerate overnight. Remove from the refrigerator 30 minutes before baking. Cover and bake at 350° for 15 minutes; stir. Top with pimientos if desired. Bake, uncovered, 10 minutes longer or until bubbly and heated through. **Yield:** 4-6 servings.

Colorful Veggie Casserole

(Pictured at right)

When I retired from the U.S. Army a few years ago, I began tinkering in the kitchen and now work in there regularly. This casserole is chock-full of vegetables and flavor and couldn't be easier to prepare.

—Marion White
La Center, Washington

1 cup chopped green onions
1 large carrot, shredded
2 celery ribs, chopped
1 small green pepper, chopped
1 small sweet red pepper, chopped
6 garlic cloves, minced
2 tablespoons vegetable oil
3 pounds frozen cubed hash brown potatoes, thawed
2 cans (10-3/4 ounces *each*) condensed cream of chicken soup, undiluted
1-1/2 cups (6 ounces) shredded cheddar cheese, *divided*
1-1/2 cups (6 ounces) shredded mozzarella cheese, *divided*

2 tablespoons minced fresh parsley *or* 2 teaspoons dried parsley flakes
1 teaspoon salt
Paprika

In a large skillet, saute onions, carrot, celery, peppers and garlic in oil until crisp-tender. Transfer to a large bowl; add hash browns, soup, 1 cup cheddar cheese, 1 cup mozzarella cheese, parsley and salt; mix well.

Pour into a greased 3-qt. baking dish. Sprinkle with remaining cheeses and paprika. Bake, uncovered, at 350° for 1 hour or until golden brown. **Yield:** 12-16 servings.

WINTER Celebrations

Home-Baked Holiday Breads

MOST FOLKS agree the holidays just wouldn't be the same without a sweet and savory assortment of home-baked breads, rolls and muffins.

Homemade goodies not only make great gifts from the kitchen, they also add flavorful variety to any holiday breakfast, lunch, dinner...or even snack.

Family, friends and neighbors will eagerly accept a basket brimming with Easy Batter Rolls, Pineapple Cherry Loaves and Cherry-Go-Round.

From tasty quick breads and mouth-watering muffins to tender rolls and yummy yeast breads, you're sure to find an oven-fresh baked good fit for any occasion!

"FLOUR"ISHING FAVORITES

(Clockwise from top left)

Easy Batter Rolls (p. 252)

Pineapple Cherry Loaves (p. 253)

Cherry-Go-Round (p. 255)

Easy Batter Rolls

(Pictured on page 250)

The first thing my guests ask when they come for dinner is if I'm serving these dinner rolls.
The buns are so light, airy and delicious that I'm constantly asked for the recipe.
— *Thomasina Brunner, Gloversville, New York*

3 cups all-purpose flour
2 tablespoons sugar
1 package (1/4 ounce) active
  dry yeast
1 teaspoon salt
1 cup water
2 tablespoons butter
1 egg
Melted butter

In a mixing bowl, combine 2 cups flour, sugar, yeast and salt. In a saucepan, heat water and butter to 120°-130°. Add to dry ingredients; beat until blended. Add egg; beat on low speed for 30 seconds, then on high for 3 minutes. Stir in remaining flour (batter will be stiff). Do not knead. Cover and let rise in a warm place until doubled, about 30 minutes.

Stir dough down. Fill greased muffin cups half full. Cover and let rise until doubled, about 40 minutes.

Bake at 350° for 15-20 minutes or until golden brown. Cool for 1 minute before removing from pan to a wire rack. Brush tops with melted butter. **Yield:** 1 dozen.

Norwegian Christmas Bread

When my husband became the minister for a church in an area populated with Norwegians,
my father-in-law was delighted because I had easy access to recipes he enjoyed as a child.
This is a traditional Christmas bread, but I make it for any holiday we get together.
— *Deborah Petersen, Princeton, New Jersey*

1 package (1/4 ounce) active
  dry yeast
1 cup warm water
  (110° to 115°)
1/2 cup sugar
1 egg
1/4 cup butter, softened
1/2 teaspoon salt
1 teaspoon ground cardamom
3-3/4 to 4 cups all-purpose
  flour
1/2 cup raisins
1/2 cup diced citron *or* mixed
  candied fruit

In a mixing bowl, dissolve yeast in warm water. Add sugar, egg, butter, salt, cardamom and 2 cups flour; mix well. Stir in raisins, citron and enough remaining flour to form a soft dough.

Turn onto a floured surface; knead until smooth and elastic, about 6-8 minutes. Place in a greased bowl, turning once to grease top. Cover and let rise in a warm place until doubled, about 1 hour.

Punch dough down; divide in half. Shape each portion into a flattened ball. Place in two greased 9-in. round baking pans. Cover and let rise in a warm place until doubled, about 1 hour.

Bake at 350° for 30-35 minutes or until golden brown. Remove from pans to cool on wire racks. **Yield:** 2 loaves.

Pineapple Cherry Loaves

(Pictured at right and on page 251)

Pineapple adds a fun twist to this holiday quick bread, plus it makes each delicious bite nice and moist. My family prefers this to traditional fruitcake.
—Dolores Peltier, Warren, Michigan

1-3/4 cups butter, softened
2 cups sugar
8 eggs
1 teaspoon vanilla extract
3-3/4 cups all-purpose flour
1 teaspoon salt
1 teaspoon baking powder
2 cans (8 ounces *each*) pineapple chunks, drained
1 jar (10 ounces) red maraschino cherries, drained and halved
1 jar (10 ounces) green maraschino cherries, drained and halved
2 cups chopped walnuts

In a mixing bowl, cream butter and sugar. Add eggs, one at a time, beating well after each addition. Beat in vanilla. Combine the flour, salt and baking powder; add to creamed mixture until well blended. Stir in pineapple, cherries and nuts. Pour into three greased and floured 8-in. x 4-in. x 2-in. loaf pans.

Bake at 325° for 1-1/4 hours or until a toothpick comes out clean. Cool for 10 minutes before removing from pans to wire racks. **Yield:** 3 loaves.

SHORT-TERM BREAD STORAGE

TO KEEP quick and yeast breads fresh and flavorful for a few days, it's important to store them properly. (For longer storage, see "Facts About Freezing Breads" on page 261.)
- Quick breads and muffins are often quite moist. To prevent them from spoiling, let cool completely, then wrap tightly in foil or plastic wrap and let stand overnight. Refrigerate any leftovers the next day.
- Yeast breads, too, should be cooled completely and placed in an airtight container or bag. Store at room temperature in a cool dry place for 2 to 3 days. Yeast breads made with cheese or meat should be refrigerated.

Banana Buttermilk Muffins

Like my father, I love to spend time in the kitchen inventing new recipes.
There are few pleasures greater than sampling one of these warm muffins on a winter day.
—Kimberly Kronenberg, New Lenox, Illinois

1/2 cup butter, softened
1 cup sugar
2 eggs
2 large ripe bananas, mashed
    (about 1 cup)
1 teaspoon vanilla extract
2 cups all-purpose flour
1 teaspoon salt
1 teaspoon baking powder
1/2 teaspoon baking soda
1 cup buttermilk
TOPPING:
1/4 cup all-purpose flour
1/4 cup packed brown sugar
1/4 cup quick-cooking oats
2 tablespoons cold butter

In a mixing bowl, cream butter and sugar. Add eggs, one at a time, beating well after each. Add bananas and vanilla; mix well. Combine the flour, salt, baking powder and baking soda; add to creamed mixture alternately with buttermilk.

Fill greased or paper-lined muffin cups two-thirds full. For the topping, combine the flour, brown sugar and oats. Cut in butter until crumbly. Sprinkle a rounded teaspoonful over each muffin.

Bake at 400° for 16-20 minutes or until a toothpick comes out clean. Cool for 5 minutes before removing from pans to wire racks. **Yield:** 15 muffins.

Poppy Seed Cranberry Bread

I make poppy seed bread about once a month. So one Christmas, I decided to make it a little more
festive by stirring in some cranberries. My family loved the colorful addition.
—Cindy Harmon, Stuarts Draft, Virginia

2-1/2 cups all-purpose flour
3/4 cup sugar
2 tablespoons poppy seeds
3 teaspoons baking powder
1/2 teaspoon salt
1 egg
1 cup milk
1/3 cup butter, melted
2 teaspoons vanilla extract
2 teaspoons grated lemon peel
1 cup fresh *or* frozen
    cranberries, thawed and
    chopped
ICING:
1/2 cup confectioners' sugar
2 teaspoons milk

In a mixing bowl, combine the flour, sugar, poppy seeds, baking powder and salt. Combine the egg, milk, butter, vanilla and lemon peel; add to dry ingredients, beating on low speed just until moistened. Fold in cranberries. Pour into a greased 8-in. x 4-in. x 2-in. loaf pan.

Bake at 350° for 55-60 minutes or until a toothpick comes out clean. Cool for 10 minutes before removing from pan to a wire rack. Combine icing ingredients; drizzle over cooled loaf. **Yield:** 1 loaf.

Cherry-Go-Round

(Pictured at right and on page 250)

This fancy coffee cake is surprisingly easy.
It makes a great gift.
—Kathy McCreary, Wichita, Kansas

1 package (1/4 ounce) active
   dry yeast
1/4 cup warm water (110° to 115°)
1 cup warm milk (110° to 115°)
1/2 cup sugar
1/2 cup butter, softened
1 teaspoon salt
1 egg
4-1/2 to 5 cups all-purpose flour
FILLING:
   2 cans (16 ounces *each*)
     pitted tart cherries, well
     drained
1/2 cup all-purpose flour
1/2 cup packed brown sugar
1/2 cup chopped pecans
ICING:
   1 cup confectioners' sugar
1/4 teaspoon vanilla extract
1 to 2 tablespoons milk

In a mixing bowl, dissolve yeast in warm water. Add warm milk, sugar, butter, salt, egg and 2 cups flour; beat until smooth. Stir in enough remaining flour to form a soft dough.

Turn onto a lightly floured surface; knead until smooth and elastic, about 6-8 minutes. Place in a greased bowl, turning once to grease top. Cover and refrigerate for at least 2 hours or overnight.

Line two baking sheets with foil and grease well; set aside. Punch dough down. Turn onto a lightly floured sur-face; divide in half. Roll each portion into a 14-in. x 7-in. rectangle. Spread cherries over dough to within 1/2 in. of edges. Combine the flour, brown sugar and pecans; sprinkle over cherries.

Roll up jelly-roll style, starting with a long side; pinch seams and tuck ends under. Place seam side down on prepared baking sheets; pinch ends together to form a ring. With kitchen scissors, cut from outside edge two-thirds of the way toward center of ring at 1-in. intervals. Separate strips slightly and twist to allow filling to show. Cover and let rise until doubled, about 1 hour.

Bake at 350° for 20-25 minutes or until golden brown. Remove from pans to wire racks. Combine icing ingredients; drizzle over warm coffee cakes. **Yield:** 2 coffee cakes.

SHAPING A COFFEE CAKE RING

1. With a scissors, make cuts two-thirds of the way through dough at 1-inch intervals.

2. Separate the strips slightly, twisting each individually to show the filling inside.

Country White Bread

Knowing how much I like to bake bread, an aunt shared this recipe with me.
I enjoy making it on rainy days and giving the house a warm, homey feeling.
—*Nancy Perry, Sayre, Pennsylvania*

2 packages (1/4 ounce *each*)
　active dry yeast
3 cups warm water
　(110° to 115°)
1 egg
3 tablespoons shortening
3 tablespoons sugar
1 tablespoon salt
9 to 10 cups all-purpose flour
Melted butter

In a mixing bowl, dissolve yeast in warm water. Add the egg, shortening, sugar, salt and 5 cups flour; beat until smooth. Stir in enough remaining flour to form a stiff dough.

Turn onto a floured surface; knead until smooth and elastic, about 6-8 minutes. Place in a greased bowl, turning once to grease top. Cover and let rise in a warm place until doubled, about 1 hour.

Punch dough down. Turn onto a lightly floured surface; divide in half. Roll each portion into a 12-in. x 10-in. rectangle. Roll up jelly-roll style, starting with a long side; pinch seam to seal. Place seam side down on a greased baking sheet. Cover and let rise until doubled, about 30 minutes.

With a sharp knife, make five shallow diagonal slashes across the top of each loaf. Bake at 400° for 35-40 minutes or until golden brown. Remove from pans to wire racks. Brush with butter. **Yield:** 2 loaves.

Favorite Pull-Apart Rolls

I've been using this recipe for soft pull-apart rolls for over 20 years and have yet to tire of it.
This easy-to-make recipe yields wonderful results.
—*Gay Nell Nicholas, Henderson, Texas*

3/4 cup shortening
3/4 cup sugar
1 cup boiling water
2 packages (1/4 ounce *each*)
　active dry yeast
1 cup warm water
　(110° to 115°)
2 eggs
1 teaspoon salt
1 teaspoon baking powder
1/2 teaspoon baking soda
6 to 7 cups all-purpose flour

In a mixing bowl, cream shortening and sugar. Add boiling water; mix well. Cool to 110°-115°. Dissolve yeast in warm water. Add yeast mixture and eggs to creamed mixture; mix well. Add salt, baking powder, baking soda and 5 cups flour; beat until smooth. Stir in enough remaining flour to form a soft dough.

Turn onto a floured surface; knead until smooth and elastic, about 6-8 minutes. Do not let rise. Divide into 32 pieces; shape each into a ball. Place in two greased 9-in. round baking pans. Cover and let rise in a warm place until doubled, about 1-1/2 hours.

Bake at 400° for 18-22 minutes or until golden brown. Remove from pans to wire racks. **Yield:** 32 rolls.

Cranberry Apple Muffins

(Pictured at right)

It's sometimes difficult to get our daughter to eat healthy foods, but she gobbles up these fruit-filled muffins. Although these are a "must" around the holidays, I keep cranberries in the freezer so I can whip up a batch any time of year.
—Esther Bowers, Westland, Michigan

2 cups shredded peeled apples
1-1/3 cups sugar
1 cup chopped fresh *or* frozen cranberries, thawed
1 cup shredded carrots
1 cup chopped nuts
2 eggs, lightly beaten
1/2 cup vegetable oil
2-1/2 cups all-purpose flour
3 teaspoons baking powder
2 teaspoons baking soda
2 teaspoons ground cinnamon
2 teaspoons ground coriander, optional
1/2 teaspoon salt

In a bowl, combine apples and sugar; let stand for 10 minutes. Add cranberries, carrots, nuts, eggs and oil; mix well. Combine the flour, baking powder, baking soda, cinnamon, coriander if desired and salt; stir into apple mixture just until moistened. Fill paper-lined muffin cups two-thirds full.

Bake at 375° for 25-30 minutes or until a toothpick comes out clean. Cool for 5 minutes before removing from pans to wire racks. **Yield:** 1-1/2 dozen.

BAKING POWDER AND SODA SHOULD BUBBLE

IF YOU don't seem to have much success with making baked goods, there may be a simple answer—your baking powder and/or baking soda may not be fresh. The shelf life for these products is about 6 months, but here's how to test for freshness to be sure:

• For baking powder, place 1 teaspoon baking powder in a cup and add 1/3 cup hot tap water.
• For baking soda, place 1/4 teaspoon baking soda in a cup and add 2 teaspoons vinegar.

If active bubbling occurs, the products are fine to use. If not, they should be replaced. When buying a new can, check for an expiration date.

Traditional Whole Wheat Bread

With all the sweet breads that get served during the holidays, it's nice to make this nutritious wheat bread. I use it for sandwiches and also enjoy it toasted and buttered.
—*Carol Forcum, Marion, Illinois*

3 cups whole wheat flour
1/2 cup toasted wheat germ
1/4 cup mashed potato flakes
1/4 cup nonfat dry milk powder
2 tablespoons sugar
2 packages (1/4 ounce *each*)
  active dry yeast
2 teaspoons salt
2 cups water
3 tablespoons vegetable oil
3 eggs
3 to 3-1/2 cups all-purpose flour

In a mixing bowl, combine the first seven ingredients. In a saucepan, heat water and oil to 120°-130°. Add to dry ingredients; beat until blended. Beat in eggs until smooth. Stir in enough all-purpose flour to form a soft dough.

Turn onto a floured surface; knead until smooth and elastic, about 8-10 minutes. Place in a greased bowl, turning once to grease top. Cover and let rise in a warm place until doubled, about 1 hour.

Punch dough down. Turn onto a lightly floured surface; divide in half. Shape into loaves. Place in two greased 9-in. x 5-in. x 3-in. loaf pans. Cover and let rise until doubled, about 45 minutes.

Bake at 375° for 35-40 minutes or until golden brown. Remove from pans to cool on wire racks. **Yield:** 2 loaves.

Orange Chocolate Muffins

No one can resist these muffins, which feature a pleasant pairing of orange and bittersweet chocolate. They're sensational for breakfast with a warm mug of coffee or tea.
—*Anna Pidhirny, Gibsonia, Pennsylvania*

1/2 cup butter, softened
1 cup sugar
2 eggs
1/2 cup sour cream
1/2 cup orange juice
2 to 3 tablespoons grated
  orange peel
2 cups all-purpose flour
1 teaspoon baking powder
1/2 teaspoon baking soda
3 squares (1 ounce *each*)
  bittersweet chocolate, grated

In a mixing bowl, cream butter and sugar. Add eggs, one at a time, beating well after each addition. Beat in the sour cream, orange juice and peel. Combine the flour, baking powder, baking soda and grated chocolate; stir into creamed mixture just until moistened. Fill paper-lined muffin cups three-fourths full.

Bake at 400° for 15-20 minutes or until a toothpick comes out clean. Cool for 5 minutes before removing from pans to wire racks. **Yield:** about 1-1/2 dozen.

Festive Biscuit Strips

(Pictured at right)

Many people—especially children—don't care for fruitcake, so I came up with this sweet biscuit recipe. A few years ago, these strips earned high honors in a recipe contest sponsored by a local newspaper.
— Tena Huckleby, Greeneville, Tennessee

    2 cups self-rising flour
1-3/4 cups all-purpose flour
    1 teaspoon ground cinnamon
  3/4 cup cold butter
1-1/4 cups milk
  1/4 cup chopped fresh *or* frozen
        cranberries
  1/4 cup chopped navel orange
  1/4 cup crushed pineapple,
        drained
  1/4 cup chopped red maraschino
        cherries
  1/4 cup chopped green
        maraschino cherries
ICING:
  1/2 cup confectioners' sugar
    3 to 4 teaspoons milk

In a bowl, combine flours and cinnamon. Cut in butter until mixture resembles coarse crumbs. Gradually add milk, stirring with a fork until mixture forms a soft dough. Fold in the cranberries, orange, pineapple and cherries.

Turn onto a lightly floured surface; knead 4-5 times. Pat into a 13-in. x 9-in. rectangle. Cut into 3-in. x 1-in. strips; place on greased baking sheets. Bake at 425° for 11-15 minutes or until golden brown. Combine icing ingredients; drizzle over strips. Serve warm. **Yield:** about 3 dozen.

Editor's Note: As a substitute for *each* cup of self-rising flour, place 1-1/2 teaspoons baking powder and 1/2 teaspoon salt in a measuring cup. Add all-purpose flour to measure 1 cup.

Chocolate Yeast Bread

Your family will love this tender loaf of chocolate bread.
Slices are excellent when toasted and spread with butter, cream cheese or peanut butter.
—*Laura Cryts, Derry, New Hampshire*

4-1/2 cups all-purpose flour
1/3 cup baking cocoa
2 tablespoons sugar
1 package (1/4 ounce) active dry yeast
1 teaspoon salt
1/4 teaspoon baking soda
1 cup water
1/2 cup milk
1/2 cup semisweet chocolate chips
2 tablespoons butter
1 egg

In a mixing bowl, combine 1-1/4 cups flour, cocoa, sugar, yeast, salt and baking soda. In a saucepan, heat the water, milk, chocolate chips and butter; stir until chocolate is melted. Cool to 120°-130°. Add to dry ingredients; beat on medium speed for 2 minutes. Add 1/2 cup flour and egg; beat on high for 2 minutes. Stir in enough remaining flour to form a stiff dough.

Turn onto a floured surface; knead until smooth and elastic, about 6-8 minutes. Place in a greased bowl, turning once to grease top. Cover and let rise in a warm place until doubled, about 1 hour.

Punch dough down. Turn onto a lightly floured surface; divide in half. Shape into loaves. Place in two greased 8-in. x 4-in. x 2-in. loaf pans. Cover and let rise until doubled, about 1 hour.

Bake at 375° for 25-30 minutes or until browned. Remove from pans to cool on wire racks. **Yield:** 2 loaves.

Pecan Graham Muffins

These unique muffins have a little heavier texture than other varieties, making them perfect for
cool days. Although they were skeptical at first, my family now says these are their favorite muffins.
—*Kim Franzen, San Bernardino, California*

1-1/3 cups graham cracker crumbs (about 22 squares)
1-1/4 cups all-purpose flour
1/2 cup sugar
1 teaspoon baking powder
3/4 teaspoon baking soda
1/4 teaspoon salt
1 egg
1 cup milk
1/3 cup vegetable oil
1/2 cup chopped pecans

In a large bowl, combine the first six ingredients. In another bowl, beat the egg, milk and oil; stir into dry ingredients just until moistened. Fold in pecans. Fill greased or paper-lined muffin cups two-thirds full.

Bake at 375° for 18-22 minutes or until a toothpick comes out clean. Cool for 5 minutes before removing from pan to a wire rack. **Yield:** 1 dozen.

Editor's Note: Four dozen miniature muffin cups may be used; bake for 12-15 minutes.

Walnut Marmalade Mini Loaves

(Pictured at right)

The orange marmalade and fresh juice in this bread give it a citrusy aroma, moist texture and warm golden color. It's almost like giving friends a gift of home-baked sunshine!
—Michele Bragg, Palm City, Florida

2-1/2 cups all-purpose flour
1/3 cup sugar
1 tablespoon baking powder
1 teaspoon salt
1 jar (12 ounces) orange marmalade
1 cup orange juice
3 tablespoons vegetable oil
1 egg
1 cup chopped walnuts

In a mixing bowl, combine the flour, sugar, baking powder and salt. Combine the marmalade, orange juice, oil and egg; stir into dry ingredients just until moistened. Stir in walnuts. Pour into three greased 5-3/4-in. x 3-in. x 2-in. loaf pans.

Bake at 350° for 40-50 minutes or until a toothpick comes out clean. Cool for 10 minutes before removing from pans to wire racks. **Yield:** 3 loaves.

FACTS ABOUT FREEZING BREADS

DURING the hectic holiday season, it's nice to bake and freeze some breads, rolls and muffins a few weeks in advance.

After the baked goods have cooled completely, follow these steps to ensure they remain fresh and flavorful in the freezer.

- For best results, don't top bread with icing, frosting or glaze before freezing.
- Wrap baked goods tightly in freezer-safe plastic bags, airtight containers, heavy-duty aluminum foil or freezer paper. (Place coffee cakes and rolls on foil-wrapped cardboard before wrapping and freezing.)
- Make sure the temperature of your freezer is 0° or less.
- Most baked goods are fine to freeze for up to 1 month.
- To thaw, unwrap slightly and thaw at room temperature for 2 to 3 hours.
- The baked goods can be served at room temperature. Or to serve warm, wrap in foil and bake at 350° for 15 to 20 minutes.

Golden Pan Rolls

When I'm having company for dinner, I bake these rolls during the day. Then the house has a wonderful aroma when the guests arrive. The ranch dressing mix adds terrific flavor.
—*Kimm Avans, De Soto, Texas*

3-1/2 to 4 cups all-purpose flour
2 tablespoons sugar
1 envelope ranch salad dressing mix
2 packages (1/4 ounce *each*) active dry yeast
1 can (10-3/4 ounces) condensed cheddar cheese soup, undiluted
1/4 cup butter
1/4 cup milk
2 eggs
2 tablespoons cornmeal, *divided*

In a mixing bowl, combine 1-1/2 cups flour, sugar, dressing mix and yeast. In a saucepan, heat the soup, butter and milk to 120°-130°. Add to dry ingredients; beat until moistened. Add eggs; beat on medium speed for 3 minutes. Stir in enough remaining flour to form a stiff dough.

Turn onto a floured surface; knead until smooth and elastic, about 8-10 minutes. Place in a greased bowl, turning once to grease top. Cover and let rise in a warm place until doubled, about 1 hour.

Punch dough down. Turn onto a lightly floured surface. Divide into 24 pieces; shape each into a ball. Grease a 13-in. x 9-in. x 2-in. baking pan and sprinkle with 1 tablespoon cornmeal. Place rolls in pan; sprinkle with remaining cornmeal. Cover and let rise in a warm place until doubled, about 30 minutes.

Bake at 400° for 15-18 minutes or until golden brown. Remove from pan to wire racks. **Yield:** 2 dozen.

Potato Muffins

Come in from the cold to enjoy these moist parsley-flecked muffins. They're comforting and delicious with a steaming bowl of soup, a savory stew or a favorite casserole.
—*Marlene Loecke, Des Moines, Iowa*

1 egg
2/3 cup milk
1-1/2 cups all-purpose flour
2 tablespoons sugar
3 teaspoons baking powder
1 teaspoon salt
1-1/2 cups mashed potatoes (prepared with milk and butter)
1 tablespoon minced fresh parsley

In a bowl, beat egg and milk. Combine the flour, sugar, baking powder and salt; stir into egg mixture just until moistened. Fold in potatoes and parsley. Fill greased muffin cups two-thirds full.

Bake at 400° for 30-35 minutes or until a toothpick comes out clean. Cool for 5 minutes before removing from pan to a wire rack. Serve warm. **Yield:** 1 dozen.

Cardamom Braids

(Pictured at right)

This treasured recipe reflects my Norwegian heritage. The subtle hint of cardamom is undeniably good.
—Sally Nelsen, Tempe, Arizona

  2 packages (1/4 ounce *each*)
    active dry yeast
1/2 cup warm water
    (110° to 115°)
1-1/2 cups warm milk
    (110° to 115°)
1-1/2 cups sugar
1/2 cup butter, softened
  3 eggs
  2 teaspoons ground cardamom
1/2 teaspoon salt
  9 to 10 cups all-purpose
    flour
Additional sugar

In a mixing bowl, dissolve yeast in warm water. Add warm milk, sugar, butter, 2 eggs, cardamom, salt and 6 cups flour; beat until smooth. Stir in enough remaining flour to form a soft dough.

Turn onto a floured surface; knead until smooth and elastic, about 6-8 minutes. Place in a greased bowl, turning once to grease top. Cover and let rise in a warm place until doubled, about 1-1/4 hours.

Punch dough down; cover and let rest for 10 minutes. Divide into fourths. Divide each portion into thirds; shape each into a 12-in. rope. Place three ropes on a greased baking sheet and braid; pinch ends to seal and tuck under. Repeat with remaining dough. Cover and let rise in a warm place until nearly doubled, about 45 minutes.

Beat remaining egg; brush over loaves. Sprinkle with sugar. Bake at 375° for 20-25 minutes or until golden brown. Remove from pans to wire racks. **Yield:** 4 loaves.

BRAIDING BREAD

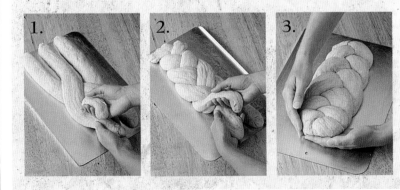

1. Place three ropes of dough almost touching on a baking sheet. Starting in the middle, loosely bring the left rope under the center rope. Bring the right rope under the new center rope and repeat until you reach the end.

2. Turn the pan and repeat braiding.

3. Press ends to seal; tuck under.

Dilly Bran Bread

My daughter, Deedee, used this recipe for her 4-H yeast bread project and received rave reviews.
This started out as a basic wheat recipe, but I eventually added dill to suit my family's tastes.
—Kathy Bock, Waterman, Illinois

3-1/2 to 4 cups all-purpose
    flour
  1 cup whole wheat flour
1/2 cup bran cereal
  2 tablespoons fresh dill *or* 2
    teaspoons dill weed
  2 packages (1/4 ounce *each*)
    active dry yeast
  2 teaspoons salt
  1 cup warm buttermilk
    (120° to 130°)
1/2 cup warm water
    (120° to 130°)
1/2 cup honey
1/2 cup shortening
  2 eggs
Butter, melted

In a mixing bowl, combine 1 cup all-purpose flour, whole wheat flour, cereal, dill, yeast and salt. Add the buttermilk, water, honey and shortening; beat until smooth. Add eggs; beat on medium speed for 3 minutes. Stir in enough remaining all-purpose flour to form a stiff dough.

Turn onto a floured surface; knead until smooth and elastic, about 5 minutes. Place in a greased bowl, turning once to grease top. Cover and let rise in a warm place until doubled, about 1 hour.

Punch dough down; divide in half. Shape into round loaves; place each in a greased 1-qt. baking dish. Cover and let rise until doubled, about 45 minutes.

Bake at 375° for 20-25 minutes or until golden brown. Remove from pans to wire racks. Brush with butter. **Yield:** 2 loaves.

Editor's Note: This recipe was tested with Post 100% Bran cereal. Warmed buttermilk will appear curdled.

Pecan Pumpkin Loaves

Pumpkin and a blend of spices make this quick bread a real holiday treat.
I can easily prepare three loaves to give to friends and neighbors as gifts.
—Leona Luecking, West Burlington, Iowa

3-1/3 cups all-purpose flour
  3 cups sugar
  2 teaspoons baking soda
  1 teaspoon salt
  1 teaspoon ground cinnamon
1/2 teaspoon ground ginger
1/4 teaspoon ground nutmeg
1/4 teaspoon ground cloves
  2 cups canned pumpkin
  4 eggs
  1 cup vegetable oil
2/3 cup water
1/2 teaspoon vanilla extract
3/4 cup chopped pecans

In a mixing bowl, combine the first eight ingredients. Add the pumpkin, eggs, oil, water and vanilla; mix well. Stir in the pecans. Pour into three greased 8-in. x 4-in. x 2-in. loaf pans.

Bake at 350° for 1 hour or until a toothpick comes out clean. Cool for 10 minutes before removing from pans to wire racks. **Yield:** 3 loaves.

Creamy Chocolate Crescents

(Pictured at right)

"Homemade" chocolate-filled treats are easy when you start with convenient refrigerated crescent rolls. They're impressive yet easy to serve for breakfast or a midday snack.
— Bill Hughes, Dolores, Colorado

2 packages (3 ounces *each*) cream cheese, softened
1/4 cup butter, softened
1/2 cup confectioners' sugar
2 tablespoons cornstarch
2 cups (12 ounces) semisweet chocolate chips, melted
1/2 teaspoon vanilla extract
4 tubes (8 ounces *each*) refrigerated crescent rolls
GLAZE:
2 eggs
1 tablespoon butter, melted
1/2 teaspoon almond extract
Confectioners' sugar, optional

In a mixing bowl, beat cream cheese, butter and sugar. Add cornstarch, melted chocolate and vanilla; beat until smooth. Unroll crescent roll dough; separate into triangles.

In a small bowl, whisk together eggs, butter and extract. Brush some over dough. Drop rounded teaspoonfuls of chocolate mixture at the wide end of each triangle; roll up from the wide end. Place point side down on greased baking sheets; curve ends slightly. Brush with remaining glaze.

Bake at 350° for 10-15 minutes or until golden. Remove from pans to cool on wire racks. Dust with confectioners' sugar if desired. **Yield:** about 2-1/2 dozen.

FESTIVE WAYS TO SERVE BUTTER

INSTEAD of having a stick of butter in a dish, impress guests with fun and festive shapes.

- To create butter cutouts, cut a chilled stick of butter into 1/4-inch slices. Cut out shapes with small cookie cutters. Simple shapes like bells, Christmas trees and circles work best.
- To make balls of butter, dip a melon baller in hot water and cut balls from a chilled 1-pound block of butter.
- Butter cutouts and balls can be made early in the day and refrigerated in an airtight container. Just before serving, arrange the cutouts or balls on a small lettuce-lined serving plate or on individual bread and butter plates.

Decked Out in Desserts

THERE IS no better way to wrap up a holiday dinner than by presenting a selection of sweets to relatives and friends.

Chocolate Truffle Dessert, Almond Puff Pastries and Peppermint Ice Cream are just a small taste of the tempting treats this chapter has to offer.

From tender cakes and pleasing pies to creamy ice cream and elegant desserts, you'll find a fitting finale for casual family suppers and special sit-down dinners for Christmas and throughout the year.

We also offer some thirst-quenching drinks and easy-to-make beverage stirrers to serve alongside all of your delectable desserts.

LAST BUT NOT LEAST
(Clockwise from top right)

Chocolate Truffle Dessert (p. 269)

Almond Puff Pastries (p. 268)

Peppermint Ice Cream (p. 270)

Decked Out in Desserts

Almond Puff Pastries

(Pictured on page 266)

My husband comes from a family of almond growers, so I use almonds often in my baking.
These puff pastries have a crisp topping and creamy filling.
— Barbara Harrison, Monte Sereno, California

1 package (17.3 ounces) frozen
    puff pastry, thawed
1 egg, *separated*
1 tablespoon water
1 cup sliced almonds
1 cup sugar
2 cups heavy whipping cream,
    whipped
Confectioners' sugar

Unfold pastry sheets onto a lightly floured surface. Cut each sheet into nine 3-in. squares. Place 1 in. apart on greased baking sheets. In a small bowl, beat egg yolk and water; brush over pastry squares. In another bowl, beat egg white; add almonds and sugar. Spread over each square. Bake at 375° for 20-25 minutes or until well puffed and browned. Cool completely on wire racks.

Split pastries in half horizontally. Fill with whipped cream; replace tops. Sprinkle with confectioners' sugar. Serve immediately. **Yield:** 18 servings.

Macaroon Cheesecake

No one can resist a slice of creamy cheesecake, especially around the holidays.
This version features coconut in the crust and topping.
— Tracy Powers, Cedar Springs, Michigan

1 cup flaked coconut, toasted
1/2 cup ground pecans
2 tablespoons butter, melted
FILLING:
3 packages (8 ounces *each*)
    cream cheese, softened
1/2 cup sugar
3 eggs
1/2 teaspoon vanilla extract
1/4 teaspoon almond extract
TOPPING:
1 egg white
1/2 teaspoon vanilla extract
1/3 cup sugar
2/3 cup flaked coconut, toasted

In a bowl, combine the coconut and pecans; stir in butter. Press onto the bottom of a greased 9-in. springform pan; set aside. In a mixing bowl, beat cream cheese and sugar until smooth. Add eggs, beating on low speed just until combined. Beat in extracts just until blended. Pour over crust. Place pan on a baking sheet. Bake at 350° for 35 minutes.

In a small mixing bowl, beat egg white and vanilla until soft peaks form. Gradually add sugar, beating until stiff peaks form. Fold in coconut. Carefully spread over top of cheesecake. Bake 20-25 minutes longer or until center is almost set. Cool on a wire rack for 10 minutes. Carefully run a knife around edge of pan to loosen; cool 1 hour longer. Refrigerate overnight. Remove sides of pan. **Yield:** 12-14 servings.

268 WINTER *Celebrations*

Chocolate Truffle Dessert

(Pictured at right and on page 267)

Chocolate lovers will savor this impressive dessert, featuring a brownie base and chocolate mousse filling.
—Lisa Otis, New Paltz, New York

1/4 cup butter, softened
1 cup sugar
2 squares (1 ounce *each*) unsweetened chocolate, melted and cooled
2 eggs, *separated*
1/4 cup milk
1 teaspoon vanilla extract
3/4 cup all-purpose flour
1/2 teaspoon baking powder
1/4 teaspoon salt
TRUFFLE MOUSSE:
2 cups (12 ounces) semisweet chocolate chips
1-1/4 cups butter
3/4 cup sugar
1 tablespoon instant coffee granules
5 egg yolks, lightly beaten
3 tablespoons vanilla extract
1 envelope unflavored gelatin
1/3 cup cold water
1 cup heavy whipping cream, whipped
14 to 16 creme-filled Pirouette cookies, cut into 1-1/2-inch pieces

In a mixing bowl, cream butter and sugar. Add chocolate; mix well. Add egg yolks, one at a time, beating well after each addition. Add milk and vanilla; mix well. Combine the flour, baking powder and salt; stir into chocolate mixture just until blended. In a small mixing bowl, beat egg whites until soft peaks form. Fold into chocolate mixture. Pour into a greased and floured 9-in. springform pan. Place pan on a baking sheet. Bake at 350° for 25-30 minutes or until a toothpick inserted near the center comes out clean. Cool completely on a wire rack.

For mousse, combine chocolate chips, butter, sugar and coffee granules in a saucepan. Cook and stir over low heat until sugar is dissolved and chips are melted. Stir a small amount of hot liquid into egg yolks; return all to pan. Cook and stir for 2 minutes or until mixture is slightly thickened. Remove from the heat; stir in vanilla. Sprinkle gelatin over cold water; let stand for 2 minutes. Add a small amount of hot liquid to gelatin; stir until gelatin is dissolved. Stir into chocolate mixture. Pour into a bowl. Set the bowl in a larger bowl of ice water; stir occasionally until thickened, about 30 minutes.

Remove sides of springform pan. Set aside 1/4 cup of mousse for garnish. Spoon half of the remaining mousse over brownie layer, spreading evenly over top and around sides.

In a mixing bowl, beat the remaining mousse and about a third of the whipped cream on low. Fold in remaining whipped cream. Spread over mousse layer. Place cookies around sides of dessert, gently pushing into mousse. Place reserved mousse in a resealable plastic bag or pastry bag; decorate top of dessert as desired. Cover and refrigerate for at least 4 hours or until firm. **Yield:** 12-16 servings.

Peppermint Ice Cream

(Pictured on page 266)

With flecks of peppermint candy, this ice cream is perfect for the holidays.
—Berneice Metcalf, Leavenworth, Washington

4 egg yolks
1-1/2 cups half-and-half cream
3/4 cup sugar
1/4 teaspoon salt
2 cups heavy whipping cream
4-1/2 to 6 teaspoons vanilla extract
1 to 1-1/4 cups crushed
    peppermint candy

In a heavy saucepan, whisk egg yolks, half-and-half, sugar and salt. Cook and stir over low heat until mixture reaches 160° and coats the back of a metal spoon. Remove from the heat. Place pan in a bowl of ice water; stir for 2 minutes. Stir in whipping cream and vanilla. Press plastic wrap onto surface of custard. Refrigerate for several hours or overnight.

Fill cylinder of ice cream freezer two-thirds full. (Refrigerate any remaining mixture until ready to freeze.) Freeze according to the manufacturer's directions. Stir in peppermint candy. Allow to ripen in ice cream freezer or firm up in the refrigerator freezer for 2-4 hours before serving. **Yield:** 1 quart.

Pineapple Dream Dessert

I often serve this creamy dessert because it's a light and refreshing end to any meal.
My mother made it when I was young, and now my daughters ask for it.
—Darlene Markel, Sublimity, Oregon

1-1/2 cups graham cracker crumbs
    (about 24 squares)
1/4 cup sugar
1/3 cup butter, melted
FILLING:
1/3 cup sugar
3 tablespoons cornstarch
2 cups milk
1 egg, beaten
1-1/2 teaspoons vanilla extract
1 can (20 ounces) crushed
    pineapple, drained
1 cup heavy whipping cream,
    whipped
1/2 cup pastel miniature
    marshmallows

In a bowl, combine the cracker crumbs, sugar and butter. Set aside 1/4 cup for topping. Press the remaining crumb mixture onto the bottom of a greased 11-in. x 7-in. x 2-in. baking dish. Bake at 350° for 10-14 minutes or until lightly browned and set. Cool on a wire rack.

For filling, combine sugar and cornstarch in a saucepan. Gradually whisk in milk until smooth. Bring to a boil; cook and stir for 2 minutes or until thickened. Remove from the heat. Stir a small amount of hot filling into egg; return all to the pan, stirring constantly. Bring to a gentle boil; cook and stir for 1 minute. Remove from the heat; stir in vanilla. Cool for 30 minutes, stirring several times.

Stir in pineapple. Pour over crust. Top with whipped cream (pan will be full). Sprinkle with marshmallows and reserved crumb mixture. Cover and refrigerate for at least 3 hours. **Yield:** 12-16 servings.

Chiffon Fruitcake

(Pictured at right)

Unlike typical fruitcakes, this tall cake is nice and light. The cinnamon whipped cream adds a bit of festive flair.
— *Tonya Farmer, Iowa City, Iowa*

2 cups plus 2 tablespoons
   all-purpose flour, *divided*
1-1/2 cups sugar
   3 teaspoons baking powder
   1 teaspoon salt
   1 teaspoon ground cinnamon
   7 eggs, *separated*
 3/4 cup water
 1/2 cup vegetable oil
   2 teaspoons grated lemon peel
   2 teaspoons vanilla extract
 1/2 teaspoon cream of tartar
 3/4 cup finely chopped candied
   cherries
 1/2 cup finely chopped pecans
 1/4 cup finely chopped mixed
   candied fruit

CINNAMON WHIPPED CREAM:
   1 cup heavy whipping cream
   2 tablespoons sugar
   1 teaspoon vanilla extract
 1/2 teaspoon ground cinnamon

In a large mixing bowl, combine 2 cups flour, sugar, baking powder, salt and cinnamon. In another bowl, whisk the egg yolks, water, oil, lemon peel and vanilla; add to dry ingredients and beat until well blended.

In another mixing bowl, beat egg whites and cream of tartar until soft peaks form; fold into batter. Toss cherries, pecans and candied fruit with remaining flour; fold into batter. Pour into an ungreased 10-in. tube pan.

Bake at 325° for 55-60 minutes or until top springs back when lightly touched. Immediately invert cake pan; cool completely. Carefully run a knife around edge of pan to loosen. Remove cake from pan and place on a serving plate.

In a small mixing bowl, beat the cream, sugar, vanilla and cinnamon until soft peaks form. Serve with cake. **Yield:** 12 servings (2 cups whipped cream).

Caramel-Chocolate Pecan Pie

This pleasing pie satisfies my family of chocoholics!
It's quick and easy to prepare, yet special enough for company.
—*Betty Thompson, Zionsville, Indiana*

1/2 cup crushed cream-filled
    chocolate sandwich cookies
    (5 cookies)
  4 teaspoons butter, melted
20 caramels
1/2 cup heavy whipping cream,
    divided
  2 cups chopped pecans
3/4 cup semisweet chocolate chips

Combine cookie crumbs and butter. Press onto the bottom of a 9-in. pie plate. Bake at 375° for 8-10 minutes or until set. Cool completely on a wire rack.

In a saucepan, melt caramels with 1/4 cup cream over low heat; stir until blended. Remove from the heat; stir in pecans. Spread evenly over crust. Refrigerate for 10 minutes or until set. In a small saucepan, melt chocolate chips with remaining cream. Drizzle over the caramel layer. Refrigerate for at least 1 hour before serving. **Yield:** 10-12 servings.

Lime Tart

For a change of pace from rich holiday desserts, try this light and cool pie.
When I'm short on time, I use a prepared graham cracker crust with equally good results.
—*Jane Dyrhaug, Andover, Minnesota*

1-1/2 cups graham cracker crumbs
    (about 24 squares)
  1/2 cup sugar
    6 tablespoons butter, melted
FILLING:
    1 cup sugar
    3 tablespoons cornstarch
    1 cup heavy whipping cream
  1/3 cup lime juice
  1/4 cup butter, cubed
    1 tablespoon grated lime peel
    1 cup (8 ounces) sour cream
TOPPING:
  1/2 cup heavy whipping cream
    2 tablespoons confectioners'
    sugar
  3/4 teaspoon vanilla extract

Combine cracker crumbs, sugar and butter; press onto the bottom and up the sides of a 9-in. pie plate. Bake at 350° for 12-15 minutes or until lightly browned. Cool completely on a wire rack.

In a saucepan, combine sugar and cornstarch. Gradually whisk in cream and lime juice until smooth. Add butter. Cook and stir over medium heat; gradually bring to a boil. Boil for 1 minute. Remove from the heat; stir in lime peel. Cool to room temperature; fold in sour cream. Pour into crust.

In a small mixing bowl, beat cream, confectioners' sugar and vanilla until stiff peaks form. Spread over filling. Chill for 4 hours or until ready to serve. **Yield:** 6-8 servings.

Minted Chocolate Torte

(Pictured at right)

Our family has enjoyed this pretty layered cake for years. It's a favorite for many occasions.
—Barbara Humiston, Tampa, Florida

1/2 cup shortening
1-1/3 cups sugar, *divided*
2-1/4 cups cake flour
3 teaspoons baking powder
1/2 teaspoon salt
1 cup milk
1-1/2 teaspoons vanilla extract
2 squares (1 ounce *each*) semisweet chocolate, finely chopped
3 egg whites

FILLING/TOPPING:
6 squares (1 ounce *each*) semisweet chocolate
1/4 cup butter
1-1/4 cups confectioners' sugar
3 tablespoons hot water
1 teaspoon vanilla extract
Dash salt

FROSTING:
2 cups whipped topping
1/2 teaspoon vanilla extract
1/8 teaspoon peppermint extract
1 to 2 drops green food coloring

In a large mixing bowl, cream shortening and 1 cup sugar. Combine the flour, baking powder and salt; add to the creamed mixture alternately with milk. Stir in vanilla and chocolate. In a small mixing bowl, beat egg whites on medium speed until soft peaks form. Gradually beat in the remaining sugar, 1 tablespoon at a time, on high until stiff peaks form. Fold into batter.

Pour into two greased and floured 9-in. round baking pans. Bake at 350° for 30-35 minutes or until a toothpick inserted near the center comes out clean. Cool for 10 minutes before removing from pans to wire racks.

In a small saucepan, melt the chocolate and butter over low heat until smooth. Remove from the heat; transfer to a mixing bowl. Beat in the confectioners' sugar, hot water, vanilla and salt.

To assemble, split each cake into two horizontal layers. Place bottom layer on a serving plate; top with 1/3 cup of filling. Repeat layers three times. In a bowl, gently combine the whipped topping, extracts and food coloring. Frost the sides of the cake. Store in the refrigerator. **Yield:** 12-16 servings.

Boston Cream Sponge Cake

I'm not a big fan of rich desserts, so I frequently make this light and fluffy cake.
—*Jan Badovinac, Harrison, Arkansas*

5 eggs
1 cup sugar
1/2 teaspoon salt
1 teaspoon vanilla extract
1-1/4 cups all-purpose flour
CUSTARD:
  3/4 cup sugar
2 tablespoons cornstarch
1-1/2 cups milk
6 egg yolks, beaten
1 teaspoon vanilla extract
1/2 cup butter, softened
CHOCOLATE FROSTING:
2 tablespoons butter, softened
1 square (1 ounce) unsweetened
  chocolate, melted and cooled
1 cup confectioners' sugar
3 tablespoons heavy whipping
  cream
1 teaspoon vanilla extract

In a mixing bowl, beat eggs until light and fluffy. Gradually add sugar and salt, beating until thick and lemon-colored. Add vanilla; mix well. Fold in flour, 2 tablespoons at a time. Pour into two greased and floured 9-in. round baking pans. Bake at 350° for 17-20 minutes or until cake springs back when lightly touched. Cool for 10 minutes before removing from pans to wire racks to cool completely.

For custard, combine sugar and cornstarch in a saucepan. Gradually stir in milk until smooth. Bring to a boil; cook and stir for 2 minutes. Remove from the heat. Stir a small amount of hot mixture into egg yolks; return all to the pan. Bring to a gentle boil, stirring constantly. Remove from the heat; stir in vanilla. Cool completely. In a mixing bowl, cream butter. Gradually beat in custard.

To assemble, split each cake into two horizontal layers. Place bottom layer on a serving plate; top with a third of the filling. Repeat layers twice. Top with remaining cake layer. In a small mixing bowl, combine frosting ingredients. Spread over top of cake. Refrigerate. **Yield:** 12-16 servings.

Toasted Almond Ice Cream Balls

You can keep these almond-coated ice cream balls on hand in the freezer for last-minute entertaining. Just whip up the sauce in minutes for a simply satisfying sweet treat.
—*Anita Curtis, Camarillo, California*

1 cup chopped almonds, toasted
1 quart French vanilla ice
  cream
HOT FUDGE SAUCE:
1 can (12 ounces) evaporated
  milk
2/3 cup semisweet chocolate chips
1/4 cup butter
2 cups confectioners' sugar

Place almonds in a shallow dish. Using an ice cream scoop, shape ice cream into balls. Roll each in almonds until well coated. Place on a waxed paper-lined baking sheet; cover and freeze.

For sauce, combine the milk, chocolate chips and butter in a saucepan. Cook and stir over low heat until melted and smooth. Add sugar; bring to a boil. Reduce heat. Simmer, stirring frequently, for 8-10 minutes or until thickened. Serve hot or cold over ice cream balls. **Yield:** 5 servings.

Candied Holly Cupcakes

(Pictured at right)

My mother often made these fruity spice cupcakes. Decorated with cherries and citron, they're so festive for Christmas.
— Pam Goodlet
Washington Island, Wisconsin

1/2 **cup shortening**
1 **cup sugar**
2 **eggs**
1-1/2 **cups all-purpose flour**
1/2 **teaspoon baking soda**
1/2 **teaspoon** *each* **ground cinnamon, allspice, nutmeg and cloves**
1/2 **cup buttermilk**
1/2 **cup cherry jam** *or* **flavor of your choice**
1/2 **cup chopped pecans**
1/4 **cup finely chopped candied cherries**
1/4 **cup finely chopped candied orange peel**
2 **cups prepared vanilla frosting**
9 **candied cherries, halved**
18 **green citron pieces** *or* **green candied pineapple pieces, cut into strips**

In a mixing bowl, cream shortening and sugar. Beat in eggs. Combine the flour, baking soda and spices; add to creamed mixture alternately with buttermilk. Stir in jam, pecans, cherries

and orange peel. Fill paper-lined muffin cups three-fourths full. Bake at 350° for 20-25 minutes or until a toothpick comes out clean. Cool for 5 minutes before removing from pans to wire racks.

Frost cooled cupcakes. Decorate with cherries for holly berries and citron for leaves. **Yield:** 1-1/2 dozen.

Cranberry Fruit Punch

This not-too-sweet punch is always a part of my Christmas buffet.
It can easily be doubled if you're having a large group.
—Ruth Andrewson, Peck, Idaho

5 cups cranberry juice, chilled
5 cups white grape juice, chilled
5 cups pineapple juice, chilled
3 cups ginger ale, chilled
1 pint orange sherbet

Just before serving, combine the juices and ginger ale in a punch bowl. Add scoops of sherbet. **Yield:** 24 servings (about 4 quarts).

Iced Coffee Slush

We have a tradition of hosting a game night during the holidays with nine other couples.
Our guests come for the camaraderie, but they sure love washing down delicious buffet
items with this sweet slush. Even non-coffee drinkers enjoy it.
—Iola Egle, McCook, Nebraska

3 cups hot strong brewed coffee
1-1/2 to 2 cups sugar
4 cups milk
2 cups half-and-half cream
1-1/2 teaspoons vanilla extract

In a freezer-safe bowl, stir coffee and sugar; until sugar is dissolved. Refrigerate until thoroughly chilled. Add the milk, cream and vanilla; freeze. Remove from the freezer several hours before serving. Chop mixture until slushy; serve immediately. **Yield:** 12 servings (2-1/4 quarts).

Sweet Citrus Punch

The wonderful rosy color of this beverage makes it a natural choice to serve at Christmas.
I keep the ingredients on hand to prepare at a moment's notice.
—Mary Ann Kosmas, Minneapolis, Minnesota

1 can (12 ounces) frozen orange juice concentrate, thawed
1 can (12 ounces) frozen lemonade concentrate, thawed
1 cup grenadine syrup
2 quarts ginger ale, chilled

Ice ring *or* shaved ice, optional

In a punch bowl, combine the first four ingredients. Add an ice ring or shaved ice to the bowl if desired. **Yield:** 10-12 servings (about 2-1/2 quarts).

Chocolate Coffee

(Pictured at right)

*A rich whipped chocolate mixture
from our Test Kitchen is used to flavor
coffee and to make hot chocolate.
Set out a small serving bowl,
spoon some of the mixture into mugs
and add hot coffee or milk.*

  1 **cup sugar**
  1 **cup baking cocoa**
  1 **cup boiling water**
  1 **teaspoon vanilla extract**
1/4 **teaspoon salt**
  4 **cups heavy whipping cream,
    whipped**
  8 **cups hot strong brewed coffee
    or whole milk**

In a large heavy saucepan, whisk the sugar, cocoa and water until smooth. Cook and whisk over medium-low heat until mixture forms soft peaks when whisk is lifted and resembles thick hot fudge sauce, about 35 minutes. Remove from the heat; stir in vanilla and salt. Transfer to a mixing bowl; refrigerate for at least 2 hours.

Beat the chocolate mixture. Add 2 cups whipped cream; mix well. Fold in remaining whipped cream. For each serving, place about 1/2 cup chocolate cream in 2/3 cup coffee or milk; stir to blend. **Yield:** 12 servings.

TIPS FOR CHOCOLATE COFFEE

THE CHOCOLATE BASE for Chocolate Coffee can be made weeks in advance and refrigerated. The morning of your party, add the whipped cream and spoon into small serving bowls. Cover with plastic wrap and refrigerate.

As a fancy garnish, place some of the chocolate cream in a pastry bag fitted with a star tip and decorate the bowls just before serving.

Set out one serving bowl at a time and replace with another after 2 hours or as needed.

Mulled Holiday Drink

(Pictured at right)

The beverage's burgundy color and tart taste are terrific for winter.
— Richell Welch, Buffalo, Texas

1 bottle (46 ounces) cranberry
   juice
1 bottle (46 ounces) white
   grape juice
6 whole cloves
2 cinnamon sticks (3 inches),
   broken
Citrus-Cinnamon Stir Sticks
   (recipe on page 279), optional

Pour juices into a Dutch oven. Place cloves and cinnamon on a double thickness of cheesecloth; bring up corners of cloth and tie with kitchen string to form a bag. Add to juice mixture. Bring to a boil. Reduce heat; cover and simmer for 30 minutes or until flavors are blended. Discard spice bag. Serve warm with stir sticks if desired. **Yield:** 10 servings (2-1/2 quarts).

Celebration Spoons

(Pictured at right)

You can easily make chocolate-covered spoons with this recipe from
our Test Kitchen. Serve them with coffee or hot chocolate.

1 cup (6 ounces) semisweet
   chocolate chips
24 metal *or* plastic spoons
Peppermints *and/or* Andes candies,
   chopped

In a microwave-safe bowl, melt chocolate chips; stir until smooth. Dip spoons into chocolate. Tap the handle of spoon on the edge of the bowl to remove excess chocolate. Place on waxed paper. Sprinkle with chopped candies. Let stand until set. **Yield:** 2 dozen.

Sparkling Candy Swizzle Sticks

(Pictured above right)

Serve these sweet sticks from our Test Kitchen with tea, cider and hot chocolate.

Assorted candy sticks (sour apple,
   cinnamon, orange *or* flavor of
   your choice)
Warm water

White *or* colored decorating sugar

Dip candy sticks halfway into warm water; sprinkle with sugar. Place on a wire rack until dry.

Citrus-Cinnamon Stir Sticks

(Pictured above)

To add a little zest to hot cider, our home economists came up with these simple stirrers.
Once the stirrer is added to the beverage, the orange strip will eventually fall off the
cinnamon stick...but that's all right. It will continue to add flavor.

3 medium navel oranges
1 cup sugar
1 cup water
12 cinnamon sticks (5 inches)
Additional sugar, optional

Using a citrus stripper or vegetable peeler, cut 12 strips of peel from or-anges, about 4-6 in. long. In a small saucepan, bring sugar and water to a boil over medium heat. Reduce heat; simmer, uncovered, for 12 minutes.

Place one orange strip at a time in hot syrup; cook for 3 minutes. Remove orange strip to waxed paper; when cool enough to handle, wrap strip around a cinnamon stick. Dip into hot syrup; place on a wire rack. Sprinkle with sugar if desired. Let stand until dry. **Yield:** 1 dozen.

Sweet Treats for Santa

KIDS of all ages quickly get into a festive frame of mind when they see a merry array of fresh-baked cookies and rich candies adorning pretty platters.

For most cooks, the jolly job of creating these confections begins weeks in advance. Families can't wait for the wonderful aroma of homemade cookies and candies to fill the house, signaling the start of the holiday season.

You'll create sweet memories in your kitchen with a magical assortment of fresh-baked cookies and dandy candies like Nutty Popcorn Party Mix, Viennese Fudge, Caramel-Filled Chocolate Cookies and Buttery Spritz Cookies.

Santa (and all the "elves" in your family) will appreciate each mouth-watering morsel!

CAPTURE CHRISTMAS MAGIC
(Clockwise from top right)

Nutty Popcorn Party Mix (p. 282)

Viennese Fudge (p. 282)

Caramel-Filled Chocolate Cookies (p. 285)

Buttery Spritz Cookies (p. 283)

Nutty Popcorn Party Mix

(Pictured on page 281)

Whoever receives this crunchy concoction is guaranteed merry munching. The snapped-up-in-seconds party mix features a combination of sweet and savory flavors.
—*Zita Wilensky, North Miami Beach, Florida*

3 quarts popped popcorn
1 cup unsalted dry roasted peanuts
1 jar (3-1/2 ounces) macadamia nuts, halved
1/2 cup slivered almonds
1/4 cup flaked coconut
3/4 cup butter
1 cup sugar
1/2 cup packed brown sugar
1/4 cup light corn syrup
1/4 cup strong brewed coffee
1/8 teaspoon ground cinnamon
2 teaspoons vanilla extract

In a large bowl, combine popcorn, nuts and coconut. In a saucepan, combine the butter, sugars, corn syrup, coffee and cinnamon. Bring to a boil over medium heat; boil and stir for 5 minutes. Remove from the heat; stir in vanilla. Pour over popcorn mixture and stir until coated.

Transfer to two greased 15-in. x 10-in. x 1-in. baking pans. Bake, uncovered, at 250° for 45-55 minutes or until golden brown, stirring every 15 minutes. Spread onto waxed paper; cool completely. Store in an airtight container. **Yield:** about 12 cups.

Viennese Fudge

(Pictured on page 281)

This fudge recipe from my mother combines two ingredients commonly found in Viennese desserts—semisweet chocolate and hazelnuts. It's a staple in my home at the holidays.
—*Loranne Weir, San Ramon, California*

1 teaspoon plus 3 tablespoons butter, *divided*
2 cups sugar
1 cup evaporated milk
1/2 teaspoon salt
1 cup miniature marshmallows
1-1/2 cups semisweet chocolate chips
2 teaspoons vanilla extract
1-1/2 cups ground hazelnuts, toasted

Line an 8-in. square pan with foil and butter foil with 1 teaspoon butter; set aside. In a large saucepan, combine sugar, milk, salt and remaining butter. Bring to a boil over medium heat, stirring constantly. Boil and stir for 6 minutes.

Remove from the heat; stir in marshmallows until melted. Add chocolate chips and stir until melted. Stir in vanilla and nuts. Pour into prepared pan. Let stand at room temperature until cool.

Using foil, lift fudge out of pan; cut into 1-in. squares. Store in an airtight container in the refrigerator. **Yield:** 2 pounds.

Buttery Spritz Cookies

(Pictured at right and on page 280)

These tender little cookies are very eye-catching on my Christmas cookie tray. The dough is easy to work with, so it's fun to make these into a variety of festive shapes.
—Beverly Launius
Sandwich, Illinois

1 cup butter, softened
1-1/4 cups confectioners' sugar
1 egg
1 teaspoon vanilla extract
1/2 teaspoon almond extract
2-1/2 cups all-purpose flour
1/2 teaspoon salt
Food coloring, optional

In a mixing bowl, cream butter and sugar until smooth. Beat in egg and extracts. Combine the flour and salt; gradually add to creamed mixture. Tint with food coloring if desired.

Using a cookie press fitted with the disk of your choice, press dough 2 in. apart onto ungreased baking sheets. Bake at 375° for 6-8 minutes or until set (do not brown). Remove to wire racks to cool. **Yield:** 7-1/2 dozen.

Almond Potato Candy

When my mother was a child, my grandmother would make this as a substitute for expensive store-bought marzipan. I've since added the melted chocolate, which gives it more richness.
—Betty Hartigan, Calgary, Alberta

1/2 cup mashed potatoes (prepared without milk and butter)
2 cups whole blanched almonds, finely ground
2 cups confectioners' sugar
1 tablespoon baking cocoa
1 teaspoon almond extract

2/3 cup semisweet chocolate chips, melted
Additional confectioners' sugar *or* ground almonds

In a bowl, combine the mashed potatoes, almonds, sugar, cocoa and almond extract; mix well. Add melted chips and stir well. Cover and refrigerate for several hours. Shape teaspoonfuls into balls; roll in sugar or almonds. **Yield:** about 5 dozen.

Cherry Bonbon Cookies

This is a very old recipe from my grandma.
The sweet cherry filling surprises folks trying them for the first time.
—Pat Habiger, Spearville, Kansas

1/2 cup butter, softened
3/4 cup confectioners' sugar
2 tablespoons milk
1 teaspoon vanilla extract
1-1/2 cups all-purpose flour
1/8 teaspoon salt
24 maraschino cherries
GLAZE:
1 cup confectioners' sugar
1 tablespoon butter, melted
2 tablespoons maraschino
   cherry juice
Additional confectioners' sugar

In a mixing bowl, cream butter and sugar. Add milk and vanilla. Combine the flour and salt; gradually add to the creamed mixture.

Divide dough into 24 portions; shape each portion around a cherry, forming a ball. Place on ungreased baking sheets. Bake at 350° for 18-20 minutes or until lightly browned. Cool on wire racks.

For glaze, combine the sugar, butter and cherry juice until smooth. Drizzle over cookies. Dust with confectioners' sugar. **Yield:** 2 dozen.

Sugarcoated Meltaways

I have fond memories of my parents spending days in the kitchen baking Christmas cookies.
It's a tradition that my husband and I now happily carry on.
—Charlotte Wright, Lebanon, Connecticut

1/2 cup orange juice
1 tablespoon grated orange
   peel
3/4 cup butter, softened
1/4 cup sugar
1 tablespoon cold water
1 teaspoon vanilla extract
1-3/4 cups all-purpose flour
1/8 teaspoon salt
1 cup miniature semisweet
   chocolate chips
1 cup finely chopped walnuts
Additional sugar

In a small bowl, combine orange juice and peel; set aside. In a mixing bowl, cream butter and sugar. Beat in water and vanilla. Combine flour and salt; gradually add to creamed mixture. Stir in chocolate chips and walnuts.

Roll into 1-in. balls. Place 1 in. apart on ungreased baking sheets. Bake at 325° for 12-15 minutes or until lightly browned. Remove to wire racks to cool.

Strain reserved orange juice. Dip cookies in juice, then roll in additional sugar. Let dry. Store in an airtight container. **Yield:** 3-1/2 dozen.

Caramel-Filled Chocolate Cookies

(Pictured at right and on page 280)

These yummy chocolate cookies have a tasty caramel surprise inside. With pecans on top and a contrasting white chocolate drizzle, they're almost too pretty to eat!
— Deb Walsh, Cabery, Illinois

  1 **cup butter, softened**
  1 **cup plus 1 tablespoon sugar,** *divided*
  1 **cup packed brown sugar**
  2 **eggs**
  1 **teaspoon vanilla extract**
2-1/2 **cups all-purpose flour**
  3/4 **cup baking cocoa**
  1 **teaspoon baking soda**
1-1/4 **cups chopped pecans,** *divided*
  1 **package (13 ounces) Rolo candies**
  4 **squares (1 ounce** *each***) white baking chocolate, melted**

In a mixing bowl, cream butter, 1 cup sugar and brown sugar. Add the eggs, one at a time, beating well after each addition. Beat in vanilla. Combine the flour, cocoa and baking soda; gradually add to the creamed mixture, beating just until combined. Stir in 1/2 cup pecans.

Shape a tablespoonful of dough around each candy, forming a ball. In a small bowl, combine the remaining sugar and pecans; dip each cookie halfway. Place nut side up 2 in. apart on greased baking sheets.

Bake at 375° for 7-10 minutes or until tops are slightly cracked. Cool for 3 minutes before removing to wire racks to cool completely. Drizzle with melted white chocolate. **Yield:** about 5 dozen.

FREEZING HOLIDAY COOKIES

TO PREPARE for holiday mania, begin your cookie-baking marathon a few weeks before Christmas. Store cooled, baked cookies in an airtight container at room temperature for about 3 days. To freeze cookies for up to 3 months, wrap the cookies in plastic, stack in an airtight container, seal and freeze. Thaw wrapped cookies at room temperature before serving.

Pecan Clusters

Toasting the pecans before stirring in the chocolate adds to the richness of this easy-to-make candy. I usually make four batches each Christmas and never have leftovers.
—*Collette Reynolds, Raleigh, North Carolina*

3 tablespoons butter, melted
3 cups chopped pecans
12 ounces chocolate candy
    coating, melted

In a 15-in. x 10-in. x 1-in. baking pan, combine butter and pecans. Bake at 250° for 20-30 minutes, stirring every 10 minutes. Remove from the oven; transfer to a bowl. Add candy coating and stir until evenly coated. Drop by rounded teaspoonfuls onto waxed paper. Cool completely. Store in an airtight container. **Yield:** about 4 dozen.

PACKING COOKIES FOR SHIPPING

NOTHING WARMS the hearts of out-of-town relatives and friends at holiday time like receiving a package from home. And when the parcel contains a pretty tin packed with home-baked cookies, their delight is undeniable. To ensure the mouth-watering morsels are at their best upon arrival, review these packing pointers.

- Bake and completely cool cookies just before packing and shipping so they're as fresh as possible.
- Determine which cookies to mail based on their fragility. Many bars, brownies and drop, refrigerator and sandwich cookies are fairly sturdy and travel well. Some cutouts and shaped varieties are a little more delicate and more likely to break. Cookies requiring refrigeration are poor choices to ship because they'll spoil.
- To help the cookies stay fresh and intact, wrap them in bundles of two (for drop cookies, place their bottoms together) with plastic wrap. It's best to wrap bars individually.
- Pack crisp and soft cookies in separate tins. If they're packed together, the moisture from the soft cookies will seep into the crisp cookies, making them lose their crunch. Consider shipping soft cookies by express mail so they'll be moist upon arrival.
- To help retain the best flavor, don't put strong-flavored cookies (like gingersnaps) and mild-flavored ones (like sugar cookies) in the same tin.
- Line a festive tin or box with crumpled waxed paper to help cushion the cookies. Snugly pack the cookies to within 1 inch of the top. Use crumpled waxed paper or bubble wrap to fill any gaps between the cookies. Add more waxed paper or bubble wrap over the last layer to cushion the cookies and prevent them from shifting during shipping. Close the tin or box.
- Place a layer of crumpled paper, bubble wrap or foam shipping peanuts in the bottom of a cardboard box that is slightly larger than your cookie tin. Set the tin on top, then add more paper, bubble wrap or shipping peanuts.
- Seal the box tightly with tape, label the top and sides of the package "Fragile and Perishable" and adhere a mailing label.

Sugar Cookie Cutouts

(Pictured at right)

I must have over 100 different cookie cutters and have fun putting them to use with this recipe over the years. Each Christmas, my brother, sister and I would eagerly wait for Grandpa and Grandma to arrive with these cookies in tow.
—Elizabeth Walters, Waterloo, Iowa

1 cup butter, softened
1 cup sugar
2 eggs
1/4 cup half-and-half cream
3 cups all-purpose flour
2 teaspoons baking powder
1 teaspoon baking soda
1/2 teaspoon salt
FROSTING:
1/2 cup butter, softened
4 cups confectioners' sugar
1 teaspoon vanilla extract
2 to 4 tablespoons half-and-half cream
Food coloring and colored sugar, optional

In a mixing bowl, cream butter and sugar. Add eggs, one at a time, beating well after each addition. Beat in cream. Combine the flour, baking powder, baking soda and salt; gradually add to creamed mixture. Cover and refrigerate for 3 hours or until easy to handle.

On a lightly floured surface, roll out dough to 1/8-in. thickness. Cut with 2-1/2-in. cookie cutters dipped in flour. Place 1 in. apart on ungreased baking sheets. Bake at 325° for 6-8 minutes or until edges are lightly browned. Remove to wire racks to cool.

In a mixing bowl, cream butter, sugar, vanilla and enough cream to achieve desired frosting consistency. Add food coloring if desired. Frost cookies. Sprinkle with colored sugar if desired. **Yield:** 8 dozen.

White Chocolate Holiday Cookies

At first glance, these look a bit like traditional chocolate chip cookies.
But one bite quickly reveals white chocolate chunks plus spicy dashes of ginger and cinnamon.
—*Bonnie Baumgardner, Sylva, North Carolina*

1/2 cup butter, softened
1/2 cup shortening
3/4 cup packed brown sugar
1/2 cup sugar
　1 egg
1/2 teaspoon almond extract
　2 cups all-purpose flour
　1 teaspoon baking soda
1/4 teaspoon salt
1/4 teaspoon ground cinnamon
1/4 teaspoon ground ginger
　6 squares (1 ounce *each*) white
　　baking chocolate, chopped
1-1/2 cups chopped pecans

In a mixing bowl, cream the butter, shortening and sugars. Add egg and almond extract; mix well. Combine the dry ingredients; add to creamed mixture. Stir in white chocolate and pecans. Drop by rounded teaspoonfuls 2 in. apart onto greased baking sheets. Bake at 350° for 8-10 minutes or until lightly browned. Remove to wire racks to cool. **Yield:** 10 dozen.

Caramel Snack Mix

Instead of the usual savory cereal snack mix, this version gets just the
right amount of sweetness from brown sugar and corn syrup.
—*Barbara Strohbehn, Gladbrook, Iowa*

　6 cups Rice Chex
　6 cups Corn Chex
　6 cups Crispix
　1 cup butter
　1 cup packed brown sugar
1/2 cup corn syrup
　1 teaspoon vanilla extract

Grease three 15-in. x 10-in. x 1-in. baking pans; set aside. In a large heatproof bowl, combine the cereals; set aside.

In a heavy saucepan over medium heat, bring butter, brown sugar and corn syrup to a boil, stirring constantly. Reduce heat. Simmer, uncovered, for 5 minutes, stirring occasionally. Remove from the heat; stir in vanilla. Pour over cereal and stir until well coated.

Transfer to prepared pans. Bake, uncovered, at 200° for 1 hour, stirring every 15 minutes. Cool completely. Break apart and store in airtight containers. **Yield:** 4-1/2 quarts.

Triple-Nut Diamonds

(Pictured at right)

My dad has always been crazy about nuts, so when I came upon this recipe, I knew I had to try it. The diamond shape is a nice addition to the Christmas cookie tray.
—*Darlene King, Estevan, Saskatchewan*

1 cup all-purpose flour
1/2 cup sugar
1/2 cup cold butter, *divided*
1/2 cup packed brown sugar
2 tablespoons honey
1/4 cup heavy whipping cream
2/3 cup *each* chopped pecans, walnuts and almonds

Line a greased 9-in. square baking pan with foil; grease the foil and set aside. In a bowl, combine the flour and sugar. Cut in 1/4 cup butter until mixture resembles coarse crumbs; press into prepared pan. Bake at 350° for 10 minutes.

In a saucepan, heat the brown sugar, honey and remaining butter until bubbly. Boil for 1 minute. Remove from the heat; stir in cream and nuts. Pour over crust. Bake at 350° for 16-20 minutes or until surface is bubbly. Cool on a wire rack.

Refrigerate for 30 minutes. Using foil, lift bars out of the pan; cut into 1-in. diamonds. Store in an airtight container. **Yield:** 4 dozen.

Orange Walnut Candy

A friend shared the recipe for these tangy goodies. Whenever I need a guaranteed crowd-pleaser, I roll them out by the dozens.
—*Betty Hostetler, Ocean Park, Washington*

3-3/4 cups (1 pound) confectioners' sugar
1 package (12 ounces) vanilla wafers, crushed
1 can (6 ounces) frozen orange juice concentrate, thawed

1/2 cup butter, melted
1-1/2 to 2 cups ground walnuts

In a bowl, combine the sugar, wafer crumbs, orange juice concentrate and butter; mix well. Shape into 3/4-in. balls; roll in walnuts. Cover and refrigerate in an airtight container for at least 24 hours before serving. **Yield:** 8 dozen.

Peanut Oat Cookies

I'm not surprised when people say these are the best cookies they've ever had. . . I agree!
Oats make them hearty and more delicious than traditional peanut butter cookies.
—Stacia McLimore, Indianapolis, Indiana

1-1/4 cups butter-flavored
    shortening
1-1/4 cups chunky peanut butter
1-1/2 cups packed brown sugar
   1 cup sugar
   3 eggs
4-1/2 cups old-fashioned oats
   2 teaspoons baking soda
   1 package (11-1/2 ounces) milk
    chocolate chips
   1 cup chopped peanuts

In a mixing bowl, cream shortening, peanut butter and sugars. Add eggs, one at a time, beating well after each addition. Combine oats and baking soda; gradually add to creamed mixture. Stir in chocolate chips and peanuts. Drop by tablespoonfuls 2 in. apart onto greased baking sheets. Bake at 350° for 10-12 minutes or until golden brown. Remove to wire racks to cool. **Yield:** about 8 dozen.

    Editor's Note: This recipe does not contain flour. Reduced-fat or generic brands of peanut butter are not recommended for this recipe.

Mamie Eisenhower's Fudge

My mother came across this recipe in a newspaper some 40 years ago.
One taste and you'll see why it doesn't take long for a big batch to disappear.
—Linda First, Hinsdale, Illinois

   1 tablespoon plus 1/2 cup
    butter, *divided*
   3 milk chocolate candy bars
    (two 7 ounces, one 1.55
    ounces), broken into pieces
   4 cups (24 ounces) semisweet
    chocolate chips
   1 jar (7 ounces) marshmallow
    creme
   1 can (12 ounces) evaporated
    milk
4-1/2 cups sugar
   2 cups chopped walnuts

Line a 13-in. x 9-in. x 2-in. pan with foil and butter the foil with 1 tablespoon butter; set aside. In a large heatproof bowl, combine the candy bars, chocolate chips and marshmallow creme; set aside.

    In a large heavy saucepan over medium-low heat, combine the milk, sugar and remaining butter. Bring to a boil, stirring constantly. Boil and stir for 4-1/2 minutes. Pour over chocolate mixture; stir until chocolate is melted and mixture is smooth and creamy. Stir in walnuts. Pour into prepared pan. Cover and refrigerate until firm.

    Using foil, lift fudge out of pan; cut into 1-in. squares. Store in an airtight container in the refrigerator. **Yield:** about 6 pounds.

Date-Filled
Sandwich
Cookies

(Pictured at right)

Of all the cookies I've baked over the years, these have remained one of my all-time favorites. The dough is very easy to work with, and the result is eye-catching.
—Debbie Rode, Oxbow, Saskatchewan

1 cup butter, softened
2 cups packed brown sugar
2 eggs
2 teaspoons vanilla extract
3-1/2 cups all-purpose flour
1 teaspoon baking powder
1 teaspoon baking soda
FILLING:
2 cups chopped dates
3/4 cup sugar
3/4 cup water

In a mixing bowl, cream butter and brown sugar. Add eggs, one at a time, beating well after each addition. Beat in vanilla. Combine the flour, baking powder and baking soda; gradually add to creamed mixture. Refrigerate for 1 hour or until easy to handle.

On a lightly floured surface, roll out dough to 1/8-in. thickness. Cut with a 2-1/2-in. cookie cutter dipped in flour. Place 1 in. apart on greased baking sheets. Bake at 350° for 10-12 minutes or until edges are lightly browned. Remove to wire racks to cool.

In a saucepan, combine filling ingredients. Cook over medium heat for 3 minutes or until thickened and bubbly. Cool to room temperature. Spread on the bottom of half of the cookies; top with remaining cookies. **Yield:** 3 dozen.

German Chocolate Caramel Bars

I get at least one recipe request every time I take these cookies to a church potluck.
The caramel and cream cheese filling is a winner.
—Hazel Baldner, Austin, Minnesota

1 package (18-1/4 ounces)
   German sweet chocolate
   cake mix
1 cup quick-cooking oats
6 tablespoons cold butter
1 egg, beaten
FILLING:
1 package (8 ounces) cream
   cheese, softened
1/2 cup caramel ice cream topping
1 egg
TOPPING:
1/2 cup chopped pecans
1/4 cup packed brown sugar
1/4 cup quick-cooking oats
2 tablespoons butter

In a bowl, combine cake mix and oats; cut in butter until crumbly. Set aside 1 cup. Stir the egg into remaining oat mixture (mixture will be crumbly). Press into a greased 13-in. x 9-in. x 2-in. baking pan. Bake at 350° for 12 minutes or until almost set. Cool on a wire rack for 10 minutes.

Combine filling ingredients; spread over crust. For topping, combine the pecans, brown sugar, oats, butter and reserved oat mixture until crumbly. Sprinkle over filling. Bake 15 minutes longer. Cool on a wire rack. Refrigerate until firm before cutting. **Yield:** 3 dozen.

Hazelnut Crescents

My mom and I make these delicate cookies every Christmas.
Hazelnuts give a little different flavor from the usual pecans.
—Beverly Launius, Sandwich, Illinois

1 cup butter, softened
1/4 cup sugar
1 teaspoon vanilla extract
2 cups all-purpose flour
1 cup whole hazelnuts, ground
Confectioners' sugar

In a mixing bowl, cream butter, sugar and vanilla. Gradually add the flour and nuts. Cover and refrigerate for 2 hours or until easy to handle.

Shape dough by teaspoonfuls into 2-in. rolls. Form into crescents. Place 2 in. apart on ungreased baking sheets. Bake at 350° for 12 minutes or until lightly browned. Cool for 2 minutes before removing from pans to wire racks. Dust with confectioners' sugar. **Yield:** about 10 dozen.

Toasted Almond Caramels

(Pictured at right)

Preparing these caramels never fails to put me in the holiday spirit. Later, when I'm passing them around, that cheerful feeling becomes contagious.
— *Mae Ondracek, Pahrump, Nevada*

1 teaspoon plus 1/4 cup butter, *divided*
2 cups sugar
1 cup light corn syrup
1/4 teaspoon salt
1 cup heavy whipping cream
1 teaspoon vanilla extract
1 cup chopped almonds, toasted

Line an 8-in. square pan with foil and butter the foil with 1 teaspoon butter; set aside. In a heavy saucepan, combine the sugar, corn syrup, salt and remaining butter. Bring to a boil over medium heat, stirring constantly. Reduce heat to medium-low; boil gently without stirring for 4 minutes.

Remove from the heat; slowly stir in cream. Return to the heat; cook, without stirring, over medium-low heat until a candy thermometer reads 245° (firm-ball stage). Remove from the heat; stir in vanilla and almonds. Pour into prepared pan (do not scrape sides of saucepan). Cool completely.

Cut into squares. Wrap individually in waxed paper or foil; twist ends. **Yield:** about 4 dozen.

CANDY MAKING TIPS

IT'S ACTUALLY quite easy to make candy from scratch if you keep in mind these pointers.

- Make sure that you test your candy thermometer before each use by bringing water to a boil; the thermometer should read 212°. Adjust your recipe temperature up or down based on your test.
- Measure and assemble all ingredients for a recipe before beginning. Do not substitute or alter the basic ingredients.
- Use heavy-gauge saucepans that are deep enough to allow candy mixtures to boil freely without boiling over.
- For safe stirring when preparing recipes with hot boiling sugar, use wooden spoons with long handles.
- Humid weather affects results when making candy that is cooked to a specific temperature or that contains egg whites. For best results, make candy on days when the humidity is less than 60%.
- Store homemade candies in tightly covered containers unless otherwise directed. Don't store more than one kind of candy in a single container.

Truffle Topiary Centerpiece

(Pictured on opposite page)

*This impressive, edible centerpiece from our Test Kitchen takes truffles
to new heights! Set out the extras on plates or package them for guests to take home.*

Gold spray paint
5-inch clay pot
Floral foam to fit inside pot
New small flat paintbrush
5-inch Styrofoam ball
**Milk chocolate candy coating,
    melted (about 1/2 cup)**
**12-inch length of 3/8-inch wooden
    dowel**
Double-sided transparent tape
2-1/3 yards of gold metallic cord
Craft scissors
White (tacky) glue
**18-inch square of gold-flecked tulle
    netting**
Craft wire
Two large wire-edged bows
Toothpicks
**60 to 70 Coconut Truffles (recipe
    on opposite page)**
60 to 70 paper *or* foil candy cups

Spray-paint clay pot gold. When dry,
fill pot with floral foam.

Use paintbrush to cover Styrofoam
ball with melted chocolate. Let harden.

With a pencil, mark dowel about 1-
1/2 inches from one end and 4-1/2
inches from the other end. Place several
pieces of double-sided tape on dowel
between markings. Wrap gold
metallic cord around dowel between
markings. Cut away excess cord and
glue ends to secure.

Insert long unwrapped end of dowel
straight up and down into center of
floral foam. Place pot in center of tulle
netting. Bring up netting on all sides to
cover pot. Use craft wire to secure net-
ting to dowel just above top of pot. Arrange netting to cover wire, trimming excess netting as desired. Attach bows to
opposite sides of top of pot. Trim ribbon ends as desired.

Use a pencil to make a hole in chocolate-covered Styrofoam ball, centering hole inside ball. Push ball onto end of
dowel until wood on dowel is covered, making sure ball and
dowel are centered and straight.

Insert a toothpick into top center of ball, leaving about a
third of the toothpick exposed. Set a truffle into a candy cup;
carefully push truffle and cup onto exposed end of toothpick. Repeat until ball is completely covered with truffles.

MAKING A TRUFFLE TOPIARY

1. Insert long unwrapped end of dowel into center of
floral foam in painted clay pot.
2. Center clay pot on top of tulle netting. Bring netting up around sides of clay pot to cover.

3. Push chocolate-covered ball onto end of dowel until wood on dowel is covered.
4. Insert toothpicks into ball, leaving about a third
of toothpick exposed. Set truffles into candy cups
and push onto ends of toothpicks.

Coconut Truffles

(Pictured at right)

These chocolate-covered coconut truffles can be flavored with a variety of extracts with delicious results. Making candy is a favorite pastime of mine.
—Janelle Johnson, Muncy, Pennsylvania

1-1/2 cups butter
    6 cups confectioners' sugar
  3/4 cup heavy whipping cream
    6 cups flaked coconut
  1/2 teaspoon almond extract
  1/2 teaspoon rum extract
  1/2 teaspoon peppermint extract
    1 teaspoon cherry extract
    2 pounds milk chocolate candy coating, melted
  1/2 cup ground almonds
    4 ounces white candy coating, melted
Red and green candy coating disks, melted

In a Dutch oven, heat butter over medium heat until golden brown, about 7 minutes. Remove from the heat; stir in confectioners' sugar, cream and coconut. Divide mixture between four bowls; stir a different flavor extract into each bowl. Cover and refrigerate for 45 minutes or until easy to handle.

Shape chilled mixtures into 1-in. balls; place on four separate waxed paper-lined baking sheets. Chill for 1-2 hours or until firm.

Dip the almond-flavored balls in milk chocolate coating; sprinkle with ground almonds. Place on waxed paper to harden.

Dip remaining balls in milk chocolate coating; place on waxed paper to harden. Drizzle white coating over rum truffles, red coating over cherry truffles and green coating over mint truffles. **Yield:** about 9 dozen.

Editor's Note: Colored candy coating disks can be obtained by mail from Wilton Industries Inc., 2240 W. 75th St., Woodridge IL 60517. To order, call 1-800/794-5866 (fax 1-888/824-9520). Or visit their Web site at *www.wilton.com*.

In Canada, contact Wilton Industries, Canada Ltd., 98 Carrier Dr., Etobicoke ON Canada M9W 5R1. Phone 1-416/679-0798.

TIME-SAVING TRUFFLES

YOU CAN make the coconut centers for these truffles and freeze them in airtight containers for up to 2 months. Thaw in the refrigerator; dip in chocolate and decorate as directed.

Soft Chocolate Mint Cookies

If you don't care for crisp cookies that crumble when you take a bite, give this soft variety a try.
No one can resist the fudgy, minty flavor.
—Kristin Vincent, Orem, Utah

1/2 cup butter
3 squares (1 ounce *each*) unsweetened chocolate
1/2 cup sugar
1/2 cup packed brown sugar
1 egg
1/4 cup buttermilk
1 teaspoon peppermint extract
1-3/4 cups all-purpose flour
1/2 teaspoon baking powder
1/4 teaspoon baking soda
1/4 teaspoon salt

In a microwave or heavy saucepan, melt butter and chocolate; stir until smooth. In a mixing bowl, beat sugars and egg; add buttermilk and peppermint extract. Beat in chocolate mixture. Combine the flour, baking powder, baking soda and salt; gradually add to sugar mixture. Let stand for 15 minutes or until dough becomes firmer.

Drop by tablespoonfuls 3 in. apart onto ungreased baking sheets. Bake at 350° for 8-10 minutes or until edges are firm. Cool for 2 minutes before removing from pans to wire racks. **Yield:** about 3 dozen.

Brown Sugar Pecan Candies

These sweet candies are similar to those served at Mexican restaurants in our area.
The recipe comes from a cookbook put together by the staff of the school where I teach.
—Barbara Windham, Houston, Texas

1-1/2 cups sugar
1/2 cup packed brown sugar
1/2 cup evaporated milk
3 tablespoons light corn syrup
4 large marshmallows, cut into quarters
2 tablespoons butter
2 cups coarsely chopped pecans
1/2 teaspoon vanilla extract

In a large heavy saucepan, combine the sugars, milk and corn syrup. Cook over medium-low heat, stirring occasionally, until a candy thermometer reads 238° (soft-ball stage).

Remove from the heat; stir in marshmallows and butter until melted. Add pecans and vanilla; stir only until mixture begins to thicken. Quickly drop by tablespoonfuls onto waxed paper. Cool until set. Store in an airtight container at room temperature. **Yield:** 5 dozen.

Editor's Note: If mixture begins to thicken, stir in hot water, a teaspoon at a time. We recommend that you test your candy thermometer before each use by bringing water to a boil; the thermometer should read 212°. Adjust your recipe temperature up or down based on your test.

Snowmen Cookies

(Pictured at right)

These cute snowmen cookies make great treats for children's parties. Kids are always willing to chip in and help decorate them.
—Sherri Johnson, Burns, Tennessee

1 package (16 ounces) Nutter Butter cookies
1-1/4 pounds white candy coating, melted
Miniature chocolate chips
M&M miniature baking bits
Pretzel sticks, halved
Orange and red decorating gel *or* frosting

Using tongs, dip cookies in candy coating; shake off excess. Place on waxed paper. Place two chocolate chips on one end of cookies for eyes. Place baking bits down middle for buttons. For arms, dip ends of two pretzel stick halves into coating; attach one to each side. Let stand until hardened. Pipe nose and scarf with gel or frosting. **Yield:** 32 cookies.

Popcorn Christmas Trees

(Pictured above)

The kids in my family like these popcorn trees instead of traditional popcorn balls. You can substitute red-hot candies for the M&M's if you like.
—Nicole Clayton, Las Vegas, Nevada

6 cups popped popcorn
1/2 cup sugar
1/2 cup light corn syrup
1/4 cup creamy peanut butter
10 to 12 drops green food coloring
2 to 3 tablespoons red M&M miniature baking bits

Place popcorn in a large bowl; set aside. In a heavy saucepan over medium heat, bring sugar and corn syrup to a boil, stirring occasionally. Boil and stir for 1 minute. Remove from the heat; stir in peanut butter and food coloring until blended. Pour over popcorn and stir to coat.

With wet hands, shape mixture by 3/4 cupfuls into evergreen tree shapes. While warm, press a few baking bits into each tree. Place on a greased baking sheet; let stand until firm, about 30 minutes. **Yield:** 8 servings.

Spiced Pecans

(Pictured at right)

The combination of spices on these nuts seems to warm everyone on cold winter days. I make this recipe several times over the holidays.
— *Tammi Simpson*
Greensburg, Kentucky

2 cups pecan halves
1/4 cup butter
1/4 cup sugar
1 teaspoon ground cinnamon
1/4 teaspoon ground nutmeg
1/4 teaspoon ground cloves

In a skillet over low heat, toast pecans in butter for 15 minutes or until lightly browned, stirring often. Drain on paper towels. In a bowl, combine the sugar and spices. Add pecans and toss to coat. Spread on a foil-lined baking sheet. Bake at 325° for 10 minutes. Cool. Store in an airtight container. **Yield:** 2 cups.

Sugar-Topped Walnut Bars

If I haven't set out these nutty treats at a holiday gathering, family and friends are sure to notice—and to ask where my bars are! They travel well to potluck dinners.
—*Gloria Siddiqui, Houston, Texas*

2-1/4 cups all-purpose flour
1 cup sugar
1 cup butter, softened
2 egg yolks
FILLING:
4 eggs
2 cups finely ground walnuts
1-1/3 cups sugar
1 teaspoon vanilla extract

Confectioners' sugar

In a mixing bowl, combine flour and sugar. Beat in butter and egg yolks. Press into an ungreased 15-in. x 10-in. x 1-in. baking pan. For filling, in a bowl, beat eggs. Stir in the walnuts, sugar and vanilla. Pour over crust. Bake at 300° for 55-60 minutes or until lightly browned. Cool completely on a wire rack. Dust with confectioners' sugar. Cut into bars. **Yield:** 6 dozen.

Wrap Up Cookies and Candies as Gifts

YOU DON'T have to spend a fortune or valuable time at the mall in search of perfect Christmas gifts. Quite often the most priceless treasures are your own homemade cookies and candies presented in decorative tins or in one of the pretty packages suggested below and shown at right.

• You'll have a handle on decorating gifts from the kitchen if you rely on baskets. They come in a variety of styles, shapes and sizes and are commonly found on sale at craft and variety stores—so be on the lookout for them throughout the year. And save any baskets you've acquired either from a gift you've received or from a purchase you've made for yourself.

Line the basket with white or colored tissue paper, then top with cookies that have been bundled in plastic wrap. Place the basket on a large piece of clear, colored or patterned cellophane; bring the edges of the cellophane up and tie with a ribbon. Add a decorative bow if desired.

• At Christmastime, craft and variety stores sell a variety of papier-mache boxes perfect for gift giving. In the photo (above right), we stacked star-shaped sugar cookies in a star-shaped papier-mache box that's been lined with wax-coated tissue paper. (Wax-coated tissue paper can be found at specialty cooking stores. It's sturdier than regular tissue paper and won't absorb the cookie's flavor and oils.) If you care to show your creativity, spray-paint the box and/or stamp it with festive designs. Let the box dry completely before adding tissue paper and cookies.

• Little dressing up is needed when you fill inexpensive clear jars with colorful snack mixes and individually wrapped candies. Simply tie a festive ribbon and some tiny ornaments around the top for an easy-to-prepare present.

Don't limit your creativity to the suggestions shown above. Consider these other ideas:

• Decorative tins, plates and candy dishes can often be found at bargain prices throughout the year at stores and rummage sales and at after-Christmas sales. Keep them on hand for last-minute gifts.

• Stack cookies in a wide-mouth canning jar, cover the lid with fabric and screw on the band. You may also want to include the recipe for the cookies.

• Instead of discarding potato chip cans, coffee tins or shortening cans, wash them, decorate the outside with wrapping paper or Con-Tact paper and fill with cookies or candies. Attach a bow to the lid and close.

• Wrap cookies in plastic wrap, place a bow on top and tuck inside a pretty coffee mug or teacup.

Neighborhood Round-Robin

ARE YOU and your neighbors looking for an alternative to the traditional progressive dinner party, where each family hosts a different course in the meal?

This holiday season, consider organizing an appetizer round-robin, where families "make the rounds" to each other's homes to enjoy hearty hors d'oeuvres.

This is a great way to entertain because no family has to cook an elaborate part of the meal.

Oven-fresh fare like Chili Artichoke Dip really warms you up, while Herbed Cheesecake and Antipasto Platter can conveniently be made ahead and refrigerated.

This chapter offers a host of innovative appetizers, from hot and cold to fancy and casual.

Seasonal Snacking
(Clockwise from top right)

Herbed Cheesecake (p. 305)

Antipasto Platter (p. 303)

Chili Artichoke Dip (p. 302)

Chili Artichoke Dip

(Pictured on page 300)

*It's not tricky to prepare this warm, tempting dip. It's cheesy and satisfying with
a bit of zip from the chilies and marinated artichokes.*
—*Leanne Mueller, Stockton, California*

1 can (14 ounces) water-packed
artichoke hearts, drained and
chopped
1 jar (6-1/2 ounces) marinated
artichoke hearts, drained and
chopped
1 can (4 ounces) chopped green
chilies
3 cups (12 ounces) shredded
cheddar cheese

1/4 cup mayonnaise
Assorted crackers *or* tortilla chips

In a bowl, combine the artichokes, chilies, cheese and mayonnaise. Transfer to a greased 8-in. square baking dish. Bake, uncovered, at 350° for 20-25 minutes or until cheese is melted. Serve warm with crackers or tortilla chips. **Yield:** about 3-1/2 cups.

Editor's Note: Reduced-fat or fat-free mayonnaise may not be substituted for regular mayonnaise in this recipe.

PLANNING A NEIGHBORHOOD ROUND-ROBIN

ORGANIZING a holiday gathering is simple when others help with the hosting. Here are some pointers for planning a successful round-robin for you and your neighbors:

- Early in fall, send a note to your neighbors inviting them to participate in an appetizer round-robin, where neighbors go from house to house (staying about 1 hour at each) to enjoy an assortment of appetizers (two to three per house). You may want to list several possible dates or just offer one date and see who can attend.

- Six weeks before the party, send the participating neighbors a schedule for the evening. You may want to ask each family what appetizers they plan on serving to avoid duplicates.

- When selecting recipes, think about the schedule of the evening. If company comes to your house first, you can prepare a recipe that has a little more last-minute fussing. If not, choose dishes that can either be completely prepared and refrigerated before serving or that can be partially assembled before baking.

- A month before the party, make some outdoor Holiday Luminaries for your walkway (see page 315). You might want to tell your neighbors about this enlightened idea! Or if you're ambitious and there aren't too many families partaking in the event, think about making enough luminaries for each stop along the way.

- The day before the party, do whatever food preparation you can. Set the table with serving trays, plates, napkins and utensils. Although the focus is on the food, you'll want to offer a variety of beverages as well.

Antipasto Platter

(Pictured at right and on page 301)

We entertain often, and this is one of our favorite "party pleasers." It's such a refreshing change from the usual chips and dip.
— *Teri Lindquist, Gurnee, Illinois*

1 jar (24 ounces) pepperoncinis, drained
1 can (15 ounces) garbanzo beans *or* chickpeas, rinsed and drained
2 cups halved fresh mushrooms
2 cups halved cherry tomatoes
1/2 pound provolone cheese, cubed
1 can (6 ounces) pitted ripe olives, drained

1 package (3-1/2 ounces) sliced pepperoni
1 bottle (8 ounces) Italian vinaigrette dressing
Lettuce leaves

In a large bowl, combine the peppers, beans, mushrooms, tomatoes, cheese, olives and pepperoni. Pour vinaigrette over mixture and gently toss to coat. Refrigerate for at least 30 minutes or overnight. Arrange on a lettuce-lined platter. Serve with toothpicks. **Yield:** 14-16 servings.

Garlic Herb Spread

Garlic and a host of herbs pleasantly season this savory spread. It's a "must" on my holiday menu because I can make it in advance.
— *Cheryl Fortier, Athabasca, Alberta*

1 package (8 ounces) cream cheese, softened
1/2 cup butter, softened
2 tablespoons minced fresh parsley
1 garlic clove, minced
1/4 teaspoon salt
1/4 teaspoon dill weed

1/4 teaspoon *each* dried basil, thyme and marjoram
Assorted crackers *or* raw vegetables

In a small mixing bowl, combine the cream cheese, butter, parsley, garlic and seasonings. Beat until blended. Refrigerate overnight. Serve with crackers or vegetables. **Yield:** 1-1/2 cups.

Eggplant Dip

*This deliciously different appetizer is loved by family and friends...even by those who
usually avoid eggplant. The pretty red color makes it great for the holidays.*
—Linda Roberson, Cordova, Tennessee

3 cups cubed eggplant
1 medium onion, chopped
1/3 cup finely chopped sweet
  red pepper
1 jar (4-1/2 ounces) sliced
  mushrooms, drained
4 garlic cloves, minced
1/3 cup olive oil
1 jar (6 ounces) stuffed olives,
  drained and chopped
1 can (6 ounces) tomato paste
2 tablespoons red wine
  vinegar
1-1/2 teaspoons sugar
1 teaspoon salt
1/2 teaspoon dried oregano
Hot pepper sauce to taste
Pita bread wedges *or* tortilla
  or corn chips

In a large skillet, combine the eggplant, onion, red pepper, mushrooms, garlic and oil. Cover and cook over medium heat for 10 minutes or until tender. Stir in the next seven ingredients; bring to a boil. Reduce heat; cover and simmer for 20-30 minutes or until flavors are blended. Serve warm or at room temperature with pita wedges or chips. **Yield:** 3 cups.

ADVICE ABOUT EGGPLANT

SELECT EGGPLANT with smooth skin; avoid those with soft or brown spots. Store eggplant in a cool dry place for 1 to 2 days. To store up to 5 days, place in a plastic bag and refrigerate. A 1-pound eggplant yields 3 to 4 cups cubed. You don't need to peel an eggplant before using.

Meaty Chili Dip

*A meaty dish like this is a must for the men in my family.
They scrape the serving bowl clean! For the best dipping, use large corn chips.*
—Karen Kiel, Camdenton, Missouri

1 pound ground beef
1 medium green pepper,
  chopped
1 cup water
1 can (6 ounces) tomato paste
1 package (3 ounces) cream
  cheese, cubed
1 envelope chili seasoning mix
Corn chips

In a large skillet, cook beef and green pepper over medium heat until meat is no longer pink; drain. Add the water, tomato paste, cream cheese and chili seasoning mix. Bring to a boil. Reduce heat; simmer, uncovered, until cheese is melted. Transfer to a small slow cooker or chafing dish to keep warm. Serve with corn chips. **Yield:** 3 cups.

Herbed Cheesecake

(Pictured at right and on page 301)

Cheesecake isn't just for dessert! This savory version is my family's favorite for merry munching around the holidays.
—Julie Tomlin, Watkinsville, Georgia

3 packages (8 ounces *each*) cream cheese, softened
2 cups (16 ounces) sour cream, *divided*
1 can (10-3/4 ounces) condensed cream of celery soup, undiluted
3 eggs
1/2 cup grated Romano cheese
3 garlic cloves, minced
1 tablespoon cornstarch
2 tablespoons minced fresh basil *or* 2 teaspoons dried basil
1 tablespoon minced fresh thyme *or* 1 teaspoon dried thyme
1/2 teaspoon Italian seasoning
1/2 teaspoon coarsely ground pepper
Assorted crackers

In a large mixing bowl, beat the cream cheese, 1 cup sour cream and soup until smooth. Add the eggs, Romano cheese, garlic, cornstarch, basil, thyme, Italian seasoning and pepper; beat until smooth.

Pour into a greased 9-in. springform pan. Place pan on a baking sheet. Bake at 350° for 55-60 minutes or until center is almost set. Cool on a wire rack for 10 minutes. Carefully run a knife around edge of pan to loosen; cool 1 hour longer.

Refrigerate for at least 4 hours or overnight. Remove sides of pan. Spread remaining sour cream over top. Serve with crackers. Refrigerate leftovers. **Yield:** 24 servings.

MAKING A POINSETTIA GARNISH

A POINSETTIA GARNISH (shown above and at right) is a great way to add color to a dish during the holidays. Here's how to make it:

Place six fresh basil leaves in a circle with the stems toward the center. Cut five petal-shaped pieces from a sweet red pepper; set between the basil leaves. Chop some sweet yellow pepper; place in the center of the "poinsettia."

Taco Roll-Ups

Our friend made these roll-ups for a Mexican-themed garden party.
A sprinkling of onion soup mix makes them a little different.
—Denice Louk, Garnett, Kansas

2 packages (8 ounces *each*)
   cream cheese, softened
1 cup (8 ounces) sour cream
2 cups (8 ounces) finely
   shredded cheddar cheese
1/2 cup picante sauce
1 can (4-1/2 ounces) chopped
   ripe olives, drained
2 tablespoons taco seasoning
1 tablespoon onion soup mix
8 flour tortillas (10 inches)

In a small mixing bowl, beat cream cheese and sour cream until smooth; stir in the cheddar cheese, picante sauce, olives, taco seasoning and soup mix. Spread over tortillas; roll up jelly-roll style. Wrap in plastic wrap; refrigerate for at least 1 hour. Just before serving, cut into 1-in. pieces. **Yield:** about 3-1/2 dozen.

Marinated Mushrooms

These are a nice addition to an appetizer buffet table. For the best flavor,
allow the mushrooms to marinate a few days before serving.
—JoAnn Stevens, Durham, North Carolina

1 pound fresh whole
   mushrooms
1 large onion, sliced
3/4 cup olive oil
1/4 cup white vinegar
2 garlic cloves, minced
1/2 teaspoon salt
1/4 teaspoon ground mustard
1/8 teaspoon pepper
Crushed red pepper flakes to taste

In a large bowl, combine all ingredients. Cover and refrigerate for 1 to 2 days. Serve with a slotted spoon. **Yield:** 6-8 servings.

Baked Brie

(Pictured at right)

I always come home with an empty plate when I take this special appetizer to holiday parties. It looks fancy but is actually quite easy to make.
—Carolyn DeKryger, Fremont, Michigan

1/4 cup butter, softened
1 package (3 ounces) cream
   cheese, softened
3/4 cup all-purpose flour
1 round (8 ounces) Brie
1 egg
1 teaspoon water
Assorted crackers and fresh fruit

In a large mixing bowl, beat the butter, cream cheese and flour on low speed until mixture forms a ball. Divide in half and wrap each portion in plastic wrap; refrigerate for 30 minutes.

On a lightly floured surface, roll out each portion into a 7-in. circle about 1/8 in. thick. Place one circle on an un-greased baking sheet. Place Brie on pastry and top with remaining pastry circle; pinch edges to seal. Flute bottom edge if desired.

In a small bowl, beat egg and water; brush over top and sides of pastry. Bake at 400° for 15-20 minutes or until golden brown. Immediately remove from the baking sheet. Let stand for 30 minutes before serving. Serve with crackers and fruit. **Yield:** 8 servings.

Holiday Vegetable Dip

This dip is sure to tickle your taste buds. When I got the recipe, I was warned one batch is never enough. So whenever I make it, I double the recipe and never have any left over.
—Nancy Hofman, Lethbridge, Alberta

1 cup mayonnaise
1 tablespoon grated onion
2 teaspoons cider vinegar
2 teaspoons chili sauce
1/4 teaspoon pepper
1/4 teaspoon dried thyme

2 teaspoons minced chives
Assorted raw vegetables *or* potato chips

In a bowl, combine the first six ingredients; cover and refrigerate for at least 1 hour. Sprinkle with chives. Serve with vegetables or chips. **Yield:** 1 cup.

Toasted Almond Party Spread

This rich spread goes a long way at holiday parties. Almonds and Swiss cheese
are a classic combination that never goes out of style.
—Kim Sobota, Plymouth, Minnesota

1 package (8 ounces) cream
   cheese, softened
1-1/2 cups (6 ounces) shredded
   Swiss cheese
1/2 cup sliced almonds, toasted,
   divided
1/3 cup mayonnaise
  2 tablespoons sliced green
   onions
1/8 teaspoon pepper

1/8 teaspoon ground nutmeg
Assorted crackers

In a small mixing bowl, beat the cream cheese until smooth. Stir in the Swiss cheese, 1/3 cup almonds, mayonnaise, onions, pepper and nutmeg. Spoon onto a lightly greased pie plate. Bake at 350° for 14-15 minutes or until heated through. Sprinkle with remaining almonds. Serve warm with crackers. **Yield:** 1-1/2 cups.

Luscious Fruit Platter

I often make this fruit-and-dip dish in summer, when the finest fruits are at their best.
Paired with angel food cake, this also makes a marvelous dessert.
—Dixie Terry, Marion, Illinois

1 package (8 ounces) cream
   cheese, softened
1/2 cup milk
  2 tablespoons lemon juice
  4 teaspoons sugar
1/4 teaspoon salt
  1 medium honeydew, peeled,
   seeded and cut into wedges
1-1/2 cups halved fresh
   strawberries

1-1/2 cups cubed seeded watermelon
  1 cup fresh blueberries
  1 medium firm banana, cut into 1-inch pieces
  2 medium ripe peaches, pitted and quartered
Clusters of red and green seedless grapes

In a small mixing bowl, beat cream cheese. Add milk, lemon juice, sugar and salt; beat until smooth. Transfer to a small serving bowl. On a large serving platter, arrange honeydew wedges in a spoke pattern. Place strawberries, watermelon, blueberries, banana, peaches and grapes between the wedges. Place dip in the center. Serve immediately. **Yield:** 8-10 servings (2 cups dip).

Bacon-Wrapped Scallops

(Pictured at right)

When I'm looking for a more special appetizer, this is the recipe I reach for. I've also served these savory scallops for dinner.
—Pamela MacCumbee
Berkeley Springs, West Virginia

20 fresh baby spinach leaves
10 uncooked sea scallops, halved
10 bacon strips, halved widthwise
Lemon wedges

Fold a spinach leaf around each scallop half. Wrap bacon over spinach and secure with a toothpick. Place on a baking sheet or broiler pan. Broil 3-4 in. from the heat for 6 minutes on each side or until bacon is crisp. Squeeze lemon over each. Serve immediately. **Yield:** 20 appetizers.

Fiesta Corn Dip

I first came across this recipe at a friend's bridge party. To give it a little more flair, I added the cilantro and olives.
—Shirley Herring, Conroe, Texas

2 cups (16 ounces) sour cream
1/2 cup mayonnaise
2 cans (11 ounces *each*) Mexicorn, drained
2-1/2 cups (10 ounces) shredded cheddar cheese
4 green onions, chopped
1/4 cup diced canned jalapeno peppers, drained
2 tablespoons chopped ripe olives
2 tablespoons minced fresh cilantro
Corn chips

In a bowl, combine the first eight ingredients. Cover and refrigerate for at least 2 hours. Serve with corn chips. **Yield:** 5-1/2 cups.

Peppered Meatballs

Plenty of ground pepper gives these saucy meatballs their irresistible zest.
They're so hearty, I sometimes serve them over noodles as a main course.
—*Darla Schroeder, Stanley, North Dakota*

1/2 cup sour cream
2 teaspoons grated Parmesan *or* Romano cheese
2 to 3 teaspoons pepper
1 teaspoon salt
1 teaspoon dry bread crumbs
1/2 teaspoon garlic powder
1-1/2 pounds ground beef
SAUCE:
  1 cup (8 ounces) sour cream
  1 can (10-3/4 ounces) condensed cream of mushroom soup, undiluted
  2 teaspoons dill weed

1/2 teaspoon sugar
1/2 teaspoon pepper
1/4 teaspoon garlic powder

In a bowl, combine sour cream and Parmesan cheese. Add pepper, salt, bread crumbs and garlic powder. Crumble meat over mixture and mix well. Shape into 1-in. balls. Place in a greased 15-in. x 10-in. x 1-in. baking pan. Bake at 350° for 20-25 minutes or until no longer pink.

Transfer meatballs to a slow cooker. Combine the sauce ingredients; pour over meatballs. Cover and cook on high for 2 hours or until heated through. **Yield:** 1-1/2 dozen (2 cups sauce).

Tomato Spinach Spread

Tomatoes add a tasty twist to a traditional spinach spread.
The red and green colors make this an appropriate appetizer for Christmas.
—*Connie Buzzard, Colony, Kansas*

1 package (8 ounces) cream cheese, softened
1 package (10 ounces) frozen chopped spinach, thawed and squeezed dry
1 cup (4 ounces) shredded Monterey Jack cheese
2 medium tomatoes, seeded and chopped
1/3 cup half-and-half cream
1 small onion, chopped
1/2 teaspoon garlic salt
Assorted crackers

In a mixing bowl, beat cream cheese until fluffy. Stir in the spinach, cheese, tomatoes, cream, onion and garlic salt. Transfer to a greased 1-qt. baking dish.

Bake, uncovered, at 350° for 20-25 minutes or until heated through. Serve with crackers. **Yield:** 4 cups.

Macaroon Fruit Dip

(Pictured at right)

I rely on make-ahead dishes like this when entertaining. Serving the dip in a pineapple shell makes for a pretty presentation.
—*Jean Forster, Elmhurst, Illinois*

2 cups (16 ounces) sour cream
1/4 cup packed brown sugar
1-1/2 cups crumbled macaroons
Assorted fresh fruit
Small macaroon cookies

In a bowl, combine the sour cream, brown sugar and crumbled cookies. Cover and refrigerate for 12 hours or overnight. Serve with fruit and macaroons. **Yield:** 3 cups.

PINEAPPLE SERVING BOWL

TO MAKE a Pineapple Serving Bowl (pictured above with Macaroon Fruit Dip), stand a medium fresh pineapple upright; cut in half lengthwise, leaving top attached. Cut pineapple from one section and discard shell. Cut pineapple from the other half, leaving a 1/2-in. shell. Spoon fruit dip into shell. Serve pineapple with dip or save for another use.

BLT Dip

Fans of bacon, lettuce and tomato sandwiches will fall for this creamy dip. It's easy to transport to different functions and always draws recipe requests.
—*Emalee Payne, Eau Claire, Wisconsin*

2 cups (16 ounces) sour cream
2 cups mayonnaise
2 pounds sliced bacon, cooked and crumbled
6 plum tomatoes, chopped

3 green onions, chopped
Assorted crackers *or* chips

In a bowl, combine the sour cream, mayonnaise, bacon, tomatoes and onions. Refrigerate until serving. Serve with crackers or chips. **Yield:** 6 cups.

Southwestern Seafood Egg Rolls

Scallops, shrimp, spicy seasonings and phyllo dough combine to make these unique egg rolls.
Assemble them in the morning, refrigerate, then bake as guests arrive.
—*Lori Coeling, Hudsonville, Michigan*

1/4 pound uncooked bay scallops
1/4 pound uncooked medium shrimp, peeled and deveined
1 teaspoon minced garlic, *divided*
2 tablespoons olive oil, *divided*
1 large tomato, peeled, seeded and chopped
1/4 cup finely chopped onion
3 tablespoons minced fresh parsley
3 tablespoons minced fresh cilantro
3/4 teaspoon ground cumin
1/2 teaspoon paprika
1/4 teaspoon salt
1/8 teaspoon pepper
Dash cayenne pepper
Dash ground turmeric
1/4 cup soft bread crumbs

1/2 pound frozen phyllo dough, thawed
1/2 cup butter, melted

In a large skillet, saute scallops, shrimp and 1/2 teaspoon garlic in 1 tablespoon oil for 2 minutes or until seafood is opaque. With a slotted spoon, remove from the pan and coarsely chop; set aside. In the same skillet, combine the tomato, onion and remaining garlic and oil; simmer for 5 minutes. Stir in parsley, cilantro, cumin, paprika, salt, pepper, cayenne and turmeric. Simmer, uncovered, until liquid is evaporated, about 5 minutes. Stir in seafood mixture and bread crumbs.

Cut the phyllo dough into 14-in. x 4-1/2-in. strips. Cover with a damp towel until ready to use. Lightly brush one strip with butter. Top with another strip; brush with butter. Place a tablespoonful of seafood mixture near one short side; fold in the long sides and roll up. Brush lightly with butter. Place on a greased baking sheet. Repeat with remaining phyllo and filling. Bake at 375° for 12-15 minutes or until golden brown. **Yield:** 2 dozen.

Baked Cheddar Bacon Spread

Potlucks at work just aren't the same without this deliciously rich spread.
—*Kathy Fehr, Fairbury, Illinois*

2 packages (8 ounces *each*) cream cheese, softened
2 cups (16 ounces) sour cream
1 medium onion, chopped
2 tablespoons mayonnaise
1 pound sliced bacon, cooked and crumbled

4 cups (16 ounces) shredded cheddar cheese, *divided*
Assorted crackers

In a mixing bowl, beat the cream cheese, sour cream, onion and mayonnaise until smooth. Fold in bacon and 3 cups of cheddar cheese. Transfer to a 2-qt. baking dish. Sprinkle with the remaining cheese. Bake, uncovered, at 375° for 30 minutes or until lightly browned. Serve with crackers. **Yield:** 7 cups.

Cheesy Pizza Fondue

(Pictured at right)

I keep these dip ingredients on hand for spur-of-the-moment gatherings. Folks can't resist chewy bread cubes coated with a savory sauce.
—Nel Carver, Moscow, Idaho

1 jar (29 ounces) meatless
   spaghetti sauce
2 cups (8 ounces) shredded
   mozzarella cheese
1/4 cup shredded Parmesan
   cheese
2 teaspoons dried oregano
1 teaspoon dried minced onion
1/4 teaspoon garlic powder
1 unsliced loaf (1 pound)
   Italian bread, cut into cubes

In a 1-1/2-qt. slow cooker, combine the spaghetti sauce, cheeses, oregano, onion and garlic powder. Cook for 4-6 hours or until cheese is melted and sauce is hot. Serve with bread cubes. **Yield:** 12 servings (4 cups).

Spicy Hummus

Hummus is a Middle Eastern spread made from seasoned mashed chickpeas. Served with pita wedges, this version from our Test Kitchen home economists is a simple, satisfying snack.

1/4 cup packed fresh parsley
   sprigs
2 tablespoons chopped onion
1 garlic clove
1 can (15 ounces) chickpeas *or*
   garbanzo beans, rinsed and
   drained
2 tablespoons sesame seeds,
   ground
2 tablespoons cider vinegar
2 teaspoons soy sauce
2 teaspoons lime juice
1 teaspoon honey

1 teaspoon Dijon mustard
1/4 teaspoon salt
1/4 teaspoon *each* ground cumin, ginger, coriander
   and paprika
Pita bread, cut into wedges

In a food processor or blender, combine the parsley, onion and garlic; cover and process until smooth. Add the chickpeas, sesame seeds, vinegar, soy sauce, lime juice, honey, mustard and seasonings; cover and process until smooth. Serve with pita bread. **Yield:** 1-1/2 cups.

Calico Clams Casino

A few years ago, I came across this recipe in the back of my files when I was looking for a special appetizer. Everyone raved about it. Now it's an often-requested dish.
—*Paula Sullivan, Barker, New York*

3 cans (6-1/2 ounces *each*) chopped clams
1 cup (4 ounces) shredded mozzarella cheese
1 cup (4 ounces) shredded cheddar cheese
4 bacon strips, cooked and crumbled
3 tablespoons seasoned bread crumbs
3 tablespoons butter, melted
2 tablespoons *each* finely chopped onion, celery and sweet red, yellow and green peppers
1 garlic clove, minced
Dash dried parsley flakes

Drain clams, reserving 2 tablespoons of juice. In a large bowl, combine the clams and remaining ingredients; stir in the reserved clam juice. Spoon into greased 6-oz. custard cups or clamshell dishes; place on baking sheets. Bake at 350° for 10-15 minutes or until heated through and lightly browned. **Yield:** 8 servings.

Egg Salad Wonton Cups

Crispy wonton wrappers are a nice contrast to the creamy egg salad in this appetizer from our Test Kitchen. It's a mouth-watering alternative to traditional deviled eggs.

36 wonton wrappers
3 cups prepared egg salad
1/3 cup chopped green onions
1/3 cup shredded carrot
10 bacon strips, cooked and crumbled
9 cherry tomatoes, quartered
Parsley sprigs

Coat one side of each wonton wrapper with nonstick cooking spray; gently press into miniature muffin cups, greased side down. Bake at 350° for 10-12 minutes or until golden brown. Remove to wire racks to cool.

In a bowl, combine the egg salad, onions and carrot; mix well. Stir in the bacon. Spoon about 1 tablespoon into each wonton cup. Garnish with tomatoes and parsley. **Yield:** 3 dozen.

Holiday Luminaries

As you and your neighbors make the rounds from house to house, light the way with these festive luminaries. They can be made well in advance. Simply light them just before your guests arrive.

Sand
Clear glass quart jars
Tea light candles
Red faceted plastic beads
Artificial wired pine garlands
   (13-inch lengths)

Place 1 cup sand in the bottom of each jar. Use a long-handled pastry brush to level. Place tea light candle in center of sand. Sprinkle about 1/4 cup of beads around each candle, using pastry brush to distribute them evenly. Wrap garland around outside bottom of jar and twist ends together to hold; arrange garland as desired.

A Tree Trimming Get-Together

WONDERING how to make the joyful job of decorating your evergreen even merrier? Go out on a limb and enlist the help of family and friends!

They won't need much needling to accept the invitation when you promise to reward them with some festive fare.

As your guests string the lights, hang the ornaments and drape the garland, they can nibble on Italian Meatball Hoagies and Confetti Tortellini Salad.

For sweets that appeal to the kid in everyone, set out a platter of Snowflake and Icicle Cookies (which also serve as edible ornaments) and Gingerbread Teddies.

A Casual Spread
(Clockwise from top right)

Snowflake and Icicle Cookies (p. 321)

Confetti Tortellini Salad (p. 320)

Gingerbread Teddies (p. 319)

Italian Meatball Hoagies (p. 318)

Italian Meatball Hoagies

(Pictured on page 316)

My sister and I often prepare the meals for our busy family of eight. We like recipes that are easy to prepare yet filling. Served with a salad, these sandwiches are satisfying.
—*Anna Collom, Hewitt, Minnesota*

4 eggs
1/2 cup milk
1 cup grated Parmesan cheese
2 garlic cloves, minced
2 tablespoons dried parsley flakes
1-1/2 teaspoons dried basil
1-1/2 teaspoons dried oregano
1/4 teaspoon pepper
2 pounds ground beef
2 cups crushed saltines (about 60 crackers)
SAUCE:
2 cans (15 ounces *each*) tomato sauce
1/2 cup grated Parmesan cheese
1-1/2 teaspoons dried oregano
1 teaspoon dried basil
1 teaspoon dried parsley flakes
1/2 teaspoon salt
12 submarine sandwich buns (about 6 inches), split
Sliced mozzarella cheese, optional

In a large bowl, combine the first eight ingredients. Crumble beef over mixture and sprinkle with cracker crumbs; mix gently. Shape into 1-in. balls. Place in ungreased 15-in. x 10-in. x 1-in. baking pans. Bake at 350° for 20-25 minutes or until meat is no longer pink. Drain on paper towels.

In a large saucepan, combine the tomato sauce, Parmesan cheese, oregano, basil, parsley and salt. Bring to a boil over medium heat; add meatballs. Reduce heat; cover and simmer for 20 minutes or until heated through. Serve meatballs and sauce on buns. Top with mozzarella cheese if desired. **Yield:** 12 servings.

Barley Turkey Soup

Instead of using chicken broth, I frequently make homemade stock using the leftover holiday turkey. A steaming bowl of soup takes the chill out of winter.
—*Mrs. Warren Constans, Fruitland, Idaho*

2 quarts chicken broth
1-1/2 cups diced celery
1 cup medium pearl barley
1 medium onion, diced
3/4 cup diced carrots
1/4 teaspoon salt
1/2 teaspoon dried thyme
1 bay leaf
1/8 teaspoon ground allspice
1/8 teaspoon pepper
Dash cayenne pepper
2 cups cubed cooked turkey
1/4 cup minced fresh parsley, optional

In a Dutch oven or soup kettle, combine the first 11 ingredients. Bring to a boil. Reduce heat; simmer, uncovered, for 30-40 minutes or until vegetables and barley are tender. Stir in turkey and parsley if desired; heat through. Discard bay leaf before serving. **Yield:** 9 servings.

Gingerbread Teddies

(Pictured at right and on page 317)

Kids of all ages will be delighted to see these roly-poly teddy bears adorning your holiday table! I've been using this gingerbread recipe for as long as I can remember.
—Judith Scholovich
Waukesha, Wisconsin

4-1/2 cups all-purpose flour, *divided*
    2 cups packed brown sugar
1-1/2 cups shortening
  1/2 cup molasses
    2 eggs
    2 teaspoons baking soda
    2 teaspoons ground cinnamon
    2 teaspoons ground ginger
    1 teaspoon ground cloves
Semisweet chocolate chips

In a large mixing bowl, combine 2-1/4 cups flour, brown sugar, shortening, molasses, eggs, baking soda, cinnamon, ginger and cloves. Beat on high speed until combined. Beat in remaining flour. Cover and refrigerate for at least 2 hours.

Shape dough into 12 balls, 1-3/4 in. each; 12 balls, 1-1/4 in. each; 72 balls, 1/2 in. each; and 60 balls, 3/8 in. each. Place the 1-3/4-in. balls on three foil-lined baking sheets for the body of 12 bears; flatten to 1/2-in. thickness. Position 1-1/4-in. balls for heads; flatten to 1/2-in. thickness.

Attach six 1/2-in. balls to each bear for arms, legs and ears. Attach four 3/8-in. balls for paws. Attach one 3/8-in. ball for nose. Add chocolate chips for eyes and belly buttons. Make three cuts halfway through the dough on the end of each paw; make an indendation in each ear with a wooden spoon handle.

Bake at 350° for 12-16 minutes or until set. Cool for 10 minutes before carefully removing from pans to wire racks to cool completely (cookies will be fragile while warm). **Yield:** 1 dozen.

Editor's Note: Any remaining dough may be shaped into balls and baked for 8-10 minutes.

Confetti Tortellini Salad

(Pictured on page 317)

After sampling a similar pasta salad at a market in Florida, I came home to develop my own version. This recipe is as close to the original as anything I've ever tried.
—Suzanne Zick, Lincolnton, North Carolina

1-1/2 cups refrigerated *or* frozen
    cheese tortellini
1 cup cauliflowerets
1 cup broccoli florets
2 medium carrots, cut
    into 1/4-inch slices
2 tablespoons thinly sliced
    green onions
1 garlic clove, minced
1/4 cup grated Parmesan cheese
1/2 cup Italian salad dressing
1/4 teaspoon hot pepper sauce

In a large saucepan, cook tortellini according to package directions; drain. In a bowl, combine the tortellini, vegetables and garlic. Sprinkle with cheese. Combine the salad dressing and hot pepper sauce; pour over salad and toss gently. Cover and refrigerate until serving. **Yield:** 6 servings.

TREE DECORATING TIPS

A BEAUTIFULLY decorated Christmas tree adds to the magical memories of the holidays. So spruce up your evergreen like a pro with these helpful hints:

- Instead of simply wrapping the lights around your tree, string the lights around the branches, starting at the trunk and working out.

  As you come to the end of each strand, turn on the lights, stand back and move the lights to fill in any holes. Plan on a strand of 100 lights for every foot your tree is tall.

- When hanging ornaments, the general rule of thumb is to have the larger ornaments near the bottom of the tree and the smaller ones on top.

  Add depth by placing some ornaments near the trunk and some closer to the branch tip. Use approximately 40 ornaments for every tree foot.

- The last thing to do is add the garland. String less garland near the top and add more as you work your way down. Thin garlands look best when draped from branch to branch, while thick garlands are more appealing when loosely wrapped around the tree. For every tree foot, you'll need about two strands of garland.

Snowflake and Icicle Cookies

(Pictured at right and on page 317)

Our Test Kitchen home economists bring some of winter's wonder indoors with shaped butter cookies that get their sparkle from edible glitter. These cookie ornaments are great favors for your trim-a-tree party guests.

1 cup butter, softened
1 cup confectioners' sugar
1 egg
1 teaspoon vanilla extract
1/2 to 1 teaspoon almond extract
2-1/2 cups all-purpose flour
1/2 teaspoon salt
GLAZE:
1-1/2 cups confectioners' sugar
1 tablespoon light corn syrup
1/4 teaspoon vanilla extract
2 to 3 tablespoons water
White edible glitter *or* coarse sugar
Ribbon

In a large mixing bowl, cream butter and sugar. Beat in egg and extracts until light and fluffy. Combine flour and salt; gradually add to the creamed mixture. Divide dough in half. Place one portion in a bowl; shape the other portion into a 5-in. log. Cover both and refrigerate for 1-2 hours or until easy to handle.

For snowflakes: Divide dough from bowl in half. On a lightly floured surface, roll out one portion to 1/8-in. thickness. (Refrigerate other portion until ready to use.) Cut nine medium snowflakes and six large snowflakes with cookie cutters. Carefully place 1 in. apart on ungreased baking sheets. Using small decorating cutters, cut out desired shapes to create designs in snowflakes. Use a toothpick to help remove the cutouts. Cut six small snowflakes and place 1 in. apart on another baking sheet. With a plastic straw, poke a hole in the top of each cookie. Bake medium and large snowflakes at 375° for 6-1/2 to 7 minutes and small snowflakes for 6 minutes or until bottoms are lightly browned. Remove to wire racks to cool.

For icicles: Cut log into 1/4-in. slices; roll each into a 9-in. rope, tapering from the center to each end. Fold each rope in half; twist, pinching the ends to a point. Place 2 in. apart on ungreased baking sheets. Bake at 375° for 8-10 minutes or until lightly browned. Immediately poke a hole in the top of each icicle with a plastic straw. Remove to wire racks to cool.

For glaze, combine the sugar, corn syrup and vanilla in a bowl. Gradually add enough water to make a thin glaze. Brush over icicles and snowflakes; sprinkle with glitter or sugar. Let stand for at least 5 minutes or until set. Thread ribbon through the hole in the icicles and small snowflakes and through a cutout in the medium and large snowflakes. **Yield:** about 20 icicles and 21 snowflakes.

Editor's Note: Snowflake cookie cutters and decorating tools can be ordered from Sweet Celebrations, Inc. Call 1-800/328-6722 or visit *www.sweetc.com*. Edible glitter can be found at cake decorating specialty stores.

Focaccia Sandwich

My family believes that nothing satisfies hunger like a sandwich, so I make them often for lunch,
dinner and late-night snacking. They request this version often.
— *Tina Miller, Sun Valley, Nevada*

1 loaf (1 pound) focaccia bread
1/2 cup spinach dip *or* chive and
   onion cream cheese spread
2 tablespoons Dijon mustard
8 ounces thinly sliced deli
   smoked turkey
4 ounces sliced Swiss cheese
1 medium tomato, thinly sliced

Cut bread in half horizontally. Spread 1/4 cup spinach dip on each half; spread with mustard. Layer the turkey, cheese and tomato on bottom half; replace top half. Cut into wedges. **Yield:** 10-12 servings.

Peppermint Ice Cream Dessert

With pudding, ice cream and whipped topping, this cool and creamy dessert is the perfect
complement to a rich holiday meal. You'll appreciate its make-ahead convenience.
—*Cindy Cyr, Fowler, Indiana*

2 cups graham cracker crumbs
   (about 32 squares)
3/4 cup butter, softened
3 tablespoons sugar
FILLING:
1-1/2 cups cold milk
2 packages (3.9 ounces *each*)
   instant chocolate pudding mix
1 quart peppermint ice cream,
   softened
1 carton (8 ounces) frozen
   whipped topping, thawed

In a bowl, combine the cracker crumbs, butter and sugar. Set aside 3/4 cup for topping. Press remaining crumb mixture into an ungreased 13-in. x 9-in. x 2-in. dish. In a bowl, whisk milk and pudding mix for 2 minutes. Let stand for 2 minutes or until soft-set. Stir in ice cream until smooth. Pour over crust. Chill for at least 1 hour.

Spread with whipped topping and sprinkle with reserved crumbs. Cover and refrigerate for 6-8 hours or overnight. **Yield:** 12-15 servings.

MAKING COOKIE AND CRACKER CRUMBS

PLACE cookies or crackers in a heavy-duty resealable plastic bag. Seal bag, pushing out as much air as possible. Press a rolling pin over the bag, crushing the crackers to fine crumbs. Crumbs also can be made in a blender or food processor.

Special Hot Chocolate Treats

(Pictured at right)

Dropping a whipped cream-filled chocolate cup into hot chocolate makes for an extra-special beverage. I make the chocolate cups ahead, chill them, then fill just before serving.
—Iola Egle, Bella Vista, Arkansas

HOT CHOCOLATE MIX:
- 8 **cups nonfat dry milk powder**
- 1 **package (15 ounces) instant chocolate drink mix**
- 1-1/2 **cups powdered nondairy creamer**
- 1-1/4 **cups confectioners' sugar**
- 3 **tablespoons instant coffee granules**
- 1/4 **teaspoon ground cinnamon**
- 1 **envelope unsweetened orange *or* raspberry soft drink mix**

CHOCOLATE CUPS:
- 1/2 **cup semisweet chocolate chips**
- 1 **teaspoon shortening**

Whipped cream in a can

In a large bowl, combine the first seven ingredients; mix well. Store in an airtight container for up to 6 months.

For chocolate cups, in a microwave, melt chips and shortening; stir until smooth. With a small pastry brush or 1/2 teaspoon measure, spread chocolate mixture on the inside of 1-in. foil or paper candy cups. Place on a baking sheet. Refrigerate for 45 minutes or until firm. Just before serving, remove foil or paper cups and add whipped cream. **Yield:** 11 cups hot chocolate mix and 16 chocolate cups.

To prepare hot chocolate: For each serving, combine 1/3 cup mix and 1 cup boiling water; stir to dissolve. Place one filled chocolate cup in each mug; stir until melted.

Thick 'n' Chewy Pizza

This crowd-pleasing pizza is topped with a zippy sauce and family-favorite
ingredients. A co-worker shared the recipe with me.
—Linda Pasbrig, West Bend, Wisconsin

1 package (1/4 ounce) active
 dry yeast
1/4 cup warm water (110°
 to 115°)
1 egg
1 can (8 ounces) tomato sauce,
 divided
3 tablespoons vegetable oil
1 tablespoon sugar
1 teaspoon salt
1/4 teaspoon chili powder
1/4 to 1/2 teaspoon hot pepper
 sauce, *divided*
2-1/4 to 2-1/2 cups all-purpose
 flour
1 pound ground beef
3/4 cup chopped onion
1 can (4 ounces) mushroom
 stems and pieces, drained
1/3 cup chopped stuffed olives
1/4 cup chopped green pepper

1 tablespoon butter, melted
2 cups (8 ounces) shredded mozzarella cheese

In a mixing bowl, dissolve yeast in warm water. Add egg, 1/4 cup tomato sauce, oil, sugar, salt, chili powder and 1/8 to 1/4 teaspoon hot pepper sauce; beat until smooth. Add 1 cup flour; beat for 1 minute. Stir in enough remaining flour to form a soft dough. Turn onto a floured surface; knead until smooth and elastic, about 6-8 minutes. Place in a greased bowl, turning once to grease top. Cover and let rise in a warm place until doubled, about 1 hour.

Meanwhile, in a skillet, cook beef over medium heat until no longer pink; drain. Remove from the heat; stir in onion, mushrooms, olives, green pepper and remaining tomato sauce and hot pepper sauce.

Punch dough down; turn onto a lightly floured surface. Roll into a 14-in. x 9-in. rectangle. Place in a greased 15-in. x 10-in. x 1-in. baking pan. Brush with butter. Top with meat mixture; sprinkle with cheese. Bake at 425° for 15 minutes or until crust is lightly browned and cheese is melted. **Yield:** 8-10 slices.

Snowball Eggnog Punch

Our grandchildren are thrilled when this ice cream punch appears on my brunch menu.
The tang from orange juice blends beautifully with the rich eggnog.
—Joann Johnson, Mountain View, Arkansas

2 quarts eggnog, chilled
1 quart orange juice, chilled
1 quart vanilla ice cream

Just before serving, combine the eggnog and orange juice in a punch bowl. Add scoops of ice cream. **Yield:** 3 quarts.

Editor's Note: This recipe was tested with commercially prepared eggnog.

Christmas Tree Sweet Rolls

(Pictured at right)

Every Christmas Eve, I make a special bread to enjoy the next morning while opening gifts. I often share one of the "trees" with a neighbor.
—*Lori Daniels, Beverly, West Virginia*

2 packages (1/4 ounce *each*) active dry yeast
2-1/2 cups warm water (110° to 115°), *divided*
1/2 cup nonfat dry milk powder
1/2 cup vegetable oil
2 tablespoons sugar
2 teaspoons salt
7 to 8 cups all-purpose flour
FILLING:
1 package (8 ounces) cream cheese, softened
1/3 cup sugar
1 teaspoon vanilla extract
1/4 teaspoon ground cinnamon
1 can (8 ounces) crushed pineapple, well drained
1/2 cup chopped red and green candied cherries
1/4 cup chopped pecans
GLAZE:
2 cups confectioners' sugar
2 tablespoons milk
1 tablespoon butter, softened
1 teaspoon vanilla extract
Red candied cherries and green colored sugar

In a large mixing bowl, dissolve yeast in 1/2 cup warm water. Add milk powder, oil, sugar, salt, remaining water and 2 cups flour. Beat on medium speed for 2 minutes. Stir in enough remaining flour to form a soft dough. Turn onto a floured surface; knead until smooth and elastic, about 6-8 minutes. Place in a greased bowl, turning once to grease top. Cover and let rise in a warm place until doubled, about 1 hour.

Meanwhile, in a small mixing bowl, combine the cream cheese, sugar, vanilla and cinnamon. Stir in the pineapple, cherries and pecans; set aside. Punch dough down. Turn onto a lightly floured surface; divide in half. Roll each portion into an 11-in. x 9-in. rectangle. Spread filling to within 1/2 in. of edges. Roll up each rectangle jelly-roll style, starting with a long side; pinch seam to seal.

To form a tree, cut each log into 11 slices, 1 in. each. Cover two baking sheets with foil and grease well. Center one slice near the top of each prepared baking sheet for tree-top. Arrange slices with sides touching in three more rows, adding one slice for each row, forming a tree. Center the remaining slice below the tree for trunk. Cover and let rise until doubled, about 30 minutes.

Bake at 350° for 20-25 minutes or until golden brown. Transfer foil with trees to wire racks; cool for 20 minutes. For glaze, in a bowl, combine the confectioners' sugar, milk, butter and vanilla until smooth. Transfer to a small pastry or plastic bag; cut a small hole in a corner of the bag. Pipe garlands on trees. Decorate with cherries and colored sugar. **Yield:** 2 trees (11 rolls each).

Three-Layer Gelatin Salad

My love of cooking started in high school. Now I get to try out recipes at church, where my husband is the pastor. My mother-in-law gave me the recipe for this pretty layered salad.
—*Christine Fletcher, Bronx, New York*

RASPBERRY LAYER:
   1 **package (3 ounces) raspberry gelatin**
   1 **cup boiling water**
   1 **package (10 ounces) frozen sweetened raspberries**
ORANGE LAYER:
   1 **can (11 ounces) mandarin oranges**
   1 **package (3 ounces) orange gelatin**
   1 **cup boiling water**
   1 **package (8 ounces) cream cheese, softened**
LIME LAYER:
   1 **package (3 ounces) lime gelatin**
   1 **cup boiling water**
   1 **can (8-1/2 ounces) crushed pineapple, undrained**

In a bowl, dissolve raspberry gelatin in boiling water. Stir in raspberries until thawed. Pour into an 8-in. square dish; refrigerate until set.

Drain oranges, reserving juice. In a mixing bowl, dissolve orange gelatin in boiling water. Beat in cream cheese and reserved juice; mix well. Fold in oranges. Pour over raspberry layer; refrigerate until set.

In a bowl, dissolve lime gelatin in boiling water. Stir in pineapple; cool for 10 minutes. Carefully spoon over orange layer. Refrigerate until set. **Yield:** 12-16 servings.

MAKING TABLETOP TREES

1. Wrap each cone with parchment paper, using straight pins to secure.

2. Wrap jute string and raffia around cone in a spiral pattern until desired look is achieved. Let dry.

3. With a table knife, remove parchment paper from the cone. Carefully separate the parchment paper from the jute and raffia.

Tabletop Trees

(Pictured above and on page 316)

*For a country-style centerpiece, try your hand at these jute string and raffia
Christmas trees. Tuck in a few branches from your evergreen, then add a
little garland or some ornaments for a tabletop "forest" in a flash!*

Styrofoam cones in assorted sizes
Parchment paper
Three-ply natural jute string
Green raffia
Commercial stiffener
**Large, medium and small 1/8-inch-
   thick natural wooden star cutouts**
Gold metallic acrylic craft paint
Small flat paintbrush
Craft glue

Wrap each cone shape with parchment paper, using straight
pins to secure paper to cone. Soak jute string and raffia in
stiffener as directed by manufacturer. Wrap jute string
around cone shape in a spiral pattern. Add raffia in the same
way. Continue to add jute and raffia alternately until desired
look is achieved, making sure the bottom of the cone is level. Secure any loose ends with straight pins. Let dry.

Carefully insert a table knife between the cone and parchment paper; move the cone around to loosen. Carefully remove parchment paper from the jute and raffia. Paint all sides
of each star gold; let dry. Glue a star to the top of each tree.

Casual New Year's Eve Buffet

INSTEAD of heading out to an expensive New Year's Eve gala, welcome in the New Year at home with friends and family.

After breaking the bank on Christmas gifts, you can forgo fancy and prepare a down-home spread of flavorful, frugal fare.

Marinated Beef Sandwiches, Whole Wheat Dinner Rolls, Almond Good Luck Cake, Broccoli Salad Supreme and Almond Creme fill the bill for any budget.

Or turn the page for other appealing appetizers, main courses, side dishes and desserts.

Simple decorations like balloons, streamers, horns and party hats are inexpensive additions that make the evening fun and festive.

RING IN THE NEW YEAR

(Clockwise from top left)

Marinated Beef Sandwiches (p. 332)

Whole Wheat Dinner Rolls (p. 334)

Almond Good Luck Cake (p. 333)

Broccoli Salad Supreme (p. 330)

Almond Creme (p. 331)

Broccoli Salad Supreme

(Pictured on page 329)

People can't get enough of the sweet grapes and crunchy broccoli in this colorful salad. I appreciate its make-ahead convenience.
— *Terri Twyman, Bonanza, Oregon*

10 cups broccoli florets
  (about 3-1/2 pounds)
6 cups seedless red grapes
  (about 3 pounds)
1 cup sliced celery
6 green onions, sliced
2 cups mayonnaise
2/3 cup sugar
2 tablespoons cider vinegar

1 pound sliced bacon, cooked and crumbled
1-1/3 cups slivered almonds, toasted

In a large salad bowl, combine the broccoli, grapes, celery and onions. In a small bowl, combine the mayonnaise, sugar and vinegar. Pour over broccoli mixture and toss to coat. Cover and refrigerate for at least 4 hours or overnight. Just before serving, gently stir in bacon and almonds. **Yield:** about 20 servings.

Beef 'n' Bean Egg Rolls

Unlike traditional cabbage-filled egg rolls, this version uses southwest-seasoned ground beef and beans. These are a regular part of our New Year's Eve "snack fest."
—*Laura Mahaffey, Annapolis, Maryland*

1/2 pound ground beef
1/4 cup chopped onion
2 tablespoons chopped green pepper
1 cup refried beans
1/4 cup shredded cheddar cheese
1 tablespoon ketchup
1-1/2 teaspoons chili powder
1/4 teaspoon ground cumin
32 wonton wrappers
Oil for deep-fat frying
Salsa

In a large skillet, cook the beef, onion and green pepper over medium heat until meat is no longer pink; drain. Remove from the heat; stir in beans, cheese, ketchup, chili powder and cumin.

Position a wonton wrapper with one point toward you. Place 1 tablespoon meat mixture in the center. Fold bottom corner over filling; fold sides toward center over filling. Roll toward the remaining point. Moisten top corner with water; press to seal. Repeat with remaining wrappers and filling.

In an electric skillet or deep-fat fryer, heat oil to 375°. Fry egg rolls, a few at a time, for 2 minutes or until golden brown. Drain on paper towels. Serve with salsa. **Yield:** 32 egg rolls.

Editor's Note: Fill wonton wrappers a few at a time, keeping others covered until ready to use.

Almond Creme

(Pictured at right and on page 328)

My mother often made this rich, velvety dessert for New Year's Eve. Now that I'm married, I plan to carry on the tradition.
— Marcie McEachern, Dallas, Texas

2 envelopes unflavored gelatin
1/2 cup water
3 cups heavy whipping cream
1 cup sugar
4 eggs, beaten
1 teaspoon almond extract
Fresh raspberries and chocolate
  curls, optional

In a saucepan, sprinkle gelatin over water. Let stand for 1 minute. Stir in cream and sugar. Cook and stir over medium-low heat for 5 minutes or until gelatin is dissolved.

Remove from the heat. Stir a small amount of hot mixture into eggs; return all to the pan, stirring constantly. Cook and stir over medium heat until a thermometer reads 160° (do not boil). Remove from the heat. Stir in almond extract.

Pour into dessert dishes. Refrigerate until set. Garnish with raspberries and chocolate curls if desired. **Yield:** 8 servings.

THE STRAIGHT STORY ON CHOCOLATE CURLS

FOR A SWEET TWIST, garnish your dessert with chocolate curls. There are two ways to make them.

- If you have a solid block of chocolate, warm it in the microwave for a few seconds. Then hold a vegetable peeler against a flat side of the block and carefully bring the blade toward you. Allow the curls to fall onto a plate or piece of waxed paper in a single layer.

- If you don't have a block of chocolate, melt chocolate chips, chocolate candy coating or chocolate bars. (The amount needed depends on the number of curls you want.)

  Pour the chocolate onto the back of an inverted cookie sheet and spread to a smooth, thin layer. Let cool until firm and pliable, not brittle. With a cheese slicer, metal spatula or pancake turner and using even pressure, scrape a thin layer of chocolate. The chocolate will curl as you go. The slower you scrape, the wider your curls will be.

  Slide a toothpick or wooden skewer through each curl to carefully lift it onto the dessert and arrange as desired.

Marinated Beef Sandwiches

(Pictured on page 328)

This recipe from my sister-in-law is especially good when entertaining for New Year's and football games. No one walks away hungry after eating one of these hearty sandwiches.
—*Elizabeth Stoddart, West Lafayette, Indiana*

1-1/2 cups water
  3/4 cup packed dark brown sugar
  3/4 cup soy sauce
    2 tablespoons lemon juice
    3 small onions, sliced
    3 garlic cloves, minced
1-1/2 teaspoons ground ginger
    1 boneless beef rump roast
      (about 4 pounds)
  12 to 14 sandwich rolls, split

In a gallon-size resealable plastic bag, combine the first seven ingredients; add roast. Seal bag and turn to coat; refrigerate overnight, turning occasionally. Transfer roast and marinade to a Dutch oven. Cover and bake at 325° for 2-1/2 to 3 hours or until meat is tender. Thinly slice; serve beef and juice on rolls. **Yield:** 12-14 servings.

SERVING IN A SLOW COOKER

YOU CAN BAKE the beef for Marinated Beef Sandwiches the day before your party. Transfer the sliced beef and cooking juices to a slow cooker and refrigerate. The next day, reheat on low before your guests arrive. Serve on rolls.

Black-Eyed Pea Soup

Since we raise our own pigs, I like to use ground pork in this zesty soup. But I've used ground beef with equally good results. Green chilies give this dish some southwestern flair.
—*Mary Lou Chernik, Taos, New Mexico*

1-1/2 pounds ground pork
    1 large onion, chopped
    2 garlic cloves, minced
    3 cans (15-1/2 ounces *each*)
      black-eyed peas, rinsed and
      drained
    2 cups water
    1 can (14-1/2 ounces) stewed
      tomatoes
    1 can (10 ounces) diced
      tomatoes and green chilies
    1 can (4 ounces) chopped green
      chilies

    1 tablespoon beef bouillon granules
    1 tablespoon molasses
    1 teaspoon Worcestershire sauce
  1/2 teaspoon salt
  1/4 teaspoon pepper
  1/4 teaspoon ground cumin

In a large soup kettle or Dutch oven, cook the pork, onion and garlic over medium heat until meat is no longer pink; drain. Stir in the remaining ingredients; bring to a boil. Reduce heat; cover and simmer for 45 minutes. **Yield:** 12 servings (about 3 quarts).

Almond Good Luck Cake

(Pictured at right and on page 329)

I make this cake for every New Year's Eve dinner. It's said that the person who finds the one whole almond inside will have good luck during the upcoming year.
— *Vivian Nikanow, Chicago, Illinois*

1/2 cup chopped almonds
1 tablespoon plus 2-1/3 cups
    all-purpose flour, *divided*
1/3 cup butter, softened
1/3 cup shortening
1-1/4 cups sugar, *divided*
3 eggs, *separated*
2 tablespoons lemon juice
1 teaspoon grated lemon peel
1 teaspoon vanilla extract
1 teaspoon almond extract
2 teaspoons baking powder
1/2 teaspoon salt
1/4 teaspoon baking soda
3/4 cup milk
1/2 teaspoon cream of tartar
1 whole almond
APRICOT GLAZE:
1/2 cup apricot preserves
1 tablespoon orange juice

Combine almonds and 1 tablespoon flour; sprinkle into a well-greased 10-in. fluted tube pan. Set aside. In a large mixing bowl, cream the butter, shortening and 1 cup sugar. Add egg yolks, one at a time, beating well after each addition. Stir in lemon juice, peel and extracts. Combine the baking powder, salt, baking soda and remaining flour; add to the creamed mixture alternately with milk.

In a small mixing bowl, beat egg whites and cream of tartar until soft peaks form. Beat in the remaining sugar, 1 tablespoon at a time, until stiff. Fold into batter. Pour into prepared pan. Insert whole almond into batter.

Bake at 350° for 40-45 minutes or until a toothpick inserted near the center comes out clean. Cool for 10 minutes before removing from pan to a wire rack.

For glaze, melt preserves in a microwave or saucepan; strain. Add orange juice; drizzle over warm cake. **Yield:** 12 servings.

Whole Wheat Dinner Rolls

(Pictured on page 329)

Our family has come to expect my husband's grandma to make these rolls for every gathering.
With their simple down-home flavor, they're great for sandwiches or just topped with butter.
—Kerry Luce, Woodstock, Vermont

3 to 4 cups all-purpose flour
3 cups whole wheat flour
1/2 cup sugar
2 packages (1/4 ounce *each*)
   active dry yeast
1 tablespoon salt
2 cups milk
1/2 cup vegetable oil
2 tablespoons molasses
2 eggs
GLAZE:
1 egg white
1 tablespoon water
Sesame *or* poppy seeds, optional

In a large mixing bowl, combine 1/2 cup all-purpose flour, whole wheat flour, sugar, yeast and salt. In a saucepan, heat milk, oil and molasses to 120°-130°. Add to dry ingredients. Add eggs; beat on low speed until moistened. Beat on medium for 3 minutes. Stir in enough remaining all-purpose flour to form a soft dough.

Turn onto a floured surface; knead until smooth and elastic, about 6-8 minutes. Place in a greased bowl, turning once to grease top. Cover and let rise in a warm place until doubled, about 1 hour.

Punch dough down. Divide in half; shape each portion into 12 balls. Place 1 in. apart in two greased 13-in. x 9-in. x 2-in. baking pans. Cover and let rise until doubled, about 45 minutes. Beat egg white and water until foamy; lightly brush over dough. Sprinkle with sesame or poppy seeds if desired. Bake at 350° for 20-25 minutes or until golden brown. **Yield:** 2 dozen.

Lacy Oat Sandwich Wafers

These cookies appear on my table for various special occasions. I'm often asked for the recipe,
so I'm sure to have a few copies on hand.
—Ruth Lee, Troy, Ontario

2/3 cup butter
2 cups quick-cooking oats
1 cup sugar
2/3 cup all-purpose flour
1/4 cup milk
1/4 cup corn syrup
2 cups semisweet chocolate,
   milk chocolate, vanilla *or*
   white chips, melted

In a saucepan, melt butter over low heat. Remove from the heat. Stir in the oats, sugar, flour, milk and corn syrup; mix well. Drop by teaspoonfuls 2 in. apart onto foil-lined baking sheets. Bake at 375° for 8-10 minutes or until golden brown. Cool completely; peel cookies off foil.

Spread melted chocolate on the bottom of half of the cookies; top with remaining cookies. **Yield:** about 3-1/2 dozen.

Baked Deli Sandwich

(Pictured at right)

Frozen bread dough, easy assembly and quick baking time make this stuffed sandwich an appetizer I rely on often. This is one of my most-requested recipes. It's easy to double for a crowd or to try with different meats and cheeses.
—Sandra McKenzie
Braham, Minnesota

1 loaf (1 pound) frozen bread dough, thawed
2 tablespoons butter, melted
1/4 teaspoon garlic salt
1/4 teaspoon dried basil
1/4 teaspoon dried oregano
1/4 teaspoon pizza seasoning
1/4 pound sliced deli ham
6 thin slices mozzarella cheese
1/4 pound sliced deli smoked turkey breast
6 thin slices cheddar cheese
Pizza sauce, warmed, optional

On a baking sheet coated with non-stick cooking spray, roll dough into a small rectangle. Let rest for 5-10 minutes. In a small bowl, combine the butter and seasonings. Roll out dough into a 14-in. x 10-in. rectangle. Brush with half of the butter mixture.

Layer the ham, mozzarella cheese, turkey and cheddar cheese lengthwise over half of the dough to within 1/2 in. of edges. Fold dough over and pinch firmly to seal. Brush with remaining butter mixture.

Bake at 400° for 10-12 minutes or until golden brown. Cut into 1-in. slices. Serve immediately with pizza sauce if desired. **Yield:** 4-6 servings.

Family Traditions

WHEN my husband's Polish-Austrian parents immigrated to the United States, they brought along a wonderful New Year's Eve custom. Before the stroke of midnight, a coin is placed on every window ledge and above every doorway in the house. As the New Year enters the home through windows and doors, it carries along blessings of prosperity in the year to come. It's a fun tradition our two grown daughters now follow.
—Bonnie Ziolecki, Menomonee Falls, Wisconsin

Wild Rice Bread

Wild rice gives this tender bread a tasty nutty flavor. This recipe makes five loaves,
which are great for sharing. We enjoy slices warmed for dinner and toasted for breakfast.
—Susan Schock, Hibbing, Minnesota

2 packages (1/4 ounce *each*)
   active dry yeast
4-1/2 cups warm water (110°
   to 115°), *divided*
8 tablespoons sugar, *divided*
1/2 cup molasses
1/2 cup vegetable oil
2 tablespoons salt
1-1/2 cups cooked wild rice
14 to 15 cups all-purpose flour

In a mixing bowl, dissolve yeast in 1 cup warm water. Add 1 tablespoon sugar; let stand for 5 minutes. Add the molasses, oil, salt and remaining water and sugar; mix well. Add wild rice. Stir in enough flour to form a soft dough. Turn onto a floured surface; knead until smooth and elastic, about 6-8 minutes. Place in a greased bowl, turning once to grease top. Cover and let rise in a warm place until doubled, about 1-1/2 hours.

Punch dough down. Cover and let rise until doubled, about 1 hour. Punch dough down. Turn onto a lightly floured surface; divide into five portions. Shape each into a loaf. Place in five greased 9-in. x 5-in. x 3-in. loaf pans. Cover and let rise until doubled, about 1 hour.

Bake at 375° for 25-35 minutes or golden brown. Remove from pans to wire racks to cool. **Yield:** 5 loaves.

Make-Ahead Coleslaw

A blend of vegetables adds pretty color and pleasant crunch to this coleslaw.
It's nice to rely on make-ahead dishes like this when feeding a crowd.
—Andrea Hutchison, Canton, Oklahoma

1 large head cabbage, shredded
   (about 20 cups)
2 large onions, thinly sliced
2 celery ribs, thinly sliced
2 large carrots, shredded
1 large cucumber, thinly sliced
1 large green pepper, chopped
1 jar (4 ounces) diced
   pimientos, drained
1-1/2 cups sugar
1-1/2 cups vinegar
1/2 cup vegetable oil
1 teaspoon salt

1 teaspoon celery seed
1 teaspoon ground mustard
1/2 teaspoon dried basil
1/2 teaspoon dried marjoram
1/4 teaspoon pepper

In a large salad bowl, combine the first seven ingredients; set aside. In a large saucepan, combine the remaining ingredients. Bring to a boil; boil for 1-2 minutes or until the sugar is dissolved. Pour over cabbage mixture and toss to coat. Cover and refrigerate overnight or up to 1 week. **Yield:** about 20 servings.

Black-Eyed Pea Salsa

(Pictured at right)

Colorful tomatoes, green pepper and red onion contrast nicely with black-eyed peas.
—Lynn McAllister
Mt. Ulla, North Carolina

2 cans (15-1/2 ounces *each*) black-eyed peas, rinsed and drained
2 medium tomatoes, chopped
1 cup chopped green pepper
1/2 cup chopped red onion
4 green onions, sliced
1 garlic clove, minced
1 cup Italian salad dressing
1/4 cup sour cream
1/4 cup minced fresh parsley
Tortilla chips

In a bowl, combine the first six ingredients. Combine the salad dressing, sour cream and parsley. Add to the pea mixture; toss to coat. Cover and refrigerate for at least 4 hours. Serve with tortilla chips. **Yield:** 5 cups.

Golden Shrimp Puffs

I first served these at a New Year's Eve get-together a few years ago. After receiving raves, they became part of my regular appetizer offerings throughout the year.
—Patricia Slater, Baldwin, Ontario

6 tablespoons butter
3/4 cup water
1/4 teaspoon garlic salt
3/4 cup all-purpose flour
3 eggs
1 package (5 ounces) frozen cooked salad shrimp, thawed
1/4 cup chopped green onions
5 tablespoons grated Parmesan cheese, *divided*

In a saucepan, bring butter, water and garlic salt to a boil. Add flour all at once; stir until a smooth ball forms. Remove from the heat; let stand for 5 minutes. Add eggs, one at a time, beating well after each addition. Continue beating until mixture is smooth and shiny.

Stir in the shrimp, onions and 4 tablespoons Parmesan cheese. Drop by rounded teaspoonfuls 2 in. apart onto ungreased baking sheets. Sprinkle with remaining Parmesan cheese. Bake at 400° for 25-30 minutes or until golden brown. Serve warm. **Yield:** 4 dozen.

Cheddar Cheese Spread

A simple spread like this with some crackers is often all you need when entertaining.
Letting the spread refrigerate overnight blends the flavors beautifully.
—Kathy Rairigh, Milford, Indiana

 2 cartons (8 ounces *each*) sharp
   cheddar cheese spread
 1 package (8 ounces) cream
   cheese, softened
 1 teaspoon Worcestershire
   sauce
 1/2 teaspoon garlic powder
 1/2 teaspoon onion powder

 1/8 teaspoon salt
 1/8 teaspoon white pepper
 Assorted crackers

In a mixing bowl, combine the first seven ingredients; beat until smooth. Cover and refrigerate overnight. Serve with crackers. **Yield:** 3 cups.

Crunchy Caramel Corn

Kids at our New Year's Eve parties gobble up this sweet and crunchy popcorn.
—Shelly Gromer, Long Beach, California

 6 cups popped popcorn
 3/4 cup salted peanuts
 1/2 cup packed brown sugar
 1/4 cup butter
 2 tablespoons light corn syrup
 1/4 teaspoon salt
 1/2 teaspoon vanilla extract
 1/4 teaspoon baking soda

Place popcorn and peanuts in a large microwave-safe bowl; set aside. In another microwave-safe bowl, combine the brown sugar, butter, corn syrup and salt. Cover and microwave on high for 1 minute; stir. Microwave 2 minutes longer.

Stir in vanilla and baking soda. Pour over popcorn mixture. Microwave, uncovered, on high for 3 minutes, stirring several times. Spread on greased baking sheets to cool. Store in an airtight container. **Yield:** about 2 quarts.

Editor's Note: This recipe was tested in an 850-watt microwave.

POPCORN POINTERS

LEAN your ears this way for a few kernels of wisdom that will steer you toward perfect popcorn.

- 1 cup of unpopped kernels equals about 8 cups of popped popcorn.
- To pop popcorn on the stove, use a 3- or 4-quart pan with a loose-fitting lid to allow the steam to escape. Add 1/3 cup vegetable oil for every cup of kernels.
- Heat the oil to between 400° and 460° (if the oil smokes, it's too hot). Drop in one kernel, and when it pops, add the rest—just enough to cover the bottom of the pan with a single layer.
- Cover the pan and shake to spread the oil. When the popping begins to slow, remove the pan from the heat. The hot oil will continue to pop the remaining kernels.
- Don't pre-salt the kernels—this toughens the popcorn. If desired, salt the corn after it's popped.

Stuffed Shells Florentine

(Pictured at right)

For a little fancier New Year's gathering, I like to serve these pasta shells stuffed with cheese and spinach and topped with spaghetti sauce. Complete the meal with breadsticks and a tossed salad. Italian food is loved by all, and the aroma is warm and inviting.

— Trisha Kuster, Macomb, Illinois

1 package (12 ounces) jumbo pasta shells
1 egg, beaten
2 cartons (15 ounces *each*) ricotta cheese
1 package (10 ounces) frozen chopped spinach, thawed and squeezed dry
1/2 cup grated Parmesan cheese
1/2 teaspoon salt
1/2 teaspoon dried oregano
1/4 teaspoon pepper
1 jar (32 ounces) spaghetti sauce
Thin breadsticks, optional

Cook pasta shells according to package directions. Meanwhile, in a bowl, combine the egg, ricotta cheese, spinach, Parmesan cheese, salt, oregano and pepper; mix well. Drain shells; stuff with spinach mixture.

Place shells in a greased 13-in. x 9-in. x 2-in. baking dish. Pour spaghetti sauce over shells. Cover and bake at 350° for 30-40 minutes or until heated through. Serve with breadsticks if desired. **Yield:** 8-10 servings.

DRAINING JUMBO PASTA SHELLS

INSTEAD of draining jumbo pasta shells in a colander (which can cause them to tear), carefully remove them from the boiling water with a tongs. Pour out any water inside the shells and drain on lightly greased waxed paper until you're ready to stuff them.

Meatball Sub Sandwiches

*Making these saucy meatballs in advance and reheating them saves me precious time when
expecting company. These sandwiches are great casual fare for any get-together.*
—*Deena Hubler, Jasper, Indiana*

2 eggs
1 cup dry bread crumbs
2 tablespoons finely chopped
  onion
2 tablespoons grated Parmesan
  cheese
1 teaspoon salt
1/2 teaspoon pepper
1/2 teaspoon garlic powder
1/4 teaspoon Italian seasoning
2 pounds ground beef
1 jar (28 ounces) spaghetti
  sauce
12 sandwich rolls, split

Additional Parmesan cheese, and sliced onion and
  green peppers, optional

In a large bowl, combine the first eight ingredients. Crumble beef over mixture and mix well. Shape into 1-in. balls. Place in a single layer in a 3-qt. microwave-safe dish.

Cover and microwave on high for 5 minutes. Turn meatballs; cook 5-6 minutes longer or until no longer pink. Drain. Add spaghetti sauce. Cover and microwave on high for 3-5 minutes or until heated through. Serve on rolls. Top with Parmesan cheese, onion and green peppers if desired. **Yield:** 12 servings.

Editor's Note: This recipe was tested in an 850-watt microwave.

Greek Chicken

*This recipe earned me first place in a local cooking contest a few years ago.
For special occasions, I add four to six sun-dried tomatoes (soaked and drained according
to package directions) to the cheese mixture before blending.*
—*Nina Ivanoff, Prince George, British Columbia*

4 boneless skinless chicken
  breast halves
2 packages (4 ounces *each*) feta
  cheese
1 can (4-1/4 ounces) chopped
  ripe olives, drained
2 tablespoons olive oil, *divided*
1/2 teaspoon dried oregano
2 tablespoons dry white wine *or*
  chicken broth
1 teaspoon sugar
1 teaspoon balsamic vinegar
1 garlic clove, minced
1/4 teaspoon dried thyme
1 medium onion, sliced

Flatten chicken breasts to 1/8-in. thickness; set aside. In a food processor or blender, combine the cheese, olives, 1 tablespoon oil and oregano; cover and process until mixture reaches a thick chunky paste consistency. Spread over chicken breasts; roll up and tuck in ends. Secure with a wooden toothpick.

In a bowl, combine wine or broth, sugar, vinegar, garlic, thyme and remaining oil. Pour into an ungreased 2-qt. baking dish. Top with onion. Place chicken over onion. Cover and bake at 350° for 30 minutes. Uncover and baste with pan juices. Bake 15-20 minutes longer or until chicken juices run clear. **Yield:** 4 servings.

Hazelnut Mocha Torte

(Pictured at right)

This dessert is reminiscent of fine European cakes. I recently made it for my mother, who is German, and it brought back many fond memories for her.
—Elizabeth Blondefield
San Jose, California

6 egg whites
1/4 teaspoon cream of tartar
1 cup sugar
2 cups ground hazelnuts
1/4 cup all-purpose flour
MOCHA GANACHE:
   8 squares (1 ounce *each*)
     semisweet chocolate
   1 cup heavy whipping cream
   3 tablespoons butter
   2 teaspoons instant coffee
     granules
BUTTERCREAM:
   2/3 cup sugar
   1/4 cup water
   4 egg yolks, lightly beaten
   1 teaspoon vanilla extract
   1 cup butter
   1/4 cup confectioners' sugar
Additional ground hazelnuts
Whole hazelnuts and chocolate
  leaves

CHOCOLATE LEAVES

WASH mint, lemon or rose leaves; set aside to dry. Melt 1 cup semisweet chocolate chips and 1 tablespoon shortening. Brush evenly on underside of leaves. Chill until set, about 10 minutes. Apply a second layer; chill until set. Gently peel leaf away from chocolate. Cover and refrigerate until ready to use.

In a mixing bowl, beat egg whites until foamy. Add cream of tartar; beat until soft peaks form. Gradually add sugar, beating until sugar is dissolved and stiff peaks form. Combine hazelnuts and flour; fold into batter, 1/4 cup at a time. Spoon into two greased 9-in. round baking pans lined with waxed paper. Bake at 300° for 25-30 minutes or until cake springs back when lightly touched. Cool for 10 minutes before removing from pans to wire racks.

In a heavy saucepan, combine the ganache ingredients; cook and stir over low heat until chocolate and butter are melted. Remove from the heat. Set saucepan in ice; stir for 3-4 minutes or until thickened. Remove from ice and set aside.

For buttercream, combine sugar and water in a heavy saucepan. Bring to a boil; cook over medium-high heat until sugar is dissolved. Remove from the heat. Add a small amount of hot mixture to egg yolks; return all to pan. Cook and stir 2 minutes longer. Remove from the heat; stir in vanilla. Cool to room temperature. In a mixing bowl, cream butter until fluffy. Gradually beat in cooked sugar mixture. Beat in confectioners' sugar. If necessary, refrigerate until buttercream reaches spreading consistency.

Place one cake layer on a serving plate. Spread with half of ganache to within 1/4 in. of edges. Top with second cake layer and remaining ganache. Freeze for 5 minutes. Spread buttercream over top and sides of cake. Gently press ground hazelnuts into sides of cake. Garnish with whole hazelnuts and chocolate leaves. Refrigerate. **Yield:** 12-16 servings.

Soups & Breads Warm Up Winter

AFTER you've packed away the colorful holiday decorations, a few months of winter still lay ahead.

To keep the blues at bay, host a casual dinner party for relatives and friends, featuring a slew of down-home comfort foods.

You'll chase away Old Man Winter in a flash when you ladle out hearty helpings of simmering soups like Zippy Potato Soup, Spiced Chili served in Bread Bowls and Kielbasa Bean Soup. Don't forget to pass a basket of oven-fresh Cheddar Buttermilk Biscuits.

Just place a bright bouquet of flowers on the table and you have a satisfying spread that will add a little sunshine to even the most blustery winter day.

SOUP'S ON!
(Clockwise from top right)

Zippy Potato Soup (p. 345)

Spiced Chili and
Bread Bowls (p. 346)

Cheddar
Buttermilk Biscuits (p. 344)

Kielbasa Bean Soup (p. 344)

Kielbasa Bean Soup

(Pictured on page 342)

*I usually make a double batch of this meaty vegetable soup and freeze some
in serving-size containers. It makes a nice meal for busy days or unexpected guests.*
—*Emily Chaney, Penobscot, Maine*

4-1/2 cups water
   2 cans (14-1/2 ounces *each*)
     diced tomatoes, undrained
   1 can (16 ounces) kidney beans,
     rinsed and drained
   1 can (15-1/2 ounces) great
     northern beans, rinsed
     and drained
   1 can (15 ounces) garbanzo
     beans *or* chickpeas, rinsed and
     drained
   2 medium green peppers,
     chopped
   2 medium onions, chopped
   2 celery ribs, chopped

   1 medium zucchini, sliced
   2 teaspoons chicken bouillon granules
   2 garlic cloves, minced
2-1/2 teaspoons chili powder
   2 teaspoons dried basil
1-1/2 teaspoons salt
  1/2 teaspoon pepper
   2 bay leaves
  3/4 pound fully cooked kielbasa *or* Polish sausage,
     halved lengthwise and sliced

In a soup kettle or Dutch oven, combine all ingredients except the sausage. Bring to a boil. Reduce heat; cover and simmer for 1 hour. Add sausage and heat through. Discard bay leaves. **Yield:** 12 servings (about 3 quarts).

Cheddar Buttermilk Biscuits

(Pictured on page 342)

*Every bite of these flaky biscuits gets a little kick from cayenne pepper and
sharp cheddar cheese. They're a nice accompaniment to soup and stew.*
—*Kimberly Nuttall, San Marcos, California*

   2 cups all-purpose flour
   2 tablespoons sugar
   4 teaspoons baking powder
1/2 teaspoon salt
1/4 to 1/2 teaspoon cayenne
    pepper
1/2 cup cold butter
1/2 cup shredded sharp cheddar
    cheese
3/4 cup buttermilk

In a bowl, combine the flour, sugar, baking powder, salt and cayenne. Cut in butter until mixture resembles coarse crumbs. Add the cheese and toss. Stir in buttermilk just until moistened.

Turn onto a lightly floured surface; knead 8-10 times. Pat or roll to 1 in. thickness; cut with a floured 2-1/2-in. biscuit cutter. Place 1 in. apart on an ungreased baking sheet. Bake at 425° for 15-18 minutes or until golden brown. Serve warm. **Yield:** 6-8 biscuits.

Zippy Potato Soup

(Pictured at right and on page 343)

This savory soup has a lot of substance,
especially for the men in the family.
We enjoy brimming bowls all winter long.
—Clara Lee Parsons
Terre Haute, Indiana

3/4 pound sliced bacon, diced
  1 medium onion, chopped
  8 to 10 potatoes, peeled and cut
     into chunks
  1 medium carrot, grated
  5 cups water
  1 can (12 ounces) evaporated
     milk
  2 tablespoons butter
4-1/2 teaspoons minced fresh
     parsley
  2 teaspoons Worcestershire
     sauce
1/2 teaspoon ground mustard
1/2 teaspoon ground nutmeg
1/4 teaspoon salt
1/8 to 1/4 teaspoon cayenne pepper

In a large skillet, cook bacon and onion; drain and set aside. In a soup kettle or Dutch oven, cook the potatoes and the carrot in water for 20 minutes or until tender (do not drain).

Stir in the remaining ingredients and the bacon mixture. Cook for 10 minutes or until heated through. **Yield:** 14 servings (3-1/2 quarts).

ADD WARMTH TO A WINTER TABLE

CHASE AWAY the winter blues with these colorful ideas for warming up your dinner table.

- Instead of white linens, use brightly colored cloth or paper napkins and tablecloths.
- Add an assortment of fresh flowers in vases of various shapes and sizes. Or top the table with some potted plants.
- Buy a bunch of helium balloons in an array of colors, shapes and sizes. Set them on the table and throughout the house.
- Place tea light candles on tables, counter- tops and mantels. Nothing creates a warm and inviting atmosphere quite like candles.
- Blanket the table in warmth by using an eye-catching quilt as a tablecloth.
- Clear bowls brimming with red and green apples or lemons and limes add beautiful color and a wonderful fragrance.
- Another "scent-sational" idea is to simmer some apple cider on the stove. The aroma appeals to all, adds a little coziness and serves as a super sipper.

Bread Bowls

(Pictured on page 343)

Instead of offering bread with your favorite kettle creation, our Test Kitchen home economists suggest serving it inside of these bread bowls!

2 packages (1/4 ounce *each*)
   active dry yeast
1 cup warm water
   (110° to 115°)
1 cup warm milk (110° to 115°)
1/2 cup shortening
1/2 cup sugar
2 eggs
2 teaspoons salt
6 to 6-1/2 cups all-purpose flour
Cornmeal

In a mixing bowl, dissolve yeast in warm water. Add the milk, shortening, sugar, eggs, salt and 2 cups flour. Beat until smooth. Stir in enough remaining flour to form a soft dough. Turn onto a floured surface; knead until smooth and elastic, about 6-8 minutes. Place in a greased bowl, turning once to grease top. Cover and let rise in a warm place until doubled, about 1 hour.

Punch dough down. Turn onto a lightly floured surface. Divide into eight pieces; shape each into a ball. Grease two baking sheets and sprinkle with cornmeal. Place four balls 3 in. apart on each prepared pan. Cover and let rise until doubled, about 30 minutes. Bake at 350° for 20-25 minutes or until golden brown. Remove from pans to wire racks to cool.

For bread bowls, cut a thin slice off the top of bread. Hollow out bottom half, leaving a 1/4-in. shell (discard removed bread or save for another use). Fill with chili, chowder or stew. **Yield:** 8 bread bowls.

Spiced Chili

(Pictured on page 343)

My father was a cook in the Army and taught me the basics in the kitchen. My childhood baby-sitter inspired my love of cooking, too...in fact, she gave me this recipe.
—Julie Brendt, Antelope, California

1-1/2 pounds ground beef
1/2 cup chopped onion
4 garlic cloves, minced
2 cans (16 ounces *each*) kidney
   beans, rinsed and drained
2 cans (15 ounces *each*) tomato
   sauce
2 cans (14-1/2 ounces *each*)
   stewed tomatoes, cut up
1 cup water
2 bay leaves

1/4 cup chili powder
1 tablespoon salt
1 tablespoon brown sugar
1 tablespoon dried basil
1 tablespoon Italian seasoning
1 tablespoon dried thyme
1 tablespoon pepper
1 teaspoon dried oregano
1 teaspoon dried marjoram
Shredded cheddar cheese and additional chopped
   onions, optional

In a large skillet, cook beef, onion and garlic over medium heat until meat is no longer pink; drain. Transfer to a 5-qt. slow cooker. Stir in the beans, tomato sauce, tomatoes, water and seasonings. Cover and cook on low for 4-5 hours. Discard bay leaves. If desired, serve in bread bowls and garnish with cheese and onions. **Yield:** 12 servings (about 3 quarts).

Tomato Basil Bread

(Pictured at right)

This round breads' chewy crust pairs well with a steaming mug of soup. The pretty color and robust flavor are great conversation starters.
—Darlene Hoefs, Schofield, Wisconsin

1 package (1/4 ounce) active
  dry yeast
3/4 cup warm water
  (110° to 115°)
1/4 cup minced fresh basil
1/4 cup grated Parmesan cheese
2 tablespoons tomato paste
1 tablespoon sugar
1 tablespoon olive oil
1 teaspoon salt
1/8 to 1/4 teaspoon crushed red
  pepper flakes
2-1/4 to 2-1/2 cups bread flour

In a mixing bowl, dissolve yeast in water. Stir in basil, Parmesan cheese, tomato paste, sugar, oil, salt, pepper flakes and 2 cups of flour. Stir in enough remaining flour to form a stiff dough. Turn onto a floured surface; knead until smooth and elastic, about 3-5 minutes. Place in a greased bowl, turning once to grease top. Cover and let rise in a warm place until doubled, about 1 hour.

Punch dough down; knead for 1 minute. Shape into a round loaf. Place on a greased baking sheet. Cover and let rise until doubled, about 1 hour. With a sharp knife, cut a large X in top of loaf. Bake at 375° for 35-40 minutes or until golden brown. Remove from pan to a wire rack to cool. **Yield:** 1 loaf.

Double Sausage Stromboli

*When the winter winds blow, my family loves this stuffed bread that
I created. Serve it as an appetizer or entree.*
—Connie Atchley, Westport, Indiana

1 pound bulk pork sausage
28 pepperoni slices, chopped
3/4 cup shredded mozzarella *or*
   cheddar cheese
1 package (16 ounces) hot roll
   mix
1 cup warm water
   (120° to 130°)
2 tablespooons butter, softened
1 egg, beaten
1 tablespoon dried oregano
1-1/2 teaspoons vegetable oil

In a large skillet, cook sausage over medium heat until no longer pink; add pepperoni. Drain well and pat dry with paper towels; stir in cheese and set aside.

In a bowl, combine contents of hot roll mix, water, butter and egg until dough pulls away from side of bowl and holds together. Turn onto a lightly floured surface; knead until smooth and elastic, about 5 minutes. Cover and let rest for 5 minutes. Pat dough into a greased 15-in. x 10-in. x 1-in. baking pan. Spread sausage mixture lengthwise down the center third of dough; sprinkle with oregano. Fold sides over filling; press edges lightly to seal. Cover and let rise until doubled, about 30 minutes. Brush with oil. Bake at 375° for 20-25 minutes or until golden brown. **Yield:** 6-8 servings.

Shrimp Chowder

*Pretty pink shrimp and green parsley dot this golden chowder.
It's a rich and satisfying first course or main meal.*
—Anne Bennett, Hockessin, Delaware

2 large onions, cut into thin
   wedges
1/4 cup butter
3 cups cubed peeled potatoes
1 cup water
2 teaspoons salt
1/2 teaspoon seasoned pepper
2 pounds uncooked small
   shrimp, peeled and deveined
6 cups milk
2 cups (8 ounces) shredded
   sharp cheddar cheese
1/4 cup minced fresh parsley

In a soup kettle or Dutch oven, saute onions in butter until tender. Add potatoes, water, salt and pepper; bring to a boil. Reduce heat; cover and simmer for 15-20 minutes or until potatoes are tender (do not drain). Add shrimp; cook until shrimp turn pink, about 5 minutes.

In a large saucepan over low heat, heat milk. Stir in cheese until melted (do not boil). Add to potato mixture; heat through (do not boil). Stir in parsley. **Yield:** 12 servings (about 3 quarts).

Apple Cider Chicken 'n' Dumplings

(Pictured at right)

*I came up with this recipe one fall when
I had an abundance of apple cider.
Adding some to a down-home classic
was a delectable decision.*
—Margaret Sumner-Wichmann
Questa, New Mexico

8 chicken thighs (about 3
    pounds), skin removed
2 tablespoons butter
1 medium red onion, chopped
1 celery rib, chopped
2 tablespoons minced fresh
    parsley
Salt and pepper to taste
3 tablespoons all-purpose flour
3 cups chicken broth
1 cup apple cider *or* apple juice
DUMPLINGS:
2 cups all-purpose flour
1 tablespoon baking powder
1/2 teaspoon salt
1 tablespoon cold butter
1 egg, lightly beaten
2/3 cup milk

In a Dutch oven, brown chicken in butter; remove and set aside. In the same pan, combine the onion, celery, parsley, salt and pepper; cook and stir until vegetables are tender. Sprinkle with flour and mix well. Add broth and cider. Bring to a boil; cook and stir for 2 minutes or until thickened. Add chicken. Cover and bake at 350° for 45-50 minutes.

    Increase heat to 425°. For dumplings, combine the flour, baking powder and salt in a bowl; cut in butter until crumbly. Combine the egg and milk; stir into dry ingredients just until moistened. Drop batter into 12 mounds onto hot broth. Bake, uncovered, at 425° for 10 minutes. Cover and bake 10 minutes longer or until a toothpick inserted into a dumpling comes out clean. **Yield:** 4 servings.

WINTER
Celebrations

Super Bowl Pizza Party

IF YOU want to a score a touchdown with the Super Bowl fans in your family, just quarterback a pizza party!

To defeat hunger in a hurry, turn to this guaranteed-to-please game plan: Start with a winning combination of appetizing "pies"…then toss in a bowl brimming with salad greens or fresh fruit, generous slices of buttery garlic bread or some potato chips and, for dessert, homemade or store-bought cookies or brownies.

With tender crusts and a variety of toppings, Four-Cheese Pizza, Pepper Sausage Pizza and Deluxe Turkey Club Pizza will score points with football followers of every age.

350 WINTER *Celebrations*

FOOTBALL FAN FAVORITES

(Clockwise from top right)

Four-Cheese Pizza (p. 354)

Pepper Sausage Pizza (p. 353)

Deluxe Turkey Club Pizza (p. 352)

Deluxe Turkey Club Pizza

(Pictured on page 350)

This unique recipe has become my family's favorite. In winter, we often stay home on Saturday nights to rent movies and indulge in generous slices of this pizza.
—*Philis Bukovcik, Lansing, Michigan*

1 tube (10 ounces) refrigerated pizza crust
1 tablespoon sesame seeds
1/4 cup mayonnaise
1 teaspoon grated lemon peel
1 medium tomato, thinly sliced
1/2 cup cubed cooked turkey
4 bacon strips, cooked and crumbled
2 medium fresh mushrooms, thinly sliced
1/4 cup chopped onion
1-1/2 cups (6 ounces) shredded Colby-Monterey Jack cheese

Unroll pizza dough and press onto a greased 12-in. pizza pan; build up edges slightly. Sprinkle with sesame seeds. Bake at 425° for 12-14 minutes or until edges are lightly browned.

Combine mayonnaise and lemon peel; spread over crust. Top with tomato, turkey, bacon, mushrooms, onion and cheese. Bake for 6-8 minutes or until cheese is melted. Cut into slices. **Yield:** 8 slices.

Editor's Note: Reduced-fat or fat-free mayonnaise may not be substituted for regular mayonnaise.

GAME PLAN FOR YOUR PARTY

YOU WON'T be defeated by last-minute details at your pizza party if you follow these timely tips.

- If you plan on baking more than one pizza at a time, look for recipes with the same baking temperature.
- Instead of serving only hot pizzas, offer a cold variety (like Pesto Pizza Squares on page 354 or Taco Pan Pizza on page 357) that can be made ahead.
- For each pizza, chop and measure as many ingredients as you can the night before and refrigerate in small resealable plastic bags. Write the name of each pizza on a large resealable plastic bag and fill with the appropriate smaller bags. This not only saves you time, but also makes it easier for guests to jump in and help assemble pizzas on party day.
- If a recipe instructs you to prebake the crust, do so the morning of the party. Store the cooled crust loosely covered at room temperature.

Pepper Sausage Pizza

(Pictured at right and on page 351)

Fresh spinach gives this recipe from our Test Kitchen a tasty twist. That leafy green plus yellow peppers, snow-white mushrooms and tomato sauce make this a colorful addition to your pizza buffet table.

3 to 4 cups all-purpose flour, *divided*
1 package (1/4 ounce) quick-rise yeast
1 teaspoon sugar
1 cup warm water (120° to 130°)
1/4 cup olive oil
2 teaspoons salt
1 teaspoon dried basil
1/2 teaspoon pepper
1/2 cup shredded Parmesan cheese, *divided*
3 cups torn fresh spinach
1 can (15 ounces) pizza sauce
4 cups (16 ounces) shredded mozzarella cheese, *divided*
1/2 pound bulk pork sausage, cooked and drained
1 medium onion, chopped
1/2 pound fresh mushrooms, sliced
1/2 medium sweet yellow pepper, chopped
1-1/2 teaspoons pizza seasoning
3 tablespoons minced fresh basil, optional

In a mixing bowl, combine 1 cup flour, yeast and sugar. Add water; beat until smooth. Add the oil, salt, dried basil, pepper, 1/4 cup Parmesan cheese and 2 cups flour; beat until blended. Stir in enough remaining flour to form a soft dough. Turn onto a floured surface; knead until smooth and elastic, about 6-8 minutes. Cover and let rest for 5 minutes.

Meanwhile, place spinach in a microwave-safe bowl; cover and microwave on high for 30 seconds or just until wilted. Uncover and set aside.

Press dough into a greased 15-in. x 10-in. x 1-in. baking pan. Spread with pizza sauce; sprinkle with 2-1/2 cups mozzarella cheese, sausage, onion, spinach, mushrooms and yellow pepper. Top with remaining Parmesan and mozzarella. Sprinkle with pizza seasoning. Bake at 450° for 20 minutes or until crust is golden brown. Sprinkle with fresh basil if desired. Cut into squares. **Yield:** 12-15 slices.

Four-Cheese Pizza

(Pictured on page 351)

Although this pizza doesn't have sauce, it gets unforgettable flavor from a blend of cheeses, vegetables and garlic. Using frozen bread dough appeals to folks who don't care to bake.
— Doris Johns, Hurst, Texas

1 loaf (16 ounces) frozen bread dough, thawed
1 large sweet red pepper, chopped
1 large green pepper, chopped
1 cup (4 ounces) shredded mozzarella cheese
3/4 cup shredded Swiss cheese
1/2 cup grated Parmesan cheese
1/2 cup crumbled feta cheese
2 tablespoons minced fresh parsley
1 tablespoon minced fresh basil *or* 1 teaspoon dried basil
3 plum tomatoes, thinly sliced
1 tablespoon olive oil
2 garlic cloves, minced

On a lightly floured surface, roll dough into a 15-in. circle. Transfer to a greased 14-in. pizza pan; build up edges slightly. Prick dough several times with a fork. Bake at 400° for 8-10 minutes or until lightly browned. Remove from the oven.

Reduce heat to 375°. Sprinkle chopped peppers, cheeses, parsley and basil over crust. Arrange tomato slices over top. In a small bowl, combine oil and garlic; brush over tomatoes. Bake for 15-20 minutes or until cheese is melted. Let stand for 5 minutes before cutting. **Yield:** 8 slices.

Pesto Pizza Squares

Our Test Kitchen offers this alternative to traditional baked pizzas. With pesto sauce, tomatoes, olives and fresh mushrooms, it's a flavorful variation of the more common vegetable pizza.

2 tubes (8 ounces *each*) refrigerated crescent rolls
1 cup tightly packed fresh basil
1/4 cup tightly packed fresh parsley
1/4 cup tightly packed fresh cilantro
2 garlic cloves
1/3 cup olive oil
1/4 cup grated Parmesan cheese
1/4 cup sour cream
1/4 cup whipped cream cheese
3 plum tomatoes
3/4 cup chopped fresh mushrooms
1/3 cup sliced ripe olives

Unroll crescent dough into a greased 15-in. x 10-in. x 1-in. baking pan; press seams together and build up edges. Prick dough with a fork. Bake at 375° for 11-13 minutes or until golden brown; cool completely on a wire rack.

In a food processor, combine the basil, parsley, cilantro, garlic, oil and Parmesan cheese; cover and puree until smooth. Transfer to a bowl; add sour cream and cream cheese. Spread over crust.

Halve tomatoes lengthwise and thinly slice widthwise; arrange over basil mixture. Top with mushrooms and olives. Refrigerate until serving. Cut into bite-size squares. **Yield:** 3 dozen.

Baked Potato Pizza

(Pictured at right)

I make this creative pizza for Super Bowl parties. The sour cream, bacon, onions and cheese make every bite taste just like a loaded baked potato.
—Gina Pierson, Centralia, Missouri

1 package (6 ounces) pizza crust mix
3 medium unpeeled potatoes, baked and cooled
1 tablespoon butter, melted
1/4 teaspoon garlic powder
1/4 teaspoon Italian seasoning *or* dried oregano
1 cup (8 ounces) sour cream
6 bacon strips, cooked and crumbled
3 to 5 green onions, chopped
1-1/2 cups (6 ounces) shredded mozzarella cheese
1/2 cup shredded cheddar cheese

Prepare crust according to package directions. Press dough into a lightly greased 14-in. pizza pan; build up edges slightly. Bake at 400° for 5-6 minutes or until crust is firm and begins to brown.

Cut potatoes into 1/2-in. cubes. In a bowl, combine butter, garlic powder and Italian seasoning. Add potatoes and toss. Spread sour cream over crust; top with potato mixture, bacon, onions and cheeses. Bake at 400° for 15-20 minutes or until cheese is lightly browned. Let stand for 5 minutes before cutting. **Yield:** 8 slices.

SUGGESTIONS FOR SERVING PIZZAS

YOU WON'T FUMBLE getting food on the table with these guidelines.

- Put two pizzas with the same baking temperature into the oven. (If possible, have two different varieties for folks to sample.) Each pizza should be on its own shelf. Halfway through the baking time, rotate the pizzas, moving the pizza on the higher rack to the lower rack and vice versa. You may need to add 5 to 10 minutes to the baking time.
- Bake other pizzas as soon as the first two come out of the oven. This gives people a chance to finish their first plate of food and allows you to add hot fresh food to the table.
- While pizzas are baking, set out the cold pizzas and other food.

Buffalo Chicken Calzones

I'm always looking for creative ways to jazz up pizza. I came up with this
"pizza turnover" to incorporate my love of buffalo chicken wings.
—Ruth Ann Riendeau, Twin Mountain, New Hampshire

  1 **can (8 ounces) pizza sauce**
  2 **teaspoons plus 1/2 cup hot**
    pepper sauce, *divided*
1-1/4 **pounds boneless skinless**
    chicken breasts, cubed
  3 **celery ribs, chopped**
  3 **tablespoons butter**
Dash Cajun seasoning
  2 **tubes (10 ounces** *each***)**
    refrigerated pizza crust dough
1-1/2 **cups (6 ounces) shredded**
    Monterey Jack cheese
  4 **ounces crumbled blue cheese**
Cornmeal

In a bowl, combine pizza sauce and 2 teaspoons hot pepper sauce; set aside. In a skillet, saute chicken and celery in butter for 3-5 minutes or until chicken is no longer pink. Stir in Cajun seasoning and remaining hot pepper sauce; cover and simmer for 10-15 minutes or until heated through.

Unroll pizza dough; divide each portion in half. On a floured surface, roll each into an 8-in. circle. Spread pizza sauce mixture over half of each circle to within 1 in. of edges. Top with chicken mixture and cheeses. Fold dough over filling; pinch edges to seal.

Sprinkle greased baking sheets with cornmeal. Place calzones over cornmeal. Bake at 400° for 10-12 minutes or until golden brown. **Yield:** 4 calzones.

Breakfast Pizza

When my boys were in high school, they often tired of traditional breakfast foods.
To keep them interested, I would make this pizza. It's also a great appetizer.
—Judy Skinner, Fort Collins, Colorado

1 **tube (8 ounces) refrigerated**
  crescent rolls
1 **pound bulk pork sausage**
1 **cup frozen shredded hash**
  brown potatoes, thawed
1 **jar (4-1/2 ounces) sliced**
  mushrooms, drained
6 **bacon strips, cooked and**
  crumbled
1/2 **cup sliced ripe olives**
1 **cup (4 ounces) shredded**
  cheddar cheese
1 **cup (4 ounces) shredded**
  mozzarella cheese
5 **eggs**

1/4 **cup milk**
1/2 **teaspoon salt**
  2 **tablespoons grated Parmesan cheese**

Unroll crescent dough and separate into triangles; place on a greased 12-in. pizza pan. Press seams together and build up edges; set aside.

In a skillet, cook sausage over medium heat until no longer pink; drain and cool slightly. Sprinkle sausage, hash browns, mushrooms, bacon and olives over dough. Top with cheddar and mozzarella cheeses.

In a bowl, beat eggs, milk and salt; pour over pizza. Sprinkle with Parmesan cheese. Bake at 375° for 25-30 minutes or until golden brown. Let stand for 10 minutes before cutting. **Yield:** 6-8 slices.

Taco Pan Pizza

(Pictured at right)

Our Test Kitchen knows that pizza and tacos are favorite foods in lots of families. So they came up with this recipe that cleverly combines the two. A variety of toppings can be used to suit your tastes.

1 tube (10 ounces) refrigerated pizza crust
1/2 cup sour cream
1/3 cup mayonnaise
2 tablespoons minced fresh cilantro
1 jalapeno pepper, seeded and chopped
1 teaspoon sugar
1/2 teaspoon chili powder
1/4 teaspoon salt
1/4 teaspoon ground cumin
1 medium ripe avocado, peeled and cubed
2 teaspoons lime juice
2 medium tomatoes, chopped
1/4 cup chopped green onions
1/3 cup sliced ripe olives
1 cup (4 ounces) shredded Mexican cheese blend

Unroll pizza dough and place in a greased 15-in. x 10-in. x 1-in. baking pan; flatten dough and build up edges slightly. Prick dough several times with a fork. Bake at 425° for 10-11 minutes or until lightly browned. Cool on a wire rack.

Meanwhile, in a bowl, combine the sour cream, mayonnaise, cilantro, jalapeno, sugar, chili powder, salt and cumin. Spread over cooled crust. Toss avocado with lime juice; arrange over sour cream mixture. Sprinkle with tomatoes, onions, olives and cheese. Refrigerate until serving. Cut into squares. **Yield:** 16-20 slices.

Editor's Note: When cutting or seeding hot peppers, use rubber or plastic gloves to protect your hands. Avoid touching your face.

PERSONAL "PIES" FOR KIDS

CONSIDER having some small Italian bread shells and assorted toppings for the kids. They can have fun making pizzas to suit their tastes, and you don't have to worry about them not liking the pizzas you've prepared.

Valentine's Day Dinner For Two

MAKING DINNER FROM scratch on Valentine's Day is one of the finest ways to display your love for that special someone.

And everything will be coming up rosy when you serve this magical meal for just the two of you.

The first course of Shrimp with Basil-Mango Sauce will bring romance to the table. Notice how two shrimp come together to form a heart?

Then, after dining on rich Veal Scallopini and nicely seasoned Apricot-Ginger Asparagus, dish out dreamy Orange Cheesecake Mousse garnished with easy-to-prepare chocolate hearts.

ENCHANTED EATING
(Clockwise from top left)

Veal Scallopini (p. 360)

Apricot-Ginger Asparagus (p. 360)

Orange Cheesecake Mousse (p. 361)

Shrimp with Basil-Mango Sauce (p. 362)

Veal Scallopini

(Pictured on page 358)

My husband and I prepare this veal dish for birthdays and other special occasions.
We love to cook and often entertain friends and family.
—*Karen Bridges, Downers Grove, Illinois*

2 tablespoons all-purpose flour
1/8 teaspoon salt
1/8 teaspoon pepper
1 egg
1/2 to 3/4 pound veal cutlets *or* boneless skinless chicken breasts, flattened to 1-inch thickness
2 tablespoons olive oil
4 ounces fresh mushrooms, halved
1 cup chicken broth
2 tablespoons marsala wine *or* apple juice
Hot cooked spaghetti

In a small bowl, combine the flour, salt, and pepper. In another bowl, lightly beat the egg. Dip veal in egg, then coat with flour mixture.

In a large skillet, brown veal in oil on both sides. Stir in the mushrooms, broth and wine or apple juice. Bring to a boil. Reduce heat; simmer, uncovered, for 5-10 minutes or until mushrooms are tender. Serve over spaghetti. **Yield:** 2 servings.

Apricot-Ginger Asparagus

(Pictured on page 359)

Our Test Kitchen home economists blend apricot preserves and a few simple seasonings to dress up tender asparagus spears. This succulent side dish goes great with any entree.

1/2 pound fresh asparagus, trimmed
1/4 cup apricot preserves
1 tablespoon red wine vinegar
1/8 teaspoon ground cinnamon
1/8 teaspoon minced fresh gingerroot

In a large skillet, bring 1 in. of water to a boil; place asparagus in a steamer basket over water. Cover and steam for 5 minutes or until crisp-tender; drain and keep warm.

In a small skillet over medium heat, bring the preserves, vinegar, cinnamon and ginger to a boil. Reduce heat; simmer, uncovered, for 2-4 minutes or until glaze begins to thicken. Pour over asparagus. **Yield:** 2 servings.

Orange Cheesecake Mousse

(Pictured at right and on page 359)

This creamy dessert from our Test Kitchen will make your mouth water. It's especially pleasant after a rich meal.

1/2 cup orange marmalade
1/4 cup orange juice
1/2 teaspoon cornstarch
1 tablespoon cold water
1/2 teaspoon orange extract
1 carton (8 ounces) frozen
   whipped topping, thawed
Yellow and red liquid food coloring,
   optional
1 package (8 ounces) cream
   cheese, softened
1 cup (8 ounces) sour cream
1/2 cup cold milk
1 package (3.4 ounces) instant
   vanilla pudding mix
Chocolate hearts, optional

In a large saucepan, combine the orange marmalade and juice; cook and stir over medium heat until melted and blended.

In a small bowl, combine cornstarch and water until smooth. Gradually stir into marmalade mixture. Bring to a boil; cook and stir for 4 minutes or until thickened. Remove from the heat; stir in extract. Cool completely. Fold in whipped topping. Tint orange with yellow and red food coloring if desired.

In a large mixing bowl, beat cream cheese until smooth. Add the sour cream; mix well. In a small mixing bowl, beat the milk and pudding mix on low speed for 2 minutes. Stir into cream cheese mixture. Cut a large hole in the corner of a pastry or plastic bag; fill half full with cream cheese mixture. Press bag slightly to flatten. Cut a small hole in another bag; insert star tip No. 21. Place filled bag in empty bag; fill empty bag with orange mixture. Pipe in a swirled design in parfait glasses; chill. Garnish with chocolate hearts if desired. **Yield:** 4 servings.

CHOCOLATE HEARTS ADORN DESSERTS

IF YOUR HEART'S DESIRE is to be creative in the kitchen, try your hand at this simple garnish.

In a microwave or heavy saucepan, melt 1/2 cup semisweet chocolate chips and 1/4 teaspoon shortening; stir until smooth. Cut a small hole in the corner of a pastry or plastic bag; fill with melted chocolate. Pipe two overlapping 1-in. hearts onto waxed paper. Repeat to make three more sets of hearts. Let dry for 2-3 minutes.

Store at room temperature in an airtight container. Use as a garnish for Orange Chocolate Mousse or another dessert.

Shrimp with Basil-Mango Sauce

(Pictured on page 358)

*Instead of serving cold shrimp with cocktail sauce, prepare this simple basil sauce
and top it with tender cooked shrimp. It's a fun and fancy appetizer.*
—*Ken Hulme, Prescott, Arizona*

 1 medium ripe mango *or* 2
   medium peaches, peeled and
   sliced
 2 to 4 tablespoons minced fresh
   basil
 1 tablespoon lemon juice
12 cooked medium shrimp,
   peeled and deveined
 1 tablespoon butter
Basil sprigs, optional

In a blender or food processor, combine the mango, basil and lemon juice; cover and process until blended. Pour onto two serving plates; set aside.

Skewer two shrimp each onto six 4- to 6-in. metal or soaked wooden skewers, forming a heart shape. Cook in a large skillet in butter over medium-high heat for 4-5 minutes or until shrimp turn pink, turning once. Place over mango sauce. Garnish with basil sprigs if desired. **Yield:** 2 servings.

Chocolate Truffles

*It's hard to eat just one of these chocolaty, silky candies.
I like to keep some on hand for a quick sweet treat.*
—*DeAnn Alleva, Hudson, Wisconsin*

14 squares (1 ounce *each*)
   semisweet chocolate, *divided*
 1 cup heavy whipping cream
1/3 cup butter, softened
 1 teaspoon rum extract *or*
   vanilla extract
1/2 cup finely chopped pecans *or*
   walnuts, toasted

Coarsely chop 12 squares of chocolate; set aside. In a saucepan, heat cream over low heat until bubbles form around sides of the pan. Remove from the heat; add chopped chocolate, stirring until melted and smooth. Cool to room temperature. Stir in butter and extract. Cover tightly and refrigerate for at least 6 hours or until firm.

Grate remaining chocolate; place in a shallow dish. Add nuts; set aside. Shape tablespoonfuls of chilled chocolate mixture into balls. Place on waxed paper-lined baking sheets. (If truffles are soft, refrigerate until easy to handle.) Roll truffles in chocolate-nut mixture. Store in an airtight container in the refrigerator. **Yield:** 3 dozen.

Cupid's Breadsticks

(Pictured at right)

Our Test Kitchen home economists encourage you to play with your food and shape refrigerated breadsticks into hearts and arrows! A sprinkling of seasonings provides the finishing touch.

1 tube (11 ounces) refrigerated breadsticks
2 tablespoons butter, melted
1/2 teaspoon dried minced onion
1/2 teaspoon dried tarragon
1/2 teaspoon dried oregano
1/2 teaspoon dried thyme
1/2 teaspoon dried parsley flakes
1/8 teaspoon onion powder

Separate breadstick dough into six pieces. For each heart, unroll four pieces and twist if desired; seal perforations and pinch ends together. Shape into hearts on an ungreased baking sheet.

For arrows, unroll remaining two pieces and separate into four breadsticks. With scissors, cut one end of each breadstick into a point. About 2 in. from the point, cut out a triangle from both sides of breadsticks (discard removed pieces). At the other end of the breadstick, make diagonal cuts on each side, creating feathers. Place on baking sheet with hearts.

In a small bowl, combine butter and seasonings. Brush over the dough. Bake at 375° for 12-14 minutes or until golden brown. **Yield:** 4 hearts and 4 arrows.

Editor's Note: This recipe was tested with Pillsbury refrigerated breadsticks.

Chocolate Chip Meringue Cookies

This is one of my most popular recipes. Shape them into hearts for Valentine's Day or make them as drop cookies for other occasions.
— Debbie Tilley, Riverview, Florida

3 egg whites
1/4 teaspoon cream of tartar
1/4 teaspoon salt
1 cup sugar
3 tablespoons baking cocoa
3 tablespoons miniature semisweet chocolate chips
3 tablespoons finely crushed almonds *or* walnuts, optional

Place egg whites in a large mixing bowl; let stand at room temperature for 30 minutes. Beat egg whites until foamy. Add cream of tartar and salt; beat until soft peaks form. Gradually add sugar, 1 tablespoon at a time, beating on high until stiff peaks form, about 6 minutes. Beat in cocoa. Fold in chocolate chips and nuts if desired.

Cut a small hole in the corner of a pastry or plastic bag; insert No. 806 round tip. Spoon meringue into bag. Pipe 1-1/2-in. hearts 2 in. apart onto lightly greased baking sheets. Bake at 300° for 20-25 minutes or until firm to the touch. Remove to wire racks to cool. Store in an airtight container. **Yield:** 2 dozen.

Editor's Note: Meringue can be dropped by rounded tablespoonfuls onto lightly greased baking sheets. Bake as directed.

MAKE MERINGUE ON DRY DAYS

HUMIDITY is the most critical factor when making a successful meringue, so choose a dry day. Meringues can absorb moisture on a humid day and become limp and sticky.

Ruby-Red Strawberry Sauce

(Pictured at right)

My best friend, Lynn Young, and I came up with this recipe after our husbands requested it. In addition to ice cream, it can be served over pancakes and waffles.
— Terri Zobel, Raleigh, North Carolina

1/2 cup sugar
4-1/2 teaspoons cornstarch
1/4 cup orange juice concentrate
4 cups sliced fresh strawberries
1/2 teaspoon vanilla extract

In a large saucepan, combine the sugar and cornstarch. Stir in orange juice concentrate until smooth; add strawberries. Bring to a boil; cook and stir for 2 minutes or until thickened. Remove from the heat; stir in vanilla. Cool. Store in the refrigerator. **Yield:** 2-1/2 cups.

Engaging Heart Cookies

(Pictured at right)

My husband, Brian, is an excellent cook. The first time he made these elegant cookies was the night we got engaged. He took them to the restaurant and had the staff arrange them on a plate along with my ring!
— Beth Kelley, Indianapolis, Indiana

1 cup butter, softened
1/2 cup sugar
1/2 cup packed brown sugar
2 eggs
1 teaspoon vanilla extract
2-1/4 cups all-purpose flour
1/4 cup baking cocoa
1/4 teaspoon salt
3/4 cup ground toasted hazelnuts
3/4 cup semisweet chocolate chips
2 tablespoons shortening, *divided*
3/4 cup vanilla *or* white chips

In a mixing bowl, cream butter and sugars. Beat in eggs and vanilla. Combine the flour, cocoa and salt; add to creamed mixture. Stir in hazelnuts. Divide dough in half. Cover and refrigerate for 1 hour or until easy to handle.

Working with one portion of dough at a time, roll to 1/4-in. thickness on a lightly floured surface. Cut with a 2-in. heart-shaped cookie cutter. Place 1 in. apart on ungreased baking sheets. Bake at 350° for 9-10 minutes (cookies will be soft). Cool for 1 minute before removing to wire racks.

In a microwave-safe bowl, melt chocolate chips and 1 tablespoon shortening; stir until smooth. Repeat with vanilla chips and remaining shortening. Dip right side of half of the cookies in semisweet chocolate; dip the left side of remaining cookies in white chocolate. Overlap two hearts before the chocolate is set. Place on waxed paper until set. **Yield:** about 3-1/2 dozen.

Be-Mine Sandwich Cookies

These simple cookies are the first thing to disappear from dessert tables.
They're cute, colorful and extremely fast to make.
—Darcie Cross, Novi, Michigan

6 ounces white *or* chocolate
  candy coating
50 to 55 chocolate cream-filled
  sandwich cookies
Assorted candy hearts, sprinkles *or*
  decorations

In a microwave-safe bowl or heavy saucepan, melt 2 ounces of candy coating at a time, stirring until smooth. Spread over cookie tops; decorate immediately. Place on waxed paper to harden. **Yield:** 50-55 cookies.

Queen-of-Hearts Salad

Red raspberries and heart-shaped croutons make this salad from our Test Kitchen
perfect for Valentine's Day. The creamy dressing hints of Dijon and lemon.

2 slices whole wheat bread
4-1/2 teaspoons butter, melted
1/4 teaspoon garlic powder
1/4 teaspoon dill weed
1/8 teaspoon salt
3 cups torn salad greens
1 jar (4-1/2 ounces) marinated
  artichoke hearts, drained and
  quartered
1/2 cup fresh raspberries
DRESSING:
1 tablespoon sugar
2-1/2 teaspoons lemon juice
1-1/2 teaspoons tarragon vinegar
1/2 teaspoon salt

1 tablespoon Dijon mustard
1/4 teaspoon minced garlic
Dash coarsely ground pepper
1/4 cup vegetable oil

For croutons, cut bread into hearts with a 1-in. heart-shaped cookie cutter. In a bowl, combine butter, garlic powder, dill and salt. Add the bread hearts; toss to coat. Place in a single layer on a baking sheet. Bake at 400° for 3 minutes on each side.

On two salad plates, arrange the greens, artichokes, raspberries and croutons. In a bowl, combine sugar, lemon juice, vinegar and salt. Add mustard, garlic and pepper. Slowly whisk in oil. Drizzle over salads. Serve immediately. **Yield:** 2 servings.

Strawberry Pavlova

(Pictured at right)

I eat lots of fruits, and this recipe showcasing strawberries is a favorite. It's an impressive dessert that never fails.
—Mary Pead, Ocala, Florida

- **4 egg whites**
- **1/4 teaspoon cream of tartar**
- **1-1/4 cups plus 2 tablespoons sugar,** *divided*
- **2 teaspoons cornstarch**
- **1 teaspoon lemon juice**
- **1/2 to 1 teaspoon almond extract**
- **2 cups heavy whipping cream**
- **1 quart fresh strawberries, sliced**

PAVLOVA FOLKLORE

BOTH Australia and New Zealand claim pavlova as a national dish. It's been said that this meringue dessert with whipped cream and fruit was named after the famous Russian ballerina Anna Pavlova.

Place egg whites in a large mixing bowl; let stand at room temperature for 30 minutes. Beat egg whites on medium speed until foamy. Add cream of tartar; beat until soft peaks form. Gradually add 1-1/4 cups sugar, 1 tablespoon at a time, beating on high until stiff peaks form. Sprinkle cornstarch over egg white mixture; fold in. Fold in lemon juice and extract.

Coat a 14-in. pizza pan with nonstick cooking spray. Spoon meringue onto pan, forming a 12-in. heart; build up edges slightly. Bake at 250° for 45-55 minutes or until crisp. Cool on pan on a wire rack.

In a mixing bowl, beat cream until soft peaks form. Gradually add the remaining sugar, beating until stiff peaks form. Spoon over meringue; arrange strawberries over top. Serve immediately. **Yield:** 12 servings.

Caramel Fondue

My brothers can't get enough of this caramel dip. We gather around the table,
dipping pieces of pound cake and fruit until the fondue pot is clean!
—Leora Miller, Milford, Indiana

1 **cup heavy whipping cream,**
   divided
3/4 **cup sugar**
1/2 **cup light corn syrup**
1/4 **cup butter**
1/4 **teaspoon salt**
1/2 **teaspoon vanilla extract**
Pound cake and assorted fresh
   fruit, cut into pieces

In a heavy saucepan, combine 1/2 cup cream, sugar, corn syrup, butter and salt. Bring to a boil over medium heat until a candy thermometer reads 234° (soft-ball stage), stirring constantly. Cool to 220°; stir in remaining cream. Bring to a boil. Remove from the heat; stir in vanilla.

Transfer to a fondue pot and keep warm. Serve with pound cake and fruit. **Yield:** 1-3/4 cups.

Editor's Note: We recommend that you test your candy thermometer before each use by bringing water to a boil; the thermometer should read 212°. Adjust your recipe temperature up or down based on your test.

HEART-SHAPED DIPPERS

INSTEAD of simply serving cubes of pound cake with Caramel Fondue (recipe above), make some heart-shaped dippers. Thaw a 10-3/4-ounce loaf of pound cake. Slice the cake, then cut with a 1-in. heart-shaped cookie cutter.

Valentine's Day Snack Mix

Kids of all ages will gobble up this sweet snack mix from our Test Kitchen. Best of all,
because it requires no cooking, they can help combine the ingredients.

1 **package (12.7 ounces)**
   Valentine's M&M's
1 **can (9-3/4 ounces) whole**
   cashews
1 **package (8 ounces)**
   yogurt-covered raisins
1 **package (3.53 ounces) dried**
   cranberries
1 **cup miniature pretzels**
1 **cup chocolate-flavored bear-shaped graham**
   crackers

In a large bowl, combine all ingredients. Store in an airtight container. **Yield:** 7 cups.

Arranging Fresh Roses

ROSES can cost a pretty penny, especially around Valentine's Day. To lengthen their life — and enhance their beauty — properly prepare them for an arrangement.

- Select a vase that is about half as tall as your flowers.
- Using floral tape, create a grid on your vase. (See "Using a Grid to Arrange Flowers" below.) Then fill with water and add a floral preservative. The water should be slightly higher than your body temperature.
- With a garden shears or sharp knife, cut off any leaves and thorns that will be below the water line. Wear gardening gloves to protect your hands.
- While holding the stems under running water, cut off at least 1 inch. The flowers should be about twice the height of your vase with several stems an inch or two longer for the center of your bouquet.
- Arrange the flowers in the water as

you cut them, starting in the center and working toward the rim. Fill in with other flowers and greens as desired.

- Keep roses away from direct heat or sunlight and drafts. Add fresh water regularly and replenish the floral preservative from time to time.

USING A GRID TO ARRANGE FLOWERS

HERE'S HOW TO arrange your long-stemmed roses like a pro.

1. Place strips of waterproof floral tape parallel to one another across the top of the vase. Then place strips perpendicular to the first set to form a grid. Wrap a piece of tape to secure ends around the rim of the vase.

2. Fill the vase with water. Insert flowers, placing taller ones near the center and shorter ones near the rim to create a rounded form. Fill in with greens and baby's breath, making sure to cover the tape on the rim of the vase.

YEAR-ROUND
Celebrations

Birthday Treats Take the Cake 372-383

Bridal Shower Reigns Supreme 384-395

It's a Girl! 396-405

25th Wedding Anniversary 406-417

Birthday Treats Take the Cake

FOR young and old alike, birthday celebrations revolve around friends and family, prettily wrapped packages and—most importantly—a scrumptious cake topped with candles!

Make someone's day extra special by taking a little time to prepare showstopping treats like Raspberry Fudge Torte, Cookies 'n' Cream Cake and Posy Cupcakes.

This chapter also provides some do-it-yourself decorating techniques that let you easily create impressive cakes.

So turn the pages and spread the fun with innovative ideas for fancy layered cakes, creative cupcakes and more!

EYE-CATCHING CAKES
(Clockwise from top)

Raspberry Fudge Torte (p. 376)

Cookies 'n' Cream Cake (p. 374)

Posy Cupcakes (p. 375)

Cookies 'n' Cream Cake

(Pictured on page 373)

This cake is the perfect size when you're feeding a smaller crowd and don't want leftovers.
Chunks of chocolate sandwich cookies are in every bite.
—Dorothy Smith, El Dorado, Arkansas

1/4 cup butter, softened
3/4 cup sugar
1 egg
3/4 cup sour cream
1 cup all-purpose flour
1/2 teaspoon baking soda
1/2 teaspoon baking powder
1/4 cup water
8 cream-filled chocolate sandwich cookies, coarsely chopped

WHIPPED CREAM TOPPING:
3/4 cup heavy whipping cream
2 tablespoons sugar

Additional coarsely chopped cream-filled chocolate sandwich cookies, optional

In a small mixing bowl, cream butter and sugar. Add egg; beat well. Beat in sour cream. Combine the flour, baking soda and baking powder; add to creamed mixture alternately with water. Stir in chopped cookies. Pour into a greased and floured 9-in. round baking pan. Bake at 350° for 30-35 minutes or until a toothpick inserted near the center comes out clean. Cool for 10 minutes before removing from pan to a wire rack to cool completely.

For topping, beat cream in a small mixing bowl until soft peaks form. Gradually add sugar, beating until stiff peaks form. Spread over top of cake; sprinkle with additional chopped cookies if desired. **Yield:** 6-8 servings.

Clove Bundt Cake

This old-fashioned bundt cake is so moist, it doesn't need any frosting.
But I sometimes sprinkle it with confectioners' sugar for a pretty presentation.
—Mary Zawlocki, Gig Harbor, Washington

1 cup butter, softened
2 cups sugar
3 eggs, lightly beaten
3 cups all-purpose flour
1 tablespoon ground cinnamon
2 to 3 teaspoons ground cloves
3/4 teaspoon baking soda
1/4 teaspoon salt
1 cup buttermilk
Confectioners' sugar, optional

In a mixing bowl, cream butter and sugar. Add eggs; mix well (mixture will appear curdled). Combine the flour, cinnamon, cloves, baking soda and salt; add to creamed mixture alternately with buttermilk.

Pour into a greased and floured 10-in. fluted tube pan. Bake at 350° for 50-55 minutes or until a toothpick inserted near the center comes out clean. Cool for 10 minutes before inverting onto a wire rack; cool completely. Dust with confectioners' sugar if desired. **Yield:** 12-14 servings.

Posy Cupcakes

(Pictured at right and on page 372)

Our Test Kitchen staff suggests dressing up cupcakes from a mix with canned frosting and candied flowers. Don't want to fuss with perfectly placing the flowers? Crumble them for a fun confetti look.

1 package (18-1/4 ounces) white *or* yellow cake mix
1 can (16 ounces) white *or* vanilla frosting
40 to 50 Candied Flowers (recipe below)

Prepare cake batter according to package directions. Fill greased, foil or paper-lined muffin cups two-thirds full. Bake at 350° for 18-24 minutes or until a toothpick comes out clean. Cool for 5 minutes before removing from pans to wire racks to cool completely. Frost cupcakes. Decorate with candied flowers. **Yield:** 2 dozen.

Candied Flowers

(Pictured above and on page 372)

Sugarcoated edible flowers are a quick and easy way to add a little flair to many desserts and serving trays. They need to be made in advance, which is a real time-saver on party day.

2 teaspoons meringue powder
2 tablespoons water
40 to 50 edible blossoms of your choice, such as rose petals, violas (Johnny-jump-ups), calendula petals (pot marigold) and dianthus
1-1/4 cups superfine sugar

In a small bowl, dissolve meringue powder in water. Lightly brush over all sides of flowers to coat completely. Sprinkle with sugar. Allow to dry on a waxed paper-lined baking sheet for 1 to 2 days. Use as a garnish for desserts. **Yield:** 40 to 50 candied flowers.

Editor's Note: Meringue powder can be ordered by mail from Wilton Industries, Inc. Call 1-800/794-5866 or visit their Web site at *www.wilton.com*.

Superfine sugar can be found in the baking aisle alongside granulated sugar. As a substitute for superfine sugar, place granulated sugar in a blender or food processor; cover and pulse until fine.

EDIBLE FLOWER REMINDER

ONLY harvest blooms from plants that have not been treated with chemicals. When using any flowers for cooking, be certain of what you are picking.

Raspberry Fudge Torte

(Pictured on page 373)

This special-occasion cake impresses all who see and taste it. People are surprised to hear
this torte starts with a simple cake mix…they're sure I bought it at a bakery.
—Julie Hein, York, Pennsylvania

1 package (18-1/4 ounces)
  devil's food cake mix
1 cup (8 ounces) sour cream
3/4 cup water
3 eggs
1/3 cup vegetable oil
1 teaspoon vanilla extract
1 cup miniature semisweet
  chocolate chips
GANACHE:
1 cup semisweet chocolate chips
1/2 cup heavy whipping cream
1 tablespoon butter
RASPBERRY CREAM:
1 package (10 ounces) frozen
  sweetened raspberries,
  thawed
3 tablespoons sugar
4 teaspoons cornstarch
1/2 cup heavy whipping cream,
  whipped
Fresh raspberries and mint,
  optional

In a mixing bowl, combine the cake mix, sour cream, water, eggs, oil and vanilla; beat on low speed until moistened. Beat for 2 minutes on medium. Fold in miniature chips. Pour into three greased and floured 9-in. round baking pans. Bake at 350° for 25-30 minutes or until a toothpick inserted near the center comes out clean. Cool for 10 minutes before removing from pans to wire racks to cool completely.

For ganache, combine chips and cream in a small saucepan. Cook and stir over low heat until melted and smooth. Remove from the heat; stir in butter. Refrigerate for 1-2 hours or until cold, stirring occasionally. Beat for 1-2 minutes or until mixture achieves spreading consistency.

For raspberry cream, mash and strain raspberries, reserving juice; discard seeds. In a small saucepan, combine sugar and cornstarch; stir in raspberry juice. Cook and stir over low heat for 1-2 minutes until thickened and bubbly. Cover and refrigerate for 30 minutes or until cold. Fold in whipped cream.

To assemble, place one cake layer on serving plate; spread with half of the ganache. Place second cake layer over ganache; spread with raspberry cream. Top with remaining cake; spread with remaining ganache. Garnish with raspberries and mint if desired. Cover and store in the refrigerator. **Yield:** 12 servings.

Scaredy Cakes

(Pictured at right)

Our Test Kitchen home economists guarantee kids of all ages will delight in these funny-faced cupcakes. You can even enlist your little ones to help decorate them, using the candies we suggest or other candies to suit your tastes.

1 package (18-1/4 ounces) yellow cake mix
1 can (16 ounces) vanilla frosting
Green gel food coloring, optional
Assorted candies of your choice (Chiclets, black licorice nips, red shoestring licorice, Gummi Worms, M&M's, Life Savers, gumballs, strawberry sour belts, Tart 'n' Tangy's, Tic Tacs)

Prepare cake batter according to package directions. Fill greased or paper-lined muffin cups two-thirds full. Bake at 350° for 18-24 minutes or until a toothpick comes out clean. Cool for 5 minutes before removing from pans to wire racks to cool completely.

Tint some of the frosting green if desired. Frost cupcakes. Decorate with assorted candy to create monster faces. **Yield:** 2 dozen.

CAKE DECORATING TIPS

EVEN a novice can master decorating techniques to create impressive cakes. To make the task easier, use pastry bags or heavy-duty resealable bags, metal or plastic cake decorating tips and a coupler. A coupler lets you switch tips without changing pastry bags when using the same color frosting.

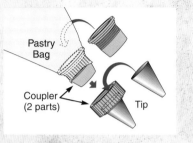

To use a coupler, place the large part of the coupler inside the pastry bag (see illustration at right). Trim the top of the bag if necessary in order to let the coupler extend about 1/4 inch outside the bag. Place the coupler ring over the tip and screw both parts of the coupler together. To change tips and continue using the same color frosting, unscrew the coupler ring, replace tip and screw on the ring.

Below are some common cake decorating techniques. Unless otherwise noted, hold the pastry bag at a 45° angle.

1. Shell Border. Using a No. 16-21 star tip, hold the bag just above the surface. Squeeze bag; slightly lift tip as frosting builds and fans out. Relax pressure as you lower tip to make tail. Stop pressure completely and pull tip away. Work from left to right, resting the head of one shell on the tail of the previous shell.

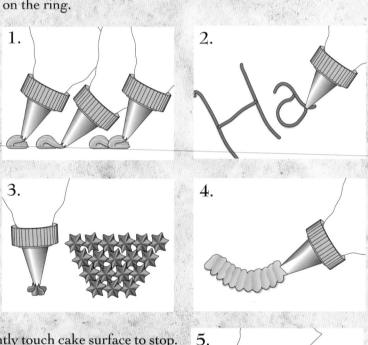

2. Writing, Outline, Facial Features, Zigzag. Using a No. 1-3 round tip, touch surface lightly, squeezing frosting out evenly as you go. Release pressure and gently touch cake surface to stop. To zigzag, continue piping up and down with steady pressure.

3. Star Fill-in. Using a No. 16-21 star tip, hold bag at a 90° angle with tip just above the surface. Squeeze bag; hold tip in place as star is formed. Stop pressure and pull tip up. Pipe rows of stars evenly and close together until entire area is filled.

4. Ruffle Garland. Using a No. 102-104 tip, angle the narrow end of the tip slightly away from the surface. Squeeze bag, moving your hand up and down slightly to ruffle the icing and positioning the bag to form the curve.

5. Sotas (Lace). Using a No. 1-3 round tip, squeeze bag and allow frosting to drop randomly in a series of overlapping loops.

Clown Cake

(Pictured at right)

You can't go wrong planning a circus theme for your child's birthday party, especially with this colorful cake from our Test Kitchen. Use some of the clown cookies on the cake and serve the remainder alongside.

1 tube (18 ounces) refrigerated
   sugar cookie dough
1 package (18-1/4 ounces)
   yellow *or* chocolate cake mix
3/4 cup butter, softened
6 tablespoons shortening
9 cups confectioners' sugar
3 teaspoons vanilla extract
1/8 teaspoon salt
1/2 cup milk
Red, blue, yellow and green gel *or*
  paste food coloring

On a lightly floured surface, roll out cookie dough to 1/4-in. thickness. Cut out with a 3-in. to 3-1/2-in. gingerbread man cookie cutter. Bake according to package directions. Cool on wire racks.

Prepare and bake cake according to the package directions, using two greased and floured 9-in. round baking pans. Cool for 10 minutes before removing from pans to wire racks to cool completely.

For frosting, in a large mixing bowl, cream butter and shortening. Beat in the confectioners' sugar, vanilla and salt. Beat in the milk until smooth. Place 1/2 cup of frosting each in four small bowls; tint one red, one blue, one yellow and one green. Place 3/4 cup of frosting in a small bowl and leave white. Cover the bowls with plastic wrap and set aside.

To assemble, place one cake layer on a 10-in. round serving plate. Using some of the remaining frosting, frost top of cake. Top with second layer; frost top and sides of cake.

Using 1/2 cup of the reserved white frosting, spread a thin layer on the front side of nine cookies; let stand until dry. (Set aside remaining cookies for another use or decorate and serve alongside.) Cut a small hole in the corner of four pastry or plastic bags; insert a tip and fill each bag with a tinted frosting. Decorate frosted side of cookies with zigzag, star fill-in, ruffle garland or sotas (lace) to resemble clowns. Let stand until dry.

Gently press a clown cookie into the lower left side of top of cake. Using frosting, make three balloons. Pipe strings from the balloons to the clown's hand. Pipe "Happy Birthday" on cake. Pipe a shell border around top edge. Pipe two large dots on the back of each clown with remaining white frosting. Evenly space clowns around sides of cake; gently press into the cake. **Yield:** 8-10 servings (about 2 dozen cookies).

Coconut Pecan Torte

An apricot filling is the sweet surprise in this moist, pretty cake.
Every forkful is filled with a wonderful combination of flavors.
—*Mary Somers, Enid, Oklahoma*

1/2 cup butter, softened
1/2 cup shortening
2 cups sugar
5 eggs, *separated*
1/2 teaspoon almond extract
1/2 teaspoon vanilla extract
2 cups all-purpose flour
1 teaspoon baking soda
1 cup buttermilk
1 cup flaked coconut
1 cup finely chopped pecans,
  toasted
APRICOT FILLING:
1 cup dried apricots
1 cup boiling water
1/4 cup packed brown sugar
1/8 teaspoon ground mace
FROSTING:
1/2 cup butter, softened
1 package (8 ounces) cream
  cheese, softened
3-3/4 cups confectioners' sugar
1 teaspoon vanilla extract
1 cup chopped pecans,
  toasted

In a mixing bowl, cream butter, shortening and sugar. Add egg yolks, one at a time, beating well after each. Beat in extracts. Combine flour and baking soda; add to the creamed mixture alternately with buttermilk. Stir in the coconut and pecans.

In a mixing bowl, beat egg whites until stiff peaks form; fold into cake batter. Pour into three greased and floured 9-in. round baking pans. Bake at 325° for 25-30 minutes or until a toothpick inserted near the center comes out clean. Cool for 10 minutes before removing from pans to wire racks to cool completely.

For filling, place apricots and boiling water in a small bowl; let stand until completely cooled. Drain, reserving 1/3 cup liquid. In a small saucepan, combine apricots, brown sugar and reserved liquid. Cook over medium heat for 20 minutes or until thickened, stirring frequently. Remove from the heat; stir in mace. Cool completely. Place in a blender or food processor; cover and process until smooth.

For frosting, in a mixing bowl, cream the butter, cream cheese and confectioners' sugar. Beat in vanilla.

To assemble, place bottom cake layer on a serving plate; spread with half of the filling. Repeat layers. Top with the third cake layer; spread frosting over top and sides of cake. Garnish with pecans. Cover and store in the refrigerator.
Yield: 12-15 servings.

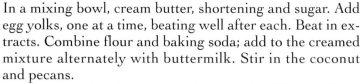

Family Traditions

I PURCHASED a plate with "Happy Birthday" painted on it. On each of my son's birthdays, they get to eat off of this special plate for breakfast, lunch, dinner and snacks. I've even toted it to restaurants! It's the first thing my kids run to get as soon as they wake up on their birthday.
—*Chris Kallies, Oldsmar, Florida*

Checkerboard Birthday Cake

(Pictured at right)

Although this cake from our Test Kitchen does take some time to prepare, no special pan is needed. The different batters are simply added in rings in three 9-inch round pans.

1 cup butter, softened
2 cups sugar
4 eggs
3 cups cake flour, *divided*
4 teaspoons baking powder
1/4 teaspoon salt
1 cup milk
1 square (1 ounce) unsweetened chocolate, melted and cooled
1/2 teaspoon vanilla extract
1/2 teaspoon almond extract
Red liquid food coloring
1/2 teaspoon lemon extract
Yellow liquid food coloring
FROSTING:
6 tablespoons butter, softened
6-1/2 to 7-1/2 cups confectioners' sugar, *divided*
5 squares (1 ounce *each*) unsweetened chocolate, melted and cooled
3/4 cup milk
1-1/2 teaspoons vanilla extract

Grease three 9-in. round baking pans; set aside. In a mixing bowl, cream butter and sugar. Add eggs, one at a time, beating well after each addition. Combine 2-1/2 cups of cake flour, baking powder and salt; add to the creamed mixture alternately with milk.

Divide batter into thirds. To one portion, fold in melted chocolate and vanilla. To second portion, fold in 1/4 cup flour, almond extract and 3-4 drops red food coloring. To third portion, fold in lemon extract, 3-4 drops yellow food coloring and remaining flour.

Spoon a ring of chocolate batter around edge of one prepared pan; spoon a ring of pink batter inside chocolate ring and fill center with yellow batter. Spoon a ring of yellow batter around edge of second pan; add a chocolate middle ring and a pink center. Spoon a ring of pink batter around edge of third pan; add a yellow middle ring and a chocolate center.

Bake at 350° for 20-25 minutes or until a toothpick inserted near the center comes out clean. Cool for 10 minutes before removing from pans to wire racks to cool completely.

For frosting, in a mixing bowl, cream butter and 2 cups confectioners' sugar. Beat in melted chocolate until smooth. Add milk and vanilla. Beat in enough of the remaining confectioners' sugar until frosting achieves spreading consistency. Spread between layers and over top and sides of cake. **Yield:** 12-14 servings.

Chocolate Fudge Cake

(Pictured at right)

I first made this cake in my junior high home economics class. I've changed the recipe through the years to make the cake a little richer, and the icing is my own invention.
— *Katarina Greer*
Victoria, British Columbia

1/2 cup butter, softened
1-1/4 cups packed brown sugar
1 egg
1 teaspoon vanilla extract
3/4 cup water
1/2 cup milk
1-1/2 cups all-purpose flour
6 tablespoons baking cocoa
1-1/2 teaspoons cream of tartar
1 teaspoon baking soda
1 teaspoon baking powder
1/4 teaspoon salt
FROSTING:
1/2 cup butter, softened
1 cup confectioners' sugar
1/4 cup baking cocoa
1 to 2 tablespoons milk
1 can (16 ounces) vanilla
frosting

Grease a 13-in. x 9-in. x 2-in. baking pan; line with parchment paper. Grease the paper; set aside. In a mixing bowl, cream butter and brown sugar. Beat in egg and vanilla. Combine water and milk. Combine the flour, cocoa, cream of tartar, baking soda, baking powder and salt; add to creamed mixture alternately with milk mixture.

Pour into prepared pan. Bake at 350° for 22-27 minutes or until a toothpick inserted near the center comes out clean. Cool for 10 minutes before inverting onto a wire rack. Remove and discard parchment paper. Cool cake completely.

For frosting, in a mixing bowl, cream butter, confectioners' sugar and cocoa until smooth. Beat in enough milk to achieve spreading consistency. Transfer cake to a serving platter or covered board. Spread with chocolate frosting; decorate with vanilla frosting. **Yield:** 16-20 servings.

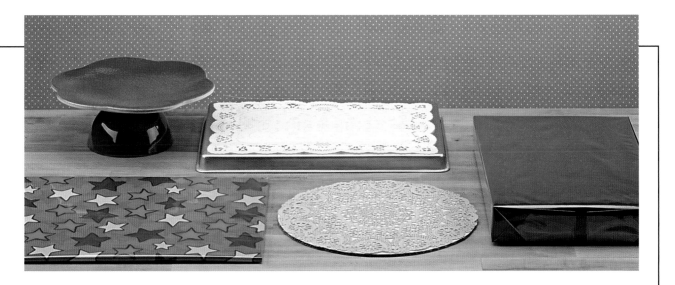

Creative Cake Boards

(Pictured above)

CAKES baked in convenient 13-inch x 9-inch x 2-inch baking pans are great because they don't call for any tricky layering and they often feed a larger group. But to make the cake look a little more special for occasions like birthday parties, you may want to take it out of the pan (see "Removing a Cake from a Pan" at right) and serve it on a cake board.

While the cake cools on the wire rack, prepare your cake board, making sure it's large enough to hold your cake.

For the Chocolate Fudge Cake shown on opposite page, we covered a piece of foam core with wrapping paper, then with clear cellophane. The same can be done with a sturdy gift box. Another option is to invert an everyday jelly roll pan and top it with an inexpensive paper doily. You can also place the cake directly onto a clean marble or plastic cutting board.

If you're serving a round cake but don't have a traditional cake plate or pedestal, any large round plate will do.

Or to make your own pedestal, invert a soup bowl, custard cup, footed dessert dish, ice cream sundae dish or a similar bowl and top it with a coordinating cake plate, dinner plate or round serving plate. Although you can use florist's clay between the inverted dish and plate to add some stability, this type of cake pedestal is for presentation only, and the plate should be removed from the pedestal dish before cutting and serving the cake.

REMOVING A CAKE FROM A PAN

HERE'S a trick that will make it easy to remove a cake from a baking pan. Before adding the batter, grease the pan. Line the bottom only with parchment paper, trimming the paper as needed to fit; grease the paper. Add batter and bake as directed.

1. Let the cake cool in the pan for 10 minutes. Carefully run a knife around the edges of the pan. Invert the pan onto a wire rack and lift up.

2. Lift off the parchment paper and discard. Let the cake cool completely before transferring to a serving plate for frosting.

Bridal Shower Reigns Supreme

EVERYTHING will be coming up roses for the bride-to-be when you shower her with a party and presents!

Hosting this get-together is a breeze when you rely on the appetizers, entrees, side dishes and desserts featured on the following pages.

As guests arrive, offer dainty cups of refreshing Cranberry Raspberry Punch, then call the ladies to the linen-topped table showcasing Orange-Avocado Chicken Salad, Creamy Crab Salad and Parmesan Cheese Straws. This menu is especially easy because much of the preparation can be done ahead of time.

While the guest of honor opens pretty packages, present some delectable desserts and freshly brewed coffee or tea.

HERE COMES THE BRIDE
(Clockwise from top right)

Cranberry Raspberry Punch (p. 388)

Creamy Crab Salad (p. 388)

Parmesan Cheese Straws (p. 386)

Orange-Avocado
Chicken Salad (p. 387)

Parmesan Cheese Straws

(Pictured on page 384)

*These rich and buttery breadsticks are a fun change from regular dinner rolls
and are fairly easy to make. They're great alongside salads and soups.*
—*Mitzi Sentiff, Greenville, North Carolina*

1/2 cup butter, softened
2/3 cup grated Parmesan cheese
1 cup all-purpose flour
1/4 teaspoon salt
1/8 teaspoon cayenne pepper
1/4 cup milk

In a small mixing bowl, beat butter and Parmesan cheese until well blended. Add the flour, salt and cayenne; mix well. Divide dough in half. On a lightly floured surface, roll each portion into an 18-in. x 3-in. rectangle. Cut into 3-in. x 1/2-in. strips.

Place 1 in. apart on lightly greased baking sheets; brush with milk. Bake at 350° for 8-10 minutes or until lightly browned. Remove to wire racks to cool. Store in an airtight container. **Yield:** 6 dozen.

Creamy Coconut Chocolate Pie

*I've used this recipe many times through the years for showers and luncheons.
The women I've served it to like the fluffy chocolate filling.*
—*Joan Sturrus, Grand Rapids, Michigan*

3 cups finely crushed cream-filled sandwich cookies (about 30 cookies)
1/2 cup butter, melted
FILLING:
5 cups miniature marshmallows
1 cup milk
Pinch salt
1 teaspoon vanilla extract
1/2 cup chopped pecans
1 square (1 ounce) unsweetened chocolate, grated
1 cup heavy whipping cream, whipped

TOPPING:
1/2 cup flaked coconut, toasted
1/3 cup confectioners' sugar
1 cup heavy whipping cream, whipped
Chocolate curls *or* grated chocolate

For crust, combine crushed cookies and butter; press onto the bottom and up the sides of a 9-in. pie plate. Chill until firm. For filling, combine marshmallows, milk and salt in a heavy saucepan. Cook and stir over low heat until marshmallows are melted. Refrigerate until cool, about 1-1/2 hours.

In a bowl, gently fold vanilla, pecans and grated chocolate into whipped cream. Fold into chilled marshmallow mixture. Pour into crust. Sprinkle with coconut. Fold confectioners' sugar into whipped cream; spread over coconut. Garnish with chocolate curls or grated chocolate. Refrigerate for at least 2 hours before serving. **Yield:** 8 servings.

Orange-Avocado Chicken Salad

(Pictured at right and on page 384)

Orange sections and avocado slices surround this hearty salad, making for a pretty presentation. It's a refreshing summer main dish for both lunch and dinner.
—*Shelia Garcia, Mantachie, Mississippi*

1/4 cup lime juice
2 teaspoons salt, *divided*
4 cups cubed cooked chicken
2 cups frozen peas, thawed
1 cup coarsely chopped carrots
1/2 cup thinly sliced celery
1/3 cup minced fresh parsley
1 cup mayonnaise
3 tablespoons orange juice
1/4 teaspoon pepper
Torn salad greens
6 medium navel oranges, peeled and sectioned
4 medium ripe avocados, peeled and sliced
1/4 cup thinly sliced green onions

In a small bowl, combine lime juice and 3/4 teaspoon salt; cover and refrigerate. In a large bowl, combine the chicken, peas, carrots, celery and parsley. Combine the mayonnaise, orange juice, pepper and remaining salt; pour over chicken mixture and toss to coat.

Cover and refrigerate for at least 1 hour.

Place greens on a serving platter or individual plates. Top with chicken salad; arrange orange sections and avocado slices around salad. Sprinkle with green onions. Drizzle with lime juice mixture. **Yield:** 12 servings.

SEEDING AND PEELING AVOCADOS

THE EASIEST avocados to peel and slice are those that are ripe yet firm. (Very ripe, soft avocados are best used for mashing.)

Cut the avocado in half lengthwise. Twist the halves in opposite directions to separate. Carefully tap the seed with the blade of a sharp knife. Rotate the knife to loosen the seed and lift it out.

To remove the peel, scoop out the flesh from each half with a large metal spoon, staying close to the peel. Slice; dip slices in lemon juice to prevent them from turning brown.

Creamy Crab Salad

(Pictured on page 385)

This easy-on-the-pocket salad beautifully dresses up economical imitation crab.
My husband's grandmother gladly shared the recipe.
—Barb Stanton, Winona, Minnesota

1 package (16 ounces) medium
  shell pasta
1 package (16 ounces) imitation
  crabmeat, flaked
3 green onions, thinly sliced
1/2 cup chopped carrot
1/2 cup chopped cucumber
1/2 cup chopped green pepper
1 cup (8 ounces) sour cream
1 cup mayonnaise
1/3 cup sugar
1 tablespoon seasoned salt
2 teaspoons cider vinegar
1-1/2 to 2 teaspoons pepper
Leaf lettuce, optional

Cook pasta according to package directions; drain and rinse in cold water. Place in a large bowl; add crab, onions, carrot, cucumber and green pepper. Combine the sour cream, mayonnaise, sugar, seasoned salt, vinegar and pepper; pour over salad and toss to coat. Cover and chill for at least 2 hours. Serve in a lettuce-lined bowl if desired. **Yield:** 10-12 servings.

Cranberry Raspberry Punch

(Pictured on page 385)

The blushing bride-to-be and her guests will ask for refills of this pretty pink punch.
It's not too sweet, so my family never tires of it at events throughout the year.
—Susan Rogers, Wilmington, Massachusetts

1 package (16 ounces) frozen
  sweetened sliced strawberries,
  thawed
1 can (12 ounces) frozen
  lemonade concentrate, thawed
1 can (11-1/2 ounces) frozen
  cranberry raspberry juice
  concentrate, thawed
2 liters ginger ale, chilled

2 liters club soda, chilled
1 quart raspberry *or* orange sherbet

Place the strawberries, lemonade concentrate and cranberry raspberry concentrate in a blender; cover and process until smooth. Transfer to a punch bowl. Gently stir in ginger ale and club soda. Top with scoops of sherbet. Serve immediately. **Yield:** about 5 quarts.

Pretty Petit Fours

(Pictured at right)

Add a delicate touch to your dessert table with these bite-size cakes from our Test Kitchen. We decorated the tops with roses to follow our floral theme, but feel free to try your hand at other designs.

1/4 cup butter, melted
1/4 cup shortening
1 cup sugar
1 teaspoon vanilla extract
1-1/3 cups all-purpose flour
2 teaspoons baking powder
1/2 teaspoon salt
2/3 cup milk
3 egg whites
GLAZE:
2 pounds confectioners' sugar
2/3 cup plus 2 tablespoons water
2 teaspoons orange extract
FROSTING:
6 tablespoons butter, softened
2 tablespoons shortening
1/2 teaspoon vanilla extract
3 cups confectioners' sugar
3 to 4 tablespoons milk
Gel, liquid *or* paste food coloring

In a large mixing bowl, cream the butter, shortening and sugar. Beat in vanilla. Combine the flour, baking powder and salt; add to creamed mixture alternately with milk. In a small mixing bowl, beat egg whites until soft peaks form; gently fold into batter.

Pour into a greased 9-in. square

baking pan. Bake at 350° for 20-25 minutes or until a toothpick inserted near the center comes out clean. Cool for 10 minutes before removing from pan to a wire rack to cool completely.

Cut a thin slice off each side of cake. Cut cake into 1-1/4-in. squares. Place 1/2 in. apart on a rack in a 15-in. x 10-in. x 1-in. pan.

In a mixing bowl, combine glaze ingredients. Beat on low speed just until blended; beat on high until smooth. Apply glaze evenly over tops and sides of cake squares, allowing excess to drip off. Let dry. Repeat if necessary to thoroughly coat squares. Let dry completely.

For frosting, in a mixing bowl, cream butter, shortening and vanilla. Beat in confectioners' sugar and enough milk to achieve desired consistency. Place 1/2 cup each in two bowls; tint one pink and one green.

Cut a small hole in the corner of a pastry or plastic bag; insert #104 tip. Fill with pink frosting; pipe a rosebud on each petit four. Insert #3 round tip into another pastry or plastic bag; fill with green frosting. Pipe a leaf under each rose. **Yield:** 2-1/2 dozen (3 cups frosting).

Puff Pillow Buns

I entered this recipe at the 1971 Iowa State Fair and won first place. You can conveniently make the dough the night before, then shape and bake the buns the next morning.
—*Shirley Marti, Lansing, Iowa*

1 package (1/4 ounce) active dry yeast
1/4 cup warm water (110° to 115°)
1/2 cup warm milk (110° to 115°)
1/3 cup butter, melted
1/4 cup sugar
1 teaspoon salt
1/2 teaspoon lemon extract
2 eggs
3 to 3-1/2 cups all-purpose flour
FILLING:
1 package (8 ounces) cream cheese, softened
1/4 cup milk
1 teaspoon vanilla extract
2 tablespoons butter, melted
ICING:
1 cup confectioners' sugar
2 tablespoons butter, softened
1/2 teaspoon vanilla extract
1 to 2 tablespoons milk

In a mixing bowl, dissolve yeast in warm water. Add the milk, butter, sugar, salt, lemon extract, eggs and 1 cup flour. Beat until smooth. Stir in enough remaining flour to form a soft dough. Turn onto a floured surface; gently knead for 2-3 minutes. Place in a greased bowl, turning once to grease top. Cover and refrigerate for 2 hours or overnight.

Punch dough down. Turn onto a floured surface; divide into four portions. Roll one portion into a 9-in. x 6-in. rectangle (refrigerate remaining portions until ready to roll out). Cut into 3-in. squares.

In a mixing bowl, beat cream cheese, milk and vanilla until smooth. Place about 2 teaspoons filling in the center of each square. Moisten corners with water; bring over center of filling and pinch corners tightly in center. Repeat with remaining dough and filling. Place seam side up 2 in. apart on greased baking sheets; brush with melted butter. Cover and let rise in a warm place until doubled, about 45 minutes.

Bake at 400° for 10-12 minutes or until lightly browned. Remove from pans to wire racks. Combine icing ingredients; spread over warm buns. **Yield:** 2 dozen.

Mexican Wedding Cakes

As part of a Mexican tradition, I tucked these tender cookies into small gift boxes for the guests at my sister's wedding a few years ago. Most folks gobbled them up before they ever got home!
—*Sarita Johnston, San Antonio, Texas*

2 cups butter, softened
1 cup confectioners' sugar
4 cups all-purpose flour
1 teaspoon vanilla extract
1 cup finely chopped pecans
Additional confectioners' sugar

In a mixing bowl, cream butter and sugar. Gradually add flour; mix well. Beat in vanilla. Stir in pecans. Shape tablespoonfuls into 2-in. crescents. Place 2 in. apart on ungreased baking sheets. Bake at 350° for 12-15 minutes or until lightly browned. Roll warm cookies in confectioners' sugar; cool on wire racks. **Yield:** about 6 dozen.

Strawberry Wedding Bell Cookies

(Pictured at right)

To ring in a joyous occasion like a bridal shower or wedding, I'm often asked to make these festive cookies. You can use different flavors of jam to suit your tastes.
—Laurie Messer, Bonifay, Florida

1 cup butter, softened
1 package (3 ounces) cream cheese, softened
1/4 cup sugar
1 teaspoon vanilla extract
2 cups all-purpose flour
1/4 teaspoon salt
1/2 cup strawberry jam
Confectioners' sugar

In a mixing bowl, cream butter, cream cheese and sugar. Beat in vanilla. Combine flour and salt; gradually add to the creamed mixture. Divide dough into fourths. Cover and refrigerate for 2 hours or until easy to handle.

On a lightly floured surface, roll out each portion of dough to 1/8-in. thickness. Cut with floured 2-in. round cookie cutters. Place 1 in. apart on ungreased baking sheets. Spoon 1/4 teaspoon jam in the center and spread to within 1/4 in. of edge.

Shape into a bell by folding edges of dough to meet over filling. Bake at 375° for 8-10 minutes or until lightly browned. Remove to wire racks to cool. Dust with confectioners' sugar. **Yield:** about 5 dozen.

Family Traditions

INSTEAD of making a "bouquet" from ribbons and bows at the bridal shower, our family gives the guest of honor a nosegay of silk flowers with silver dollars (minted in the year of the wedding) tied on with colorful ribbon. The bride-to-be then uses this memento at the wedding rehearsal and saves it as a keepsake for years.
—Betty McLean, Fort Myers, Florida

Shrimp Pasta Salad

A Thousand Island-type dressing adds some zip to this pasta and shrimp salad.
My family prefers it to oil-based salad dressings.
—*Mrs. Herbert Waalkens, Albert Lea, Minnesota*

1 package (16 ounces) small
   shell pasta
1 package (10 ounces) frozen
   cooked salad shrimp, thawed
1/2 cup chopped celery
1/2 cup chopped onion, *divided*
  2 hard-cooked eggs, chopped,
   divided
1/4 cup minced fresh parsley
  1 cup mayonnaise
1/4 cup chili sauce

1 tablespoon chopped dill pickle *or* dill pickle relish
1/2 teaspoon Worcestershire sauce
1/2 teaspoon seasoned salt

Cook pasta according to package directions; drain and rinse in cold water. Place in a bowl; add the shrimp, celery, 1/4 cup onion, half of the chopped eggs and parsley.

In a small bowl, combine the mayonnaise, chili sauce, pickle, Worcestershire sauce, seasoned salt, and remaining onion and eggs. Stir into pasta mixture. Cover and refrigerate until serving. **Yield:** 10 servings.

Marinated Mozzarella Cubes

(Pictured on opposite page)

Being from America's Dairyland, I'm always on the lookout for new ways to serve cheese.
I received this delicious recipe from a friend a few years ago and am happy to share it with others.
—*Arline Roggenbuck, Shawano, Wisconsin*

1 pound mozzarella cheese, cut
   into 1-inch cubes
1 jar (7 ounces) roasted red
   peppers, drained and cut into
   bite-size pieces
  6 fresh thyme sprigs
  2 garlic cloves, minced
1-1/4 cups olive oil
  2 tablespoons minced fresh
   rosemary
  2 teaspoons Italian seasoning
1/4 teaspoon crushed red pepper
   flakes
Bread *or* crackers

In a quart jar with a tight-fitting lid, layer a third of the cheese, peppers,

thyme and garlic. Repeat layers twice. In a small bowl, combine the oil, rosemary, Italian seasoning and pepper flakes; mix well. Pour into jar; seal and turn upside down. Refrigerate overnight, turning several times. Serve with bread or crackers. **Yield:** 12-16 servings.

Mmmmarinated Mozzarella!

MAKE a few extra batches of Marinated Mozzarella Cubes; divide among quart or pint jars. Tuck each jar into a pretty basket along with bread or crackers and give away the baskets as party favors.

After eating the cheese and peppers from the jar, use the olive oil for cooking or as a dip for fresh bread.

Spinach-Cheese Mushroom Caps

(Pictured at right)

Dainty finger foods like these mushrooms are a nice way to welcome guests into your home. A hearty spinach filling will tide folks over until the meal is served.
—Sandy Herman, Marietta, Georgia

24 large fresh mushrooms
1/4 cup chopped onion
2 garlic cloves, minced
1 tablespoon olive oil
1 package (8 ounces) cream cheese, softened
1 package (10 ounces) frozen chopped spinach, thawed and well drained
1/2 cup plus 2 tablespoons shredded Parmesan cheese, *divided*
1/2 cup crumbled feta cheese
1 bacon strip, cooked and crumbled
1/2 teaspoon salt

Remove stems from mushrooms; set caps aside. Finely chop the stems. In a skillet, saute the chopped mushroom stems, onion and garlic in oil until tender.

In a mixing bowl, beat cream cheese until smooth. Add the spinach, 1/2 cup Parmesan cheese, feta cheese, bacon, salt and mushroom mixture. Spoon into mushroom caps. Sprinkle with the remaining Parmesan cheese. Place on a baking sheet. Bake at 400° for 15 minutes or until golden brown. **Yield:** 2 dozen.

MAKE THE MUSHROOMS AHEAD

INSTEAD of assembling Spinach-Cheese Mushroom Caps as guests arrive, stuff them in the morning and place on a baking sheet. Cover with a damp paper towel; refrigerate until baking time.

Artichoke Chicken Lasagna

*Chicken, artichokes and a cream sauce make this lasagna more special
than the usual tomato and beef variety. Everyone will love it!*
— Donna Boellner, Annapolis, Maryland

2/3 cup butter, *divided*
1/3 cup all-purpose flour
1 teaspoon salt, *divided*
1/4 teaspoon ground nutmeg
1/8 teaspoon pepper
3 cups milk
1-3/4 pounds boneless skinless
  chicken breasts, cut into thin
  strips and halved
2 cans (14 ounces *each*)
  water-packed artichoke
  hearts, drained and
  quartered
1 teaspoon dried thyme
9 lasagna noodles, cooked and
  drained
1 cup grated Parmesan cheese

In a saucepan, melt 1/3 cup butter. Stir in flour, 1/2 teaspoon salt, nutmeg and pepper until smooth. Gradually stir in milk. Bring to a boil; cook and stir for 2 minutes or until thickened. In a skillet, cook chicken in remaining butter until juices run clear. Stir in artichokes, thyme and remaining salt; heat through.

  In a greased 13-in. x 9-in. x 2-in. baking dish, layer about 1/3 cup white sauce, three noodles, 1/2 cup sauce, 1/3 cup Parmesan cheese and about 3 cups chicken mixture. Repeat layers. Top with remaining noodles, sauce and Parmesan cheese. Bake, uncovered, at 350° for 35-40 minutes or until bubbly and golden brown. Let stand for 10 minutes before cutting. **Yield:** 12 servings.

Frozen Fruit Slush

*A fresh fruit salad can take some time to prepare and needs last-minute assembly.
That's why I often rely on this make-ahead frozen fruit dish when entertaining a crowd.*
—Judy McHone, Springfield, Illinois

2-1/2 cups water
1 cup sugar
1 can (6 ounces) frozen orange
  juice concentrate, thawed
3/4 cup lemonade concentrate
4 large firm bananas, sliced
1 can (29 ounces) sliced
  peaches, undrained and
  chopped

1 can (20 ounces) pineapple chunks, undrained
1 can (15 ounces) mandarin oranges, drained
1 package (10 ounces) frozen sweetened sliced
  strawberries, thawed
1 jar (6 ounces) maraschino cherries, undrained

In a large bowl, combine all ingredients. Cover and freeze for at least 8 hours or until firm. Remove from the freezer 45 minutes before serving. **Yield:** 18 servings (3/4 cup each).

Lovely Table For the Ladies

(Pictured above)

WHEN hosting a party just for women, add a little more feminine flair. For starters, place white or ivory linen cloths on your table, then drape tulle netting over the top. Place Napkin Roses (instructions at right) on each plate.

You can further enhance the floral effect by setting out a spray of fresh flowers. Or beside each place setting, put the blossom of a fresh-cut flower in a small, shallow clear bowl filled with water. (To prop up the flower, we first filled the bowl with clear marbles.)

CREATING NAPKIN ROSES

GUESTS will shower you with compliments when they see this fresh idea for Napkin Roses. To start, lay a square napkin flat with the right side down.

1. Fold napkin in half diagonally. Fold right corner three-quarters of the way up, aligning open edges.

2. Hold newly folded edge a few inches from the bottom; alternately finger-pleat and roll napkin to opposite corner, following bottom edge. Secure rose with ribbon and tie in a bow.

It's a Girl!

BABY SHOWERS don't always have to be a surprise. In fact, planning the party after the bundle of joy arrives gives friends and relatives an opportunity to meet the tiny guest of honor.

No matter when you host the shower, you won't get rattled thinking about the menu if you turn to these lovely lunch items.

As guests arrive, serve Celebration Punch, then top the table with Tropical Chicken Salad and Spinach Salad with Honey Dressing. The Watermelon Baby Carriage not only holds a beautiful blend of fruit but serves as a centerpiece as well.

In addition to a rich dessert, pass around pretty plates piled high with refreshing Party Mint Patties.

PRETTY IN PINK
(Clockwise from top right)

Celebration Punch (p. 399)

Party Mint Patties (p. 400)

Tropical Chicken Salad (p. 398)

Spinach Salad with
Honey Dressing (p. 400)

Watermelon Baby
Carriage (p. 401)

Tropical Chicken Salad

(Pictured on page 397)

Pineapple and almonds give this chicken salad its tropical taste.
Every forkful is loaded with chicken, making this a hearty luncheon entree.
—*Russell Moffett, Irvine, California*

1 can (20 ounces) pineapple
   tidbits
4 cups cubed cooked chicken
4 hard-cooked eggs, chopped
1 cup thinly sliced celery
1 cup slivered almonds
1/2 cup mayonnaise
1/2 cup sour cream

1 teaspoon poppy seeds
Salt and pepper to taste

Drain pineapple, reserving 1 tablespoon juice (discard remaining juice or save for another use). In a large bowl, combine the pineapple, chicken, eggs, celery and almonds. In a small bowl, combine the remaining ingredients; stir in reserved pineapple juice. Pour over chicken mixture; mix well. Refrigerate until serving. **Yield:** 8 servings.

Chocolate Cheesecake Squares

These bite-size bars are very rich, so small servings are satisfying.
They're perfect for parties because they don't require a fork and plate to eat.
—*Helen Longmire, Austin, Texas*

1 cup all-purpose flour
1/2 cup sugar
3 tablespoons baking cocoa
1 teaspoon baking powder
1/4 teaspoon salt
1/2 cup cold butter
1 egg yolk
1 teaspoon vanilla extract
1/2 cup finely chopped walnuts
FILLING:
1 package (8 ounces) cream
   cheese, softened
1/3 cup sugar
1/2 cup sour cream
1 tablespoon all-purpose flour
2 teaspoons grated orange peel
1/4 teaspoon salt
1 egg

1 egg white
1/2 teaspoon vanilla extract
Chocolate sprinkles, optional

Line a 9-in. square baking pan with foil; grease the foil and set aside. In a bowl, combine the first five ingredients. Cut in butter until fine crumbs form. Stir in egg yolk, vanilla and walnuts; mix well. Press onto the bottom of the prepared pan. Bake at 325° for 15 minutes.

In a small mixing bowl, beat cream cheese and sugar until smooth. Add the sour cream, flour, orange peel and salt; mix well. Add egg, egg white and vanilla; beat on low speed just until combined. Pour over warm crust. Bake for 20-25 minutes or until center is almost set. Cool on a wire rack for 1 hour.

Garnish top with chocolate sprinkles if desired. Refrigerate overnight. Using foil, lift out of pan. Discard foil; cut into 1-in. squares. **Yield:** 25 servings.

Celebration Punch

(Pictured at right and on page 397)

This pretty fruit punch has just the right amount of sweetness. The ice ring keeps it cool for hours without diluting the flavor.
—Marci Carl
Northern Cambria, Pennsylvania

ICE RING:
1-3/4 cups orange juice
1-1/2 cups water
    1 cup halved fresh strawberries
Fresh mint springs
PUNCH:
    2 packages (10 ounces *each*)
       frozen sweetened
       strawberries, thawed
    4 cans (5-1/2 ounces *each*)
       apricot nectar
3/4 cup orange juice concentrate
    3 cups cold water
    1 cup lemon juice
3/4 cup sugar
    1 liter ginger ale, chilled

For ice ring, in a bowl, combine orange juice and water. Pour 2 cups into a 4-1/2-cup ring mold. Freeze until solid. Top with fresh strawberries and mint. Slowly pour remaining juice mixture into mold to almost cover strawberries and mint. Freeze until solid.

For punch, place thawed strawberries in a blender; cover and puree until smooth. Pour into a large serving bowl or punch bowl. Add the apricot nectar, orange juice concentrate, water, lemon juice and sugar; stir until sugar is dissolved. Just before serving, stir in ginger ale and add ice ring. **Yield:** about 1 gallon.

UNMOLDING AN ICE RING

TO REMOVE an ice ring from a mold, wrap the bottom of the mold with a hot, damp dish towel. Invert onto a baking sheet; place fruit side up in a punch bowl.

Spinach Salad with Honey Dressing

(Pictured on page 397)

Guests are always impressed by this elegant salad's taste and appearance.
They never leave the table without requesting the recipe.
—*Emilie Hinton, Bradley, Illinois*

1 medium red apple
Lemon juice
6 cups torn fresh spinach
6 cups torn red leaf lettuce
1 small red onion, sliced and
  separated into rings
1 can (11 ounces) mandarin
  oranges, drained
1/3 cup sunflower kernels,
  toasted
6 bacon strips, cooked and
  crumbled
DRESSING:
1/2 cup vegetable oil
1/4 to 1/3 cup sugar

2 tablespoons plus 1-1/2 teaspoons cider vinegar
2 tablespoons plus 1-1/2 teaspoons honey
1/2 teaspoon celery salt
1/2 teaspoon onion salt
1/2 teaspoon paprika
1/2 teaspoon ground mustard
1/2 teaspoon lemon juice

Thinly slice apple; brush with lemon juice. In a large salad bowl, toss the spinach, lettuce, onion, oranges and apple slices. Sprinkle with sunflower kernels and bacon.

In a microwave-safe bowl, whisk the dressing ingredients. Microwave, uncovered, on high for 1 minute. Stir and drizzle over salad. Serve immediately. **Yield:** 12 servings.

Party Mint Patties

(Pictured on page 397)

These easy-to-make mint candies are perfect for any occasion throughout the year.
Simply tint the dough the appropriate color. Friends and family will gobble these up in a jiffy!
—*Mrs. William Yoder, Bloomfield, Iowa*

1/4 cup butter, softened
1/3 cup light corn syrup
4 cups confectioners' sugar,
  divided
1/2 to 1 teaspoon peppermint
  extract
2 drops red food coloring
2 drops yellow food coloring
Granulated sugar (about 1 cup)

In a small mixing bowl, combine butter and corn syrup. Add 2 cups confectioners' sugar and extract; beat well. Stir in 1 cup confectioners' sugar. Turn onto a work surface sprinkled with remaining confectioners' sugar; knead until sugar is absorbed and mixture is smooth.

Divide into three portions. Tint one portion pink and one yellow; leave remaining portion white. Shape into 3/4-in. balls; roll in granulated sugar. Flatten with a fork. Let stand, uncovered, at room temperature for 1 day. Store in an airtight container. **Yield:** about 7-1/2 dozen.

Watermelon Baby Carriage

(Pictured at right and on page 396)

This fruit-filled carriage was made for my daughter's baby shower and was a huge hit. Fill it with any fruit you fancy and serve purchased poppy seed dressing alongside if you desire.
—Angie Schaff
St. Anthony, North Dakota

1 medium watermelon
5 toothpicks
4 orange slices
4 lime slices
2 cups seedless red grapes, *divided*
1 medium cantaloupe, cut into balls *or* cubes
2 cups seedless green grapes
2 cups halved fresh strawberries
Poppy seed salad dressing

With a sharp knife, cut a thin slice from bottom of melon so it sits flat. Lightly score a horizontal line halfway up sides and around the melon, leaving 5 in. from one end unmarked on each side for baby carriage hood.

For hood, make another line around top of watermelon, connecting both sides of the horizontal line. Using the rounded edge of a biscuit cutter as a guide, mark a scalloped edge along all straight lines. With a long sharp knife, cut into melon along the scalloped lines, making sure to cut all the way through the melon rind. Gently pull off rind. Remove fruit from melon and removed section; cut fruit into balls or cubes and set aside.

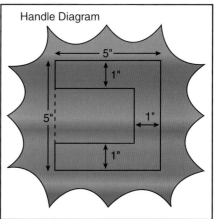

For the U-shaped handle (see diagram at right), cut out a 5-in. square from the removed section of rind. Cut out the center and one end, leaving a 1-in.-wide handle. Break one toothpick in half. Attach handle to watermelon with toothpick halves.

For wheels, position orange slices at base of watermelon and attach with toothpicks. Top each orange slice with a lime slice and a red grape.

In a large bowl, combine the cantaloupe, green grapes, strawberries, remaining red grapes and reserved watermelon. Spoon into baby carriage. Serve with poppy seed salad dressing. **Yield:** 20-24 servings.

Lemon Squares

I'm expected to bring these bars to bridal showers and family gatherings.
The combination of sweet and tart tastes is sure to please.
—Mary Larson, Maplewood, Minnesota

3 cups all-purpose flour
3/4 cup confectioners' sugar
1/2 teaspoon salt
1-1/2 cups cold butter
TOPPING:
  6 eggs, lightly beaten
  3 cups sugar
  1/2 cup lemon juice
1-1/2 teaspoons baking powder
  1/2 teaspoon salt
Confectioners' sugar

In a bowl, combine the flour, confectioners' sugar and salt. Cut in butter until crumbly. Pat into a greased 15-in. x 10-in. x 1-in. baking pan. Bake at 350° for 16-20 minutes or until set and top is golden brown.

For topping, combine the eggs, sugar, lemon juice, baking powder and salt in a bowl. Pour over crust (pan will be full). Bake 16-20 minutes longer or until set and top is golden brown. Cool. Dust with confectioners' sugar. Cut into squares. **Yield:** 4 dozen.

STARTING A TIME CAPSULE FOR THE BABY

LOOKING for a fun tradition to begin at a baby shower? Help the parents start a "time capsule" of the baby's first year of life.

- Select a durable container that will last for years, such as a heavy cardboard box or plastic container with tight-fitting lid.
- When you send out the invitations, inform the guests you're starting a time capsule and ask each guest to bring an item to add. Assign a specific object to each guest or provide them with a list of possibilities to spark their creativity. Here are some ideas:

    Newspapers and television guides with the year of the child's birth
    Magazines featuring current clothing styles
    Grocery store ads showing food prices
    Stamps or coins
    Music compact discs
    Television video tapes or DVDs
    Popular toys (Beanie Babies, etc.)
    Copy of the baby's family tree
    Handwritten letters to baby
    Copies of family-favorite recipes
    Recent pictures of family and friends
    Clean newborn diapers or clothes

- In lieu of party games, present the time capsule container to the mother-to-be. Go around the room and have each guest add their own item.
- After the party, encourage Mom and Dad to add pictures from the shower and other mementos from the baby's first year (lock of hair, favorite rattle, discarded pacifiers, etc.).

  Note: To avoid yellowing, place all papers in resealable plastic bags. Put photos on acid-free pages to prevent deterioration.

- On the baby's first birthday, have the parents seal the capsule, adhere a "Do Not Open Until" label (indicating a special date in the future, such as the child's 16th birthday, high school graduation day or birth of their own baby) and tuck it away in a cool dry place like a closet.

Strawberry Cheese Bundles

(Pictured at right)

When I first served these turnovers, folks thought I bought them from a bakery. Everyone was surprised to hear they start with refrigerated crescent rolls and pie filling.
—Jolene Spray, Van Wert, Ohio

1 package (3 ounces) cream cheese, softened
2 tablespoons confectioners' sugar
1/4 teaspoon almond extract
1 tube (8 ounces) refrigerated crescent rolls
1/3 cup strawberry pie filling
1/3 cup crushed pineapple, drained
2 to 3 tablespoons apricot spreadable fruit

In a small mixing bowl, beat the cream cheese, sugar and extract until smooth. Unroll crescent dough and separate into eight triangles. Place 1 heaping teaspoonful of cream cheese mixture in the center of each triangle. Top with 1 teaspoon of pie filling and 1 teaspoon of pineapple.

With one long side of pastry facing you, fold right and left corners over filling to top corner, forming a square. Seal edges. Place on an ungreased baking sheet. Bake at 375° for 15-17 minutes or until lightly browned. Brush with spreadable fruit. Serve warm or cold. **Yield:** 8 servings.

Candy Pacifiers

(Pictured at right)

These cute candy pacifiers are a clever addition to any baby shower.
—Lori Vigstol
Thief River Falls, Minnesota

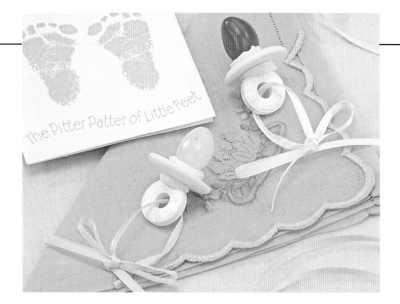

The Pitter Patter of Little Feet

1/4 cup vanilla frosting
Liquid food coloring, optional
  24 candy coating wafers
  24 jelly beans
  24 peppermint Life Savers
   8 feet of ribbon (1/8 inch), cut into 4-inch lengths

Tint frosting with food coloring if desired. Place a pea-size amount of frosting on the rounded side of each candy wafer; position a jelly bean standing upright in the frosting. Let stand for 10-20 minutes or until set. Place wafers jelly bean side down on a wire rack with jelly beans between the wires.

Carefully place another pea-size amount of frosting on the flat side of each candy wafer; position a Life Saver on edge in the frosting. Let stand for at least 1 day to dry. Tie a ribbon through each Life Saver. **Yield:** 2 dozen.

PAPER CLIP STOPS KNOTS

TO PREVENT the knot from slipping when making a loop on the Candy Pacifiers, place a paper clip on ribbon about 1 inch above top of pacifier; tie a knot. Remove paper clip. Tie ends of ribbon into a bow.

Cucumber Party Sandwiches

When I serve these refreshing sandwiches at ladies' luncheons and potlucks, the platter is always emptied. They are so simple to prepare that you'll find yourself making them often.
—Veronica Smith, Donnelly, Minnesota

1 package (8 ounces) cream cheese, softened
2 teaspoons Italian salad dressing mix
1 loaf (16 ounces) snack rye bread
2 large cucumbers, thinly sliced

2 tablespoons minced fresh dill *or* 2 teaspoons dill weed

In a small mixing bowl, beat the cream cheese and salad dressing mix until smooth. Spread on one side of each slice of bread. Top with a cucumber slice and sprinkle with dill. Serve immediately. **Yield:** about 3-1/2 dozen.

Broccoli Chicken Braid

(Pictured at right)

I work outside the home, so I appreciate recipes like this that are fast and delicious.
—Diane Wampler
Morristown, Tennessee

2 cups chopped cooked chicken
1 cup chopped fresh broccoli florets
1 cup (4 ounces) shredded cheddar cheese
1/4 cup chopped green pepper
1/4 cup chopped sweet red pepper
1 garlic clove, minced
1 teaspoon dill weed
1/4 teaspoon salt
1/2 cup mayonnaise

2 tubes (8 ounces *each*) refrigerated crescent rolls
1 egg white, lightly beaten
2 tablespoons slivered almonds

In a bowl, combine the first eight ingredients. Stir in mayonnaise. Unroll both tubes of crescent roll dough into one long rectangle on an ungreased baking sheet. Roll into a 15-in. x 12-in. rectangle, sealing seams and perforations. Spoon chicken mixture down center third of dough.

On each long side, cut eight strips about 3-1/2 in. into the center. Bring one strip from each side over filling and pinch ends to seal; repeat. Brush with egg white. Sprinkle with almonds. Bake at 375° for 15-20 minutes or until filling is heated through and top is golden brown. **Yield:** 8 servings.

Sunflower Cheese Ball

Having lived in the Sunflower State all my life, I've loved using sunflower kernels in a variety of recipes. Here, those crunchy kernels coat a creamy cheese spread.
—Karen Ann Bland, Gove, Kansas

1 package (8 ounces) cream cheese, softened
1 teaspoon Dijon mustard
1/2 teaspoon garlic powder
2 cups (8 ounces) shredded cheddar cheese
1/2 cup chopped ripe olives
2 tablespoons minced fresh parsley

1/2 cup salted sunflower kernels
Assorted crackers

In a small mixing bowl, beat cream cheese and mustard until smooth. Add garlic powder. Stir in the cheese, olives and parsley. Cover and refrigerate for 15 minutes. Shape into a ball; roll in sunflower kernels. Store in the refrigerator. Serve with crackers. **Yield:** 2-1/2 cups.

25th Wedding Anniversary

IF YOU'RE planning a party to celebrate the 25th wedding anniversary of either you and your spouse or a close relative, you can spare the cost of a caterer and forgo the fees of renting a hall.

Just open up your home and celebrate in style! It's easy to entertain a large group when you turn to this chapter's crowd-pleasing recipes.

Turkey Breast Roulade is an elegant entree that features a hearty ham and artichoke filling.

Partner slices of the main course with Garlic Potato Bake and Mandarin Orange Spinach Salad.

Then leave a lasting impression by presenting an eye-catching Anniversary Cake.

SILVER CELEBRATION

(Clockwise from top)

Anniversary Cake (p. 414)

Garlic Potato Bake (p. 408)

Turkey Breast Roulade (p. 409)

Mandarin Orange Spinach Salad (p. 410)

Garlic Potato Bake

(Pictured on page 407)

I created this recipe for an end-of-summer harvest picnic. Everyone loved it.
—Shelly Lehman, Powell, Wyoming

18 medium potatoes, peeled and
   diced
3 whole garlic bulbs, separated
   into cloves and peeled
3 cups (12 ounces) shredded
   cheddar cheese
1 package (8 ounces) cream
   cheese, cubed
6 eggs, beaten
1 tablespoon minced chives
1-1/2 to 2 teaspoons salt
1/4 teaspoon white pepper
Diced sweet red, yellow and
   orange peppers, rosemary sprigs
   and additional minced chives,
   optional

Place potatoes and garlic in a large kettle; cover with water. Bring to a boil. Reduce heat; cover and simmer for 15-20 minutes or until potatoes and garlic are tender. Drain.

In a large mixing bowl, combine potatoes and garlic, cheddar cheese, cream cheese, eggs, chives, salt and pepper; beat until smooth. Spoon into two greased shallow 3-qt. baking dishes. Bake, uncovered, at 350° for 30-35 minutes or until a thermometer reads 160°. Garnish with peppers, rosemary and chives if desired. **Yield:** 25 servings.

STEMWARE SERVERS

TO ADD a little elegance to a special-occasion dinner, present servings of Garlic Potato Bake in casual stemmed glasses (shown on page 407).

After baking the potatoes as directed, scoop servings into goblets or glasses. If you don't have enough of the same pattern, you can mix and match stemware.

Editor's Note: Do not use crystal stemware to serve hot food because the heat may cause breakage.

Lemon Burst Broccoli

This lemon dressing is great on any vegetable, especially broccoli.
—Kim Morren, Carrollton, Texas

3/4 cup lemon juice
3/4 cup vegetable oil
3 tablespoons sugar
3 tablespoons finely chopped
   onion
3 garlic cloves, minced
1-1/2 teaspoons salt
3/4 teaspoon paprika
6 pounds fresh broccoli, cut
   into florets

In a jar with a tight-fitting lid, combine the lemon juice, oil, sugar, onion, garlic, salt and paprika; shake well. Refrigerate for at least 1 hour.

Place broccoli in a steamer basket over 1 in. of boiling water in a large kettle or Dutch oven. Cover and steam for 8-10 minutes or until crisp-tender. Transfer broccoli to a serving dish. Shake lemon dressing and pour over broccoli; toss to coat. **Yield:** 24 servings.

Turkey Breast Roulade

(Pictured at right and on page 407)

The original recipe for this roulade called for tomatoes, which our son is allergic to. I substituted artichokes and mushrooms with wonderful results.
—Carol Earl, Brewster, New York

3 jars (7-1/2 ounces *each*) marinated artichoke hearts, drained and chopped
3 cans (4 ounces *each*) mushroom stems and pieces, drained and chopped
3 tablespoons chopped sweet onion
3 boneless turkey breast halves (3 to 3-1/2 pounds *each*)
2-1/4 pounds thinly sliced deli ham
1 cup butter, melted
1-1/2 teaspoons dried thyme

In a bowl, combine the artichokes, mushrooms and onion; set aside. With skin side down, cut a lengthwise slit through the thickest portion of each turkey breast to within 1/2 in. of bottom. Open the turkey breasts so they lie flat; cover with plastic wrap. Flatten to 3/4- to 1-in. thickness; remove plastic.

Place ham slices over turkey to within 1 in. of edges. Spoon vegetable mixture lengthwise down the center of the ham. Roll each turkey breast, starting from a side where the fold is in the center. Secure with kitchen string at 3-in. intervals. Place the turkey rolls seam side down in one greased 15-in. x 10-in. x 1-in. baking pan and one 13-in. x 9-in. x 2-in. baking pan.

In a small bowl, combine the butter and thyme; spoon over the turkey rolls. Bake, uncovered, at 350° for 1-1/4 to 1-3/4 hours or until a meat thermometer reads 170°, basting frequently. Cover and let stand for 10 minutes before slicing. **Yield:** 24-30 servings.

Mandarin Orange Spinach Salad

(Pictured on page 406)

With mandarin oranges and a slightly sweet dressing, this spinach salad is a refreshing change of pace. I frequently take it along to summer picnics.
—*Georgiann Franklin, Canfield, Ohio*

1/2 cup vegetable oil
1/3 cup sugar
1/3 cup white vinegar
2 tablespoons minced fresh parsley
3/4 teaspoon salt
SALAD:
3/4 cup slivered almonds
4-1/2 teaspoons sugar
7 cups torn romaine
7 cups torn spinach
1-1/2 cups sliced celery
1-1/2 cups sliced green onions
3 cans (11 ounces *each*) mandarin oranges, drained

In a jar with a tight-fitting lid, combine the first five ingredients; shake well. Set aside. In a skillet, cook and stir the almonds and sugar over medium heat until sugar is melted and almonds are coated. Spread on foil to cool completely.

In a large salad bowl, combine the romaine, spinach, celery and onions. Add oranges and sugared almonds; toss gently. Shake dressing; drizzle over salad and toss to coat. **Yield:** 24 servings.

Creamy Onion Soup

I enjoy inviting people into my home to sample flavorful foods like this creamy soup. You'll find it's a nice twist on the traditional version.
—*Minnie Paulson, Stanley, North Dakota*

8 medium onions, thinly sliced
1/3 cup butter
2 tablespoons all-purpose flour
1 teaspoon salt
1/2 teaspoon pepper
8 cups chicken broth
1 cup (8 ounces) sour cream
1/2 cup milk
12 slices French bread (1 inch thick), toasted
1 cup (4 ounces) shredded mozzarella cheese

In a large kettle or Dutch oven, saute onions in butter until tender. Sprinkle with flour, salt and pepper; cook and stir for 1 minute. Gradually add broth. Bring to a boil; cook and stir for 2 minutes. Reduce heat; simmer, uncovered, for 30 minutes. Combine sour cream and milk. Stir into soup; heat through (do not boil). Place a slice of toasted bread in each soup bowl; ladle soup over bread. Sprinkle with cheese. **Yield:** 12 servings.

Ham Cream Cheese Balls

(Pictured at right)

It seems like I'm always hosting a shower, birthday party or other celebration. This spread is fast to fix.
—Jill Kirby, Calhoun, Georgia

- 2 packages (8 ounces *each*) cream cheese, softened
- 1 package (2-1/2 ounces) thinly sliced deli ham, finely chopped
- 3 green onions, finely chopped
- 2 tablespoons Worcestershire sauce
- 1 cup finely chopped peanuts

Crackers and raw vegetables

In a bowl, combine the cream cheese, ham, onions and Worcestershire sauce; mix well. Shape into 3/4-in. balls. Roll in peanuts. Cover and refrigerate until serving. Serve with crackers and vegetables. **Yield:** about 5 dozen.

Refrigerator Rolls

I taught my teenage son how to make these soft rolls for a 4-H project. Everyone was surprised when this big brawny fellow, who shows Brahman cattle, was named Grand Champion!
— Deanna Naivar, Temple, Texas

- 2 packages (1/4 ounce *each*) active dry yeast
- 2 cups warm water (110° to 115°)
- 1/2 cup sugar
- 1 teaspoon salt
- 6 cups all-purpose flour
- 1 egg
- 1/4 cup shortening

In a mixing bowl, dissolve yeast in warm water. Add the sugar, salt and 2 cups flour. Beat on medium speed for 2 minutes. Add egg and shortening; mix well. Stir in enough remaining flour to form a soft dough (do not knead). Place in a greased bowl, turning once to grease top. Cover and refrigerate overnight.

Punch dough down. Turn onto a lightly floured surface; divide into 24 pieces. Shape each into a ball. Place 2 in. apart on greased baking sheets. Cover and let rise in a warm place until doubled, about 2 hours. Bake at 400° for 12-15 minutes or until golden brown. Remove from pans to wire racks to cool. **Yield:** 2 dozen.

Three-Cheese Manicotti

Family and friends love the rich cheese filling tucked inside tender pasta shells.
— Vikki Rebholz, West Chester, Ohio

2 cartons (15 ounces *each*)
  ricotta cheese
5 cups (20 ounces) shredded
  mozzarella cheese, *divided*
1 cup grated Parmesan cheese
2 eggs, beaten
2 teaspoons dried basil
2 teaspoons dried oregano
1 teaspoon onion powder
1 teaspoon garlic powder
1 teaspoon seasoned salt
2 jars (26 ounces *each*) spaghetti
  sauce
20 manicotti shells, cooked and
  drained

In a bowl, combine the ricotta cheese, 3 cups mozzarella cheese, Parmesan cheese, eggs and seasonings. Spread 1 cup spaghetti sauce each in two ungreased 13-in. x 9-in. x 2-in. baking dishes. Stuff manicotti shells with cheese mixture; arrange over sauce. Top with remaining sauce.

Cover and bake at 375° for 35-40 minutes. Uncover; sprinkle with remaining mozzarella cheese. Bake 10 minutes longer or until cheese is melted and manicotti is heated through. **Yield:** 10 servings.

STUFFING MANICOTTI SHELLS

TO EASILY STUFF manicotti shells, place the filling in a large resealable plastic bag; seal the bag. Cut off a small part of one bottom corner. Squeeze the filling into each shell.

Stuffed Bread Appetizers

You may want to double the recipe for this hearty cold appetizer because
I've found that folks just can't seem to stop eating it!
— Tracey Wesstrom, Lansdale, Pennsylvania

2 packages (one 8 ounces,
  one 3 ounces) cream cheese,
  softened
1 cup chopped celery
1 cup (4 ounces) shredded
  cheddar cheese
1/2 cup chopped sweet red pepper
1/2 cup chopped water chestnuts
1 teaspoon garlic salt
1 loaf (26 inches) French bread,
  halved lengthwise
Mayonnaise
Dried parsley flakes

4 dill pickle spears
4 slices deli ham

In a bowl, combine the first six ingredients. Hollow out top and bottom of bread, leaving a 1/2-in. shell (discard removed bread or save for another use). Spread a thin layer of mayonnaise over bread; sprinkle with parsley. Fill each half with cheese mixture.

Wrap pickle spears in ham; place lengthwise over cheese mixture on bottom half of loaf. Replace top; press together to seal. Wrap in foil; refrigerate overnight. Just before serving, cut into 1-in. slices. **Yield:** about 2 dozen.

Cheesecake Dessert Squares

(Pictured at right)

These creamy squares are a nice alternative for folks who are intimidated to make a cheesecake or other fancy dessert. Fresh fruit on top gives them a little more elegance.
—Sharon Skildum
Maple Grove, Minnesota

2 cups graham cracker crumbs
  (about 32 squares)
1/3 cup sugar
1/2 teaspoon ground cinnamon
1/2 cup butter, melted
FILLING:
3 packages (8 ounces *each*)
  cream cheese, softened
1-1/2 cups sugar
1 teaspoon vanilla extract
4 eggs, *separated*
Fresh fruit

In a small bowl, combine the cracker crumbs, sugar and cinnamon; stir in butter. Press into a greased 15-in. x 10-in. x 1-in. baking pan. Bake at 350° for 5 minutes.

In a large mixing bowl, beat cream cheese, sugar and vanilla until smooth. Add egg yolks; beat on low speed just until combined. In a small mixing bowl, beat egg whites until soft peaks form; fold into cream cheese mixture. Pour over crust. Bake for 28-30 minutes or until center is almost set. Cool on a wire rack for 30 minutes. Refrigerate overnight. Garnish with fruit. **Yield:** 24 servings.

Anniversary Cake

(Pictured on opposite page and page 407)

You can make this lovely single layer cake from our Test Kitchen with or without the cake topper. Flavor the cake as you wish, and if possible, tint the frosting to match the wedding colors.

ROYAL ICING:
- 4 cups confectioners' sugar
- 1/3 cup plus 2 to 3 teaspoons water, *divided*
- 3 tablespoons meringue powder
- 1/2 teaspoon cream of tartar

CAKE:
- 2 cups shortening
- 3-1/2 cups sugar
- 6 eggs
- 5-1/2 cups all-purpose flour
- 6 teaspoons baking powder
- 3 teaspoons salt
- 3 cups milk

ADDITIONAL INGREDIENTS FOR YELLOW CAKE:
- 3 teaspoons vanilla extract

ADDITIONAL INGREDIENTS FOR LEMON CAKE:
- 4-1/2 teaspoons grated lemon peel
- 3 teaspoons lemon extract

ADDITIONAL INGREDIENTS FOR SPICE CAKE:
- 3 teaspoons ground cinnamon
- 1-1/2 teaspoons ground allspice
- 1-1/2 teaspoons ground cloves

BUTTERCREAM FROSTING:
- 1 cup butter, softened
- 1 cup shortening
- 12 cups confectioners' sugar
- 3/4 cup plus 3 tablespoons milk
- 3 teaspoons vanilla extract

- 1/4 teaspoon salt
- 2-1/4 cups lemon curd, raspberry filling, apricot filling, poppy seed filling *or* filling of your choice
- Gel *or* paste food coloring

In a mixing bowl, combine the confectioners' sugar, 1/3 cup water, meringue powder and cream of tartar; beat on low speed just until combined. Beat on high for 7-10 minutes or until stiff peaks form. (Keep icing covered at all times with a damp cloth to keep from drying out. If necessary to restore texture later, beat again on high speed. Prepare only half of the icing recipe if using store-bought candy roses or edible flowers to decorate.)

ROSES: Divide icing in half; set half aside. If using store-bought roses, refer to photo for position and attach roses to top of cake using a dab of icing. If making icing roses, cut a hole in the corner of pastry or plastic bag; insert round tip #12 and fill with remaining icing. Holding the bag straight up, pipe a dome-shaped mound of icing on the flower nail.

With petal tip #103 and icing, hold pastry bag at a 45-degree angle, wide end of tip down. Turn nail and squeeze bag to form bud. Holding pastry bag with narrow end farther away from the rose tip and turning the nail, pipe a row of three standing petals. Pipe a second row of petals, holding the narrow tip end at a greater angle. Repeat for a third row.

Gently slide scissor ends underneath rose and remove it from nail to waxed paper; let dry completely. Repeat with remaining icing to make 20-22 roses. (Flowers can be made several weeks in advance and stored in an airtight container.)

NUMERALS AND CAKE TOPPER: Set aside 1/2 cup of reserved icing. With round tip #4 and remaining reserved icing, pipe at least ten 3/4-in.-square "25"s, making sure to connect the 2 and 5 at the base of each.

For cake topper, place pattern of your choice under waxed paper; tape both to work surface. Completely outline edges; let dry for 10 minutes. To reserved 1/2 cup icing, stir in remaining 2-3 teaspoons water to thin. Fill in outline of cake topper with thinned icing, using the same tip. Let dry completely, then place in an airtight container to store before use.

CAKE: Line two greased 12-in. round baking pans with parchment or waxed paper; grease and flour paper and set aside. In a mixing bowl, cream shortening and sugar. Add eggs, one at a time, beating well after each. Combine the flour, baking powder and salt; add to the creamed mixture alternately with the milk. Stir in additional cake ingredients based

on the desired cake flavor. Pour into prepared pans. Bake at 350° for 50-55 minutes or until a toothpick inserted near the center comes out clean. Cool for 10 minutes before removing from pans to wire racks to cool completely.

FROSTING: In a large mixing bowl, cream the butter, shortening and confectioners' sugar until well combined. Beat in milk, vanilla and salt until mixture becomes light and fluffy.

ASSEMBLING: Split each cooled cake into two horizontal layers. Place bottom layer on serving plate; spread with a thin layer of frosting. Top with 3/4 cup filling of your choice. Spread a thin layer of frosting over the bottom of next layer; place cake, frosted side down, over filling. Repeat layers twice. Top with remaining cake layer.

Set aside 3 cups frosting. Tint remaining frosting with color of your choice; set aside 1/2 cup. Spread remaining tinted frosting over top and sides of cake. Place reserved tinted frosting in a pastry or plastic bag with round tip #4. Pipe lettering and outlines over cake topper. Let dry.

FINISHING: Place reserved white frosting in a pastry or plastic bag with star tip #21. Pipe eight vertical columns around sides of cake. With the same tip,

pipe a shell border around top and bottom of cake.

Just before serving, use small dabs of frosting to attach numerals between columns and roses at top of columns. Stand cake topper up in center of cake; continue to hold while piping two large dollops of frosting on either side of cake topper. Position remaining roses with frosting around base of cake topper. Using leaf tip #69, pipe leaves around cluster of roses. (Dried decorations will collapse upon refrigeration. Remove to save.) **Yield:** 25-30 servings.

Editor's Note: Meringue powder can be ordered by mail from Wilton Industries, Inc. Call 1-800/794-5866 or visit their Web site, *www.wilton.com*.

ASSEMBLING THE ANNIVERSARY CAKE TOPPER

1. Place cake topper pattern under a sheet of waxed paper; tape both to work surface. Pipe icing along outside and inside edges of the design; let dry.

2. Thin remaining icing with water. Pipe icing inside the edges of the design to fill in; let dry.

3. Using tinted frosting, pipe lettering and outlines over cake topper; let dry.

Peppered Rib Eye Roast

Roast recipes are a fuss-free entree to serve when entertaining. After marinating the meat overnight, simply pop in the oven and bake for a couple of hours. It turns out terrific every time.
—Ruth Andrewson, Leavenworth, Washington

1/3 to 1/2 cup coarsely ground pepper
1 teaspoon ground cardamom
2 boneless rib eye roasts (5 to 6 pounds *each*)
2 cups soy sauce
1-1/2 cups cider vinegar
2 tablespoons tomato paste
2 teaspoons garlic powder
2 teaspoons paprika

Combine the pepper and cardamom; rub over roasts. Place each in a shallow baking dish. In a bowl, combine the soy sauce, vinegar, tomato paste, garlic powder and paprika. Pour over the roasts; turn several times. Cover and refrigerate overnight.

Place each roast in a roasting pan. Bake, uncovered, at 350° for 2 hours or until meat reaches desired doneness (for rare, a meat thermometer should read 140°; medium, 160°; well-done, 170°). **Yield:** 24-30 servings.

Vegetable Rice Casserole

As an avid gardener and occasional cook, I use fresh vegetables and herbs when trying out new recipes on my wife and children. This zesty rice dish always pleases.
—Blaine Baker, Kelseyville, California

6 cups water
2 tablespoons butter
3 cups uncooked long grain rice
2 tablespoons dried parsley flakes
3 teaspoons dill weed, *divided*
2 teaspoons celery salt, *divided*
1 cup diced carrots
1 cup diced fresh tomato
1 cup diced green pepper
1 cup diced onion
1 cup diced celery
1/4 to 1/2 cup diced hot banana peppers *or* hot peppers of your choice
2 tablespoons olive oil
2 cans (10-3/4 ounces *each*) condensed cream of chicken soup, undiluted
1/2 cup milk
2 teaspoons dried basil
1 teaspoon dried thyme
1/2 teaspoon pepper

In a large saucepan, bring water and butter to a boil; add rice. Cover and simmer for 20 minutes or until liquid is absorbed. Stir in the parsley, 2 teaspoons dill and 1 teaspoon celery salt; set aside.

In a skillet, saute carrots, tomato, green pepper, onion, celery and hot peppers in oil until vegetables are crisp-tender. Stir in soup, milk, basil, thyme, pepper and remaining dill and celery salt. Divide half of the rice mixture between two greased 11-in. x 7-in. x 2-in. baking dishes. Top with vegetable mixture and remaining rice mixture. Cover and bake at 350° for 45 minutes or until heated through. **Yield:** 24 servings.

Editor's Note: When cutting or seeding hot peppers, use rubber or plastic gloves to protect your hands. Avoid touching your face.

Circle of Love Centerpiece

(Pictured above)

WHEN you celebrate the anniversary of two people who are the light of each other's lives, add a romantic touch to the dinner table with this easy-to-assemble luminary.

First, apply a strip of double-sided transparent tape down the length of a clear glass cylinder vase. Wrap parchment paper around the outside of the vase, securing the short ends over the tape. (We used off-white parchment paper, but you could use paper with a little more color or with a pattern corresponding to the colors of the day.) Wrap a colored narrow ribbon around the vase and tie in a bow. Place a small pillar candle inside the vase.

Set a small bowl upside down in the center of the table. Drape a cloth dinner napkin (in the same color as the table napkins you're using) over the bowl. Position a 12-inch round mirror on top of the covered bowl.

Place the vase in the center of the mirror. Add greens and fresh flowers in a circle around the vase. (We used leather and Italian ferns, purple wax flowers, tinted baby's breath and white tea roses.) Light the candles just before guests sit down to dinner.

There's very little last-minute preparation for this centerpiece. You can wrap the vase with paper, tie on the ribbon and set the candle inside the vase weeks in advance. The day before the party, set up the display on the table, but don't add the fresh flowers and greens. Those should be added just before guests arrive so they stay fresh longer.

You can put together this elegant display whenever you're entertaining. For Christmas, use a red or green napkin, pine boughs and holly berries. A wreath of silk fall leaves is great for Thanksgiving. And for a springtime celebration, a pretty pastel napkin and daffodils or tulips are a nice touch.

REFERENCE INDEX

Use this index as a guide to the many helpful hints, food facts, decorating ideas and step-by-step instructions throughout the book.

BREADS & ROLLS

Baking Powder and Soda Should Bubble, 257
Braiding Bread, 263
Facts About Freezing Breads, 261
Festive Ways to Serve Butter, 265
Shaping a Coffee Cake Ring, 255
Short-Term Bread Storage, 253
The Irish Soda Bread Story, 8

CENTERPIECES

Arranging Fresh Roses, 369
Berry Beautiful Centerpiece, 75
Candy Corn Clay Pot, 140
Carrot and Daisy Bouquet, 38
Circle of Love Centerpiece, 417
Cookie-Cutter Pumpkin Carving, 152
Cranberries & Boughs Centerpiece, 221
Harvest Centerpiece, 159
Making a Candy Corn Clay Pot, 140
Making a Truffle Topiary, 294
Making Tabletop Trees, 326
Making the Harvest Centerpiece, 159
Soda Bottle Flower Vases, 113
Spine-Tingling Table Topper, 153
Tabletop Trees, 327
Truffle Topiary Centerpiece, 294
Using a Grid to Arrange Flowers, 369

COOKIES, BROWNIES & CANDIES

Candy Making Tips, 293
Fast Frosting, 118
Foiled Again!, 120
Freezing Holiday Cookies, 285
Packing Cookies for Shipping, 286
Time-Saving Truffles, 295
Wrap Up Cookies and Candies as Gifts, 299

COOKOUT & PICNIC POINTERS

Chilling Dip at Picnics, 96
Food Safety Tips for Summer, 92
Great Grilling Tips, 84
Hints for Making Hamburgers, 104
Properly Packing a Cooler, 98

DECORATING IDEAS

Creepy Cauldron, 143
Devilish Decorations, 139
Holiday Luminaries, 315
Tree Decorating Tips, 320

DESSERTS

Cake Decorating Tips, 378
Decorating Pie with Pastry Cutouts, 181
Heart-Shaped Dippers, 368
Make Meringue on Dry Days, 364
Making and Shaping Single- and Double-Crust Pie Pastry, 187
Making Cookie and Cracker Crumbs, 322
Pavlova Folklore, 367
Removing a Cake from a Pan, 383

EGGS

Chopping Hard-Cooked Eggs, 59
Early Easter Eggs, 21
Storing Hard-Cooked Easter Eggs, 57

FRUIT

Cranberry Basics, 219
Fast Fruit Salad, 18
Peach Pointers, 29
Star Fruit Facts, 201

GARNISHES

Assembling the Anniversary Cake Topper, 415
Chocolate Hearts Adorn Desserts, 361
Chocolate Leaves, 341
Edible Flower Reminder, 375
Great Garnishes, 231
Making a Poinsettia Garnish, 305
Making Pots o' Gold, 15
Making Red Radish Rosettes, 109
Simple Soup Garnishes, 246
Spinning a Spiderweb Garnish, 146
The Straight Story on Chocolate Curls, 331

HERBS & SPICES
Homemade Pumpkin Pie Spice, 191
Learn About Cilantro, 68
The History of Worcestershire
  Sauce, 132

MEAL & PARTY PLANNING
Avoid a Brunch Crunch, 30
Christmas Dinner Countdown, 220
Easter Dinner Timeline, 34
Food Quantities for a Crowd, 124
Game Plan for Your Party, 352
Holiday Menu Suggestions, 226
How Your Easter Egg Hunt
  Can Be a Hit, 50
Planning a Neighborhood
  Round-Robin, 302
Starting a Time Capsule for
  the Baby, 402
Thanksgiving Day Dinner
  Timeline, 156
Thanksgiving Dinner Agenda, 162
Timetable for Hanukkah
  Dinner, 210

MEAT
Buying and Storing Bacon, 44
Turkey and Stuffing Tips, 170
Turkey-Carving Basics, 216

MISCELLANEOUS FOOD & COOKING TIPS
Deep-Fat Frying Facts, 211
Draining Jumbo Pasta Shells, 339
Making Homemade Tortillas, 65
Safely Storing Thanksgiving
  Leftovers, 198
Stuffing Manicotti Shells, 412

PARTY FAVORS
Chili Pepper Place Card, 69
Easter Egg Invitation, 51

SERVING SUGGESTIONS
Burger Bar Topping Tray, 107
Creative Cake Boards, 383
Making a Floral Ice Bowl, 19
Personal "Pies" for Kids, 357
Pineapple Serving Bowl, 311
Serving in a Slow Cooker, 332
Stemware Servers, 408
Suggestions for Serving Pizzas, 355

SIDE DISHES & VEGETABLES
Advice About Eggplant, 304
Baking a Winter Squash, 176
Basic Brussels Sprouts, 157
Do You Know About Colcannon?

Dressing Up Everyday
  Vegetables, 237
Potato Pointers, 46
Prepping Potatoes, 202
Seeding and Peeling Avocados, 387
Selecting Successful Side
  Dishes, 240
Sweet Potato Secrets, 174
Versatile Stuffing, 163

SNACKS & BEVERAGES
Make the Mushrooms Ahead, 393
Mmmmarinated Mozzarella!, 392
Popcorn Pointers, 338
Snack Mix Serving Suggestions, 148
Tips for Chocolate Coffee, 277
Toasting Pumpkin Seeds, 195
Unmolding an Ice Ring, 399

TABLE SETTINGS & NAPKIN FOLDS
Add Warmth to a Winter Table, 345
Creating Napkin Roses, 395
Lovely Table for the Ladies, 395
Patriotic Picnic Table, 79
Pocket Napkin Fold, 39
Simple Elegant Thanksgiving
  Table, 167
Water Goblet Napkin Bouquet, 69

GENERAL RECIPE INDEX

This handy index lists every recipe by food category, major ingredient and/or cooking method.

APPETIZERS & SNACKS
Cold Appetizers
Antipasto Platter, 303
Deviled Egg Bunnies, 51
Egg Salad Wonton Cups, 314
German-Style Pickled Eggs, 59
Hard-Cooked Eggs, 54
Herbed Cheesecake, 305
Luscious Fruit Platter, 308
Marinated Mozzarella Cubes, 392
Marinated Mushrooms, 306
Pesto Pizza Squares, 354
Stuffed Bread Appetizers, 412
Taco Pan Pizza, 357
Taco Roll-Ups, 306
Three-Cheese Deviled Eggs, 56
Dips
BLT Dip, 311
Chili Artichoke Dip, 302

Eggplant Dip, 304
Fiesta Corn Dip, 309
Gingersnap Dip, 191
Holiday Vegetable Dip, 307
Hot 'n' Spicy Cranberry Dip, 201
Macaroon Fruit Dip, 311
Meaty Chili Dip, 304
Melon with Minted Lime Dip, 96
Orange Fruit Dip, 76
Fondue
Caramel Fondue, 368
Cheesy Pizza Fondue, 313
Hot Appetizers
Bacon-Wrapped Scallops, 309
Baked Brie, 307
Beef 'n' Bean Egg Rolls, 330
Calico Clams Casino, 314
Cheese-Stuffed Jalapenos, 67
Golden Shrimp Puffs, 337

Hot Wings, 86
Peppered Meatballs, 310
Pepperoncini Firecrackers, 110
Potato Chip Chicken Strips, 74
Southwestern Seafood Egg
  Rolls, 312
Spinach-Cheese Mushroom
  Caps, 393
Salsa
Black-Eyed Pea Salsa, 337
Summertime Salsa, 100
Tangy Fruit Salsa with
  Cinnamon Chips, 27
Snacks
Caramel Snack Mix, 288
Crunchy Caramel Corn, 338
Nacho Popcorn, 112
Nutty Popcorn Party Mix, 282
Popcorn Christmas Trees, 297

APPETIZERS & SNACKS (cont.)

Spiced Pecans, 298
Sweet 'n' Spicy Halloween
  Munch, 148
Three-in-One Popcorn
  Crunch, 142
Valentine's Day Snack Mix, 368

Spreads

Baked Cheddar Bacon
  Spread, 312
Cheddar Cheese Spread, 338
Garlic Herb Spread, 303
Ham Cream Cheese Balls, 411
Hot Pastrami Spread, 11
Spicy Hummus, 313
Sunflower Cheese Ball, 405
Toasted Almond Party
  Spread, 308
Tomato Spinach Spread, 310

APPLES

Apple Broccoli Salad, 128
Apple Cider Chicken 'n'
  Dumplings, 349
Apple Cranberry Crumble, 190
Apple Pie Sandwiches, 20
Apple Pound Cake, 192
Cranberry Apple Muffins, 257
Creamy Apple Pie, 185
Crunchy Apple Salad, 177
Hot Apple Cider, 150
Tangy Baked Apples, 171
Turkey with Apple Stuffing, 157

APRICOTS

Apricot Casserole, 18
Apricot-Ginger Asparagus, 360

ARTICHOKES

Artichoke Chicken Lasagna, 394
Artichoke-Red Pepper Tossed
  Salad, 172
Chili Artichoke Dip, 302
Turkey Breast Roulade, 409

ASPARAGUS

Apricot-Ginger Asparagus, 360
Asparagus Chicken Divan, 230
Asparagus Hollandaise Puff, 23
Asparagus Rice Salad, 48
Creamy Asparagus Soup, 28
Potato Asparagus Bake, 12
Swiss 'n' Asparagus Egg Salad, 57

BACON

Bacon 'n' Egg Bundles, 44
Bacon Wild Rice Bake, 247
Bacon-Wrapped Scallops, 309
Baked Cheddar Bacon Spread, 312
BLT Dip, 311
Breakfast Pizza, 356
Fluffy Bacon-Cheese Frittata, 28

BANANAS

Banana Buttermilk Muffins, 254
White Chocolate Banana Pie, 182

BARS & BROWNIES

Bars

German Chocolate Caramel
  Bars, 292
Glazed Lebkuchen, 212
Lemon Squares, 402
Springtime Strawberry Bars, 44
Sugar-Topped Walnut Bars, 298
Triple-Nut Diamonds, 289
Witch Hat Treats, 143

Brownies

Almond Macaroon
  Brownies, 116
Brownie Pizza, 119
Brownies in a Cone, 126
Butterscotch Pecan
  Brownies, 120
Caramel Macadamia Nut
  Brownies, 118
Cinnamon Brownies, 116
Decadent Brownie Pie, 121
Frosted Brownies, 118
Ice Cream Brownie
  Mountain, 117

BASIL

Pesto Pizza Squares, 354
Shrimp with Basil-Mango
  Sauce, 362
Tomato Basil Bread, 347

BEANS

Beef 'n' Bean Egg Rolls, 330
Black Bean Chicken Tacos, 65
Family-Style Baked Beans, 129
Kielbasa Bean Soup, 344
Thyme Green Beans with
  Almonds, 162

BEEF & GROUND BEEF

(also see Corned Beef)

All-American Hamburgers, 105
Beef 'n' Bean Egg Rolls, 330
Blue Cheese Burgers, 110
Chili Burgers, 108
Festive Meat Loaf Pinwheel, 227
Greek-Style Rib Eye Steaks, 226
Hearty Meatball Soup, 238
Herb Burgers, 72
Hot Pastrami Spread, 11
Irish Beef 'n' Carrot Stew, 14
Italian Meatball Hoagies, 318
Marinated Beef Sandwiches, 332
Meatball Sub Sandwiches, 340
Meaty Chili Dip, 304
Patriotic Taco Salad, 77
Peppered Meatballs, 310
Peppered Rib Eye Roast, 416
Pumpkin Stew, 146
Savory Beef Brisket, 210
Southwest Rib Roast with
  Salsa, 62
Spiced Chili, 346
Stuffed Flank Steak, 232
Tangy Sirloin Strips, 84
Thick 'n' Chewy Pizza, 324
Veal Scallopini, 360

BEVERAGES, ICE CUBES & STIRRERS

Celebration Punch, 399
Celebration Spoons, 278
Chocolate Coffee, 277
Citrus-Cinnamon Stir Sticks, 279
Cranberry Fruit Punch, 276
Cranberry Raspberry Punch, 388
Fast Fruit Punch, 46
Floating Four-Leaf Clovers, 9
Hot Apple Cider, 150
Iced Coffee Slush, 276
Mint Tea Punch, 9
Minty Pineapple Punch, 26
Mulled Holiday Drink, 278
Old-Fashioned Lemonade, 105
Orange Witches' Brew
  Punch, 142
Refreshing Lime Slush, 63
Snowball Eggnog Punch, 324
Sparkling Candy Swizzle
  Sticks, 278
Special Hot Chocolate Treats, 323

Summertime Fruit Tea, 77
Sweet Citrus Punch, 276

BISCUITS
Cheddar Buttermilk Biscuits, 344
Festive Biscuit Strips, 259

BLUEBERRIES
Berries 'n' Cream Torte, 111
Berry Sour Cream Cake, 74
Blueberry-Rhubarb Refrigerator
    Jam, 48
Chilled Blueberry Soup, 76

BREADS (also see Biscuits; Bread-
sticks; Coffee Cakes; Corn Bread &
Cornmeal; Doughnuts & Pastries;
French Toast; Muffins; Pancakes; Rolls
& Buns; Yeast Breads)
Broccoli Chicken Braid, 405
Double Sausage Stromboli, 348
Irish Soda Bread, 8
Pecan Pumpkin Loaves, 264
Pineapple Cherry Loaves, 253
Poppy Seed Cranberry Bread, 254
Scrambled Egg Brunch Bread, 31
Sopaipillas, 64
Walnut Marmalade Mini
    Loaves, 261

BREADSTICKS
Cupid's Breadsticks, 363
Parmesan Cheese Straws, 386
Witches' Broomsticks, 148

BROCCOLI &
CAULIFLOWER
Apple Broccoli Salad, 128
Broccoli Chicken Braid, 405
Broccoli Salad Supreme, 330
Broccoli Souffle, 204
Broccoli with Ginger-Orange
    Butter, 236
Cauliflower Zucchini Toss, 247
Cheddar Cauliflower Quiche, 236
Dressed-Up Broccoli, 220
Lemon Burst Broccoli, 408
Swiss-Topped Cauliflower
    Soup, 240
Walnut Broccoli Bake, 242

BURGERS
All-American Hamburgers, 105
Blue Cheese Burgers, 110
Chili Burgers, 108
Dilly Turkey Burgers, 106

Herb Burgers, 72
Tortilla Burgers, 104

BURRITOS, TACOS &
ENCHILADAS
Black Bean Chicken Tacos, 65
Breakfast Burritos, 58
Creamy Chicken Enchiladas, 66

CABBAGE & SAUERKRAUT
Colcannon Potatoes, 10
Make-Ahead Coleslaw, 336
Reuben Chicken, 11
Simple Cabbage Slaw, 87
Tangy Red Cabbage, 248
Three's-a-Charm Shamrock
    Soup, 13

CAKES & TORTES (also see
Cheesecakes; Coffee Cakes)
Almond Good Luck Cake, 333
Anniversary Cake, 414
Apple Pound Cake, 192
Berry Sour Cream Cake, 74
Boston Cream Sponge Cake, 274
Candied Holly Cupcakes, 275
Checkerboard Birthday Cake, 381
Chiffon Fruitcake, 271
Chocolate Fudge Cake, 382
Clove Bundt Cake, 374
Clown Cake, 379
Coconut Pecan Torte, 380
Cookies 'n' Cream Cake, 374
Cranberry Bundt Cake, 190
Flag Cake, 73
Fourth of July Ice Cream Cake, 101
German Chocolate Cupcakes, 78
Hazelnut Mocha Torte, 341
Minted Chocolate Torte, 273
Poppy Seed Easter Cake, 37
Posy Cupcakes, 375
Pretty Petit Fours, 389
Raspberry Fudge Torte, 376
Scaredy Cakes, 377
Three Milk Cake, 66

CANDIES
Almond Potato Candy, 283
Bird's Nests, 42

Black Widow Bites, 152
Brown Sugar Pecan Candies, 296
Candy Pacifiers, 404
Chocolate Truffles, 362
Coconut Truffles, 295
Easter Egg Candies, 47
Mamie Eisenhower's Fudge, 290
Marshmallow Ghosts, 138
Orange Walnut Candy, 289
Party Mint Patties, 400
Pecan Clusters, 286
Toasted Almond Caramels, 293
Viennese Fudge, 282

CARAMEL
Caramel Chocolate Mousse Pie, 184
Caramel-Chocolate Pecan Pie, 272
Caramel-Filled Chocolate
    Cookies, 285
Caramel Fondue, 368
Caramel Macadamia Nut
    Brownies, 118
Caramel Snack Mix, 288
Crunchy Caramel Corn, 338
German Chocolate Caramel
    Bars, 292
Toasted Almond Caramels, 293

CARROTS
Glazed Cranberry Carrots, 199
Irish Beef 'n' Carrot Stew, 14
Maple-Glazed Carrots, 158
Pecan Carrot Pie, 194

CASSEROLES
Main Dishes
    Artichoke Chicken Lasagna, 394
    Crab-Spinach Egg Casserole, 20
    Egg Bake with Sausage
        Biscuits, 56
    French Toast Strata, 24
    Ham 'n' Cheese Egg Bake, 45
    Ham 'n' Potato Casserole, 54
    Hearty Alfredo Potatoes, 202
    Nana's Chilies Rellenos, 62
Side Dishes
    Almond-Cranberry Squash
        Bake, 177
    Apricot Casserole, 18
    Bacon Wild Rice Bake, 247
    Cheesy Green Chili Rice, 63
    Colorful Veggie Casserole, 249
    Cranberry Sweet Potato
        Bake, 237
    Creamy Vegetable Medley, 246
    Family-Style Baked Beans, 129

CASSEROLES (cont.)

Garlic Potato Bake, 408
Mustard Potatoes Au Gratin, 34
Peachy Sweet Potato Bake, 156
Potato Asparagus Bake, 12
Spinach Noodle Casserole, 244
Supreme Scalloped Potatoes, 238
Sweet Potato Casserole, 174
Two-Cheese Spinach Bake, 172
Vegetable Rice Casserole, 416
Walnut Broccoli Bake, 242

CHEESE

Baked Brie, 307
Baked Cheddar Bacon Spread, 312
Blue Cheese Burgers, 110
Cheddar Buttermilk Biscuits, 344
Cheddar Cauliflower Quiche, 236
Cheddar Cheese Spread, 338
Cheddar Pan Rolls, 130
Cheddar Pancakes, 24
Cheese-Stuffed Jalapenos, 67
Cheesecake Dessert Squares, 413
Cheesy Green Chili Rice, 63
Cheesy Pizza Fondue, 313
Chocolate Cheesecake Squares, 398
Creamy Vegetable Medley, 246
Festive Meat Loaf Pinwheel, 227
Fluffy Bacon-Cheese Frittata, 28
Four-Cheese Pizza, 354
Ham 'n' Cheese Egg Bake, 45
Ham 'n' Swiss Strudel, 30
Ham Cream Cheese Balls, 411
Hearty Alfredo Potatoes, 202
Herbed Cheesecake, 305
Macaroon Cheesecake, 268
Marinated Mozzarella Cubes, 392
Mustard Potatoes Au Gratin, 34
Orange Cheesecake Mousse, 361
Parmesan Cheese Straws, 386
Pumpkin Cheesecake Dessert, 164
Sage Chicken Cordon Bleu, 224
Salad with Blue Cheese
   Dressing, 218
Spiderweb Pumpkin
   Cheesecake, 147

Spinach-Cheese Mushroom
   Caps, 393
Strawberry Cheese Bundles, 403
Stuffed Shells Florentine, 339
Sunflower Cheese Ball, 405
Supreme Scalloped Potatoes, 238
Swiss 'n' Asparagus Egg Salad, 57
Swiss Creamed Peas, 205
Swiss-Topped Cauliflower
   Soup, 240
Three-Cheese Deviled Eggs, 56
Three-Cheese Manicotti, 412
Two-Cheese Spinach Bake, 172

CHEESECAKES

Cheesecake Dessert Squares, 413
Chocolate Cheesecake Squares, 398
Herbed Cheesecake, 305
Macaroon Cheesecake, 268
Orange Cheesecake Mousse, 361
Pumpkin Cheesecake Dessert, 164
Spiderweb Pumpkin
   Cheesecake, 147

CHERRIES

Cherry Bonbon Cookies, 284
Cherry-Go-Round, 255
Cherry Meringue Pie, 182
Pineapple Cherry Loaves, 253

CHICKEN

Apple Cider Chicken 'n'
   Dumplings, 349
Artichoke Chicken Lasagna, 394
Asparagus Chicken Divan, 230
Black Bean Chicken Tacos, 65
Broccoli Chicken Braid, 405
Buffalo Chicken Calzones, 356
Caesar Chicken Potato Salad, 95
Chicken Tortilla Soup, 68
Chicken Wild Rice Soup, 243
Creamy Chicken Enchiladas, 66
Greek Chicken, 340
Grilled Picnic Chicken, 125
Honey-Glazed Chicken, 232
Hot Wings, 86
Mandarin Pasta Salad, 133
Orange-Avocado Chicken
   Salad, 387
Pepperoncini Firecrackers, 110
Potato Chip Chicken Strips, 74
Red, White and Blue Chili, 99
Reuben Chicken, 11
Sage Chicken Cordon Bleu, 224
Sesame Chicken Kabobs, 94
Tropical Chicken Salad, 398

CHOCOLATE

Almond Macaroon Brownies, 116
Almond Potato Candy, 283
Bird's Nests, 42
Black Cat Cookies, 141
Boston Cream Sponge Cake, 274
Brownie Pizza, 119
Brownies in a Cone, 126
Butterscotch Pecan Brownies, 120
Caramel Chocolate Mousse Pie, 184
Caramel-Chocolate Pecan Pie, 272
Caramel-Filled Chocolate
   Cookies, 285
Caramel Macadamia Nut
   Brownies, 118
Celebration Spoons, 278
Championship Cookies, 86
Chewy Chocolate Cookies, 112
Chocolate Cheesecake Squares, 398
Chocolate Chip Coffee Cake, 50
Chocolate Chip Meringue
   Cookies, 364
Chocolate Coffee, 277
Chocolate Fudge Cake, 382
Chocolate Lime Dessert, 14
Chocolate Truffle Dessert, 269
Chocolate Truffles, 362
Chocolate Yeast Bread, 260
Cinnamon Brownies, 116
Cinnamon Chocolate Chip
   Ice Cream, 64
Coconut Truffles, 295
Creamy Chocolate Crescents, 265
Creamy Coconut Chocolate Pie, 386
Decadent Brownie Pie, 121
Engaging Heart Cookies, 365
Frosted Brownies, 118
German Chocolate Caramel
   Bars, 292
German Chocolate Cupcakes, 78
Ice Cream Brownie Mountain, 117
Mamie Eisenhower's Fudge, 290
Minted Chocolate Torte, 273
Orange Chocolate Muffins, 258
Pecan Clusters, 286
Pots o' Gold, 15
Raspberry Fudge Torte, 376
Soft Chocolate Mint Cookies, 296
Special Hot Chocolate Treats, 323
Viennese Fudge, 282
White Chocolate Banana Pie, 182
White Chocolate Holiday
   Cookies, 288

CINNAMON

Cinnamon Brownies, 116

Cinnamon Chocolate Chip
  Ice Cream, 64
Cinnamon Gelatin Salad, 239
Cinnamon Pecan Braids, 22
Citrus-Cinnamon Stir Sticks, 279
Tangy Fruit Salsa with Cinnamon
  Chips, 27

COCONUT
Almond Macaroon Brownies, 116
Coconut Pecan Torte, 380
Coconut Truffles, 295
Creamy Coconut Chocolate Pie, 386
German Chocolate Cupcakes, 78
Macaroon Cheesecake, 268

COFFEE CAKES
Cherry-Go-Round, 255
Chocolate Chip Coffee Cake, 50
Date Crumb Cake, 22

CONDIMENTS
Blueberry-Rhubarb Refrigerator
  Jam, 48
Crisp Onion Relish, 131
Horseradish-Mustard Sauce for
  Corned Beef, 8
Maple Cranberry Sauce, 170
Ruby-Red Strawberry Sauce, 364
Smoky Barbecue Sauce, 132
Strawberry Syrup, 25

COOKIES
Cutout
  Engaging Heart Cookies, 365
  Lemon Nut Star Cookies, 93
  Sugar Cookie Cutouts, 287
Drop
  Championship Cookies, 86
  Chewy Chocolate Cookies, 112
  Jumbo Jack-o'-Lantern
    Cookies, 149
  Peanut Oat Cookies, 290
  Root Beer Cookies, 127
  Soft Chocolate Mint Cookies, 296
  Strawberry Cookies, 78
  White Chocolate Holiday
    Cookies, 288
Sandwich
  Be-Mine Sandwich Cookies, 366
  Date-Filled Sandwich
    Cookies, 291
  Lacy Oat Sandwich Wafers, 334
Shaped
  Black Cat Cookies, 141

Buttery Spritz Cookies, 283
Caramel-Filled Chocolate
  Cookies, 285
Cherry Bonbon Cookies, 284
Chocolate Chip Meringue
  Cookies, 364
Frightening Fingers, 138
Gingerbread Teddies, 319
Hazelnut Crescents, 292
Meringue Bunnies, 43
Mexican Wedding Cakes, 390
Snowflake and Icicle Cookies, 321
Snowmen Cookies, 297
Strawberry Wedding Bell
  Cookies, 391
Sugarcoated Meltaways, 284

CORN
Fiesta Corn Dip, 309
Grilled Corn with Chive Butter, 89

CORN BREAD &
CORNMEAL
Goose with Corn Bread
  Stuffing, 163
Peppered Corn Bread, 87

CORNED BEEF
Spicy Corned Beef, 12
Three's-a-Charm Shamrock
  Soup, 13

CRANBERRIES
Almond-Cranberry Squash Bake, 177
Apple Cranberry Crumble, 190
Citrus Cranberry Pie, 183
Cranberry Apple Muffins, 257
Cranberry Bundt Cake, 190
Cranberry Fruit Mold, 165
Cranberry Fruit Punch, 276
Cranberry Ice, 219

Cranberry Raspberry Punch, 388
Cranberry Sweet Potato Bake, 237
Cranberry Turkey Salad, 200
Frosty Cranberry Salad Cups, 174
Glazed Cranberry Carrots, 199
Hot 'n' Spicy Cranberry Dip, 201
Maple Cranberry Sauce, 170
Poppy Seed Cranberry Bread, 254

DESSERTS (also see specific kinds)
Almond Creme, 331
Almond Puff Pastries, 268
Apple Cranberry Crumble, 190
Baked Stuffed Pears, 194
Berries 'n' Cream Torte, 111
Bread Pudding Pumpkin, 195
Caramel Fondue, 368
Cheesecake Dessert Squares, 413
Chocolate Lime Dessert, 14
Chocolate Truffle Dessert, 269
Cranberry Ice, 219
Frozen Pumpkin Dessert, 192
Gingersnap Dip, 191
Lemon Clouds with Custard, 39
Orange Cheesecake Mousse, 361
Patriotic Fruit Pizza, 97
Peppermint Ice Cream Dessert, 322
Pineapple Dream Dessert, 270
Potluck Strawberry Trifle, 130
Pumpkin Baked Alaska, 193
Pumpkin Cheesecake Dessert, 164
Pumpkin Shortbread Dessert, 158
Rhubarb Terrine with Raspberry
  Sauce, 75
Ruby-Red Strawberry Sauce, 364
Strawberry Pavlova, 367

DILL
Dilled Duchess Potatoes, 245
Dilly Bran Bread, 264
Dilly Bread Ring, 175
Dilly Turkey Burgers, 106

DOUGHNUTS & PASTRIES
Buttermilk Potato Doughnut
  Holes, 46
Strawberry Cheese Bundles, 403

DRESSING & STUFFING
Country Potato Dressing, 204
Goose with Corn Bread
  Stuffing, 163
Oat 'n' Rye Bread Dressing, 170
Sausage Potato Dressing, 171
Turkey with Apple Stuffing, 157
Turkey with Sausage Stuffing, 217

EGGS
Bacon 'n' Egg Bundles, 44
Breakfast Burritos, 58
Breakfast Pizza, 356
Crab-Spinach Egg Casserole, 20
Deviled Egg Bunnies, 51
Egg and Spinach Side Dish, 58
Egg Bake with Sausage Biscuits, 56
Egg Salad Wonton Cups, 314
Eggnog Fruit Fluff, 244
Fluffy Bacon-Cheese Frittata, 28
German-Style Pickled Eggs, 59
Ham 'n' Cheese Egg Bake, 45
Ham 'n' Potato Casserole, 54
Hard-Cooked Eggs, 54
Lemon Clouds with Custard, 39
Meringue Bunnies, 43
Molded Egg Salad, 55
Scrambled Egg Brunch Bread, 31
Snowball Eggnog Punch, 324
Swiss 'n' Asparagus Egg Salad, 57
Three-Cheese Deviled Eggs, 56

FISH & SEAFOOD
Bacon-Wrapped Scallops, 309
Calico Clams Casino, 314
Crab-Spinach Egg Casserole, 20
Creamy Crab Salad, 388
Crispy Orange Roughy, 228
Fish Fillets with Citrus-Herb
   Butter, 233
Golden Shrimp Puffs, 337
Saucy Orange Shrimp, 88
Shrimp Chowder, 348
Shrimp Creole, 231
Shrimp Pasta Salad, 392
Shrimp with Basil-Mango
   Sauce, 362
Southwestern Seafood
   Egg Rolls, 312

FOWL
Goose with Corn Bread
   Stuffing, 163

Roast Duck with Orange
   Glaze, 228

FRENCH TOAST
French Toast Sticks, 42
French Toast Strata, 24

FRUIT (also see specific kinds)
Candied Holly Cupcakes, 275
Chiffon Fruitcake, 271
Christmas Tree Sweet Rolls, 325
Citrus-Cinnamon Stir Sticks, 279
Citrus Cranberry Pie, 183
Cranberry Fruit Mold, 165
Cranberry Fruit Punch, 276
Eggnog Fruit Fluff, 244
Fast Fruit Punch, 46
Festive Biscuit Strips, 259
Fish Fillets with Citrus-Herb
   Butter, 233
Frozen Fruit Slush, 394
Fruit Salad with Poppy Seed
   Dressing, 18
Fruited Turkey Salad, 198
Hot Fruit Soup, 245
Luscious Fruit Platter, 308
Macaroon Fruit Dip, 311
Marinated Fruit Salad, 43
Melon with Minted Lime Dip, 96
Norwegian Christmas Bread, 252
Orange Fruit Dip, 76
Patriotic Fruit Pizza, 97
Shrimp with Basil-Mango
   Sauce, 362
Summertime Fruit Tea, 77
Sweet Citrus Punch, 276
Tangy Fruit Salsa with Cinnamon
   Chips, 27
Tropical Fruit Salad, 129
Watermelon Baby Carriage, 401

GARLIC
Garlic Herb Spread, 303
Garlic Potato Bake, 408

GARNISHES
Candied Flowers, 375
Pots o' Gold, 15

GINGER
Apricot-Ginger Asparagus, 360
Broccoli with Ginger-Orange
   Butter, 236
Honey-Ginger Barbecued Ribs, 100
Plum-Glazed Gingered Ham, 36

GRILLED & BROILED
All-American Hamburgers, 105
Blue Cheese Burgers, 110
Chili Burgers, 108
Dilly Turkey Burgers, 106
Grilled Corn with Chive Butter, 89
Grilled Picnic Chicken, 125
Grilled Rack of Lamb, 230
Herb Burgers, 72
Honey-Ginger Barbecued Ribs, 100
Sesame Chicken Kabobs, 94
Skewered Potatoes, 88
Sweet 'n' Spicy Grilled Pork
   Chops, 92
Tangy Sirloin Strips, 84
Tortilla Burgers, 104
Zesty Grilled Pork Medallions, 85

HAM
Asparagus Hollandaise Puff, 23
Baked Deli Sandwich, 335
Festive Meat Loaf Pinwheel, 227
Ham 'n' Cheese Egg Bake, 45
Ham 'n' Potato Casserole, 54
Ham 'n' Swiss Strudel, 30
Ham Cream Cheese Balls, 411
Holiday Ham, 25
Plum-Glazed Gingered Ham, 36
Sage Chicken Cordon Bleu, 224
Scrambled Egg Brunch Bread, 31
Stuffed Bread Appetizers, 412
Summer Sub Sandwich, 125

HONEY
Glazed Lebkuchen, 212
Honey-Ginger Barbecued Ribs, 100
Honey-Glazed Chicken, 232
Spinach Salad with Honey
   Dressing, 400

ICE CREAM & SHERBET
Bewitching Ice Cream Cones, 139
Cinnamon Chocolate Chip
   Ice Cream, 64
Fourth of July Ice Cream Cake, 101

Ice Cream Brownie Mountain, 117
Peanut Butter Ice Cream Pie, 85
Peppermint Ice Cream, 270
Peppermint Ice Cream Dessert, 322
Pumpkin Baked Alaska, 193
Pumpkin-Face Ice Cream
    Sandwiches, 150
Sherbet Watermelon, 106
Strawberry Sherbet, 97
Toasted Almond Ice Cream
    Balls, 274

LAMB
Grilled Rack of Lamb, 230

LEMON & LIME
Chocolate Lime Dessert, 14
Floating Four-Leaf Clovers, 9
Lemon Burst Broccoli, 408
Lemon Clouds with Custard, 39
Lemon Nut Star Cookies, 93
Lemon Squares, 402
Lemony Turkey Rice Soup, 205
Lime Tart, 272
Melon with Minted Lime Dip, 96
Old-Fashioned Lemonade, 105
Refreshing Lime Slush, 63
Three-Layer Gelatin Salad, 326

MAPLE
Maple Cranberry Sauce, 170
Maple-Glazed Carrots, 158

MARSHMALLOW &
MARSHMALLOW CREME
Mamie Eisenhower's Fudge, 290
Marshmallow Ghosts, 138
Witch Hat Treats, 143

MEAT LOAF & MEATBALLS
Festive Meat Loaf Pinwheel, 227
Hearty Meatball Soup, 238
Italian Meatball Hoagies, 318
Meatball Sub Sandwiches, 340
Peppered Meatballs, 310

MEAT PIES & PIZZA
All-American Turkey Potpie, 203
Baked Potato Pizza, 355
Breakfast Pizza, 356
Buffalo Chicken Calzones, 356
Deluxe Turkey Club Pizza, 352
Four-Cheese Pizza, 354
Pepper Sausage Pizza, 353
Pesto Pizza Squares, 354
Taco Pan Pizza, 357

Thick 'n' Chewy Pizza, 324
Turkey Divan Pizza, 199
Turkey Shepherd's Pie, 202

MERINGUE
Cherry Meringue Pie, 182
Chocolate Chip Meringue
    Cookies, 364
Meringue Bunnies, 43
Strawberry Pavlova, 367

MICROWAVE RECIPES
Egg and Spinach Side Dish, 58
Meatball Sub Sandwiches, 340
Skewered Potatoes, 88

MINT
Melon with Minted Lime Dip, 96
Mint Tea Punch, 9
Minted Chocolate Torte, 273
Minty Pineapple Punch, 26
Party Mint Patties, 400
Peppermint Ice Cream, 270
Peppermint Ice Cream Dessert, 322
Soft Chocolate Mint Cookies, 296

MUFFINS
Banana Buttermilk Muffins, 254
Cranberry Apple Muffins, 257
Orange Chocolate Muffins, 258
Peach Graham Muffins, 260
Peach Praline Muffins, 29
Potato Muffins, 262

MUSHROOMS
Marinated Mushrooms, 306
Mushroom Pork Scallopini, 229
Paprika Mushrooms, 241
Sausage Mushroom Manicotti, 26
Spinach-Cheese Mushroom
    Caps, 393

MUSTARD
Horseradish-Mustard Sauce for
    Corned Beef, 8
Mustard Potatoes Au Gratin, 34

NUTS & PEANUT BUTTER
Almond-Cranberry Squash
    Bake, 177
Almond Good Luck Cake, 333
Almond Macaroon Brownies, 116
Almond Potato Candy, 283
Almond Puff Pastries, 268
Brown Sugar Pecan Candies, 296
Butterscotch Pecan Brownies, 120

Caramel-Chocolate Pecan Pie, 272
Caramel Macadamia Nut
    Brownies, 118
Cinnamon Pecan Braids, 22
Coconut Pecan Torte, 380
Crunchy Caramel Corn, 338
Hazelnut Crescents, 292
Hazelnut Mocha Torte, 341
Lemon Nut Star Cookies, 93
Nutty Popcorn Party Mix, 282
Orange Walnut Candy, 289
Peach Praline Muffins, 29
Peanut Butter Ice Cream Pie, 85
Peanut Oat Cookies, 290
Pecan Carrot Pie, 194
Pecan Clusters, 286
Pecan Pumpkin Loaves, 264
Spiced Pecans, 298
Sugar-Topped Walnut Bars, 298
Sweet 'n' Spicy Halloween
    Munch, 148
Three-in-One Popcorn Crunch, 142
Thyme Green Beans with
    Almonds, 162
Toasted Almond Caramels, 293
Toasted Almond Ice Cream
    Balls, 274
Toasted Almond Party Spread, 308
Triple-Nut Diamonds, 289
Valentine's Day Snack Mix, 368
Walnut Broccoli Bake, 242
Walnut Marmalade Mini
    Loaves, 261

OLIVES
Greek Chicken, 340
Greek-Style Rib Eye Steaks, 226
Olive Potato Salad, 126

ONIONS
Creamed Pearl Onions, 248
Creamy Onion Soup, 410
Crisp Onion Relish, 131
Eyeball Soup, 151

ORANGE
Beets in Orange Sauce, 218
Broccoli with Ginger-Orange
    Butter, 236
Mandarin Orange Spinach
    Salad, 410
Mandarin Pasta Salad, 133
Orange-Avocado Chicken
    Salad, 387
Orange Cheesecake Mousse, 361
Orange Chocolate Muffins, 258
Orange Fruit Dip, 76
Orange Walnut Candy, 289
Orange Whipped Sweet
    Potatoes, 165
Orange Witches' Brew Punch, 142
Roast Duck with Orange Glaze, 228
Saucy Orange Shrimp, 88
Sugarcoated Meltaways, 284
Three-Layer Gelatin Salad, 326
Walnut Marmalade Mini
    Loaves, 261

OVEN ENTREES (also see
Casseroles; Meat Loaf & Meatballs;
Meat Pies & Pizza)
Asparagus Chicken Divan, 230
Asparagus Hollandaise Puff, 23
Bacon 'n' Egg Bundles, 44
Crispy Orange Roughy, 228
Fish Fillets with Citrus-Herb
    Butter, 233
Goose with Corn Bread
    Stuffing, 163
Greek Chicken, 340
Ham 'n' Swiss Strudel, 30
Herb 'n' Spice Turkey Breast, 164
Holiday Ham, 25
Holiday Pork Roast, 224
Honey-Glazed Chicken, 232
Peppered Rib Eye Roast, 416
Plum-Glazed Gingered Ham, 36
Potato Chip Chicken Strips, 74
Reuben Chicken, 11
Roast Duck with Orange Glaze, 228
Sage Chicken Cordon Bleu, 224

Saucy Orange Shrimp, 88
Sausage Mushroom Manicotti, 26
Savory Beef Brisket, 210
Scrambled Egg Brunch Bread, 31
Southwest Rib Roast with Salsa, 62
Spicy Corned Beef, 12
Stuffed Crown Roast of Pork, 225
Stuffed Shells Florentine, 339
Three-Cheese Manicotti, 412
Turkey Breast Roulade, 409
Turkey with Apple Stuffing, 157
Turkey with Sausage Stuffing, 217

PANCAKES
Cheddar Pancakes, 24
Swedish Pancakes, 21

PASTA & NOODLES
Artichoke Chicken Lasagna, 394
Confetti Tortellini Salad, 320
Deli-Style Pasta Salad, 72
Mandarin Pasta Salad, 133
Mushroom Pork Scallopini, 229
Sausage Mushroom Manicotti, 26
Shrimp Pasta Salad, 392
Southwestern Pasta Salad, 128
Spinach Noodle Casserole, 244
Stuffed Shells Florentine, 339
Three-Cheese Manicotti, 412
Veal Scallopini, 360
Wagon Wheel Pasta Salad, 108

PEACHES
Peach Graham Muffins, 260
Peach Praline Muffins, 29
Peach Streusel Pie, 89
Peachy Sweet Potato Bake, 156

PEARS
Baked Stuffed Pears, 194
Rustic Pear Tart, 180

PEAS
Black-Eyed Pea Salsa, 337
Black-Eyed Pea Soup, 332
Spicy Hummus, 313
Swiss Creamed Peas, 205

PEPPERS & CHILIES
Artichoke-Red Pepper Tossed
    Salad, 172
Cheese-Stuffed Jalapenos, 67
Cheesy Green Chili Rice, 63
Chili Artichoke Dip, 302
Nana's Chilies Rellenos, 62
Pepper Sausage Pizza, 353

Peppered Corn Bread, 87
Pepperoncini Firecrackers, 110

PIES & PIE PASTRY
Apple Butter Pumpkin Pie, 184
Caramel Chocolate Mousse Pie, 184
Caramel-Chocolate Pecan Pie, 272
Cherry Meringue Pie, 182
Citrus Cranberry Pie, 183
Creamy Apple Pie, 185
Creamy Coconut Chocolate Pie, 386
Decadent Brownie Pie, 121
Lime Tart, 272
Pastry for Double-Crust Pie, 186
Pastry for Single-Crust Pie, 186
Peach Streusel Pie, 89
Peanut Butter Ice Cream Pie, 85
Pecan Carrot Pie, 194
Rustic Pear Tart, 180
Sour Cream Raisin Pie, 180
Spiced Pumpkin Pie, 181
White Chocolate Banana Pie, 182

PINEAPPLE
Minty Pineapple Punch, 26
Pineapple Cherry Loaves, 253
Pineapple Dream Dessert, 270
Tropical Chicken Salad, 398

POPCORN
Crunchy Caramel Corn, 338
Nacho Popcorn, 112
Nutty Popcorn Party Mix, 282
Popcorn Christmas Trees, 297
Three-in-One Popcorn Crunch, 142

POPPY SEEDS
Fruit Salad with Poppy Seed
    Dressing, 18
Poppy Seed Cranberry Bread, 254
Poppy Seed Easter Cake, 37

PORK (also see Bacon; Ham;
Sausage & Hot Dogs)
Barbecued Pork Sandwiches, 132
Black-Eyed Pea Soup, 332
Hearty Meatball Soup, 238
Holiday Pork Roast, 224
Honey-Ginger Barbecued
    Ribs, 100
Mushroom Pork Scallopini, 229
Stuffed Crown Roast of Pork, 225
Sweet 'n' Spicy Grilled Pork
    Chops, 92
Tortilla Burgers, 104
Zesty Grilled Pork Medallions, 85

POTATOES
(also see Sweet Potatoes)
Almond Potato Candy, 283
Baked Potato Pizza, 355
Breakfast Pizza, 356
Buttermilk Potato Doughnut
 Holes, 46
Caesar Chicken Potato Salad, 95
Colcannon Potatoes, 10
Country Potato Dressing, 204
Dilled Duchess Potatoes, 245
Garlic Potato Bake, 408
Ham 'n' Potato Casserole, 54
Hearty Alfredo Potatoes, 202
Herbed Mashed Potatoes, 216
Latkes, 211
Mustard Potatoes Au Gratin, 34
Olive Potato Salad, 126
Picnic Potato Salad, 98
Potato Asparagus Bake, 12
Potato Muffins, 262
Potato Salad Mold, 109
Sausage Potato Dressing, 171
Skewered Potatoes, 88
Slow-Cooked Chowder, 246
Supreme Scalloped Potatoes, 238
Three's-a-Charm Shamrock
 Soup, 13
Turkey Shepherd's Pie, 202
Zippy Potato Soup, 345

PUMPKIN
Apple Butter Pumpkin Pie, 184
Bread Pudding Pumpkin, 195
Frozen Pumpkin Dessert, 192
Jumbo Jack-o'-Lantern
 Cookies, 149
Pecan Pumpkin Loaves, 264
Pumpkin Baked Alaska, 193
Pumpkin Cheesecake Dessert, 164
Pumpkin Shortbread Dessert, 158
Pumpkin Stew, 146
Spiced Pumpkin Pie, 181
Spiderweb Pumpkin
 Cheesecake, 147

RAISINS & DATES
Date Crumb Cake, 22
Date-Filled Sandwich Cookies, 291
Irish Soda Bread, 8
Sour Cream Raisin Pie, 180

RASPBERRIES
Berries 'n' Cream Torte, 111
Berry Sour Cream Cake, 74
Cranberry Raspberry Punch, 388
Raspberry Fudge Torte, 376
Rhubarb Terrine with Raspberry
 Sauce, 75
Three-Layer Gelatin Salad, 326

RHUBARB
Blueberry-Rhubarb Refrigerator
 Jam, 48
Rhubarb Terrine with Raspberry
 Sauce, 75

RICE & BARLEY
Asparagus Rice Salad, 48
Bacon Wild Rice Bake, 247
Barley Turkey Soup, 318
Cheesy Green Chili Rice, 63
Chicken Wild Rice Soup, 243
Curried Rice Pilaf, 239
Lemony Turkey Rice Soup, 205
Shrimp Creole, 231
Vegetable Rice Casserole, 416
Wild Rice Bread, 336

ROLLS & BUNS
Butterfluff Rolls, 166
Cheddar Pan Rolls, 130
Christmas Tree Sweet Rolls, 325
Creamy Chocolate Crescents, 265
Easy Batter Rolls, 252
Favorite Pull-Apart Rolls, 256
Golden Pan Rolls, 262
Puff Pillow Buns, 390
Rabbit Rolls, 49
Refrigerator Rolls, 411
Whole Wheat Dinner Rolls, 334

SALADS & DRESSINGS
Coleslaw
 Make-Ahead Coleslaw, 336
 Simple Cabbage Slaw, 87

Dressing
 Favorite French Dressing, 151
Egg Salad
 Molded Egg Salad, 55
Fruit & Gelatin Salads
 Cinnamon Gelatin Salad, 239
 Cranberry Fruit Mold, 165
 Cranberry Turkey Salad, 200
 Crunchy Apple Salad, 177
 Eggnog Fruit Fluff, 244
 Frosty Cranberry Salad Cups, 174
 Frozen Fruit Slush, 394
 Fruit Salad with Poppy Seed
  Dressing, 18
 Marinated Fruit Salad, 43
 Three-Layer Gelatin Salad, 326
 Tropical Fruit Salad, 129
 Watermelon Baby Carriage, 401
Lettuce & Spinach Salads
 Artichoke-Red Pepper Tossed
  Salad, 172
 Festive Tossed Salad, 212
 Mandarin Orange Spinach
  Salad, 410
 Queen-of-Hearts Salad, 366
 Salad with Blue Cheese
  Dressing, 218
 Spinach Salad with Honey
  Dressing, 400
Main-Dish Salads
 Creamy Crab Salad, 388
 Fruited Turkey Salad, 198
 Orange-Avocado Chicken
  Salad, 387
 Patriotic Taco Salad, 77
 Tropical Chicken Salad, 398
Pasta Salads
 Confetti Tortellini Salad, 320
 Deli-Style Pasta Salad, 72
 Mandarin Pasta Salad, 133
 Shrimp Pasta Salad, 392
 Southwestern Pasta Salad, 128
 Wagon Wheel Pasta Salad, 108
Potato & Rice Salads
 Asparagus Rice Salad, 48
 Caesar Chicken Potato Salad, 95
 Olive Potato Salad, 126
 Picnic Potato Salad, 98
 Potato Salad Mold, 109
Vegetable Salads
 Apple Broccoli Salad, 128
 Broccoli Salad Supreme, 330
 Cauliflower Zucchini Toss, 247
 Marinated Vegetable Salad, 124
 Zucchini Salad, 94

SANDWICHES *(also see Burgers)*
Apple Pie Sandwiches, 20
Baked Deli Sandwich, 335
Barbecued Pork Sandwiches, 132
Broccoli Chicken Braid, 405
Cucumber Party Sandwiches, 404
Double Sausage Stromboli, 348
Fiesta Chili Dogs, 131
Focaccia Sandwich, 322
Italian Meatball Hoagies, 318
Italian Veggie Turkey Pitas, 47
Marinated Beef Sandwiches, 332
Meatball Sub Sandwiches, 340
Summer Sub Sandwich, 125
Swiss 'n' Asparagus Egg Salad, 57
Thanksgiving Turkey Sandwich, 200

SAUSAGE & HOT DOGS
Antipasto Platter, 303
Breakfast Burritos, 58
Breakfast Pizza, 356
Double Sausage Stromboli, 348
Egg Bake with Sausage Biscuits, 56
Fiesta Chili Dogs, 131
Kielbasa Bean Soup, 344
Pepper Sausage Pizza, 353
Sausage Mushroom Manicotti, 26
Sausage Potato Dressing, 171
Turkey with Sausage Stuffing, 217

SIDE DISHES *(also see Casseroles)*
Apricot-Ginger Asparagus, 360
Beets in Orange Sauce, 218
Broccoli Souffle, 204
Broccoli with Ginger-Orange
    Butter, 236
Cheddar Cauliflower Quiche, 236
Colcannon Potatoes, 10
Creamed Pearl Onions, 248
Curried Rice Pilaf, 239
Dilled Duchess Potatoes, 245
Dressed-Up Broccoli, 220
Egg and Spinach Side Dish, 58
Glazed Cranberry Carrots, 199
Grilled Corn with Chive Butter, 89

Herbed Mashed Potatoes, 216
Latkes, 211
Lemon Burst Broccoli, 408
Maple-Glazed Carrots, 158
Orange Whipped Sweet
    Potatoes, 165
Paprika Mushrooms, 241
Roasted Root Vegetables, 173
Skewered Potatoes, 88
Snowcapped Butternut
    Squash, 241
Swiss Creamed Peas, 205
Tangy Baked Apples, 171
Tangy Red Cabbage, 248
Thyme Green Beans with
    Almonds, 162
Vegetable Bundles, 35
Winter Squash Souffle, 176

**SKILLET &
STOVETOP SUPPERS**
Fluffy Bacon-Cheese Frittata, 28
Greek-Style Rib Eye Steaks, 226
Mushroom Pork Scallopini, 229
Shrimp Creole, 231
Shrimp with Basil-Mango
    Sauce, 362
Stuffed Flank Steak, 232
Veal Scallopini, 360

SLOW COOKER RECIPES
Cheesy Pizza Fondue, 313
Peppered Meatballs, 310
Slow-Cooked Chowder, 246
Slow-Cooked Vegetable Soup, 242

SOUPS & CHILI
After-Thanksgiving Turkey
    Soup, 176
Apple Cider Chicken 'n'
    Dumplings, 349
Barley Turkey Soup, 318
Black-Eyed Pea Soup, 332
Chicken Tortilla Soup, 68
Chicken Wild Rice Soup, 243

Chili Burgers, 108
Chilled Blueberry Soup, 76
Creamy Asparagus Soup, 28
Creamy Onion Soup, 410
Eyeball Soup, 151
Fiesta Chili Dogs, 131
Hearty Meatball Soup, 238
Hot Fruit Soup, 245
Kielbasa Bean Soup, 344
Lemony Turkey Rice Soup, 205
Red, White and Blue Chili, 99
Shrimp Chowder, 348
Slow-Cooked Chowder, 246
Slow-Cooked Vegetable Soup, 242
Spiced Chili, 346
Swiss-Topped Cauliflower
    Soup, 240
Three's-a-Charm Shamrock Soup, 13
Zippy Potato Soup, 345

SPINACH
Crab-Spinach Egg Casserole, 20
Egg and Spinach Side Dish, 58
Mandarin Orange Spinach
    Salad, 410
Spinach-Cheese Mushroom
    Caps, 393
Spinach Noodle Casserole, 244
Spinach Salad with Honey
    Dressing, 400
Stuffed Shells Florentine, 339
Tomato Spinach Spread, 310
Two-Cheese Spinach Bake, 172

SQUASH & ZUCCHINI
Almond-Cranberry Squash
    Bake, 177
Cauliflower Zucchini Toss, 247
Snowcapped Butternut
    Squash, 241
Winter Squash Souffle, 176
Zucchini Salad, 94

STEWS
Irish Beef 'n' Carrot Stew, 14

Pumpkin Stew, 146

STRAWBERRIES
Berries 'n' Cream Torte, 111
Celebration Punch, 399
Potluck Strawberry Trifle, 130
Ruby-Red Strawberry Sauce, 364
Springtime Strawberry Bars, 44
Strawberry Cheese Bundles, 403
Strawberry Cookies, 78
Strawberry Pavlova, 367
Strawberry Sherbet, 97
Strawberry Syrup, 25
Strawberry Wedding Bell
   Cookies, 391

SWEET POTATOES
Cranberry Sweet Potato Bake, 237
Orange Whipped Sweet
   Potatoes, 165
Peachy Sweet Potato Bake, 156
Sweet Potato Casserole, 174

TOMATOES
BLT Dip, 311

Summertime Salsa, 100
Tomato Basil Bread, 347
Tomato Spinach Spread, 310

TURKEY
After-Thanksgiving Turkey Soup, 176
All-American Turkey Potpie, 203
Baked Deli Sandwich, 335
Barley Turkey Soup, 318
Cranberry Turkey Salad, 200
Deluxe Turkey Club Pizza, 352
Dilly Turkey Burgers, 106
Focaccia Sandwich, 322
Fruited Turkey Salad, 198
Hearty Alfredo Potatoes, 202
Hearty Meatball Soup, 238
Herb 'n' Spice Turkey Breast, 164
Italian Veggie Turkey Pitas, 47
Lemony Turkey Rice Soup, 205
Thanksgiving Turkey Sandwich, 200
Turkey Breast Roulade, 409
Turkey Divan Pizza, 199
Turkey Shepherd's Pie, 202
Turkey with Apple Stuffing, 157
Turkey with Sausage Stuffing, 217

VEGETABLES
(also see specific kinds)
Colorful Veggie Casserole, 249
Creamy Vegetable Medley, 246
Italian Veggie Turkey Pitas, 47
Marinated Vegetable Salad, 124
Roasted Root Vegetables, 173
Slow-Cooked Vegetable Soup, 242
Vegetable Bundles, 35
Vegetable Rice Casserole, 416

YEAST BREADS
Bread Bowls, 346
Cardamom Braids, 263
Challah, 213
Chocolate Yeast Bread, 260
Cinnamon Pecan Braids, 22
Country White Bread, 256
Dilly Bran Bread, 264
Dilly Bread Ring, 175
Norwegian Christmas Bread, 252
Tomato Basil Bread, 347
Traditional Whole Wheat
   Bread, 258
Wild Rice Bread, 336

ALPHABETICAL INDEX

Refer to this index for a complete alphabetical listing of all recipes in this book.

A

After-Thanksgiving Turkey
   Soup, 176
All-American Hamburgers, 105
All-American Turkey Potpie, 203
Almond-Cranberry Squash
   Bake, 177
Almond Creme, 331
Almond Good Luck Cake, 333
Almond Macaroon Brownies, 116
Almond Potato Candy, 283
Almond Puff Pastries, 268
Anniversary Cake, 414
Antipasto Platter, 303
Apple Broccoli Salad, 128
Apple Butter Pumpkin Pie, 184
Apple Cider Chicken 'n'
   Dumplings, 349
Apple Cranberry Crumble, 190
Apple Pie Sandwiches, 20
Apple Pound Cake, 192
Apricot Casserole, 18
Apricot-Ginger Asparagus, 360
Artichoke Chicken Lasagna, 394

Artichoke-Red Pepper Tossed
   Salad, 172
Asparagus Chicken Divan, 230
Asparagus Hollandaise Puff, 23
Asparagus Rice Salad, 48

B

Bacon 'n' Egg Bundles, 44
Bacon Wild Rice Bake, 247
Bacon-Wrapped Scallops, 309
Baked Brie, 307
Baked Cheddar Bacon Spread, 312
Baked Deli Sandwich, 335
Baked Potato Pizza, 355
Baked Stuffed Pears, 194
Banana Buttermilk Muffins, 254
Barbecued Pork Sandwiches, 132
Barley Turkey Soup, 318
Be-Mine Sandwich Cookies, 366
Beef 'n' Bean Egg Rolls, 330
Beets in Orange Sauce, 218
Berries 'n' Cream Torte, 111
Berry Sour Cream Cake, 74
Bewitching Ice Cream Cones, 139

Bird's Nests, 42
Black Bean Chicken Tacos, 65
Black Cat Cookies, 141
Black-Eyed Pea Salsa, 337
Black-Eyed Pea Soup, 332
Black Widow Bites, 152
BLT Dip, 311
Blue Cheese Burgers, 110
Blueberry-Rhubarb Refrigerator
   Jam, 48
Boston Cream Sponge Cake, 274
Bread Bowls, 346
Bread Pudding Pumpkin, 195
Breakfast Burritos, 58
Breakfast Pizza, 356
Broccoli Chicken Braid, 405
Broccoli Salad Supreme, 330
Broccoli Souffle, 204
Broccoli with Ginger-Orange
   Butter, 236
Brown Sugar Pecan Candies, 296
Brownie Pizza, 119
Brownies in a Cone, 126
Buffalo Chicken Calzones, 356
Butterfluff Rolls, 166

Buttermilk Potato Doughnut Holes, 46
Butterscotch Pecan Brownies, 120
Buttery Spritz Cookies, 283

C

Caesar Chicken Potato Salad, 95
Calico Clams Casino, 314
Candied Flowers, 375
Candied Holly Cupcakes, 275
Candy Pacifiers, 404
Caramel Chocolate Mousse Pie, 184
Caramel-Chocolate Pecan Pie, 272
Caramel-Filled Chocolate Cookies, 285
Caramel Fondue, 368
Caramel Macadamia Nut Brownies, 118
Caramel Snack Mix, 288
Cardamom Braids, 263
Cauliflower Zucchini Toss, 247
Celebration Punch, 399
Celebration Spoons, 278
Challah, 213
Championship Cookies, 86
Checkerboard Birthday Cake, 381
Cheddar Buttermilk Biscuits, 344
Cheddar Cauliflower Quiche, 236
Cheddar Cheese Spread, 338
Cheddar Pan Rolls, 130
Cheddar Pancakes, 24
Cheese-Stuffed Jalapenos, 67
Cheesecake Dessert Squares, 413
Cheesy Green Chili Rice, 63
Cheesy Pizza Fondue, 313
Cherry Bonbon Cookies, 284
Cherry-Go-Round, 255
Cherry Meringue Pie, 182
Chewy Chocolate Cookies, 112
Chicken Tortilla Soup, 68
Chicken Wild Rice Soup, 243
Chiffon Fruitcake, 271

Chili Artichoke Dip, 302
Chili Burgers, 108
Chilled Blueberry Soup, 76
Chocolate Cheesecake Squares, 398
Chocolate Chip Coffee Cake, 50
Chocolate Chip Meringue Cookies, 364
Chocolate Coffee, 277
Chocolate Fudge Cake, 382
Chocolate Lime Dessert, 14
Chocolate Truffle Dessert, 269
Chocolate Truffles, 362
Chocolate Yeast Bread, 260
Christmas Tree Sweet Rolls, 325
Cinnamon Brownies, 116
Cinnamon Chocolate Chip Ice Cream, 64
Cinnamon Gelatin Salad, 239
Cinnamon Pecan Braids, 22
Citrus-Cinnamon Stir Sticks, 279
Citrus Cranberry Pie, 183
Clove Bundt Cake, 374
Clown Cake, 379
Coconut Pecan Torte, 380
Coconut Truffles, 295
Colcannon Potatoes, 10
Colorful Veggie Casserole, 249
Confetti Tortellini Salad, 320
Cookies 'n' Cream Cake, 374
Country Potato Dressing, 204
Country White Bread, 256
Crab-Spinach Egg Casserole, 20
Cranberry Apple Muffins, 257
Cranberry Bundt Cake, 190
Cranberry Fruit Mold, 165
Cranberry Fruit Punch, 276
Cranberry Ice, 219
Cranberry Raspberry Punch, 388
Cranberry Sweet Potato Bake, 237
Cranberry Turkey Salad, 200
Creamed Pearl Onions, 248
Creamy Apple Pie, 185
Creamy Asparagus Soup, 28
Creamy Chicken Enchiladas, 66
Creamy Chocolate Crescents, 265
Creamy Coconut Chocolate Pie, 386
Creamy Crab Salad, 388
Creamy Onion Soup, 410
Creamy Vegetable Medley, 246
Crisp Onion Relish, 131
Crispy Orange Roughy, 228
Crunchy Apple Salad, 177
Crunchy Caramel Corn, 338
Cucumber Party Sandwiches, 404
Cupid's Breadsticks, 363

Curried Rice Pilaf, 239

D

Date Crumb Cake, 22
Date-Filled Sandwich Cookies, 291
Decadent Brownie Pie, 121
Deli-Style Pasta Salad, 72
Deluxe Turkey Club Pizza, 352
Deviled Egg Bunnies, 51
Dilled Duchess Potatoes, 245
Dilly Bran Bread, 264
Dilly Bread Ring, 175
Dilly Turkey Burgers, 106
Double Sausage Stromboli, 348
Dressed-Up Broccoli, 220

E

Easter Egg Candies, 47
Easy Batter Rolls, 252
Egg and Spinach Side Dish, 58
Egg Bake with Sausage Biscuits, 56
Egg Salad Wonton Cups, 314
Eggnog Fruit Fluff, 244
Eggplant Dip, 304
Engaging Heart Cookies, 365
Eyeball Soup, 151

F

Family-Style Baked Beans, 129
Fast Fruit Punch, 46
Favorite French Dressing, 151
Favorite Pull-Apart Rolls, 256
Festive Biscuit Strips, 259
Festive Meat Loaf Pinwheel, 227
Festive Tossed Salad, 212
Fiesta Chili Dogs, 131
Fiesta Corn Dip, 309
Fish Fillets with Citrus-Herb Butter, 233
Flag Cake, 73
Floating Four-Leaf Clovers, 9
Fluffy Bacon-Cheese Frittata, 28
Focaccia Sandwich, 322
Four-Cheese Pizza, 354
Fourth of July Ice Cream Cake, 101
French Toast Sticks, 42
French Toast Strata, 24
Frightening Fingers, 138
Frosted Brownies, 118
Frosty Cranberry Salad Cups, 174
Frozen Fruit Slush, 394
Frozen Pumpkin Dessert, 192
Fruit Salad with Poppy Seed Dressing, 18
Fruited Turkey Salad, 198

G

Garlic Herb Spread, 303
Garlic Potato Bake, 408
German Chocolate Caramel
  Bars, 292
German Chocolate Cupcakes, 78
German-Style Pickled Eggs, 59
Gingerbread Teddies, 319
Gingersnap Dip, 191
Glazed Cranberry Carrots, 199
Glazed Lebkuchen, 212
Golden Pan Rolls, 262
Golden Shrimp Puffs, 337
Goose with Corn Bread Stuffing, 163
Greek Chicken, 340
Greek-Style Rib Eye Steaks, 226
Grilled Corn with Chive Butter, 89
Grilled Picnic Chicken, 125
Grilled Rack of Lamb, 230

H

Ham 'n' Cheese Egg Bake, 45
Ham 'n' Potato Casserole, 54
Ham 'n' Swiss Strudel, 30
Ham Cream Cheese Balls, 411
Hard-Cooked Eggs, 54
Hazelnut Crescents, 292
Hazelnut Mocha Torte, 341
Hearty Alfredo Potatoes, 202
Hearty Meatball Soup, 238
Herb 'n' Spice Turkey Breast, 164
Herb Burgers, 72
Herbed Cheesecake, 305
Herbed Mashed Potatoes, 216
Holiday Ham, 25
Holiday Pork Roast, 224
Holiday Vegetable Dip, 307
Honey-Ginger Barbecued Ribs, 100
Honey-Glazed Chicken, 232
Horseradish-Mustard Sauce for
  Corned Beef, 8
Hot 'n' Spicy Cranberry Dip, 201
Hot Apple Cider, 150
Hot Fruit Soup, 245
Hot Pastrami Spread, 11
Hot Wings, 86

I

Ice Cream Brownie Mountain, 117
Iced Coffee Slush, 276
Irish Beef 'n' Carrot Stew, 14
Irish Soda Bread, 8
Italian Meatball Hoagies, 318
Italian Veggie Turkey Pitas, 47

J

Jumbo Jack-o'-Lantern
  Cookies, 149

K

Kielbasa Bean Soup, 344

L

Lacy Oat Sandwich Wafers, 334
Latkes, 211
Lemon Burst Broccoli, 408
Lemon Clouds with Custard, 39
Lemon Nut Star Cookies, 93
Lemon Squares, 402
Lemony Turkey Rice Soup, 205
Lime Tart, 272
Luscious Fruit Platter, 308

M

Macaroon Cheesecake, 268
Macaroon Fruit Dip, 311
Make-Ahead Coleslaw, 336
Mamie Eisenhower's Fudge, 290
Mandarin Orange Spinach
  Salad, 410
Mandarin Pasta Salad, 133
Maple Cranberry Sauce, 170
Maple-Glazed Carrots, 158
Marinated Beef Sandwiches, 332
Marinated Fruit Salad, 43
Marinated Mozzarella
  Cubes, 392
Marinated Mushrooms, 306
Marinated Vegetable Salad, 124
Marshmallow Ghosts, 138
Meatball Sub Sandwiches, 340
Meaty Chili Dip, 304
Melon with Minted Lime Dip, 96
Meringue Bunnies, 43
Mexican Wedding Cakes, 390
Mint Tea Punch, 9
Minted Chocolate Torte, 273
Minty Pineapple Punch, 26
Molded Egg Salad, 55
Mulled Holiday Drink, 278
Mushroom Pork Scallopini, 229
Mustard Potatoes Au Gratin, 34

N

Nacho Popcorn, 112
Nana's Chilies Rellenos, 62
Norwegian Christmas Bread, 252
Nutty Popcorn Party Mix, 282

O

Oat 'n' Rye Bread Dressing, 170
Old-Fashioned Lemonade, 105
Olive Potato Salad, 126
Orange-Avocado Chicken Salad, 387
Orange Cheesecake Mousse, 361
Orange Chocolate Muffins, 258
Orange Fruit Dip, 76
Orange Walnut Candy, 289
Orange Whipped Sweet
  Potatoes, 165
Orange Witches' Brew Punch, 142

P

Paprika Mushrooms, 241
Parmesan Cheese Straws, 386
Party Mint Patties, 400
Pastry for Double-Crust Pie, 186
Pastry for Single-Crust Pie, 186
Patriotic Fruit Pizza, 97
Patriotic Taco Salad, 77
Peach Graham Muffins, 260
Peach Praline Muffins, 29
Peach Streusel Pie, 89
Peachy Sweet Potato Bake, 156
Peanut Butter Ice Cream Pie, 85
Peanut Oat Cookies, 290
Pecan Carrot Pie, 194
Pecan Clusters, 286
Pecan Pumpkin Loaves, 264
Pepper Sausage Pizza, 353
Peppered Corn Bread, 87
Peppered Meatballs, 310
Peppered Rib Eye Roast, 416
Peppermint Ice Cream, 270
Peppermint Ice Cream Dessert, 322
Pepperoncini Firecrackers, 110
Pesto Pizza Squares, 354
Picnic Potato Salad, 98
Pineapple Cherry Loaves, 253
Pineapple Dream Dessert, 270
Plum-Glazed Gingered Ham, 36
Popcorn Christmas Trees, 297
Poppy Seed Cranberry Bread, 254
Poppy Seed Easter Cake, 37
Posy Cupcakes, 375
Potato Asparagus Bake, 12
Potato Chip Chicken Strips, 74
Potato Muffins, 262
Potato Salad Mold, 109
Potluck Strawberry Trifle, 130
Pots o' Gold, 15
Pretty Petit Fours, 389
Puff Pillow Buns, 390
Pumpkin Baked Alaska, 193

Pumpkin Cheesecake Dessert, 164
Pumpkin-Face Ice Cream
   Sandwiches, 150
Pumpkin Shortbread Dessert, 158
Pumpkin Stew, 146

Q

Queen-of-Hearts Salad, 366

R

Rabbit Rolls, 49
Raspberry Fudge Torte, 376
Red, White and Blue Chili, 99
Refreshing Lime Slush, 63
Refrigerator Rolls, 411
Reuben Chicken, 11
Rhubarb Terrine with Raspberry
   Sauce, 75
Roast Duck with Orange Glaze, 228
Roasted Root Vegetables, 173
Root Beer Cookies, 127
Ruby-Red Strawberry Sauce, 364
Rustic Pear Tart, 180

S

Sage Chicken Cordon Bleu, 224
Salad with Blue Cheese
   Dressing, 218
Saucy Orange Shrimp, 88
Sausage Mushroom Manicotti, 26
Sausage Potato Dressing, 171
Savory Beef Brisket, 210
Scaredy Cakes, 377
Scrambled Egg Brunch Bread, 31
Sesame Chicken Kabobs, 94
Sherbet Watermelon, 106
Shrimp Chowder, 348
Shrimp Creole, 231
Shrimp Pasta Salad, 392
Shrimp with Basil-Mango
   Sauce, 362
Simple Cabbage Slaw, 87
Skewered Potatoes, 88
Slow-Cooked Chowder, 246
Slow-Cooked Vegetable Soup, 242
Smoky Barbecue Sauce, 132
Snowball Eggnog Punch, 324
Snowcapped Butternut Squash, 241
Snowflake and Icicle Cookies, 321
Snowmen Cookies, 297
Soft Chocolate Mint Cookies, 296
Sopaipillas, 64
Sour Cream Raisin Pie, 180
Southwest Rib Roast with Salsa, 62
Southwestern Pasta Salad, 128

Southwestern Seafood Egg
   Rolls, 312
Sparkling Candy Swizzle Sticks, 278
Special Hot Chocolate Treats, 323
Spiced Chili, 346
Spiced Pecans, 298
Spiced Pumpkin Pie, 181
Spicy Corned Beef, 12
Spicy Hummus, 313
Spiderweb Pumpkin
   Cheesecake, 147
Spinach-Cheese Mushroom
   Caps, 393
Spinach Noodle Casserole, 244
Spinach Salad with Honey
   Dressing, 400
Springtime Strawberry Bars, 44
Strawberry Cheese Bundles, 403
Strawberry Cookies, 78
Strawberry Pavlova, 367
Strawberry Sherbet, 97
Strawberry Syrup, 25
Strawberry Wedding Bell
   Cookies, 391
Stuffed Bread Appetizers, 412
Stuffed Crown Roast of Pork, 225
Stuffed Flank Steak, 232
Stuffed Shells Florentine, 339
Sugar Cookie Cutouts, 287
Sugar-Topped Walnut Bars, 298
Sugarcoated Meltaways, 284
Summer Sub Sandwich, 125
Summertime Fruit Tea, 77
Summertime Salsa, 100
Sunflower Cheese Ball, 405
Supreme Scalloped Potatoes, 238
Swedish Pancakes, 21
Sweet 'n' Spicy Grilled Pork
   Chops, 92
Sweet 'n' Spicy Halloween
   Munch, 148
Sweet Citrus Punch, 276
Sweet Potato Casserole, 174
Swiss 'n' Asparagus Egg Salad, 57
Swiss Creamed Peas, 205
Swiss-Topped Cauliflower
   Soup, 240

T

Taco Pan Pizza, 357
Taco Roll-Ups, 306
Tangy Baked Apples, 171
Tangy Fruit Salsa with Cinnamon
   Chips, 27
Tangy Red Cabbage, 248
Tangy Sirloin Strips, 84

Thanksgiving Turkey
   Sandwich, 200
Thick 'n' Chewy Pizza, 324
Three Milk Cake, 66
Three's-a-Charm Shamrock Soup, 13
Three-Cheese Deviled Eggs, 56
Three-Cheese Manicotti, 412
Three-in-One Popcorn Crunch, 142
Three-Layer Gelatin Salad, 326
Thyme Green Beans with
   Almonds, 162
Toasted Almond Caramels, 293
Toasted Almond Ice Cream
   Balls, 274
Toasted Almond Party Spread, 308
Tomato Basil Bread, 347
Tomato Spinach Spread, 310
Tortilla Burgers, 104
Traditional Whole Wheat Bread, 258
Triple-Nut Diamonds, 289
Tropical Chicken Salad, 398
Tropical Fruit Salad, 129
Turkey Breast Roulade, 409
Turkey Divan Pizza, 199
Turkey Shepherd's Pie, 202
Turkey with Apple Stuffing, 157
Turkey with Sausage Stuffing, 217
Two-Cheese Spinach Bake, 172

V

Valentine's Day Snack Mix, 368
Veal Scallopini, 360
Vegetable Bundles, 35
Vegetable Rice Casserole, 416
Viennese Fudge, 282

W

Wagon Wheel Pasta Salad, 108
Walnut Broccoli Bake, 242
Walnut Marmalade Mini
   Loaves, 261
Watermelon Baby Carriage, 401
White Chocolate Banana Pie, 182
White Chocolate Holiday
   Cookies, 288
Whole Wheat Dinner Rolls, 334
Wild Rice Bread, 336
Winter Squash Souffle, 176
Witch Hat Treats, 143
Witches' Broomsticks, 148

Z

Zesty Grilled Pork Medallions, 85
Zippy Potato Soup, 345
Zucchini Salad, 94

Metric Equivalents

VOLUME

IMPERIAL	METRIC
⅛ teaspoon	0.5 milliliter
¼ teaspoon	1 milliliter
½ teaspoon	2 milliliters
1 teaspoon	5 milliliters
1 tablespoon (½ fluid ounce)	1 tablespoon (15 milliliters)*
¼ cup (2 fluid ounces)	2 tablespoons (50 milliliters)
⅓ cup (3 fluid ounces)	¼ cup (75 milliliters)
½ cup (4 fluid ounces)	⅓ cup (125 milliliters)
¾ cup (6 fluid ounces)	¾ cup (200 milliliters)
1 cup (8 fluid ounces)	1 cup (250 milliliters)
1 pint (16 fluid ounces)	500 milliliters
1 quart (32 fluid ounces)	1 liter minus 3 tablespoons

The Australian tablespoon is 20 milliliters, but the difference is negligible in most recipes.

TEMPERATURE

IMPERIAL	METRIC
0°F (freezer temperature)	minus 18°C
32°F (temperature water freezes)	0°C
180°F (temperature water simmers)*	82°C
212°F (temperature water boils)*	100°C
250°F (low oven temperature)	120°C
350°F (moderate oven temperature)	180°C
425°F (hot oven temperature)	220°C
500°F (very hot oven temperature)	260°C

At sea level

WEIGHT

IMPERIAL	METRIC
¼ ounce	7 grams
½ ounce	15 grams
¾ ounce	20 grams
1 ounce	30 grams
6 ounces	170 grams
8 ounces (½ pound)	225 grams
12 ounces (¾ pound)	340 grams
16 ounces (1 pound)	450 grams
35 ounces (2 ¼ pounds)	1 kilogram

LENGTH

IMPERIAL	METRIC
½ inch	12 millimeters
1 inch	2.5 centimeters
6 inches	15 centimeters
12 inches (1 foot)	30 centimeters

BAKING PAN SIZES

IMPERIAL	METRIC
8 x 1½-inch round cake pan	20 x 5-centimeter cake tin
9 x 1½-inch round cake pan	23 x 5-centimeter cake tin
11 x 7 x 1½-inch baking pan	28 x 18 x 4-centimeter baking tin
13 x 9 x 2-inch baking pan	30 x 20 x 3-centimeter baking tin
15 x 10 x 1-inch baking pan (jelly-roll pan)	38 x 25 x 2.5-centimeter baking tin (Swiss-roll tin)
9 x 5 x 3-inch loaf pan	25 x 7.5-centimeter loaf tin in Canada
	19 x 12 x 9-centimeter loaf tin in Australia
9-inch pie plate	23 x 3-centimeter pie plate
7- or 8-inch springform pan or loose-bottom tin	20-centimeter springform tin
10-inch tube or Bundt pan	26-centimeter (15-cup capacity) ring tin

NOTE: *Pan sizes vary between manufacturers, so use this list as an approximate guide only. Always use the nearest equivalent available.*